THE
HARLEY-DAVIDSON
MOTOR COMPANY
An Official Ninety-Year History

David K. Wright
Foreword by Willie G. Davidson

Motorbooks International
Publishers & Wholesalers

To the people of Harley-Davidson

A NOTE ON THE OFFICIALLY AUTHORIZED HARLEY-DAVIDSON HISTORY.

In the development of this book, Harley-Davidson, Inc., agreed to allow full access to company archives by the publishers and the author, David Wright. Harley-Davidson also arranged for interviews with Harley-Davidson officials past and present. Finally, Harley-Davidson received review rights of the manuscript in order to clarify questions that otherwise would not have been answerable.

Final editorial content, including statements of opinion on Harley-Davidson products and policies, and speculation on events relating to the company's history, their causes and effects, are based on the author's interpretation of the facts and do not necessarily reflect the stated position of Harley-Davidson, Inc.

First published in 1993 by Motorbooks International Publishers & Wholesalers, PO Box 2, 729 Prospect Avenue, Osceola, WI 54020 USA

Motorbooks International books are also available at discounts in bulk quantity for industrial or sales-promotional use. For details write to Special Sales Manager at the Publisher's address

Library of Congress Cataloging-in-Publication Data
Wright, David.
    The Harley-Davidson Motor Company : a ninety-year history / David Wright.
        p.   cm.
    Includes index.
    ISBN 0-87938-764-5
    1. Harley-Davidson Motor Company—History.   2. Motorcycle industry—United States—History.   3. Motorcycle racing—History.
    I. Title.
HD9710.5.U64H378   1993
338.7'6292275'0973—dc20   93-8138

On the front cover: The fabulous 1993 Harley-Davidson FLSTN limited-production model, often nicknamed the "Cow-Glide" or "Moo-Glide" for its cowhide seat and saddlebag inserts. Only 2,700 of this special edition model were built in 1993; this is motorcycle number 2628 owned by Kathy Nelson of Amery, Wisconsin, and purchased from "R" Harley of Rice Lake, Wisconsin. *Michael Dregni*

On the back cover: The first Harley-Davidson motorcycle, built in 1903. Harley-Davidson enthusiasts celebrating at the Daytona Beach races in the late 1940s. Harley racer Arthur "Babe" Tancrede on his flathead prior to a 1940 Class C race.

Printed and bound in the United States of America

Contents

Acknowledgments

It's impossible to list all the people who helped me piece this book together. But let me try. Once they were assured I had the blessing of Harley-Davidson, the following persons exerted themselves on my behalf:

Ronnie Alexander; Jim Allin; Bill Amick; Kathy Anderson; Gerald S. Arenberg; Del Austin; Gary Ball; George Balmer; W. P. Barlow; Louis Bartley; Doc Batsleer; Francis G. Blake; Bob Bolfert; Tom Bolfert; J. J. Born; Phil Boydston; Scott Brown; John and Linda Burger; John Cameron; Frank Cimermancic; Bill Cleary; Bob Conway; Richard Creed; John Crowell; John Davidson; Frank Densmoor; Clyde Denzer; Ed DeVilbis; Herbert D. Dickey; Elsie Dinsmore; Darrell Dovel; Jim Dricken; Bill Dutcher; M. F. Egan; John Endrizzi; Alice and Joseph Espada; Chris Fensham; Clyde Fessler; John Finstad; Harold Foster; Sharon Garrison; Tom Gelb; Chester Geller; Steven Getz; Nobleena and Lawrence Glanton, Jr.; Herb Glass; Larry Gutjahr; Ronald D. Hall; Chris Halla; Juanita and Glenn Harding; Rick Hauser; Chris Haynes; John Heidt; James C. Hester; Ted A. Hodgdon, Jr.; J. C. Hoel; Arnold Hoffman; Andy Huffer; Allen Hunsicker; Roger Jaynes; Lori Johnson; Arthur Kauper; H. A. Kendall; Frank Kern; John R. King; Bill Kirmec; Bob Klein; Jerry Knackert; Henry Koster; Jay Kraemer; George Kragel; Jim Kruse; Cindy Kruske; Chris Kusto; William Lally; and Leon Landry.

Also, Linda Lange; Tom Laughlin; Kathleen Lawler; Ronni Logge; Armando and Lew Magri; Jack L. Martin; Joe Martin; Randy Mason; Bob Masten; Barry Matteson; Ken McCoy; Bill McMahon; Bill Mensch; Rick Miller; Eddy Mills; Harry Molenaar; Harry W. Moore, Jr.; Richard A. Muller; Arlen Ness; Louis Netz; John Nowak; Andy Oberle; Dick O'Brien; Tim O'Day; Mary Oelstrom; Dave Pader; Ann Paluso; Steve Parker; Tom Parsons; Dudley Perkins, Jr.; James Perkins; Peter Petrali; Wilbur Petri; Steve Piehl; Paul Poberezny; John W. Powers; Sarah Protz; Dick Reiter; Otto Resech; Carroll Resweber; Bob, John and Pat Ross; Jeannie, John and Mark Ruther; Mike Sanko; Cristine and Ruth E. Sarno; Conrad Schlemmer; Ken Schneider; Sue and Tom Snyder; Gary Spears; Nancy Springer; William R. Stewart; Arthur Tancrede; Mel Thornton; Doyle Tollison; Benton Thomas Tucker; Louis Tuttle; Mark Tuttle; Vinnie in Littleton; Les Waterman; Jerry Wilke; Charles Wolverton; Scott Zampach; and Pieter Zylstra.

Special thanks to William H. Davidson, for his powers of recall, enthusiasm, energy and patience; to William ("Willie G.") Davidson, for being exactly what he appears to be, with all the good things that connotes; to John Harley, for the sheer amount of information he has amassed; to Bill Kosfeld, for going to bat on behalf of this book; and to Michael Lange, whose age belies his knowledge and devotion to Harley-Davidson.

Oh yeah—thanks to Grace, Austin and Monica Wright, who put up with it.

5

Foreword

As a boy, it didn't take me long to realize that I was related to a very special company. Born a son of H-D President William H. Davidson and a grandson of founder William A. Davidson, I recall seeing my father attired in a conservative business suit as he pulled away from the door each morning on a motorcycle. Not just any motorcycle but—as it has turned out—the only American motorcycle that remains in production today. Why and how did Harley-Davidson survive when all the others failed? Were the Davidsons and the Harleys smarter or did they work harder than others? Has there always been a bit more demand, a bit more prestige connected with Harley-Davidson? If the company and the product are special, in what ways are they so special?

I don't have any single, definitive answer, but this book may provide a hint. In a century where the only constant is change, Harley-Davidson has succeeded by remembering its heritage, even as it offers riders a unique blend of usable technology. We're keenly aware of the degree of loyalty the motorcycle has developed over the years, and we keep an eye on that heritage as each new design comes off the drawing board.

The four founders were committed to making the best motorcycle possible. Along the way, they wanted to have some fun and make some money. That was ninety years ago, but the goals aren't much changed. Nor will they change as we look toward our 100th anniversary. But that's another chapter in a story that continues to evolve.

Ride free.

Introduction

It was a warm evening in May 1966. College graduation and my draft notice were a month away. Though I didn't know it, Vietnam lay only ten months down the road. But the road on that particular evening led to a drive-in movie theater in Springfield, Ohio. A dozen of us took up three parking spaces with a Chevrolet, a Volkswagen and a Harley-Davidson. We spread blankets on car hoods and on the gravel, popped tab tops and watched Frankie Avalon fill Annette Funicello's cleavage with sand. After the movie, the guy with the H-D staggered under the weight of a twelve pack consumed. So we eased him into the back seat of the Chevy and I was elected to ride his bike home. Why me? I owned a small Italian bike, and all cycles were alike, right?

The first kick nearly tossed me into the next row of cars. Fiddling in the glare of an occasional headlight, I somehow got the Harley running. My girl climbed aboard and we eased off. Three feet later, I noticed a pronounced lurch that shook the handlebars; it went away as quickly as it appeared. We moved into traffic and somehow made it through the Midwest midnight to the bike owner's apartment. The next day, the guy who owned the Volkswagen called, upset. Somehow, in the darkness, the footpeg or the safety bar had caught his front fender, ripping it completely off the car. That accounted for the twitch in the handlebars, all right.

When the idea of writing about Harley-Davidson was suggested, fifteen years after my first ride, the fender assault came immediately to mind. No one thinks of stuff like that when you mention Harley, I believed. But that's wrong. Everyone conjures a definite mental image when H-D is brought up. Except for maybe tattoos or communism, nothing on earth fosters a stronger reaction, one way or the other. If a foreign bike is vanilla, a Harley-Davidson is rich, dark chocolate. If any other bike is elevator music, a Harley-Davidson is the Grateful Dead. If a Honda or Kawasaki or Suzuki or Yamaha is a nap in the middle of an uneventful day, a Harley-Davidson is the deep and dream-filled sleep of a laborer after working a double shift in a steel mill. Who wouldn't want to write about something as up-front as a Harley-Davidson? Everyone from Hulk Hogan to Elizabeth Taylor knows—you don't just show up on a Harley. You *arrive*.

I never did pay for that fender.

David Wright
Spring, 1983

Chapter 1

Beginnings

The Industrial Revolution was less than a century old in 1903 when Arthur and Walter Davidson and Bill Harley decided they would build a motorcycle. Arthur Davidson and William Harley and a German immigrant whose name is lost all were employed at Milwaukee's Barth Manufacturing Company. They spent long hours after work studying French blueprints and other designs before producing a spindly machine with a De-Dion-type, single-cylinder engine. The 3-horsepower motor compressed and detonated air mixed with gasoline to move a piston, a crankshaft, a chain and a belt that resulted in power to the back wheel. These were shade-tree mechanics who could figure out how things worked. They were savvy enough to find friends or friends of friends to machine or fabricate the parts they could envision but did not have the machinery to make as production began in the Davidson parents' garage.

The cycle was painted gloss black, as were the two identical machines the Davidsons and Harley managed to construct—and sell—the following year. Aunt Janet Davidson hand-applied red striping and created the original "Harley-Davidson Motor Company" logo seen on the fuel tanks. The initial bike not only looked good, but it had several things going for it that would separate it from the many other powered cycles then under construction in garages, barns and basements throughout the country.

Perhaps through luck, the trio had hit upon internal dimensions that proved reliable, if not very quick, the first time the engine was produced. However, Bill Harley realized that the spiderlike bicycle frame would soon be obsolete, so he designed a loop frame that eliminated the stresses to which diamond-shaped frames were subjected. The crucial factor, though, may have been economic—none of the three left his job immediately to embark on a career as a motorcycle manufacturer. Rather, they worked evenings and weekends on their creations. That accounts for the fact that the pair of bikes made in 1904 was followed by just eight machines in 1905. But by 1906, fifty Harley-Davidsons were made and quickly sold. One man (neither a Harley nor a Davidson) was employed full time in the ten-by-fifteen-foot shed bearing the Harley-Davidson Motor Company name. That structure was built for the boys by the Davidsons' father, a cabinetmaker who must have been confident of their future. The hum of machinery echoed daily from the Davidson backyard at 38th and Highland Boulevard, on land now owned by the Miller Brewing Company. Among fellow residents of the area was Ole Evinrude, who was busy attempting to build a reliable marine engine and who imparted to Harley and the Davidsons vital carburetor knowledge.

Joined by the eldest Davidson brother, William A., the four filed incorporation papers after completing approximately 150 machines in 1907. Walter was transformed from machinist to president, Bill Harley from draftsman to chief engineer, Arthur from patternmaker to secretary and general sales manager, and latecomer William ceased being a railroad tool room foreman for the superior title of works manager.

Harley decided at this time to pursue a degree in automotive engineering at the University of Wisconsin and left for Madison, 100 miles west.

The three Davidsons, living modestly in flats in the vicinity of their work, put in long, grimy hours in the shed. Arthur and Walter, still bachelors, lived with their parents, keeping the proceeds from sales of cycles in a large jar in a medicine cabinet. Their mother, appalled at the dirt and grease they tracked in each night, hired a maid to clean up after them. Unfortunately, the maid also knew where the company treasury was stored. Somehow, her repeated trips to the jar did not cause the company to founder; quite the contrary.

Some 450 Harley-Davidsons were built to run the rutted U.S. roads in 1908. Eighteen persons were employed and a 2,380-square-foot brick

The first Harley-Davidson was created in this shed in 1903. The site, at 38th and Highland Boulevard, is now owned by the Miller Brewing Company. *Harley-Davidson, Inc.*

A very early photo of founders and employees, proving among other things that some very young men started H-D. That's Bill Harley sitting with arms crossed. Behind him is Bill Davidson and behind them is Walter. Sherbie Becker, far left, and Bill Manz, left; Oscar Becker is astride bike, with Max Kobs behind him. The two fellows over Sherbie's shoulder are John Pfannerstill, left, and Charles Menzel. The two at right are not identified. *William H. Davidson collection*

9

building was erected for production purposes. It's hard for contemporary Americans, used to stagflation, to conceive of the speed with which the company grew. William H. Davidson, president of the company from 1942 to 1971 and son of William A., remembers his father "putting machinery in place and starting production as soon as the cement was dry" on a new floor of an H-D factory. Production grew every year but one through 1920, when 28,189 cycles were delivered to a network of domestic and foreign dealers recruited largely by Arthur Davidson.

Just thirteen years after incorporation, sales had increased 5,000 percent! What kind of men could parlay a shed, borrowed tools and some metal into the largest motorcycle company in existence at the time? They were conservative, as their 1908 letterhead indicated: The company hedged its bets by offering not only motorcycles but such items as "automatic float feed carburetors, marine motors and reversible propellors." But merely attaching labels such as conservative or industrious doesn't do these very human people justice. . . .

Ole Evinrude, who lived in the same part of Milwaukee as the founders, is said to have taught them how to make a carburetor work. *Outboard Marine Corporation*

The four founders with three unidentified employees in 1910. Walter is second from left, Arthur is in the middle, William A. is second from right and William Harley is at right. *William H. Davidson collection*

10

Arthur was usually charitable to his dealers, too. "A Harley-Davidson dealer must make money," he stated repeatedly in meetings with dealers and factory personnel alike. The late former H-D President William H. Davidson said Arthur firmly believed that the well being of dealers was crucial to the success of the company. Arthur also believed the American Motorcycle Association (AMA) was important to the company and so became a pillar of that organization. "We didn't do it [assume control of the AMA in the early days] because we wanted to," according to William H. "We did it because there was no one else around." Ever the salesman, Arthur was instrumental in signing dealers as far away as Australia and New Zealand while he recruited corporate members in the U.S. for the AMA. "Look—you make our castings, we want your support." That was Arthur's approach when all else failed.

Following World War II, he spent an increasing amount of time on his farm. A visitor recalls the satisfaction Arthur could not conceal as he ducked through a fence, walked up to the largest bull in his herd of cattle and, grabbing it by the nose ring, led it like a puppy around the barnyard. The zest he showed for life ended on the evening of December 30, 1950, when he and his wife were killed in a grinding, two-car crash in Milwaukee. Arthur was sixty-nine years old. Like his brothers and Bill Harley, he remained active in the company until his death. He could not know that his own son, James, and James' wife, would also die in an automobile accident in 1966.

William S. Harley

If there is one photo in the Harley-Davidson archives that tells about Bill Harley it is the picture showing him with William A. Davidson after a day spent fishing. Harley is at the helm of the cycle, with William A. in the sidecar. The two had just returned, on this summer day in 1920, from a successful fishing trip, as the pike draped over the sidecar indicate. In addition to being a highly skilled rider, Bill Harley was an outdoorsman of the first rank. A draftsman at the time he and Arthur Davidson produced the first bike, Harley served as the company's chief engineer and treasurer until his death from heart failure on September 18, 1943. Hunting, fishing and golf may have been even more enjoyable than motorcycling. The sole college graduate among the four founders, he was prevented from much recreation until well into the twenties, after company growth stabilized. And while he had many friends, he preferred the solitary sports that would take him into the birch- and pine-studded Wisconsin lake country.

Bill Harley earned his recreation, having started work at the age of fifteen in a Milwaukee bicycle factory. He ran some of the first Harley-Davidson motorcycles in endurance contests, finishing consistently and well. More important, his talent as an engineer resulted in many of the classic H-D models throughout his tenure. During both world wars, Harley was responsible for contact between the War Department and the factory. He had the foresight in 1939 to realize that war was inevitable; prototype H-D's were in the hands of the military at Fort Knox more than a year before Pearl Harbor. It is a tribute to him that the H-D 45 needed only a crankcase plate and extended forks to become virtually indestructible in the hands of GI's fighting from Japan to Germany.

Working long hours with the military, Harley nevertheless found time to retreat to the woodlands. He purchased a Leica 35mm camera, mounted it on a gun stock and stalked ducks and other birds, pulling the trigger and capturing them on film. After examining his prints, Harley would sketch the birds and other animals he had seen and photographed. His interpretations of wildlife etched on copper often were given to his friends. Harley continued to play a vigorous game of handball and participate in AMA activities until his death, which occurred before he could know that his efforts on behalf of the military contributed to the end of the Second World War.

Arthur Davidson, right, poses with another Harley-mounted cyclist, identified as P. Olson, about 1906 in Cambridge, Wisconsin, fifty miles west of Milwaukee. *Harley-Davidson, Inc.*

Walter Davidson, Sr.

Harley-Davidson's first president probably wasn't aware of his future when he crawled from beneath a locomotive in Parsons, Kansas, to receive a letter from Arthur inviting him to ride a new motorcycle. Walter was headed for Milwaukee anyway, to attend elder brother William's wedding, so he looked forward to the bike ride. On arrival in the Brew City, he discovered that the cycle was in pieces and that brother Arthur and Bill Harley had hoped he'd precede his ride by putting the machine together. That delayed, probably shaky, ride changed his life, fascinating him in two ways: As a machinist, he appreciated the close tolerances of the small DeDion-type engine, and he quickly discovered that he was a natural rider. Walter went immediately to the Chicago, Milwaukee and St. Paul Railroad and secured a machinist's post so that he could assist Arthur and Bill Harley with their hobby.

"Harley-Davidson was his life," said William H. Without formal business training of any kind, Walter grew with his title. He was extremely generous, giving disproportionately to charity, but his honesty was almost excessive. At a business luncheon once, in a swank New York hotel, Walter looked at the tab, deducted his own meal and listed as a business expense only the meals consumed by his fellow diners. Hank Syvertson, who ran the H-D racing department in the thirties, once wanted to ride to an assignment in Los Angeles aboard the luxurious Super Chief train. Walter examined railroad rates and then informed Syvertson he was welcome aboard—if the extra $12 came out of Syvertson's own pocket.

Toward the end of his life, Walter became recognized for his business ability. He was a trustee of Milwaukee's highly successful Northwestern Mutual Insurance Company and a director of First Wisconsin, the state's largest bank. He died at the helm of the company on February 7, 1942, at age sixty-five. While he will be remembered as the first president of H-D, his overwhelming 1908 win in that New York endurance run may have been his most important contribution. Many believe his perfect score on one of only three H-D's in the contest put the motorcycle on the map.

William A. Davidson

If Walter was the head of the company, William was the heart. A rider only briefly, he quit a responsible job as a Milwaukee Road railroad toolmaker and foreman to join his younger brothers and Bill Harley. A family man at the time, William became works manager in a motorcycle company during a decade when even the automobile industry was considered a question mark. He purchased the presses and other machines necessary to meet production needs that increased at a bewildering rate.

His employees called him "Old Bill," and he apparently relished his paternal role. One of his numerous pockets held a small black notebook filled with the names of employees who borrowed money from him "just till payday." He seldom collected any of the debts from the lengthy list of machinists, tool-and-die makers, welders and assemblers. A large man who enjoyed hunting and fishing, he liked to tell employees

William S. Harley on the cycle, William A. Davidson in the sidecar, on a trip through New England in the early twenties. They crashed the rig on a steep, freshly oiled hillside road. Harley gashed his head and Davidson suffered a broken kneecap. *William H. Davidson collection*

Incorporation papers, filed on September 17, 1907, indicate that Walter was the largest shareholder, with Arthur second; Bill Harley and Bill Davidson were third, perhaps because Davidson had a family to care for and Harley was spending most of his money for education. (A Davidson sister, Elizabeth, invested early and ended up with a sizeable share of the fledgling corporation.)

Bill Harley returned to Milwaukee during his studies long enough to design H-D's first twin, in 1909. His concept was light on theory and heavy on practicality: He grafted a second cylinder onto a single-cylinder engine, then modified the lower end to withstand the added power. In 1912, Harley created the first commercially successful motorcycle clutch, a rear-hub, free-wheel unit. In 1914, he introduced the "step-starter," allowing a machine to be kicked over by pushing either foot pedal, plus an internal expanding rear brake, a carburetor choke and a two-speed transmission. In 1915, the three-speed transmission was offered.

While Harley and fellow engineers were at work, the Davidsons were taking care of other facets of the business. Walter studied heat treating and taught it to employees, William mastered the oxygen-acetylene welding process and passed it on, and Arthur learned advertising techniques and recruited dealers.

The physical plant continued to grow, with 297,110 square feet devoted to manufacturing, manned by 1,574 employees—just ten years after the first H-D was assembled. So pressed to expand were the founders that they once built a 2,400-square-foot brick structure, only to raze it six months later to make room for a larger building.

During the early years, the company relied

Walter Davidson and an early single, no doubt similar to the model he used to win an important 1908 New York state endurance run. His performance in that event helped make H-D's early reputation. *William H. Davidson collection*

heavily on two Milwaukee financial institutions, the Marshall and Ilsley (M&I) and First Wisconsin National banks. The firm's first commercial loan originated at M&I, which maintained a close relationship with H-D until the AMF acquisition in 1969. When World War I orders for motorcycles came in, M&I provided crucial dollars that made Harley-Davidson the world's largest cycle company by 1918.

Everything the Milwaukee cyclemakers touched seemed to turn to gold. So they introduced sidecars and other motorcycle accessories, which sold very well, and bicycles, which did not. "Motorcycles and bicycles appeal to two different customers," said William H. Davidson, pointing out that the dealers were so busy selling motorcycles that they let the nine different bicycle models, introduced late in 1917 and produced for H-D by the Davis Sewing Machine Company, gather dust. To accommodate the ravenous public appetite for their motorized products in the late teens, the founders leased warehouse and production space wherever it was available. Prohibition dealt a nasty blow to Milwaukee because it forced the major breweries to shut down; Harley-Davidson quickly leased idle facilities at the Pabst Brewing Company to house parts.

Victory followed victory, on dusty racetracks at places such as Dodge City, Kansas, and Marion, Indiana, and even in the halls of Washington, where H-D led a successful fight for approval of sidecars for use by rural letter carriers. Not even Yellowstone National Park was safe from Harley-Davidson: The Department of the Interior purchased H-D's to patrol its vast facility in northwest Wyoming. While the racetrack successes were to continue, the economic trophies would temporarily tarnish.

A brief but severe depression occurred worldwide beginning late in 1920. Walter Davidson, addressing a national dealer meeting in the fall of that year, correctly attributed the economic stagger to readjustment following the post World War I boom. The nation and the world recovered gradually in 1922, enjoying more prosperity than would be known for the next seven years. Unfortunately, the motorcycle industry did not fully share in this prosperity. Henry Ford had his Dearborn, Michigan, assembly line in high gear by 1920. Paying premium wages, he was able to produce a reliable automobile for as little as $245, a price that compared very favorably to the two-wheelers.

Harley-Davidson sales reflected the fact that many increasingly affluent Americans were turning their backs on cycles. The 1920 model year saw H-D produce 28,189 motorcycles. The following, depression year, just 10,202 came off the Juneau Avenue line. The economy soared, but cycle sales did not. H-D's best sales year during the twenties was 1926, when 23,354 bikes were sold. The company would not exceed 1920 sales figures until 1942. Meanwhile, few houses were being built without garages, because everyone was acquiring a car.

The decision to drop factory racing support after the 1921 season was only in part economic. Throughout its history, Harley-Davidson's attitude toward competition has swung from one extreme to the other. As early as 1913, Arthur Davidson was using racing results in sales literature, despite descriptions of cycle racing gore in the daily papers. During the period 1914–21, H-D assembled a group of supremely talented riders that swept most of the significant events. "The Wrecking Crew," as they were known, altered Harley-

William A. Davidson, left, and William S. Harley mope following the finish of the 1914 Dodge City, Kansas, 300-mile road race. The factory officially entered racing later than many of its early rivals, but was winning consistently by 1915. *William H. Davidson collection*

Davidson's reputation from reliable and slow to reliable and virtually invincible. To the credit of the factory, when it did something, it did it right. William H. Davidson remembers being put on a train at age fourteen with just-produced cams clattering in his suitcase. He was to deliver said cams to racer Jim Davis in time for the 1920 300-mile road race at Dodge City, Kansas. Cams in place, Davis provided H-D with its fifth consecutive Dodge City win. That same year, Otto Walker mounted his Harley and became the first rider ever to top 100 miles per hour in competition. Walker's achievement was a fitting finale to racing, for the time being.

A source of strength during the teens and twenties was the acceptance of Harley-Davidson models overseas. By 1921, there were H-D dealers in sixty-seven countries, a figure not equaled since. The following year, export folders were printed in seven languages: English, Danish, Italian, French, Dutch, Swedish and Spanish. As early as 1913, the company produced catalogs and owners manuals for "Los Entusiastas Latinos." By 1920, there was a cadre of South American dealers. *The Enthusiast* magazine, H-D's factory publication, began in 1916 and was even briefly offered in Spanish. Even earlier, matching "Factory Facts" flyers were created for the U.S. and Canada, the only difference being in the price of the bikes. The 1913 Model 9-E, for example, was $285 fob Milwaukee and $350 fob Milwaukee if shipped to a Canadian buyer. Englishman Duncan Watson not only was selected as the British H-D distributor in 1919, but was made a company director. Despite the fact that cycles outnumbered cars in the United Kingdom at the time, Watson was forced by a new British import tariff of thirty-three percent to relinquish his distributorship just four years later, in 1923. To meet the European enthusiast's hunger for big V-twins, firms such as Anzani and JAP created H-D look-alikes. Throughout the twenties, accounts of races, brave deeds and tours of faraway places poured in to *The Enthusiast* offices and were reported to readers.

Never reported were the workings during this time of the research and development (R&D) department. Less active following the 1920–21 recession, R&D employees nevertheless constructed—and then destroyed, without so much as taking a photo—everything from a V-4 to variations on the V-twin theme. Four-cylinder Hendersons, popular at the time with police, interested H-D enough to explore a design; but not enough to tool up for such a machine. No sooner was one lightweight phased out than another was conceived, constructed by hand, tested, then assembled in quantity.

Two early twins, two early singles. The first H-D twin was actually produced in late 1907, but could not be made to run consistently with its suction valves. Mechanical valves on the 1911 and ensuing models solved the problem. *William H. Davidson collection*

Other, less-exotic experiments involved side-cars. Produced by the factory and for Harley-Davidson by the Seaman Body Company (later a part of Nash Motors), sidecars were seen as the answer to all sorts of pickup and delivery problems. They were created with bodies in the shapes of cameras, shoes, platforms and more; not as jokes but to fit the needs of different kinds of businesses. Again, the inventiveness displayed by the H-D developers was thwarted by the rock-bottom price of automobiles. R&D people have always come in handy, however. During the thirties, when National Screw Company in Cleveland was hit by a strike, Harley-Davidson engineers quickly devised machines that would pump out the spokes for wheels formerly supplied by the struck company.

In the twenties—well into the thirties, for that matter—Harley-Davidson passed up annual cosmetic changes, preferring instead to refine the product. An illustration of this emphasis can be found in the electrical system. Prior to World War I, H-D installed Bosch electrical equipment, known for its reliability. But the German-designed units were replaced with U.S.-made Remy parts, for obvious reasons. Dissatisfied with Remy, Harley-Davidson engineers created ignition coils that were the envy not only of the motorcycle industry, but of automakers as well. The increasing reliability of the H-D's made up for the fact that the same olive drab color scheme, with striping variations, was used on machines produced from 1918 through 1932.

Meanwhile, consumers with experimental blood in their veins were using Harley-Davidson motors in other ways. A fellow by the name of Harvey Mummert constructed a light plywood airplane powered by an 18-horsepower H-D motor and bravely entered it in the first national air races over Dayton, Ohio, in 1924. He won the speed and efficiency contest in spite of one forced landing. None of his competitors finished the race, local news accounts reported; they either crashed or their motors quit. Less than a decade later, in

The Harley-Davidson endurance team; date and place unknown. At right is Lacy Crolius, the company's first ad director. Second from right is Walter Davidson.
William H. Davidson collection

16

1932, Fawcett Publications' *Flying and Glider Manual* showed plans for building a propeller for a Harley-Davidson 74 cubic inch engine. Designed to power an ice boat, the motor was one of six (others included the Indian Chief, the Lawrence 28 and the Heath Henderson) deemed suitable for a hydroglider. But the most popular use of H-D on water or in the air proved to be the Harlequin.

Several hundred Harlequin-powered light planes took to the skies in the mid-thirties, sporting a horizontally opposed, two-cylinder engine that used H-D 74 cylinders. According to the 1933 edition of the Fawcett manual, the H-D parts were "noted for long life and are low priced and available. The valves are large and the valve chamber allows the best cooling possible to obtain in any design." The motor weighed ninety pounds and delivered 30 horsepower. Total cost to power a light plane was "way below $100." Before the introduction of light, four-cylinder

motors by Cessna and others, home-built Harlequins could be found in hangars across the country.

Harley-Davidson produced a number of truly memorable machines during the twenties. The very first 74 cu. in. model, the JD, came out in 1921. The fore-and-aft, horizontally opposed, 37 cu. in. Sport Twin, introduced in 1919, hung on into the early twenties and was well received overseas. Especially desirable in the States were the two-cam 61 cu. in. and 74 cu. in. road bikes of 1928 and 1929, developed from successful board-track racing machines and capable of outrunning anything street legal on two wheels, or four. Also highly regarded was any H-D single produced at the time. Significant models included the 21 cu. in. side valve and overhead valve singles, offered from 1926 into the early thirties, and the "Peashooter," the racing version of the overhead valve motor. The latter became a force on English, Australian and New Zealand speedway tracks and

Douglas Watson, son of English distributor Sir Duncan Watson, sat on the H-D board until a brief but precipitous recession in the early twenties. H-D exported as much as one-third of its production prior to the Great Depression. *William H. Davidson collection*

The four founders, from left, Arthur Davidson, Walter Davidson, William S. Harley and William A. Davidson. This photo, believed to have been taken about 1915, appeared originally in *Motorcycle Illustrated* and, later, in *The Enthusiast*. Note that the founders were still quite young, though they had been making H-D's for more than a decade. *William H. Davidson collection*

even competed successfully in the U.S. in hill-climb events—against machines with more than twice the cubic inches.

Due in large part to the appeal of the smaller displacement Sport Twin and the magneto- or coil-equipped singles, sales in foreign lands accounted for much of Harley-Davidson's revenue. Of 13,942 machines produced in 1924, for example, 6,194 were exported. Another important source of income was the sidecar; 3,257 were sold in 1924, or approximately one for every two of the V-twins created that year. An Indiana dealer at the time reported annual sales of forty-one V-twins; forty were sidecar-equipped. To make acquisition of a bike easier, the company formed a financing company in 1923 that evolved into Kilbourn Finance Corporation, an important H-D subsidiary that exists today as a dealer resource. Not even easy payments helped in 1924, however; H-D stockholders learned that year of the company's $119,143 loss, the only negative year prior to the Depression.

"The real beginning of our decline in this country," according to President Walter Davidson, addressing the board of directors in 1927, "began several years ago when we found it difficult to secure new dealers in territories where our old dealer either quit or for some reason had the agency taken away from him." To recruit new dealers, the company ran advertisements, not only in *The Enthusiast* but in such high-buck, national magazines as *The Saturday Evening Post.* Prior to the *Post* ads, national exposure was confined largely to mechanically oriented monthlies and to bicycle-motorcycle magazines. From the start, H-D provided its dealers with a variety of in-store signs and other trinkets and baubles. Because

Milwaukee also is a center for quality printing, the banners, posters and so on, sent to dealers as early as the mid-teens, had a highly professional look.

In addition to recruiting dealers (for as little as $1,200 seed money to open a shop in Clarksburg, West Virginia, for example), H-D endorsed the American Motorcycle Association as a means of maintaining public interest. Walter Davidson joined Louis Bauer of Indian and Frank Schwinn of Excelsior in 1928 to retrieve the AMA from its deficit position. That backing, primarily by Harley-Davidson, led to a solid (and very rigid) race-sanctioning, lobbying and social organization. The AMA joined H-D dealers throughout the period in putting together annual Memorial Day weekend gypsy tours and other cycle-oriented events.

Dealers did not have much leeway in their relations with the factory, as a 1925 contract signed by Walter Davidson and Emil Schott of Lewiston, Maine, attests. While Schott, who ordered fifteen bikes and six sidecars for the 1926 model year, could not sell outside his assigned territory, the contract was "not to be construed as granting . . . exclusive sale of Harley-Davidson Motorcycles in the territory herein described." Also a part of the pact was this reminder: "The Dealer agrees not to sell imitation component parts . . . and will not use imitation component parts in repairing Harley-Davidson Motorcycles, sidecars and Parcelcars."

The twenties also saw the second generation of Harleys and Davidsons begin to join the company. William H. Davidson came aboard in 1928, after completing work for his degree at the University of Wisconsin. He learned the business by starting out in the factory and was followed in the next few

A Harley-Davidson bicycle, in original condition, owned by John Harley. These bikes were offered just six years (1918–24) and were made for H-D by the Davis Sewing Machine Company. *David Wright*

years by Gordon Davidson in sales and by William J. Harley and Walter Davidson, both of whom were assigned initially to the shop. John Harley, brother of William J., began work in the office. The Davidsons, through marriage, birth and death, greatly outnumbered the Harleys on the stockholder rolls. There were seventeen persons with the Davidson surname, versus just three Harleys, on stock held at the eve of World War II.

Mechanical and styling advances continued throughout the twenties. Balloon tires, front brakes, streamlined gas tanks, Alemite lubrication, the beginning of parts standardization, greatly improved metallurgy—and related steps forward—made H-D riders forget about oil on pant legs from the total-loss system. Theodore A. Hodgdon, Jr., whose father was one of the guiding lights of the Indian Motorcycle Company, portrays this period quite accurately: "It is not generally remembered today, but of the hundreds of U.S. cycles during the teens, twenties and thirties, only a handful were worth their weight in scrap. Unreliability and simply shoddy workmanship were the norms of the period. It was rare for most makes to exceed 5,000 miles in actual service before some catastrophic failure prematurely retired them. The buyer of an Indian or Harley-Davidson did not generally suffer these indignities, and could expect his mount to perform as advertised. In addition, extensive dealer networks enabled him to ride anywhere, anytime, with reasonable confidence that he might return on the same machine that he started out on." With these comments in mind, it's easy to see how the twenties rider might buy an off brand and become permanently disillusioned with motorcycling.

Neither disillusionment nor despair but rather indignation was the emotion felt by Harley-Davidson principals in February 1929, when a federal judge decided that H-D owed the Eclipse Machine Company of Elmira, New York, $1.1 million for three patent infringements. It seems that Eclipse, formerly a manufacturer of bicycles, had perfected and patented a very sound motorcycle transmission component design. The suit, filed in 1924, dragged on in various courts for five years. Harley-Davidson, after winning approval in a lower court, continued installation of the clutch actuating device in question until the final judgment was received. Fortunately, 1929 model year sales of 20,946 motorcycles resulted in sufficient revenue to pay off the New York firm and still turn a profit. But the infringement can now be seen as a hint of things to come, not only for Harley-Davidson but for the whole, Depression-ridden world.

The 1930 models had been unveiled less than two months when the stock market plummeted in the fall of 1929. Oddly, sales did not suffer markedly that first year, slipping only to 17,662 units. Much of the decrease was due to the further decline in popularity of single-cylinder machines, which dropped from 3,882 units to 1,989. The big twins were only negligibly less popular, going at the rates of 10,842 for 1929 and 10,727 for 1930. A precipitous skid occurred the following year, as the economy continued its decline: 10,500 cycles rolled out of Juneau Avenue, and of those 3,831

A 1926 J model with a Package Truck. There is no reference in H-D parts and accessories books concerning the unusual solid wheels. The back brake was visible only from the right-hand side; front brakes were introduced in 1928. *Harley-Davidson, Inc.*

went overseas. "We may be able to keep you on until spring," said William A. Davidson in the fall of 1930. As works manager, it was his unpleasant duty to lay off not only hourly employees but foremen as well. Those fortunate enough to stay on gladly accepted a ten-percent pay cut in November 1930. Gross revenues during the period 1930–32 slid from $6,562,000 to $4,173,000 to $2,389,000. Sales in 1932 totaled just 6,841 cycles, of which 1,974 were exported. In other words, only 4,867 new H-D's were purchased in the entire U.S. in 1932. Board meeting minutes indicate extended, serious talk of whether Harley-Davidson should stay in business.

Not eager to throw in the towel, the Harleys and the Davidsons emphasized sales to police departments (more than 2,900 state and local departments were riding Harleys at the start of the Depression), personally won races (William H. Davidson, wearing a tie and boots, captured Michigan's Jack Pine Enduro in 1930) and devised new ways to sell. The latter involved creation in 1931 of coupon books for H-D riders. The enthusiasts were to jot down prospects and give them to dealers. If the tip led to a sale, the coupon provider earned points. Two sales garnered the rider a bronze medal, four sales meant silver, eight sales meant gold. Anyone who snagged eight sales for his dealer also received $500 in cash from the factory and a commission on each sale. It was a sign of the times that just one person earned the gold.

Sales in 1933 were 3,703 bikes, the lowest since 1910. It is a credit to H-D that it turned a slight profit that year. Through it all was one bright spot, a spot that moved hurriedly and consistently to the front. That was Joe Petrali. The slight-built Californian provided the factory with a morale booster by winning virtually every board-track, dirt-track and hillclimb event he entered for more than a decade. A quiet man who would not give an inch on the track, Petrali also was a technical conduit, telling William S. Harley and his engineers what worked and what did not. Petrali's input was one of the reasons that the H-D's from the Knucklehead on (1936–47) were state-of-the-art. The racer capped a brilliant career by running one of the new 1936 61 cu. in. V-twins to a speed of 136.183 miles per hour on the sands of Daytona Beach. Fewer than 100,000 cycles were registered in the U.S. at one point in the thirties, but Petrali's victories played a part in making Harley-Davidson a two-to-one choice over Indian, the only other U.S. cycle company still in business. By 1935, Indian was reduced to making 3,000 coaster wagons under subcontract for the Fisk Tire and Rubber Company.

Harley-Davidson looked for subcontract work, too, but without much success. One source of income from 1933 through 1937 was a licensing agreement brought by one of its overseas field representatives, Alfred Child. Child and a Japanese businessman signed a contract in late 1932 that turned over blueprints for current H-D models to a Japanese consortium. The factory received $3,000 for the prints in 1933, followed by sums of

The four founders (from left to right) in the early twenties: William A. Davidson, Walter Davidson, Arthur Davidson, William S. Harley. *William H. Davidson collection*

$5,000, $8,000 and $10,000 in 1934, 1935 and 1936, respectively. Precision machinery, idled by the lack of orders, also was sold to the Oriental concern, which created two- and three-wheelers under the Rikuo nameplate. President Walter Davidson grumbled over what he believed to be a real steal by the Japanese, but conceded that H-D would have lost the market anyway due to an unfavorable exchange rate. In all, the factory received $32,320 for the tools, dies and machines sold to Child and his Oriental friend. The money was put to good use, no doubt, since in November 1933 Walter observed the "complete collapse of the [U.S.] banking system." Equally auspicious, the deal with the Japanese turned that nation on to motorcycles.

Fewer than 300 motorcycle clubs existed in the country in the early thirties. Declining popularity of motorcycles, caused primarily by a lack of money, made it difficult in some parts of the U.S. to find any kind of organized group of riders whatsoever. Those who were in clubs became more and more a subculture, wearing clothing available only from a motorcycle dealer. The mid-thirties rider, done up in cycling attire, would today look like he's wearing all of the worst features seen on equestrians, police and delivery boys. Harley-Davidson parts and accessories catalogs offered an extremely wide selection of clothing and accessories. It's only a slight exaggeration to state that clothing and various extras offered through H-D dealers helped many dealers survive the Depression. While the company realized $373,000 net profit in 1934, $300,354 in 1935

and $381,227 in 1936, prices were very low on a new bike. The profit margins for garb, add-ons and parts, however, have always contributed a higher percentage than have the cycles. Production during the 1934–36 period totaled 10,231, 10,368 and 9,812 bikes, respectively. Since low inventory was next to godliness with the conservative Davidsons, the factory produced no more cycles each year than it could sell. In time, lack of inventory would prove a problem.

A larger problem surfaced on March 11, 1937, when nine employees asked to represent H-D wage earners under the banner of the United Auto Workers. Taking their cue from historic auto industry organizing, Harley-Davidson employees realized that the Depression was gradually lessening and that the company would survive. Though neither H-D nor most other major manufacturers in Milwaukee ever had a sweatshop reputation, the hourly employees sought job security and more say in such matters as safety, working conditions, vacations and compensation. Company officers were so unfamiliar with unionism initially that they failed to understand the employees' representation request. It became immediately evident in the form of a demand for a union election. Once organized, the wage earners sought and received forty-five cents per hour for women, sixty cents per hour for men and a week of paid vacation each year. Today, four labor unions represent various skills and jobs.

During this period, working with a minimum of capital, H-D managed to create several exciting new models. In 1936, the 61 cu. in. overhead valve

A 1929 Package Truck. Neither the rider nor the location is known. The dual headlights were featured just two years, in 1929 and 1930. *Harley-Davidson, Inc.*

model was introduced. It featured a circulating pressure oiling system that was seen the following year on the 45 cu. in. models and on the 74 and 80 cu. in. side-valve cycles, plus a new and improved four-speed gearbox. The big 1937's all featured full roller bearing motors, chrome-molybdenum tubular front forks, complete instrument panels and interchangeable wheels. The results were encouraging: '37 sales hit 11,674 units, the most since the Depression set in. Many long-time Harley-Davidson fans believe the mid-thirties bikes are the best looking machines ever to come out of Milwaukee. The streamlined, teardrop tanks with their Art Deco decals blend perfectly into the rear portion of the frame running to the back axle. The 45 cu. in. model received the full styling treatment, even though it was viewed by some as a utility machine. The 45, however, was about to become the star of the show.

Secure in the knowledge that the trusty 45 cu. in. solo motorcycle would fit Allied needs, William S. Harley and Walter Davidson departed for Camp Holabird, Maryland, on October 30, 1939. The military buildup was on and Harley-Davidson was in the running to create a shaft-drive, three-wheel vehicle for sandy and mucky terrain. Also under consideration for the project were Indian and Delco, the General Motors division. Delco's prototype used a BMW 750cc flathead engine in its three-wheeler, and while cost estimates were a soaring $4,600 apiece, the merits of the German powerplant impressed the military. The three-wheel project was dropped, but was followed by an order for 1,000 two-wheel shaft-drive cycles, to be built by H-D. To the credit of the factory, delivery of the last of these BMW copies was completed by July 1942, as promised.

The two Army-Navy "E" awards given to Harley-Davidson in 1943 and 1945 for supporting the war effort were due in large part to the performance of thousands of 45 cu. in. machines, to the feeling among employees that victory over the Axis hinged on the quality of their work and to the second generation of management. In addition to turning out 88,000 cycles on which soldiers could depend during the period 1942–45, they

William H. Davidson aboard the first 1930 big twin off the assembly line. This model, dubbed the VL, suffered from a series of mechanical woes that took a year to remedy. Davidson, to his credit, rode this example to Denver and back. *William H. Davidson collection*

performed such one-shot projects as secretly taking apart, assessing and somehow reassembling a Russian motorcycle for Army intelligence.

Walter Davidson died in 1942 and William S. Harley followed just over a year later. William H. Davidson, son of works manager William A., was named president on February 23, 1942. Like the founders, there was more to him than the initial impression of a shrewd, conservative and low-key man of intellect. This second-generation Davidson went to work for the company as a laborer in 1925, during his summers off from the University of Wisconsin. He performed the most menial tasks and learned to ride well enough to capture the prized Jack Pine Enduro on a 45 cu. in. machine in 1930.

Bill Davidson's recall of that event shows just how well the Harleys and the Davidsons got along. "On the final day, I had a good chance of winning," he says. "But the stopwatch I wore around my neck on a lanyard had hit my tank and shattered. So Bill [William J.] Harley [also competing on a factory bike] gave me his watch. With a working timepiece, I was able to win." That's the kind of support the Davidsons and the Harleys provided one another down through the years, enabling William H. to remain at the helm of a viable company into the seventies.

Founder Walter Davidson's two sons, Walter C. and Gordon, served in the positions of vice president/sales and vice president/manufacturing, respectively. Walter was instrumental during World War II in procuring materials that other factories couldn't seem to get. Never one to let strong language stand in the way of a good story, he did battle with an increasingly rebellious dealer network during the late forties and fifties. An excellent rider and duck hunting fanatic, he

William J. Harley, foreground, and William H. Davidson, in the sidecar, meet (from left) Allan, Gordon and Walter Davidson following a 1929 trip by the latter three from Milwaukee to the Pacific Northwest and back in 1929. The trio rode 45 cu. in. bikes; Harley and William Davidson are in a 74 cu. in. VL. *William H. Davidson collection*

retired early when AMF came aboard. Gordon, too, had a good sense of humor but was more temperate with his adjectives. He mixed easily with hourly laborers and supervisors alike and, according to at least two long-time employees, was incredibly tight with the company's money. He died of lung cancer in 1967. Founder William A. Davidson's son, Allan, worked briefly at Harley-Davidson and died prematurely. And Arthur's son, also named Arthur, carved a successful industrial career for himself outside the company.

The Harleys made important contributions, too. William J. Harley succeeded his father, William S., as vice president/engineering. He worked his way through the ranks to the position, acquiring superior riding skill along the way. He also excelled in swimming as a young man and hunted ducks with the Davidsons throughout Wisconsin's greater Mississippi flyway. In later years, he became a connoisseur of wine and cheese, due in part to his frequent trips to Varese, Italy, in connection with Aermacchi matters. Assuming

The 20th anniversary trophy presented to William H. Davidson in 1946 commemorating his 1930 win at the Jack Pine Enduro in Michigan. *William H. Davidson collection*

President Walter Davidson, with young William H., tries on the CAC cindertrack racer at a New York auto show in late 1933 or early 1934. Just 10–12 of these highly specialized bikes were sold. *William H. Davidson collection*

the title of chief engineer immediately following the death of his father, Harley was named a vice president in 1957, fourteen years before his death in 1971 from the complications of diabetes. His younger brother, John E., successfully ran the parts and accessories division for many years. Gentle, quiet and well liked, John's military school background propelled him into the U.S. Army during the Second World War, following graduation from Notre Dame. He rose to the rank of major, calling upon his years as an accomplished rider to help direct training of armored division motorcyclists at Fort Knox, Kentucky, and Fort Benning, Georgia. John was, like his brother and the Davidsons, a member of the H-D Board of Directors; ironically, he was never an officer in the company. A golfer, sailor and duck hunter throughout his life, John died of complications caused by cancer in December 1976.

Not even the then-monthly copies of *The Enthusiast* were produced in October 1945 as a forty-day strike descended upon the company. This job action resulted in delay of the 1946 model introduction until February 6, five months later than planned. Not that the '46 H-D's were anything new—the familiar 45, 61 and 74 cu. in. models were mechanically identical to their prewar brethren. Addressing the Board of Directors, President Davidson noted, "We will not be able to produce any radically new, postwar models until the beginning of 1948." Despite material shortages that plagued Harley-Davidson until after the Korean conflict, 15,554 bikes were produced in 1946. Some 20,392 units were made in 1947, the last year of the 61 cu. in. and 74 cu. in. hemispheric combustion chamber Knuckleheads, as they later became known. Ambitious plans for new models were announced repeatedly throughout the forties to directors, though these models failed to pass the prototype stage. Among them:

—A Servi-Car with the horizontally opposed XA motor and driveshaft.

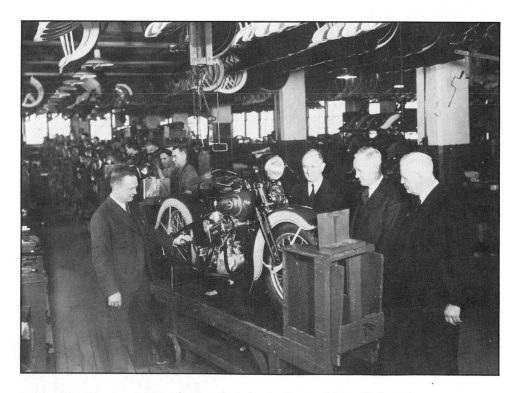

The founders size up the first 61 cu. in. overhead valve E, which rolled off the assembly line for the 1936 model year. This bike later became known to H-D aficionados as the Knucklehead. H-D's major rival, Indian, made nothing that could compete with the OHV Harleys, which were produced with few changes through 1947. *William H. Davidson collection*

—Hydraulic front forks throughout the line by 1948.

—A vertical twin with shaft drive, hydraulic forks, rear suspension, rubber-mounted handlebars, foot shift, hand clutch and more.

The latter was a response to the introduction in some quantity of British twins, ridden with gusto by GI's fortunate enough to have been stationed in

Compare the paint job on this '32 tank with the '31. Although the company had eased away from olive drab for 1931, nothing offered that year approached the scrollwork seen a year later. *David Wright*

This shapely tank is from the 1931 model year, the first cycles affected by the Depression. As the economic hard times hung on, the paint and decals became more stylized because the company was trying harder than ever to appeal to the public. *David Wright*

A 1933 model year gas tank. "There were no stylists per se at the factory at the time," says Willie G. Davidson. "But there were people who knew what looked good on a bike." Indeed, there were. *David Wright*

The early stages of Art Deco design, as seen on this 1934 model year tank. The quality of the paint and its careful application have been Harley-Davidson selling points through the years. *David Wright*

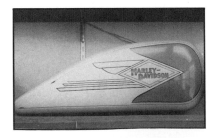

A 1935 tank. Beginning with the 1933 models, the "V" series H-D's and the 45's took on beautifully stylized tanks and color schemes. *David Wright*

This tank, from 1936, sat atop the big flathead motors. The Art Deco decal is considered a classic, with variations on this theme used throughout the mid-thirties. *David Wright*

England. The sieve-like motors and marginal quality control of the British bikes were a tradeoff for handling that made Harley-Davidsons seem agricultural by comparison. Dealers, especially along the West Coast, who sought to take on a line of British cycles, increasingly popular scooters or motorbikes such as the U.S.-made Servi-Cycle were all but terrorized by old Arthur Davidson. "If they divide their time," he told directors in 1947, ". . . we'll eventually replace them with exclusive dealers." Any long-term thoughts on a vertical twin produced in Milwaukee were shelved in the wake of the experience of the Indian Motorcycle Company, H-D's only remaining domestic competitor.

Indian appears to have had the same hot-and-cold fascination with middleweight bikes. The fascination eventually proved fatal. According to Ted A. Hodgdon, Jr., son of a long-time Indian principal, "Since 1930, Indian had been examining lighter English design engineering. The experimental shops at Springfield [Massachusetts] contained examples of these machines, such as Norton, Matchless, Velocette and Triumph. These products . . . influenced the Prince single of the thirties. While a good enough little motorcycle, it did not sell well. It should have been a warning, but the lessons of the Prince went unheeded in Springfield." Following World War II, a line of middleweight vertical twins was emphasized, with the traditional heavyweight Indian V-twin carried only as an afterthought.

"Nearly all of the 'new' machines failed quickly and resulted in massive warranty claims," Hodgdon reports. "The small displacement and fragile Arrow and Scout rewarded rough treatment by promptly reducing themselves to junk. . . . Word quickly spread and diehard devotees switched their loyalties overnight. The traditional V-twins—carryovers from prewar design—were good motorcycles and enjoyed some success, but the damage had been done. . . . Production on the offending designs ceased and stopgap imports were sold under the Indian name for a few years. It was not enough, and the wigwam folded." The final irony occurred in 1970, when Taiwanese bikes with the Indian nameplate on their tanks were offered to Harley-Davidson. AMF did not seriously consider the offer.

By the end of 1948, the company was installed in the former A. O. Smith propeller plant on Capitol Drive in west suburban Wauwatosa, Wisconsin. The 269,000-square-foot, single-story facility was purchased two years earlier for $1.5 million to meet anticipated demand for postwar models, such as the 1948 big twin models with hydraulic lifters and the 1949 Hydra-Glide, the first Harley offered with hydraulic forks. For a

John Davidson sits on a racer while Willie G. tugs at a tooth during the 1938 Milwaukee AMA flat-track races. How many kids got so close so early to competition Harley-Davidsons? *William H. Davidson collection*

couple of years in a row, officers badly misjudged public appetite for cycles; sales in 1949 totaled 23,740 units, versus an anticipated 43,250.

A year later, H-D pointed out to the U.S. Tariff Commission that foreign cycle sales amounted to nearly forty percent of new registrations. The company requested a fifty percent hike in the tariff on foreign makes. Joined by United Auto Workers and Cushman scooter executives, H-D principals argued their case in Washington, but to no avail. The commission voted four-to-two to allow trade to go on as before, in part because the former Japanese distributor for H-D, Alfred Child, provided damaging testimony concerning Harley-Davidson's inability to accurately gauge the domestic market or placate its dealers. The importer of British BSA's at the time, Child apologized for the damage years later. "Sorry, Bill," he wrote William H. Davidson, "but my future depended on being able to carry on my business."

Business was on the mind of the Federal Trade Commission at about the same time. Harley-Davidson was found guilty of preventing its dealers from selling competitive lines of vehicles and accessories. From this decision, together with dealer protection laws designed initially for car dealers in every state, Harley-Davidson franchise holders today are an independent group. The company's current attitude, according to John Finstad, field sales manager, is simply to make sure that H-D's get their share of the dealers' time and talent.

Other phenomena were occurring beyond the company's control. In 1947, members of a Hollister, California, civic organization playfully dumped a questionable substance out a second-floor window onto a group of cyclists in town to attend a race. The riders overreacted, squaring off with the town toughs, then turning on virtually anybody who happened to be on the street. The wire services and *Life* magazine picked up the story, complete with vivid photos. That riot, immortalized in Stanley Kubrick's 1953 movie *The Wild One*, starring Marlon Brando, made cyclists paranoid and appeared, to non-riders, to split all riders into only two camps. One side seemed bent on improving cycling's image; its trademark was a tidy, full-dress touring bike. The other side struck the public as an outlaw element, riding bikes in various stages of modification, ready to perform violent or outrageous behavior. Motorcycling needed fresh air. It blew in unexpectedly from the Far East.

Japan's obliterated economy was very generously primed by the U.S. immediately after World War II. Following a period when Japanese trinkets were scorned as shoddy and in poor taste, a number of quality products were exported worldwide: cameras, stereo phonographs, tape decks, television sets—and motorcycles. The Japanese cycle invasion began innocently enough about 1960 with a 50cc Honda; at the opposite end of the spectrum from either the British sports bikes or the rock-solid Harleys. These Oriental machines found favor with housewives, students and others who might or might not graduate to larger,

This 1944 photo shows a Servi-Car with the opposed-twin motor and shaft-drive transmission. The idea went no further than prototype stage, due to the declining popularity of the three-wheelers. *Harley-Davidson, Inc.*

faster, two-wheel transportation. When riders who wanted more were ready, so were the Japanese, producing larger, faster and more expensive motorcycles every year.

Earlier, following introduction of the K model in 1952, which competed sans success with the British vertical twins, Harley-Davidson was in dire straits. Consultants confirmed Gordon Davidson's contention that, "unless we lower the boom in very drastic fashion on every phase of our operations, we are headed for very serious trouble." Part of the problem appears to have been an unwillingness to sink back into the company a large share of the profits each year. Executive salaries were very low (only four company officers were paid more than $20,000 in 1950, for example), but shareholders were rewarded with dividends that frequently exceeded ten percent of the stock's value. A retired H-D employee guesses that this was a method of keeping all wages and salaries in line. "You couldn't very well ask for more money than the president of the company was making," he says. As a result, the possibilities of consolidating all operations in the Capitol Drive plant, then to moving everything back to Juneau Avenue, then to diversifying into such areas as snowblowers, lawn mowers, a motor scooter to be manufactured for Sears, even into air-conditioner compressors, were explored. Cycle production slid to 12,250 cycles in 1954 and 9,550 in 1955. H-D continued to turn a modest profit throughout the fifties before the new popularity of machines made the officers realize that there was a bike boom—worldwide and growing.

H-D's Post-War Models Committee, renamed the Development Committee, concluded on June 17, 1959, that the best way to introduce a middleweight motorcycle was to import. Of more consequence, the committee agreed to "give consideration to the 250cc model motorcycles produced by the motorcycle division of Aeronautica Macchi, SpA, of Varese, Italy." The committee decided against wedging Aermacchi motors into Sportster chassis, but to explore instead a joint venture with the firm.

William H. Davidson and his wife traveled to Varese in a circuitous route, visiting Europe's leading motorcycle manufacturers on the way. Following negotiations with Aeronautica Macchi (constructors, during World War II, of the respected Macchi fighter plane), H-D purchased half of the profitable Aermacchi cycle division for

The post-WW II single-cylinder 125cc two-stroke on the assembly line in late 1947. This model was copied from the German DKW cycle, as was the English BSA Bantam. Note union membership button on collar of worker in foreground. *William H. Davidson collection*

$247,209, a bargain even in those days. Financing was arranged through a Swiss bank and was expedited when a bank director confessed that he was a long-time H-D admirer. Net profits initially were estimated at $57,000 annually, based on the sale of 4,500 units in the 175–250cc class and 1,000 units in the 125–150cc class, plus spare parts.

The long-sought, in-between Harleys were introduced in September 1960 for the 1961 season. Chief Designer Wilbur Petri, whose father had run the H-D tool room from 1914 to 1944, was sent to Italy as technical consultant and administrative advisor. Promised that he would spend just two years in the picturesque village separated from Switzerland by an Alpine mountain, Petri had to plead with management to bring him back to Milwaukee in 1967. During his seven-year tenure, he confronted electrical systems that never lived up to expectations and the complication of fitting U.S handlebars, grips, levers and cables to the machines. Retired today after forty-three years with the company, the mechanical engineer defends the Aermacchi line. "They were well designed," he says.

Petri believes the failure of Aermacchi Harley-Davidson came about because AMF added a number of features without raising prices. "They thought they'd sell more units with more things on the bikes, but they were wrong. The machines became dated in comparison to the Japanese bikes." Also partially responsible for the demise of the Italian Harleys were the dealers themselves and the decision to switch the emphasis to two-stroke motors. Faced with the happy prospect of a superheated, Vietnam-era economy, H-D retailers consistently steered prospects toward the larger, U.S.-made machines. Asks Petri: "Would you rather sell a bike that nets $400 or $1,000?" John A. Davidson, son of William H. and president of the company at the time, announced on June 14, 1978, the closing of the lakeside plant near Varese.

Experimental hydraulic forks on a 1946 model. No details are available. *Harley-Davidson, Inc.*

Arthur Davidson congratulates rider Joe Weatherly after the latter won the 100-mile national road race at Laconia, New Hampshire, in 1949. Arthur remained active with the company until his death in an auto accident in late 1950. *William H. Davidson collection*

The factory was purchased by Italian investors and in 1982 produced 40,000 machines, primarily off-road two-strokes. The Cagiva, as the motorcycle is called today, recently began to be imported into the U.S. So these Italian bikes now compete for the tougher-to-obtain discretionary dollar with H-D and all other makes.

But I'm getting ahead of the story. Let's examine more closely some aspects in the evolution of today's machines. . . .

The handsome but sluggish 1952 K model is sized up by, from left, Gordon Davidson, vice president manufacturing; Walter C. Davidson, vice president sales; William J. Harley, vice president engineering; and William H. Davidson, president. *William H. Davidson collection*

Young Bill ("Willie G."), left, and John Davidson with their tricked-up K models in the summer of 1953. Both are the sons of William H. Davidson, late former H-D President. *William H. Davidson collection*

The first Topper scooter, surrounded by a Harley and three Davidsons. *William H. Davidson collection*

The all-aluminum 45 cu. in. KL showed promise in the mid-fifties but development time for the machine ran out. The tremendously successful Sportster, introduced in 1957, took its place. *Harley-Davidson, Inc.*

Chapter 2

Construction

The public tour of Harley-Davidson's York, Pennsylvania, assembly plant follows time spent in the Rodney C. Gott Museum, and maybe that's unfortunate. Most visitors enter the plant with their heads full of obscure facts and a lingering mental picture of Cal Rayborn's KR or Joe Petrali's record breaker. But to truly appreciate the assembly facility, it's best to start with a clean slate.

Formerly the site of a ponderous inventory system connected by a 3½-mile overhead monorail, the two main manufacturing areas total 400,000 square feet. In place of all that inventory is a series of dedicated storage carts used to move parts around the plant. Special padding in each cart protects the parts as they're taken to subassembly or assembly areas. This is all part of the MAN (material as needed) system of assembly, wherein parts must be perfect because there is no excess. All parts for all bikes arrive in York almost immediately prior to assembly. The benefit to H-D is that there is no major investment in stored inventory. Where York formerly turned its $20 million inventory just twice a year, the plant now makes seventeen turns annually.

A number of preassembly jobs are accomplished throughout the plant. Among them:

—Chrome plating. Hardware is buffed and polished here, then loaded in racks. The process, from bare metal to completion, takes approximately ninety minutes, beginning with a coat of nickel and ending with glistening chrome. Tank probes sense temperature, pH content and contaminants as parts are lowered into and raised from the toxic solutions. Monitored on a console, this system of reverse osmosis units and scrubbers allows for ninety-nine-percent use of the heavy metals in the solution. Polishing is done with three automatic machines, polishing jacks and tumblers.

—Machining. A bewildering array of pieces is machined, often in widely separated areas, throughout the plant. Parts involved include primary chain housings, brake discs and starter components. Housings arrive in York as rough castings and are machined and surface finished. Brake discs show up as blanked, circular pieces of metal and are turned to precise diameters, then hardened using magnetism and extremely high temperatures. After that, they are machined and ground for porosity and hardness. As many as sixteen distinct operations are performed on starter components by numerically controlled machines that preclude having to turn or remove the components.

—Screw machining. Steering-head bushings, axles, linkages and special screws are created from twenty-foot lengths of steel bar or hex stock, with automatic machinery.

—Grinding. Surface, cylindrical and centerless grinders precision machine such hardware as starter shafts, axles and crankpins.

—The presses. A battery of sixty-ton presses, many equipped with automatic feeders, stamps out components such as brackets, gussets, shims, battery clamps and tank and fender blanks. Even larger presses, rated as high as 1,000 tons, deep-draw such items as gas and oil tanks, fenders and air-cleaner housings. Blanking presses stamp out parts such as drive sprockets from stock as thick as $5/16$ in.

—Wheel assembly. Wire wheels, consisting of hubs, rims and spokes, are laced and tightened by hand. They are then torqued in concentric holding fixtures and trued to specifications in indicator fixtures. Brake discs, drive sprockets, tubes and tires are installed prior to final balancing.

—Welding. Various subweldments are fabricated and the frame is assembled and welded in a single, continuous line. Welding quality has taken a quantum leap forward since the buyback, for a very simple reason: Before, "No one knew what the criteria were for a weld," says Jim Wright, frame-area welding supervisor. "One of the welding operators' first suggestions was that someone explain to them exactly what they should be doing." Nowadays, the gas metal-arc welded subassemblies and mild-steel frames need no further inspection because the welders know the exact standards needed to produce the quality for all parts and frames as they travel through final assembly. But before the trip down the assembly line, several of the 20,000 different parts need painting.

—Paint. If you haven't heard, Harley-Davidson has this new, $26 million paint system that is as good as they say it is. How good is that? Before the system was installed, H-D had the finest finish on any production motorcycle. Now, says PPG, supplier of paint, "If American automobiles have a Class A finish, Harley-Davidsons are Class Triple-A." The praise is earned with an eight-stage zinc phosphate pre-treatment, followed by a coat of epoxy, followed by robotically controlled application of PPG acrylic, followed by a powder clear coat. The latter step—powder clear coat over acrylic—is entirely new technology and accounts for the strict no-photo rule in that part of the facility. Details such as hand striping and silk screening then take place.

Karl Eberly, director of manufacturing, Paul Slater, program manager, Gary Christian, project manager, and others get credit for the system, which was tough to get up and running but is producing anticipated results. Why improve a finish that was always good enough? The answer is that H-D is committed to continuous improvement, so being the best is only relative. As this is being written, new and better ways of manufacturing are being examined, not only where there are problems but where there are opportunities. Simply put, tomorrow's Harley-Davidson will be a better machine than today's.

Now we're ready for a stroll down the assembly line. . . .

A bare frame begins its trip accompanied by a Vehicle Identification Number (VIN). Assembly will take place at seventy-two stations in less than two hours, resulting in as many as 325 motorcycles a day. Assemblers trained in statistical process control are stationed at key points along the line, ensuring that each part is properly attached and that it falls within carefully set parameters that may involve only a few thousandths of an inch.

Five-speed transmissions await shipment from the Capitol Drive plant to assembly in York. *David Wright*

The end of the line results in a machine that is ready to be road tested and shipped. The road test is like nothing performed in any motorcycle magazine.

The finished, inspected H-D is wheeled into a concrete booth, hooked to a remote battery, to instruments and to ventilation equipment. The test rider climbs on, hits the starter button and the engine roars to life for the first time since it was tested in Milwaukee. This simulated road test, conducted on a roller stand that is powered by the rear wheel, lasts approximately five miles. Nearly thirty tests are conducted, including going through the gears to a "speed" of 60 miles per hour and testing such crucial functions as braking, suspension, lights, even the horn. The rider is backed up by an array of instruments that records sound level and such subtleties as the amount of vacuum in the transmission. Following this subjective and instrumental once-over, the bike is rolled forward a few feet for crating and shipping in the company's own fleet of trucks.

Harley-Davidson converted the exciting but inefficient aerial inventory to the MAN system in mid-1982. The results have included dramatic savings at a time when the money saved can be put to better use elsewhere. Chairman Vaughn Beals told dealers of this new parts binning plan in 1982, citing it as one of several ways in which the company is attempting to save money. Special mention should be made of H-D suppliers, who cooperated in the low-inventory venture following a "summit conference" between the factory and many of its 700 or so suppliers in May of '82.

So much for the assembled machines; what about the assemblers? Ralph Swenson, who formerly headed the York plant, says, "This part of Pennsylvania produces people who are proud of their work ethic. Twenty years ago, this was a farming county. It created people who were good with their hands. We conduct training, but no one can teach an attitude, to be interested and concerned about your work. These people are." Swenson adds, almost as an afterthought, that many of the assemblers, welders and machinists are also riders.

Hand in hand with the MAN system has come statistical process control and statistical operator control. Seventy-five percent of production employees have been trained in one or both systems and they employ their knowledge in quality circles. Costs have decreased and quality has climbed, says a member of the York quality audit program. Independent of the quality control processes, the quality audit people have gone from the need to audit all bikes in 1978 to subjecting only two or three percent to two-and-one-half hours of testing today. The difference is quality control. "We don't have a check list," says a team member. "It's open season—we can do anything we like to the bike." The initial going-over takes place on the bench, where anything except major disassembly is permitted. The air cleaner is unbolted, a finger probes for imprecise alignment of a gasket, the fit of the gas cap is checked. Failing to find any flaw of significance here means that the bike is ridden just to the east of the plant to the one-mile test track. From fifteen to thirty miles of acceleration, braking, handling and related functions are performed. The ribbon of asphalt is more than a mile long and winds amid rolling hills, pine trees and the tall sandbag bunkers used to test explosives by former occupants of the York plant. Speed and distance depend on the season, but the bikes are audited in rain and light snow. Following their tour through

The most expensive piece of machinery ever purchased by AMF, worth $4.5 million, takes up hundreds of square feet in the Capitol Drive plant. The machinery makes five-speed transmissions. *David Wright*

the countryside, cycle and rider meet again for a final inspection of cosmetics. Discovery of a flaw gives any employee the authority to halt shipment on as many bikes as are suspect.

"We've found a number of problems that, left unsolved, would have resulted in a major product recall," an employee notes. "For example, we discovered a bearing problem in a transmission out there on the test track. Fewer than 400 bikes with that transmission had been sold, so we were able to make the repairs quickly through the dealers or in our factory inventory while the engineers made a minor design change."

"The dealers still may find a 'onesy-twosy' flaw, but they no longer have to touch the engines or the transmissions," says an employee. "Their warranty work was decreased markedly."

A similar effort is under way in Milwaukee at the engine/transmission plant. Dynamometers, each worth $122,000, recently were installed to run a small batch of engines for approximately thirty minutes. Two engines each day will be run longer, for horsepower checks, then disassembled. "We'll test the engines in some chassis there, too, so that we can see how the engine, transmission and frame interrelate," according to an employee. "The tests in Milwaukee will tell us things that are awfully hard to detect, such as when a drill is getting dull. A small thing like that can affect the performance of a transmission."

Harley-Davidson engines and transmissions, plus a few specialized parts such as clutch and power train components, are created and assembled at the Capitol Drive plant, in the Milwaukee suburb of Wauwatosa. These components are not shipped directly to York, but instead are delayed briefly at Juneau Avenue, where high-temperature paint is applied to the engines. (Except for hand assembly of the XR racers, the engine painting procedure is the only link that remains between Juneau Avenue facilities and any actual assembly.) The Capitol plant's good work owes a lot to Thomas A. Gelb, vice president, continuous improvement, who somehow parlayed a bachelor's degree in forestry into a very successful career that began with the privately held Harley-Davidson company in 1960.

"When I joined the company, all of the assembly took place on the third floor of the Juneau Avenue plant," Gelb says, recalling that the semi-completed motorcycles were moved on elevators from floor to floor during production. Engine assembly was moved from Juneau to Capitol in 1972, even before the line was constructed in York. "We had the company's first powered assembly line," Gelb reports. He and former Chairman Vaughn Beals said in separate interviews that the increasingly oil-tight, rattle- and trouble-free H-D's of today are the result of generous investment in contemporary tools and machines, at Capitol Drive and elsewhere, during the AMF years.

One rambling piece of equipment in the middle of the Capitol Drive building automatically machines the cases for five-speed transmissions. "That cost $4.5 million, the largest single piece of machinery ever purchased by AMF for any of its operations," according to Gelb.

Approximately 1,000 persons are employed at Capitol Drive, with assembly taking place on a single shift and machining work on all three shifts. In addition to being the site for one of the largest heat-treating facilities in Wisconsin, the plant fronting U.S. Highway 41 has a just-completed

Shielded in layers of lead-impregnated plastic foam, this H-D undergoes noise emissions analysis at the Capitol Drive plant. *Buzz Buzzelli*

engine quality program. A new kind of dynamometer checks the reliability of engines and transmissions, while technicians tear down and inspect the functions of those units. The results are an audit score that is passed on to quality auditors in York—and far fewer engine problems than in the past.

Though he has been with H-D more than twenty years, Gelb probably represents the kind of supervisory employee that will become more

Assembler Gloria Cruz installs cam gears and cam covers on the new Capitol Drive XL assembly line. *Buzz Buzzelli*

Pushrods and rocker boxes are put together by employee Jim Depka. He has 20 years of experience on H-D assembly lines at the Capitol Drive plant. *Buzz Buzzelli*

common in the now-independent H-D. A compulsive worker, he ceased riding or driving anything rapid after starring in an end-over-end accident during a sports car race in 1968 that still has old-time fans talking at the Mosport, Ontario, road racing course. "I have small children. I had to quit while I was in one piece." The two-time regional driving champion has turned cautious in the extreme—he no longer fishes much in Lake Michigan because the trophy-size salmon similar to the taxidermy sample on his office wall contain questionable levels of hazardous chemicals. Such an attitude is, he hopes, reflected in the engines he ships to York. Appreciation for Gelb's outlook became evident at the culmination of the well-publicized buyback ride—from York to Milwaukee in 1981—when Vaughn Beals elevated the man who only recently climbed back on a motorcycle to a vice-presidential slot.

"You wouldn't recognize the engine plant today," Gelb says. "The new quality control system eliminated virtually all of the inspectors. We've learned during this (five-year) conversion that rewards are a very long time in coming. But they're larger than we anticipated."

The program has reached H-D's Tomahawk plant some 250 miles northwest of Milwaukee, where fiber glass and ABS side covers, wind-shields, sidecars and the electronics in fairings are crafted. When Harley-Davidson purchased the Tomahawk Boat Company in 1963, fiber glass was laid up by hand in a female mold. The following year, the use of compression molding equipment, which involved injection of fiber-glass-reinforced plastic into male and female molds and heat curing, was begun. The $250,000 in equipment paid for itself in six months, despite the fact that the products created in those early years wouldn't stand up to close scrutiny today.

Purchased primarily to create golf car bodies and for sidecars and Servi-Cars, the equipment was first used for saddlebags and fairings in 1969. Compression molding and the consequent heat curing caused the product to shrink by about six to eight percent. That shrinkage exposed the fibers in the material. The molded components were painted a matte finish, either black or white, that effectively concealed the minute fiber strands. So far, so good—until the late-seventies.

Harley-Davidson at that time began to offer TourPaks, saddlebags and fairings to match bike colors. Dealers and customers alike complained with validity that the adornments were not as well finished as either the competition's accessories or the many aftermarket products available. "It wasn't orange peel, but it didn't look right," says a

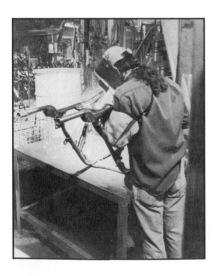

All Harley-Davidson frames are welded not by robots but by skilled employees at the York assembly plant. *David Wright*

Harley-Davidson disc brakes are attached to wheels by hand prior to assembly. *David Wright*

former employee. Then, in 1980, the Japanese entered the touring-bike market with rim-molded fairings and bags. The only way H-D could compete was to use lots of sandpaper and primer. Results were expensive and inefficient. The company then formulated its new stance toward quality with the introduction of low-profile fiber glass resin.

Shrinkage of the material is about two percent, effectively concealing the hairlike pieces of fiber glass. Efforts to make the accessories more closely match the bike were redoubled, with the result that criticism has come 180 degrees. "The finish is no longer a problem," says Robert S. Zawtocki, a Harley-Davidson executive. "We now use a new paint facility to apply urethane from either Cook, PPG or Sheboygan Paint Company to a greatly improved surface. These urethanes are also improved and they take clear coats well. Paint specifications are subjected to the statistical control program."

Not even the metallic colors cause problems, despite the fact that they formerly showed a lot of "flip." That means the paint appears to change color depending on the amount of light and the angle from which it is seen. Every color comes from a target paint sample created by the styling department. Each paint company then has to match the sample. The goal of styling, construction and assembly is to create a finished product that looks uniform, even if tiny formula adjustments have to be made in York or in Tomahawk.

All of the motorcycle products that emerge from the plant are styled by Willie G. Davidson and his H-D associates. The vice president has worked with mold makers to create distinctive parts and accessories for the bikes. Initially, Willie G. even created some new boat designs for the Tomahawk division. Weather willing, a local resident may spot one of Willie G.'s personal machines parked near the building on the east side of town.

Tomahawk isn't the end of the earth, but you can get a good view of it from there. A summer vacation destination, the year-round population shrinks like fiber glass under compression to just 3,400 hardy residents in the winter, when temperatures of forty below zero Fahrenheit are occasionally recorded. Like their Milwaukee counterparts, the 157 hourly employees are members of the Allied Industrial Workers union. There is no piecework and visitors frequently are surprised at the pace the workers maintain.

There's one more Harley-Davidson facility that should be noted. Since January 1981, the company

The Big Twin assembly line at H-D's Capitol Drive plant in Wauwatosa, WI, on Milwaukee's west side. *Buzz Buzzelli*

39

has operated road testing facilities at the Talladega (Alabama) International Motor Speedway. Durability, Environmental Protection Agency emissions testing and high-speed handling are carried out. More important, prototype models are run over railroad ties and concrete rub strips to test new frame designs. Approximately forty employees on two shifts man the leased facility, where tests continue through rain, snow and the eleven-degree weather experienced in December 1981.

A quality audit is performed on an Electra Glide Classic. The audit involves a two-and-one-half-hour test and inspection. *David Wright*

Striping is done with ¹/₁₆ in. or ¹/₈ in. paint markers at the fiber-glass plant in Tomahawk. *David Wright*

The final touches go on an FXRP police bike fairing in Tomahawk. *David Wright*

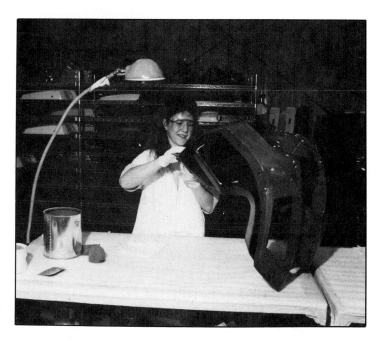

Much of the work in Tomahawk is still done by hand. *David Wright*

Glenn Christianson, manager of inventory control, looks over a sidecar before it is packed for shipping. Sidecars may go to York, to a dealer or, increasingly, to an overseas customer. *David Wright*

Chapter 3

Iron

Harley-Davidson folks in Milwaukee hear the following line all the time: "Styling carried you guys for a lot of years, right?"

They reply with a question: "What years are you talking about?"

The civilian in this case mumbles something about 1980–82 and a smile spreads across the employee's face. "Styling has done wonders for us, but during the years you mention, we came out with belt drive. That was an answer to a question that hadn't even been asked. It was particularly innovative because we had introduced the enclosed chain just a bit earlier. Other innovations during that period included the five-speed transmission in 1980 on the FLT and improved FLT front-end geometry that same year."

Under development during the years in question was everything from the Evolution engine to the fairing for the FXRT. If you're a high-tech type, you know that Harley-Davidson overcame its most pressing quality problems during that time, too. If you're the kind who simply likes to be dazzled, consider this: The early '80s saw a proliferation that resulted in more than twenty models offered in a rainbow of colors that make for 1,000 different kinds of Harley-Davidson moving down the York assembly line in 1993. That's a far cry from the lone machine created by the brothers Davidson and Mr. Harley in 1903. Here is how today's bumper crop of machines evolved. . . .

The very first model was manufactured from 1903 through 1908. It featured a 25 cu. in., three-horsepower motor that drove the rear wheel directly via a single loop of leather. In 1909, cubic inches climbed to 35 and horsepower to 4 by way of a larger bore and stroke. The year 1907 marked the appearance of the first bottom-link springer front end. Crude as this suspension system seems today, it was hailed in the young auto industry as a breakthrough in combating the country's rutted roads and was grafted onto all kinds of racers. A battery ignition was seen as early as 1908, offered on the single as an alternative to the Bosch magneto.

There is proof positive the Harley-Davidson had a working V-twin as early as 1907. However, not until 1911 was the twin perfected. An exhaust valve on the side of the cylinder created an exit for spent fuel, giving rise to the term "ioe" or inlet-over-exhaust configuration. Many have speculated on the 45-degree arrangement and 50 cu. in. size of the initial twin. The shape of the motor may well have been determined because it was the ideal depth to fit between the frame's front down tube and the seat tube. As for capacity, engineer William S. Harley probably picked 61 cu. in. because it could be constructed using two of the single cylinders and because that displacement worked out to 1,000 cubic centimeters. Sixty-one cubes were viewed by contemporaries as the ultimate reasonable size for motorcycle engines.

The company has shown a willingness to continuously improve its products down through the years; call that evolutionary if you will. H-D made its singles and V-twins more comfortable in 1912 by offering the first seat post, a patented "Ful-Floteing" device that cushioned the seat with a spring inside the seat tube. In rapid-fire succession, Harley-Davidson offered a clutch (1912), chain drive and a single-speed transmission (1913), internal expanding rear brake, gas lights, sidecars and a two-speed transmission (1914), an electrical lighting system (1915) and a three-speed transmission the same year. World War I was but a pause in technological terms. The 1918 models displayed optional hand-operated rear brakes, while 1920 bikes featured Harley-Davidson's own electrical systems; the latter were created as an answer to the dampness-prone Remy units and set standards for quality electrics for a decade. Few of the features were found on the direct-drive racers of the day, indicating that looking after the street rider was a company priority. Harley-Davidson emerged from the teens as the world's largest motorcycle company simply because its products worked better than those of the competition.

Motorcycles, like all mechanical contrivances, reach plateaus, and such a leveling off seems to have occurred in 1922. That was the year before the demise of H-D's unique 37 cu. in., 180-degree opposed twin Sport model, created in 1919. The company produced a new series of 74 cu. in. motors, the JD, in 1921, then opted for refinement rather than revelation through 1925. Styling became a factor, initially evident in 1925 when the then-new H-D's sported teardrop gas tanks. This new look worked especially well in 1926, when the company re-entered the lightweight field in a burst of new technology with 21 cu. in. models in either flathead or overhead valve configuration. Both models offered detachable heads. The homework done on the flathead was to stand Harley-Davidson in good stead.

Meanwhile, the company produced a high-output motor, even though H-D no longer financed a factory team. The 61 cu. in. two-cam began showing up in hillclimb and flat-track winner's circles in 1925. Its success resulted in production in 1928 and 1929 of only 61 and 74 cu. in. two-cam models for very sporting street riders. The first production front brake appeared in '28, but there was even bigger news the following year. Announced with twin headlights, the 1929 models included the 45 cu. in. flathead V-twin and the 30.50 cu. in. single. Singles stuck around in various forms—speedway racer, utility machine—until 1934, but the offspring of that first 45 flathead are with us still.

The 1931 bikes reverted to a single headlight and so were featured on the VL series, introduced in 1930. The VL's most interesting technical

The first Harley-Davidson. It is now believed that just one motorcycle was produced in 1903. *Harley-Davidson, Inc.*

44

innovation initially was wheel interchangeability. By 1933, the full line of bikes sported incredibly colorful Art Deco gas tanks as the factory tried desperately to sell bikes to an unemployed public. The Servi-Car, powered by the 45 cu. in. motor, came out in 1932 and was offered a year later with a reverse gear added to the three-speed transmission. This innovation was optional on all V-twins with sidecars from 1933 through 1974, when Servi-Car production ceased.

Since times were tough, the introduction of several new models in 1936 was a gamble. Foremost among them was the Knucklehead, the first overhead valve V-twin. The new, hemispherical-head motor showed a recirculating oil system and a greatly improved, welded fuel/oil tank. Companion models that memorable year included an 80 cu. in. flathead, the VLH, and the last VL, available with H-D's first four-speed transmission. Encouraged, the factory offered 74 and 80 cu. in. UL flatheads the following year, together with the first WL in the 45 cu. in. series. Generator and oil indicator lights showed up in '38, followed in '39 by a streamlined dash panel and in 1940 by the first metal nameplate and 16 in. wheels. This prewar burst of technology culminated in 1941 with the introduction of the 74 cu. in. Knucklehead, a classic among classics. Accented with metal tank strips, the '41 Knuckler is the most sought-after Harley-Davidson ever.

Paramilitary organizations and the police were the sole recipients of new civilian cycles during the war years. The ULH series 80 cu. in. motors were last produced in 1941. Civilian production resumed in November 1945. The public had to be content through 1947 with very minor alterations (such as cast aluminum tail lights and a new nameplate), but 1948 was an exciting year indeed. Hydraulic lifters beneath 74 cu. in. Panhead cylinders created interest, as did the all-new, 125cc two-stroke machine with the three-speed, foot-shift transmission. Few took note of the demise of the 74 cu. in. UL series after '48. Another surprise was in store in 1949, as H-D swapped the venerable springer front end for hydraulic suspension, dubbing such models Hydra-Glides and introducing the soft ride on a 61 cu. in. version of the Panhead. A smaller version of the same principle appeared in 1951 on the 125cc bike and was dubbed the Teleglide.

The evolutionary process was at work in 1952, as foot shift was offered optionally on FL Panheads and on the EL, even though '52 was the last year for that 61 cu. in. series. More important, the K model blended the heritage of the 45 cu. in. motor with European styling and a four-speed foot-shift transmission in a dramatic departure in thinking for the utilitarian W series engine. The company's first off-the-shelf scrambler, the KRM, followed in 1953, the final year for the 45 cu. in. motor aboard a two-wheeler. The 1954 KH sported a 55 cu. in. (883cc) motor, making the sporting bike as fast as it was stylish. Meanwhile, H-D continued to produce several 125-165cc machines, but the stage was set for a pair of momentous mid-fifties motorcycles.

The 74 cu. in. FLH came out in 1955 and, even with its rigid frame, was the ultimate two-wheeled choice for touring enthusiasts. The FL series has evolved dramatically in its twenty-eight years of existence, yet its long-haul, luxury essence remains unchanged. Equally momentous was the introduction of the Sportster in 1957. If the FL's were the kings of the highway, the XL's were the studs of the street and strip. Overhead valves were the secret to the Sportster's thunderous performance. The following year, H-D made both the F and X series even more desirable: The former received a swinging arm frame and automotive-type shocks to become the Duo-Glide, while the latter was joined by the magneto-equipped XLCH (CH stood for "Competition Hot"). Overlooked at the time were such amenities as the new hydraulic brake on the 74 cu. in. cycle.

Nineteen fifty-nine marked the final year of domestic small-engine production, with the exception of the Topper scooter, which made its debut in 1960, the golf cart, produced initially in 1963, and the snowmobile, 1971–1975. Henceforward, all of the smaller powerplants were to come from the Aermacchi/H-D plant in Italy. The mainstay bikes continued to evolve, with the Sportster receiving a full-width front brake drum in 1964 and the FL series acquiring a 12-volt battery, electric starting, a five-gallon tank and a new name, Electra Glide, in 1965.

The Shovelhead motor was created for the Electra Glide in 1966, displaying a top end reminiscent of the Knucklehead. This evolutionary step disposed of several external oil lines, trading iron for aluminum in the process. To celebrate an increasingly oil-tight motor, H-D created the 74 cu. in. King of the Highway bike, a machine that redefined the term "full dress." By 1967, Tomahawk fiber glass technology allowed the company to produce the Servi-Car with a glass body. The first fiber-glass-bodied sidecar came along in 1968, followed by similar treatment in '69 for the golf cars. (Incidentally, the first non-leather H-D saddlebags were white plastic and were seen on the 1953 K model, just one of several special offerings in that Golden Anniversary year.) The classic FLH bar-mounted fairing first appeared in 1969.

The Sportster did not sit idle during the years preceding the merger with AMF. In 1968, the XLH received electric start, a Fairbanks-Morse magneto helped launch the XLCH, both XL models sported 150 mph speedometers and the large oval air cleaner showed up, courtesy of the federal government. By the following year, the twelve-year-old motor was producing 58 horsepower at 6,800 revs a minute.

Mid-year 1970 models bore the AMF logo, even though the designs were executed before the conglomerate acquired Harley-Davidson. The first model to be recognized, in fact, as an AMF bike was the 1971 Super Glide. More important, Willie G. Davidson did at the factory what riders themselves had been doing—he mated the XL front end to the FL frame and motor, producing an electric- (FXE) or kick-start (FX) machine that is a benchmark among H-D fans. The Super Glide proved that Willie G.'s idea of a dream bike was on target and that such a machine could proliferate models even more distinctive than the initial (optional), red-white-and-blue-bedecked Super Glide. Yes, the model carried the FX designation, indicating its descent from both series of machines.

Disc brakes up front became standard on FL models the following year, while the Sportster peaked at its present 61 cu. in. (1,000cc) size. If Harley-Davidson clutches and transmissions had by then become trouble free, shifting required some thought: Governmental insistence placed all shifting mechanisms on the rider's left for '72. XL machines ran discs up front initially in 1973, whereas FX and FL models sported disc brakes front and rear. "King of the Road" replaced "King of the Highway," including such items as windshield, spotlights, front and rear safety bars, "Pak King" fiber glass bags, bag guards and a windshield bag. The 738-pound weight made for rock-steady travel during the last full year of 70 mph interstate highway speeds.

Motorcycles generally and H-D's specifically were becoming so desirable that leaving a bike unattended was risky. So the factory in 1974 installed an alarm system on all domestically produced machines. The Sportster, said a magazine, was its own worst enemy; the bike was so reliable that owners were neglecting routine service. Juneau Avenue did not neglect the 1976

U.S. Bicentennial celebration; both the FX and FXE Super Glides were available with special commemorative paint, and the Electra Glide could be had in a Liberty Edition.

Several new models were unveiled in 1977. The FXS Low Rider was a styling sensation, as Willie G. indicated once again that he and his cohort were on the cutting edge of custom machinery. In contrast, the Sportster was made available in a striking, black XLCR Cafe Racer model, complete with all the canyon-carving amenities. While the Japanese were calling on a cadre of stylists and engineers, one small department in one small factory was beating them to the punch by several years. Also on tap from then to now were XLT's, XLT Huggers, XLS Roadsters, XLX's and XR's; each "Sportster" catering to a particular kind of rider.

The 1978 FLH became the first modern H-D with the 80 cu. in. (1,340cc) motor, just in time to join an optional XLH as a seventy-fifth anniversary model. There followed the Classic in 1979 and the present successor to the touring crown, the FLT Tour Glide, in 1980. The FLT, with its five-speed transmission, vibration-isolated motor and frame-mounted fairing, which contrasted well with the Low-Rider, which acquired the 80 cu. in. motor in 1979, with the FXEF Fat Bob running the 1,200cc motor during its inaugural year in 1979 and switching to 80 cubes the year after. The laid-back Wide Glide, also running 80 cu. in., came aboard in 1980, as did the dramatic belt-drive FXB Sturgis.

The FXR came along, winning respect from bike magazines and luring Brand X touring riders into H-D showrooms with its European-style fairing. Riders bade the Shovelhead motor adieu after the 1984 model year, welcoming the Evolution and the 1100cc Sportster motor for '85. Special model introductions included the 1985½ FXRC Low Glide Custom as H-D continued to prove that beauty was more than metal deep by offering demo cruises wherever a rider could plunk down a valid operator's license. All this caused the media and the public to respond—here and abroad.

V-twin imitations were exported in earnest by the Japanese beginning with the 1981 model year. If the economy had not taken such a downturn, perhaps Harley-Davidson would feel that imitation is indeed the sincerest form of flattery. As it stands today, the American rider is offered an Oriental imitation or a domestically produced V-twin at the peak of its development, with seventy-five years of experience behind it. Let's examine that experience on a bike-by-bike basis. . . .

The First Singles 1903–1911

The first Harley-Davidson was made entirely by hand. There simply were no engine blocks, transmissions or carburetors, aftermarket or otherwise, available. That first bike was a copy of the French DeDion motor, a single-cylinder device with a capacity of approximately 25 cu. in. (400cc) that put out 2 horsepower—the equivalent of a fast walk on level ground. There was no gearbox; drive was direct to the rear wheel by means of a two-ply leather belt hooked to a pulley. The belt encircled the rear wheel rim. To get the vehicle moving, the rider pushed up to compression, then jumped on and pedaled frantically till the engine fired. Despite the exertion and the lack of hill-climbing ability, Arthur Davidson and Bill Harley sold all they could create.

The head could not be detached from the cylinder and was characterized by an induction valve stop. The downward movement of the piston sucked open this valve, admitting fuel, before the valve was closed with a spring. The exhaust valve opened and closed via cam action.

The next step, in late 1909, was to enlarge the motor to about 35 cu. in. (475cc) and to double the size of the flywheel, which Davidson and Harley knew affected the powerplant's inclination to keep turning. This single design element added greatly to the longevity of the early H-D's, while Harley's single-loop frame looked more like a motorcycle and less like a bicycle.

By 1908, the company had conceived its own model identification system, based on years of operation. The '08 machines were considered fifth-year models, since true production did not commence until 1904. Earlier, in 1906, H-D came up with its very first option: color choice. The standard, piano finish black was supplemented with a Renault gray/carmine striping combination that created the famous "Silent Gray Fellow" impression. H-D realized quickly that quiet mufflers were appreciated by the rider and the public alike.

Here's the lowdown on a very early H-D single, taken from company archives. Because Harley-Davidson seldom fooled with success, the 35 cu. in. motor was unchanged except for valve design from its creation through 1918, when it became available only on special, commercial order.

Specifications
(From a brochure believed to have been printed in 1905. List price was $200, fob Milwaukee.)
Motor: One piece cylinder, large-diameter flywheel, starting by means of pedaling or by a crank, crankshaft covered by aluminum cap when not in use.
Frame: Wheelbase is 51 in., frame height is 21½ in., extension front forks, 2¼ in. detachable tires, spring seat post, three-coil suspension motor cycle saddle.
Carburetor: Automatic float feed enables engines to run from 5 to 45 miles per hour without adjustment.
Grip control: Allows the cyclist to control engine speed without removing his hands from the handlebars.
Transmission: A 1¼ in. endless flat belt is used to drive the machine and is furnished with a 20 in. rear drive pulley and either a 4½, 5¼ or 6 in. leather-lined

The 1993 FLHTC Electra Glide Classic (90th Anniversary Edition). *Harley-Davidson, Inc.*

47

front pulley. Idler so constructed that the belt can be tightened by the rider while the machine is in motion.

Tanks: Gasoline tank holds 1½ gallons, which is sufficient for 100 to 150 miles running. The lubricating oil tank holds two quarts and one filling is good for 750 miles. The oil is fed into the motor through a sight feed (gravity) oiler.

Muffler: Large enough to be noiseless with a minimum of back pressure.

Batteries: Three standard dry cells and a regular motor cycle coil 3 × 6 in. furnish the current.

Spark plug: ½ in. standard pipe thread; either mica or porcelain plug is furnished.

Tires and wheels: 2¼ in. G&J detachable motor cycle tires are used, and the wheels are built up with steel rims and extra heavy motor cycle spokes.

Hubs: The front is ⅜ in. in diameter and the coaster brake is ½ in. in diameter.

Guards: Both braced by ¼ in. steel rods.

Finish: In black, grip control and all bright parts nickel plated. The aluminum casing is scraped and buffed to a high polish which does not tarnish or turn dull.

The V-Twin 1907–1921

The 45-degree V-twin, the very essence of Harley-Davidson down through the years, was first offered publicly in 1909. A response to the creation of multiple-cylinder models from Thor, Reading-Standard, Indian and other long-gone marques, the 7.2 horsepower behemoth was the forefather of every American V-twin now in production.

The most important engine difference between the very first V-twin, originally seen at a cycle show in late 1907 and produced through 1909, and the twins from 1911 onward, was the inlet valves. Suction valves were tried repeatedly and without success during the period 1907–1909, whereas mechanical valves were used for the later twin. There were no twins offered in 1910, a year devoted to solving the problem. Also, careful attention to the specs will show that the first V's didn't in fact measure up to the true 61 cu. in. capacity in the early years.

But the "6-D," as the model was initially dubbed, measured up in every other way. It sported a precision Bosch magneto (replacing a trio of dry-cell batteries, coil and points), a choice of 26 or 28 in. wheels (to accommodate riders of different heights) and the Renault gray finish, all standard. The founders were sufficiently confident of the new machine to provide the same guarantee against defective parts and workmanship enjoyed by singles owners. And while production was halted briefly in 1910, a "7-E" model, the very first all-out racer, was sold to a few select customers.

In 1911, H-D introduced its patented idler. A lever and gears replaced a rod and harness to uncouple the direct drive, providing clutch-like disengagement between the pulley and the new, larger 1¾-in. belt. No longer did the rider have to overcome direct drive in order to stop; nor did he have to repeatedly restart a balky motor afterward. The 1911 motor also featured a new fuel/oil tank, superseding separate tanks and storing three quarts of oil for the total-loss lubrication system.

The oil traveled by gravity through a glass sight-tube to the crankcase, where it bathed the flywheel and the crank and was fed directly to the bearings. The force of the moving parts pushed oil

The 1993 FXDL Dyna Low Rider.
Harley-Davidson, Inc.

to the piston and the lower cylinder wall. Oil not burned in combustion fell to the bottom of the case, where it was drained by hand. A hand-operated oil pump, standard for 1912, supplemented the gravity system, which could be adjusted but which most often ran at about one drop of oil every two-and-one-half seconds. Since the motor had been increased to 61 cu. in. for 1912, more lubrication was required.

Specifications
(From a 1911 brochure)

Motor: Twin-cylinder, 6½ horsepower, bore 3 in., stroke 3½ in. Piston displacement, 49.48 cu. in.

Cylinders: Close-grained gray iron, heat-treated prior to machining. Cylinder and cylinder heads each one piece, eliminating all chances of leakage through gaskets or joints.

Piston rings: Eccentric-turned and step-cut.

Connecting rod: Modified "I" beam section of chrome vanadium steel, bushed at both ends with phosphor bronze; lower bearing is adjustable.

Inlet valve: Made of nickel steel.

Exhaust valve: Two-piece type with cast iron head and nickel steel stem.

Mechanical inlet valves: Featured on the twin-cylinder models only at this time.

Crankcase: Aluminum.

Crank pin and shafts: Special tool steel, hardened and ground to exact size.

Crankshaft bearings: Made of phosphor bronze.

Ignition: Bosch magneto.

Lubrication: Semi-automatic, vacuum-feed oiling system. Overflow valve fitted to prevent flooding the crankcase; same valve maintains partial vacuum in the crankcase while motor is running to ensure lubrication in direct proportion to requirements.

Carburetor: Schebler.

Transmission: Flat belt with shield and idler. Belts are 1¾ in., two-ply, flat, waterproof.

Frame: Double bar loop, running continuously from steering head to seat mast. Steering head made of

The first production V-twin, measuring just under 50 cu. in., was offered in 1909. This model featured the suction exhaust valve, an idea that worked only in theory before mechanical valves replaced them from 1911 onward. *F-22 Photography*

vanadium steel. All joints brazed.

Forks: All bearings provided with ball oilers. The main springs are 16½ in. long and 1 in. in diameter. The recoil springs are 4½ in. long and 1 in. in diameter.

Handlebars: Made of seamless steel tubing. Double grip control entirely enclosed within handlebars.

Oil and gasoline tanks: Individual units; top and lower frame bars are completely covered by the tanks. Gasoline tank capacity is 2½ gals., oil tank 1 gal.

Tool box: Standard.

Mud guards: 3¾ in. wide with a raised center front. Front fitted with large splasher.

Muffler: Cutout provided.

Wheelbase: 56½ in.

Front hub: Equipped with knock-out type axle.

Rear hub: Coaster brake.

Equipment: Either Troxel, Mesinger or Persons saddle. G&J, Morgan & Wright, Goodyear or Goodrich tires. Studded or corrugated tread may be had at regular prices, but if any other special tread is wanted, extra charge will be made. Tires are 2½ in. Large, rubber-tread motorcycle pedals are regular equipment. A canvas tool roll containing a complete set of tools is supplied with each machine, together with an instruction book carefully written.

Single-Cylinder Models 1913–1918

This series of single-cylinder, four-cycle machines was known collectively as the 5-35, which stood for 5 horsepower and 35 cubic inches (or 3500 rpm). Like virtually all H-D's past and present, the stroke (4 in.) was larger than the bore (3⁵⁄₁₆ in.). The cylinder and its integral head were of gray iron and featured a heat-treated steel piston with three rings and a hollow steel wrist pin. A chrome steel I-beam served as the connecting rod and there were separate camshafts for the inlet and exhaust valves. The crankcase was aluminum, with a tool steel crankshaft riding on phosphor-bronze bushings. Ignition was provided by a Bosch high-tension magneto.

A Schebler carburetor was standard equipment, with a priming petcock on the left side of the cylinder head. The tank between the "Ful-Floteing" seat and the steering head held both gasoline and oil, with separate, screw-type filler caps. Lubrication for the engine descended through a sight glass that told the rider how many seconds elapsed between drops of oil. One drop every five seconds is sufficient to lube the motor without throwing out a blue exhaust cloud, according to Bill McMahon, owner of a 1914 model.

The shock of hitting a chuckhole was mitigated just a bit by the front suspension, which featured main and recoil springs, but with only about two inches of travel. The tires measured 2.5 × 28 in. and therefore did little to cushion bike or rider. Rear suspension was of course nonexistent, though the spring beneath the patented seat was

A 1914 61 cu. in. twin, as displayed in the York museum. *David Wright*

of some consolation to the owner's posterior. Drive was by roller chain from a sprocket on the crankshaft to a sprocket on the rear hub. The clutch, also on that hub, was engaged by moving a lever on the left side of the machine. The same pedals used to start the motor (with the rear wheel on the stand) activated the internal expanding rear coaster brake by backward force. With the clutch disengaged, the machine could be pedaled forward when all else failed.

Top speed in low gear was approximately 35 miles per hour, with speeds exceeding 60 mph in high. The two-speed transmission made its appearance on one single and one V-twin in 1914. By 1915, singles and twins alike were hooked to the H-D three-speed. This sliding-gear unit allowed the step starter to be routed directly through the transmission instead of its former attachment to the frame. A single, backward kick could turn the motor over.

Except for commercial use, no singles were produced from 1918 until 1926. Some confusion has arisen over the serial numbers on the early bikes, since the 1915 models began with "12" and the 1916 models bore "16" designations. H-D merely brought its serial numbers in line with the current year from 1916 onward. For example, "C16S10115" indicates that the model in question had a two-speed transmission with chain drive, was made in 1916, was a single and was one of at least 10,115 motorcycles produced that year. This system continued through 1969.

The Sidecar 1914—

There were sidecars before there were Harley-Davidsons. The first consisted of a large wagon towed by the bike, but this school of sidecar thought ended when passengers complained of oil, gravel and mud showers. There followed a seat between two wheels up front, but this arrangement prevented the rider from seeing around his passenger. The English came up with the first true sidecar, a wicker-bodied unit, built in 1913.

An early H-D sidecar began life as a sheet of steel on which a pattern had been marked. Following trimming, the sheet was shaped into a pointed cowl. Reinforcement was provided by a $\frac{1}{4}$ in. rod that was enclosed around the perimeter of the cowl, which was joined to the scoop-shaped body via the rods and spot welding. Metal braces and supports were added, since the pieces were subjected to torsion. A triple-veneered hardwood floor was added and rough edges hand-

sanded prior to receiving a coat of primer and baking in a 225-degree oven. The bodies then were spray painted by hand. The seat consisted of a wood base, springs and a leather cover. It was sewn on electric machines, a rarity for the time. The only screws on the cars—two dozen of them—were used to attach the seat to a body flange. The frame consisted of $1\frac{1}{4}$ in. steel tubing and was shaped on a series of jigs and fixtures. Since no early photos show finished sidecars within the factory, it can be assumed that the frame, body, axle, wheel and tire were shipped as a ready-to-assemble package to dealers. The price was $85.

How times change. The modern sidecar consists of a one-piece body laid up in a mold. The frame carries the body lower, just inches above the car's fender. The passenger, with no plastic windscreen for protection, formerly sat as high as the rider; today, he or she is seated about eighteen inches below the bike's saddle for added stability. A long leaf spring carries the Big Twin body (sidecars with sprung wheels were made by Goulding prior to WWII but were available only for 45 cu. in. models). With sixty years of sidecar experience, H-D sets up bikes for sidecar use quite differently from its solo mounts. The forks have slightly less trail, the steering damper is snugged up a bit, ball joints long ago replaced nuts and bolts as means of affixing the car to the bike's special braces, the wiring connection for the sidecar tail light is made and the hydraulic brake system is filled and adjusted. Only at this point, and if the rider is experienced, does the factory advise motoring off into the sunset. The current sidecar manual, complete with directions for finding the VIN number, lists all of the quirks peculiar to riding a three-wheeler: reduced acceleration and lower gas mileage, pulling to the right under acceleration and to the left when decelerating, increased wear on tires and chains and the necessity of steering rather than leaning the machine. Finally, the bike will appear to be canted away from the car when viewed from the front or rear.

The golden age of the "chair" began in 1915. Cycles were authorized for Rural Free Delivery; the sidecar was a natural for carrying the mail. That same year, H-D produced the first van body on a sidecar chassis and by 1918 offered vans with capacities of as much as 600 pounds. By 1919, 16,400 sidecars were constructed—more than seven sidecars for every ten H-D's produced. Export literature first appeared in 1917, with left-hand bodies featured, for the English market. In the twenties, sidecars constituted the main thrust in advertising and were sufficiently popular to necessitate fliers written in German, Spanish and Japanese.

Goulding created its first sidehack in 1929 for the new 45 cu. in. models. Seaman, a Milwaukee firm later absorbed by Nash (American Motors), made the bodies during the twenties and earlier. Abrash Body Shop introduced a new-design unit in 1936, and steel body production continued

through 1966 at Abresh in Milwaukee. The latter had for years created special-order sidecar and van bodies for the factory. Fiber glass bodies, laid up in the former boat-building facility in H-D's Tomahawk plant, were introduced in 1967.

Virtually all H-D's headed for the front in World War I were three-wheelers, in contrast to the virtual absence of sidecars in World War II. A small exception is the batch of military "U" models ordered by the U.S. Navy. According to a notation

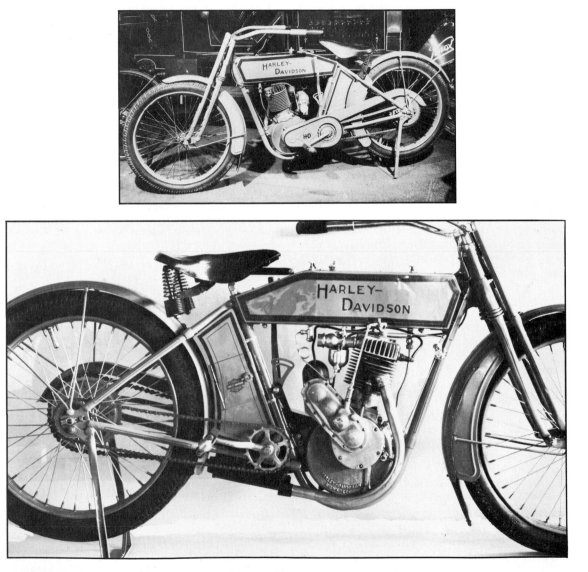

A 1913 Harley-Davidson single. This example is on display at the Smithsonian Institution in Washington, D.C. *Smithsonian Institution photos by Rolfe Baggett*

found in the Harley-Davidson archives, only 136 such machines, attached to 74 cu. in. side valve bikes, were ordered, all in battleship gray.

Harley-Davidson is the only major motorcycle company that makes its own sidecars. For 1993, there are three models—one for Low Rider (FXR) motorcycles with tall suspensions and two that fit all touring (FL) motorcycles. They're available in two interior styles and a range of cycle-matching colors, and all frames are powder-painted.

37 Cu. In. Flat Twin Sport Model 1919–1922

"This new motor has the distinction of developing the highest motor speed of any gasoline engine motor ever built, so far as we know. We are not going to tell you what it is—you would not believe it."

The new motor, a front-to-rear opposed Sport Twin, *had* to turn over rapidly; otherwise, it pumped out so little power that the lightweight cycle was left in the dust by more powerful competition, namely, the Indian Scout. The lightweight, conceived during World War I and introduced late in 1918, carried its 37 cu. in. engine and three-speed transmission low in the frame. Equipped with 26 in. tires, only the handlebars and fork springs protruded above the level of the fenders. In addition to a fully enclosed drive chain that ran in a spray of oil emitted from a breather pipe, the Sport could be had with full electric lights and coil ignition, or magneto ignition and accessory gas lights. The machine was quiet, provided good fuel economy, displayed a distinct lack of vibration—and was slow. "What will it do

on the road?" asked a copywriter. "Let's say 50 miles an hour and let it go at that—it will do better." Let's forgive the copywriter, who probably pushed a pencil better than he rode.

The Sport Twin was offered four years, from 1919 through 1922. In addition to being down on power, it represented very little that the Roaring Twenties rider wanted—the thump of the traditional V-twin, eye-watering acceleration and a top end of more than 45 or 50 mph. Nevertheless, the bike contributed important income from the export market, where the opposed twin found favor with European riders prior to the creation of autobahns and such. The electrically equipped 22WJ sold for $340, while the magneto 22WF was offered for $310 during its final year of production.

Specifications
(From a 1922 brochure)
  Motor: Six-horsepower, opposed (front to rear) twin, 2 3/4 in. (68.94mm) bore, 3 in. (76.20mm) stroke, displacement 35.64 cu. in. (584cc).
  Carburetor: Schebler.
  Three-speed transmission: Three-speed sliding gear transmission, multiple disc steel plate clutch running in oil.
  Lubrication: Automatic oil pump.
  Step starter: Rear stroke, mechanical, spring return.
  Handlebars: One-piece welded, 1 in. tubular steel, double stem. Grip, double-acting wire control entirely enclosed within handlebars.
  Frame: Keystone.
  Driving chain: Duckworth roller, 3/8 in. wide, 5/8 in. pitch.
  Brake: Internal expanding, double-acting band brake, 7 15/16-in. diameter, 1-in. face. Front external contracting brake available where required by law.

An early-twenties sidecar. Milwaukee's Seaman Body Company, later absorbed by Nash, built bodies for H-D from 1914 until World War II. *Harley-Davidson, Inc.*

Saddle: Mesinger, Ful-Floteing seat post.
Tires: 26 in. × 3 in.
Wheelbase: 53½ in.
Tanks: Capacity 2¾ gallon capacity for gasoline, 2 quarts for oil.
Mudguards: Pressed steel.
Finish: Brewster green, striped in gold.

74 Cu. In. Twin 1921–1929

The first 74 cu. in. twin, introduced in 1921, remained essentially unchanged through 1929. Dubbed the Superpowered Twin, the new motor was first featured in the 22JD, which was electrically equipped, and in the 22FD, which ran a magneto. Prices (fob Milwaukee) were $390 and $360, respectively, only $25 higher than the 61 cu. in. J and F models offered the same year. Harley-Davidson claimed 18 horsepower from the new, bigger twin. The bore was 3⁷/₁₆ in. (86.97mm) and the stroke was an even 4 in. (101.60mm). The machine was advertised as ideal for sidecars, "especially for use with the two-passenger sidecar (Model 22QT) and where traveling conditions are the worst," a '22 brochure stated. The big twin was a response to four-cylinder Hendersons in particular, which had more, if less dependable, power than the trusty 61, which by then was a thirteen-year-old design.

The company noted that the new model was capable of 40-60 miles on a gallon of the low-octane gasoline almost universally available by 1920. The lighting and ignition system consisted of a 6-volt generator-ignition unit, a storage battery, headlight, tail light and motor-driven oil warning signal. The ignition system consisted of a circuit breaker, a distributor and a high-tension spark coil. The system was mounted directly behind the motor, probably to reduce the chance of contact with water.

Two important, non-cosmetic changes on the 74 were introduced in 1924 and were the kinds of amenities riders had on Harleys and wanted on other bikes. Alemite lubrication on all bearing surfaces except within the motor greatly extended the life of the running gear. The cap of the Alemite gun was hooked over the fitting and the handle turned, forcing grease onto the surface with 500 pounds of pressure. An Alemite gun and a one-pound can of grease were furnished gratis with each new twin.

The second improvement was the use of aluminum for the 74's pistons. This lightweight metal with superior heat-dissipating properties meant more power and less chance of seizing. More evident additions included the handsome tear-

drop tank in 1925 and balloon tires in 1926 and throttle-regulated oil pressure and a front brake, standard on 1928 models.

Performance, by all accounts, was excellent. In fact, J models intended for sidecar use sported a spacer plate between the cylinders and the lower end. This ⅛-in. plate prolonged engine life by slightly lowering compression.

Specifications
(From a 1922 brochure)
Motor: Air-cooled, high-speed, high-efficiency, two cylinder, four cycle "L" head, pocket valve, "V" type motor. For sidecar use, motors are fitted with ⅛-in. compression shims, Letter "S" in model number designates sidecar motor.
Carburetor: Schebler.
Battery: Exide.
Three-speed transmission: Sliding gear type, gears of chrome nickel steel, transmission box of aluminum. Transmission main shaft mounted on large, heavy duty roller bearing on the left or drive side and a ball bearing on the right side. Main drive gear runs on a high-duty phosphor-bronze bearing. Uses same type lubrication oil as the motor.
Lubrication: Automatic oil pump. Average 800-1,000 miles per gallon of oil.
Step starter: Rear stroke mechanical starter, spring return.
Clutch: Multiple dry disc.
Handlebars: One-piece, welded, 1 in. tubular steel, double stem.
Controls: Grip, double-acting wire control entirely enclosed within the handlebars.
Frame: Extra heavy duty gauge high carbon steel seamless tubular loop, rigidly reinforced.
Driving chain: Duckworth roller, ⅜-in. width, ⅝-in. pitch.
Brake: Controlled by lever on right footboard. Internal expanding, double-acting band brake, operating on a steel drum 7⁵/₁₆ in. diameter with 1 in. face. Where the law calls for two brakes, an external contracting brake can be furnished in addition.
Saddle: Mesinger saddle, Ful-Floteing seat.
Suspension: Double spring front fork.
Tires: 28 in. × 3 in.
Wheelbase: 59½ in.
Tanks: Gasoline capacity 3¼ gallons, lubricating oil 1 gallon.
Mudguards: Pressed steel, extra wide and substantial. Flat military front mudguard available.
Finish: Brewster green, tastily double striped in gold.

21 Cu. In. Single 1926–1935

The 21 cu. in. single was produced for ten years, though the average U.S. Harley-Davidson rider was hardly aware of its prolonged existence. The dependable little machine, available in side valve or overhead valve configurations, was infinitely more popular with Europeans, Australians and

New Zealanders than in its native land. Again, the ribbons of long, straight North American highways beckoned the rider astride large, slow-turning motors.

Created simultaneously with similar Indian models, the single helped lure racer Joe Petrali from Excelsior to run the Peashooter—the nickname for H-D's overhead valve model—in competition. And run it he did. Petrali swept every national dirt-track event in the country in 1935, thirteen races in all. His success on the little machine prompted the AMA to create a new competition class made up of larger, nearly stock motorcycles.

The single was offered initially in four versions, a side valve magneto model, a side valve generator model, an overhead valve magneto model and an overhead valve generator model. The side valves featured iron alloy pistons, while the overheads sported lightweight, racing-type aluminum. The side-valve A and B singles were created with patented, aircraft-type Ricardo heads that squeezed the air-fuel mixture toward the plug for better combustion. All models were fully equipped and appeared to be scaled-down, single versions of the big bikes. While the overhead valve had plenty of punch, the side valve was slow. Top end on the overhead, produced as a 21-incher

through 1929, was a reported 65 miles per hour in stock form; the side valve struggled to exceed 50. Prices ranged from $210 to $275 in 1926.

Specifications
(From a 1926 brochure)
Motor: Four-stroke cycle, single cylinder, air cooled, 21.098 cu. in. (350 cc) displacement. $2^7/_8$ in. bore., $3^1/_4$ in. stroke. Side by side valves in models A and B. Overhead valves in models AA and BA.
Carburetor: Schebler DeLuxe.
Transmission: Three-speed progressive sliding gear.
Lubrication: Motor lubricated by mechanical pump, supplemented by hand pump. Transmission lubricated by separate oil splash. Nine-place Alemite fitted.
Ignition: Harley-Davidson generator-battery on electrically equipped models. Robert Bosch magneto on magneto models.
Electrical equipment: (On electric models only) Harley-Davidson generator, coil, timer-distributor, four-plate storage battery, vibrator horn, two-bulb headlight, standard tail lamp, ignition and light switch panel located back of steering head. Relay cutout that automatically opens and closes battery-generator circuit.
Starter: H-D rear stroke on right side.
Clutch: Single-plate dry disc, foot operated.
Handlebars: One piece, 1 in. tubular double stem with closed end grips.
Frame: High carbon, seamless, tubular steel with wide trussed loop. Drop forged head.

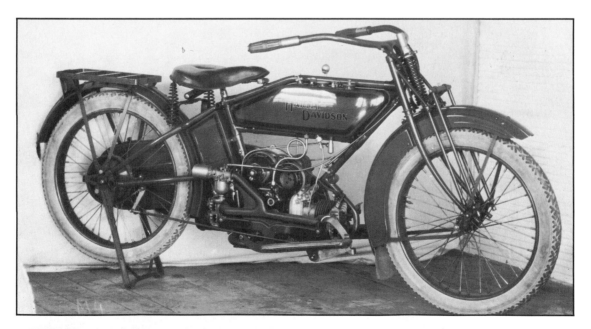

A 1921 Sport model. This front-to-back opposed twin featured a 37 cu. in. motor. *Harley-Davidson, Inc.*

Controls: Grip, double-acting wire controls entirely enclosed within handlebars. Toe operated compression relief.

Brake: External contracting, foot operated. Drum 5¾ in. diameter, 3³⁄₁₆ in. × 1 in. lining.

Driving chains: Roller ⅝ in. pitch and 1¼ in. wide.

Seat: Mesinger top. Full spring seat post.

Tires: Full balloon, 26 in. × 3.30 in.

Wheelbase: 55 in.

Tanks: Gasoline capacity, three gallons. Lubricating oil, three quarts. Reserve gasoline tank.

Mudguards: Pressed steel.

Footboards: Standard Harley-Davidson.

Tool equipment: Tool and tire repair kit.

Finish: Harley-Davidson olive green. Tanks, wide maroon striping with center gold stripe.

45 Cu. In. V-Twin 1929–1951

Nineteen twenty-nine may have been a bad year for the stock market, but it was a vintage year for Harley-Davidson. The 30.50 cu. in. single was introduced, the powerful two-cam was in its second year of road bike production and—most meaningful of all—the 45 cu. in. motor made its debut.

Three 45 models for 1929 indicated that the factory was serious about this bike. There was a low-compression D model for sidecar work, a standard DL and a high-compression DLD. Aluminum or magnesium pistons were provided for all 45's from 1929. The "R" designated machines remained mechanically the same through 1936. They then received a new letter designation, "W," and displayed the recirculating oil system proven on the 1936 Knucklehead. Special alloy heads, for the WR and WLDR, were the only other thirties mechanical innovations. The W series dominated U.S. racing until two-wheel 45 production ceased in 1951.

The motor evolved into a real winner. Throughout its forty-five years of production (the last twenty-two in the Servi-Car only), the 750cc sidevalve twin was characterized by massively oversized cooling fins on the heads, which allowed a machine to idle all day without seizure from overheating. Charles Darling, Sodus, New York, rode 45's from 1930 through 1951. Here are his impressions of those models through the years:

"The model years 1930–1935 had quite acceptable handling characteristics. . . . Even the deeply

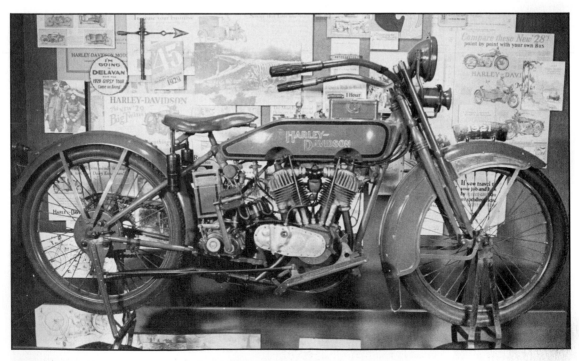

The first 74 cu. in. machine was introduced in 1921. If the 1936 Knucklehead is the father of today's big twins, this motorcycle is the grandfather. *F-22 Photography*

rutted dirt roads, which were fairly common in those days, did not present much of a problem when negotiated at reasonable speeds. However, beginning with the 1936 model year and continuing through the last 1951 WL models, the steering head angle was decreased by a few degrees, making the forks assume a more nearly vertical position. This decreased the 'caster' angle and had a decidedly negative effect on stability. It was even worse when the machines were equipped with 5.00 × 16 in. tires.

"Another handicap of the 45 R and W series were the three-speed transmissions. They had a wide ratio gap between second and third, making it necessary to really wind out the motor in second so it wouldn't bog down when the clutch was engaged in third gear. . . . The transmission itself on these models was notoriously weak, too. Despite this, the Harley 45 was a nice little machine to ride and provided economical transportation for thousands of people."

Police aboard Servi-Cars and soldiers aboard WLA 45's in World War II would agree with Darling's last statement. U.S. riders, accustomed to the power of the 61 and 74 cu. in. bikes, frequently abused the 45 to make it run with the big twins. The motor refused to react in any negative way except to leak a bit of oil from around the head gaskets, though this may have been aggravated by the owner or dealer who inadvertently scratched the gasket after cleaning carbon from the heads or grinding the valves. A low-compression motor (6.5:1), the 45 ran faultlessly on regular or Ethyl gasoline; it continued to do so in the thirties, when several compression choices were offered for those desiring more speed or pulling power for sidecar work. And because the factory produced as many as twenty sets of spares for each WLA (Army) model, 45 cu. in. parts remain easy to find.

Harley-Davidson certainly has made faster and flashier bikes. It has yet to produce a machine that endeared itself to more people.

Specifications
(From a 1929 dealer brochure)

Motor: V type twin cylinder air-cooled four stroke cycle—bore 2 3/4 in., stroke 3 13/16 in., displacement 45.32 cu. in. Side by side valves, independent cam action on each valve. Dow metal pistons. New, plunger-type crankcase oil drain.

Carburetor: Schebler DeLuxe with self-cleaning air cleaner.

Muffler: Four tubes.

Transmission: Three-speed progressive sliding gear.

Lubrication: Throttle-controlled motor oiler that pro-

vides proper lubrication at all speeds. Transmission lubricated separately. 13 Alemite fittings.

Ignition: Harley-Davidson generator-battery with output controller.

Electrical equipment: Harley-Davidson generator with instantaneous output controller; weather and waterproof coil and timer; five plate, 22-ampere/hr. storage battery; high-frequency horn; two bullet headlights; standard tail lamp; ignition and light switch panel with built-in ammeter and hooded parking light located back of steering head. Relay cutout automatically opens and closes generator-battery circuit.

Starter: Harley-Davidson rear stroke, right side.

Clutch: Multi-plate, multi-disc, foot operated.

Handlebars: One piece, 1 in. tubular, double stem with closed end twist grips.

Controls: Grip, double-acting wire controls, enclosed in handlebars and cables.

Brakes: Foot-controlled contracting rear brake and built-in hand-controlled expanding front wheel brake.

Frame: High-carbon, seamless, tubular steel, strongly reinforced with wide trussed loop. Dropforged head and gearbox bracket.

Driving chains: Duplex engine chain 3/8 in. pitch, 3/4 in. wide, each sprocket 3/16 in. wide. Rear chain roller, 5/8 in. pitch, 3/8 in. wide. Large cushion motor sprocket.

Saddle: Mesinger form-fitting top. Adjustable spring seat post.

Tires: Standard make, 25 × 3.85 in., full balloon.

Wheelbase: 56 1/2 in.

Tanks: Saddle type. Gasoline capacity, 3 3/4 gallons; oil capacity, 7 1/2 pints. Reserve gasoline tank.

Mudguards: Extra wide valanced, rear guard hinged for easy access to wheel.

Finish: Harley-Davidson Olive Green with maroon striping with center gold stripe. Rims and handlebars black.

30.50 Cu. In. Single 1929–1936

Harley-Davidson did in 1929 what racers had been doing for more than a decade: It created a single from half of a 61 cu. in. V-twin. Unlike the go-fast guys, who yanked the head and covered the gaping hole with a steel plate, H-D engineers grafted a head of very similar dimensions onto the lower end first produced in 1926 for the sidevalve and overhead valve singles. A dissimilar 500cc H-D single, the CAC, was raced in the early thirties but, except for export, was not offered as a street bike. It appears that riders at that time would accept nothing smaller than a 750cc motor. They may have preferred a twin if their memories were long, since the first bikes on U.S. roads were singles that spewed oil and often needed leg power on steep grades.

The Model C, as it was known, used the 45-cu. in. frame in 1929. From 1930 through 1934, the C used the same frame as the 1930 and 1931 45's. In 1932, the R 45 with the horizontal generator required a bowed front down-tube, which the singles did not need. Much of the rest of the C frame was from the 45. Forks, tanks, fenders and the 18-in. drop wheels were shared with the 45; the 21 cu. in. singles retained the 20-in. clincher rims throughout their production.

Specifications
(From a 1929 dealer brochure)
   Motor: Four-stroke, single-cylinder side valve. Bore 3³/₃₂ in., stroke 4 in.; piston displacement 30.50 cu. in.
   Muffler: Four-tube "Pipes of pan."
   Carburetor: Schebler DeLuxe with self-cleaning air cleaner.
   Transmission: Three-speed progressive sliding gear.
   Lubrication: Throttle-controlled motor oiler. Transmission lubricated separately. 14 Alemite fittings.
   Ignition: Harley-Davidson generator-battery with output controller.
   Electrical equipment: H-D generator with instantaneous output controller; waterproof coil and timer; five plate storage battery; high-frequency horn; two bullet headlights; standard tail lamp; ignition and light switch panel with built-in ammeter and hooded parking light located back of steering head. Relay cutout automatically opens and closes battery-generator circuit.
   Starter: Rear stroke, right side.

   Clutch: Single-plate dry disc, foot operated.
   Handlebars: One piece, 1 in. tubular, double stem with closed end twist grips. Controls in grip, double-acting wire controls enclosed in handlebars and cables. Toe-operated compression relief.
   Brakes: Foot-controlled contracting rear brake and built-in hand controlled expanding front brake.
   Frame: High-carbon, seamless, tubular steel, strongly reinforced and with wide trussed loop. Drop-forged head and gearbox bracket.
   Driving chains: Duplex engine chain ³/₈ in. pitch, ³/₄ in. wide, each sprocket ³/₁₆ in. wide. Rear chain, roller ⁵/₈ in. pitch, ³/₈ in. wide. Large cushion motor sprocket.
   Saddle: Mesinger form-fitting top. Adjustable spring seat post.
   Tires: 25 × 3.85 in.
   Wheelbase: 56½ in.
   Finish: Harley-Davidson Olive Green with maroon striping with center gold stripe. Rims and handlebars black.

74 Cu. In. VL 1930–1940

   Harley-Davidson billed the 1930 74 cubic inch big twin as "the greatest achievement in motorcycle history." Actually, the new design may have been one of the most poorly developed H-D's ever

A 1926 or 1927 overhead valve BA model, the street version of the Peashooter. With its front number plate, front wheel stand, luggage carrier and auxiliary rear brake, this probably is an export model. *Harley-Davidson, Inc.*

to roll down Juneau Avenue. "Originally, it had a bad engine, a bad clutch, the flywheels were too small, the frames broke, the mufflers became so clogged with carbon that the engines lost power," says William H. Davidson, who recalls a frantic trip he made to New York State in late 1929, only days after the Buffalo police took delivery of a fleet of new 74's. "We replaced mufflers, valves springs, pistons, everything we'd carried from Milwaukee. The shop mechanic took one out and it ran 90 miles an hour. Then I took one of their police officers out in a sidecar and wound it up to 75. He yelled to me that 75 was fast enough, which was fortunate, because it wouldn't go any faster." Davidson points out that the initial poor performance could not have come at a worse time. The stock market's nosedive took place just two months after the new model introduction in July 1929. Dealers were asked to sell a high-priced bike with big problems to riders facing even bigger problems. To Harley-Davidson's credit, early problems were quickly corrected.

There was no single specification on the new 74 that would arouse suspicion. The bore was $3\frac{7}{16}$ inches and the stroke was 4 inches. The Ricardo heads had been proven in earlier models. Combined with side-by-side valves and a $1\frac{1}{4}$ inch Schebler carburetor, the motor developed at least 15 percent more horsepower than previous 74's. It also featured a new, plunger-type crankcase oil drain and a cam gear case vacuum that was touted as keeping the motor cleaner (spewing less oil on bike and rider). The few affluent buyers soon wished they could trade their new machines for 61 cu. in. J models, even if it meant well-lubricated boots and trousers.

By no means were all of the new ideas on the 74 bad. The primary chain was extra-heavy duplex. By loosening a single nut on either axle, a wheel could be quickly removed for service. Wheels were interchangeable, not only for the VL, but for the sidecar and Package Truck options as well. Full balloon 27 × 4.00 tires were featured on the new model. The new frame, while heavier than the J model, allowed for a lower riding position. As early as 1930, then, Harley-Davidson was touting a low and distinctive way to travel. Other amenities included a high-frequency horn, an improved 22-amp battery and a sealed coil that enhanced the H-D reputation for having waterproof electrical systems. The saddle-type tanks held four gallons of gasoline and a gallon of oil.

The finish remained olive green but was highlighted by a vermilion stripe. By 1932, the olive drab caterpillar would become a multicolored, Art Deco butterfly. List price was $340 for each of four models: the standard V, the higher-compression VL, the sidecar-geared VS and the VC, which featured nickel iron rather than Dow metal pis-

The first 45 cu. in. side valve V-twin, offered in 1929. The motor was last offered in the Servi-Car in 1974. *Harley-Davidson, Inc.*

tons and which was designed for use with the Package Truck.

It's been said that the best bikes also have the most complete tool kits. The VL is the exception that proves the rule. Here's the tool kit contents, typical of H-D models throughout this period. Unfortunately, early VL owners got to know their tools on a regular basis:

1. Registration card.
2. Rider's handbook.
3. Wrench for valve spring covers, valve tappets and various small nuts.
4. Socket wrench for cylinder head clamp screws.
5. Wrench for axle nuts and rear brake hub nut.
6. Spark plug wrench.
7. Tire patches.
8. Chain tool.
9. Screwdriver.
10. Wrench for transmission clamp nuts and transmission oil filler plug.
11. Wrench for valve tappets; also fits various small nuts.
12. Wrench for rear axle adjusting screw and lock nuts, cylinder base nuts, gas pipe nuts and clutch pull rod lock nut.
13. Wrench for footboard support rod nuts, front fork rocker plate stud nuts, oil pipe nuts and various other nuts.
14. Pliers.
15. Monkey wrench.

Two headlights were used on 1929 and 1930 models. The canister held tools and was said to have kept the rider awake at night by clanking loudly on rough roads. *Harley-Davidson, Inc.*

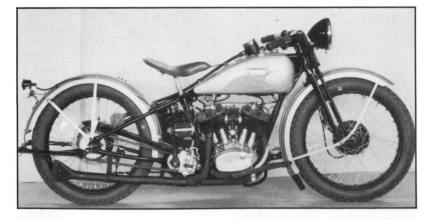

The Woolery "Bullet," a prototype, was a 1931 45 cu. in. motor in a 1933 B (single-cylinder) frame. The weight was 387 pounds with two gallons of gasoline and two quarts of oil. Top speed was a reported 88 miles per hour. Guy Webb, Inc., the Minneapolis H-D dealer at the time, ordered the bike for Mr. Woolery, a customer. The tank speedometer, incidentally, is a genuine Harley-Davidson accessory. *Harley-Davidson, Inc.*

16. Steering head lock keys.
17. Ignition and lighting switch keys.
18. Tool box key.
19. Wrench for switch box terminal nuts, also feeler gauge for adjusting circuit breaker point gap.
20. Rear chain repair links.
21. Front chain repair links.
22. Pump fastening clips.
23. Alemite grease gun.
24. Tire pump.

1930 VL Specifications
Number of cylinders: Two.
Bore: 3⁷/₁₆ in. (87.31 mm).
Stroke: 4 in. (101.6 mm).
Displacement: 73.73 in. (1,208.19 cc).
Horsepower (N.A.C.C. rating): 9.45.
Wheelbase: 60 in.
Gear ratios
Motor sprocket: 23.
Clutch sprocket: 51.
Countershaft sprocket: 28.
Rear wheel sprocket: 51.
High gear ratio: 4.04 to 1.
Tire data
Size: 4.00 in.
Inflation (solo rider): 16 lb. front, 18 lb. rear.
Motor or serial number: Stamped on left crankcase.

Servi-Car 1932–1974

The Servi-Car, introduced in 1932, made a lot of sense. It enabled someone relatively unfamiliar with two-wheelers to take advantage of the fuel economy offered by the standard 45 cu. in. R motor and the compact size of a motorcycle. Previewed to dealers in their November 9, 1931, news bulletin, the three-wheeler was "Intended primarily for use by garages and service stations in the pickup and delivery of customers' cars." Unlike other tricycle-type vehicles of the time, there seems to have been quite a bit of engineering in the Servi-Car. The frame was a complete unit; there had been no ill-planned attempt to graft a motorcycle onto a pair of wheels. Primary drive was provided by a double roller, enclosed chain leading to the three-speed transmission. A single chain transmitted power to a sprocket on the rear axle. Final drive was by means of a modified automobile differential, completely enclosed.

In addition to a hand-controlled, internal expanding brake up front, a foot pedal activated a drum brake on a larger internal expanding brake attached to the rear axle. Origin of the rear brake was no puzzle: Shoes and linings were interchangeable with the rear unit on 74 cubic inch

H-D's. An important consideration was the distance between the rear wheels, 42 inches. This allowed riders, many of whom were inexperienced, to follow the paths forged by car tires in mud and snow. The wheelbase measured 61 inches. The body of the machines, immediately behind the rider, looked like a large soft-drink cooler. It was 29 inches wide, 23 inches long, a foot high, first metal and then fiber glass and was supported on a subframe. The subframe was hinged to a tie bar fastened on the Servi-Car frame and supported in the rear by a pair of coil springs. Rear mudguards and a rear apron were attached to the body, which was hinged at the top by two latches (one of which could be locked). The flat rear end was "perfectly adapted to advertising signs and lettering," an early bulletin pointed out. The standard color initially was turquoise blue for the tanks, rear fenders and body, with the frame, chain guards, front forks, tow bar, battery box and running gear in black. Price in 1932, with tow bar, was $450 fob Milwaukee.

Options offered initially included a passenger seat and a carrier for an automobile tire (should a service station specialize in fixing flats). Never advertised as a machine designed for the highway, the three-wheeler instead offered a way for one man to drive to a parked car, hook up the Servi-Car with a standard tow bar and drive the car to a service station or garage, the tricycle in tow. As sound as this seems to be, the Servi-Car was most commonly used through 1974 by traffic police.

Changes throughout its production included making the tow bar an option in 1963 (no service station in its right mind would come to you by then), installing electric starting the following year and using fiber glass for bodies in 1966. Despite its ability to slog along at city speeds all day, the machine had a few quirks. A 1969 owner's handbook admonishes to "put shift lever in neutral before stopping engine while parking. If left in gear when engine is stopped, rock Servi-Car to shift out of gear to neutral." Neutral-only starting was a minor annoyance, but that wasn't what killed the Servi-Car. Instead, it was done in by various Cushmans and stripped-down Jeeps, which offered meter maids, postal employees and such weather protection and, usually, a heater. In its final year, only seventy Servi-Cars were sold, primarily to municipalities. A new, 74 cu. in. Servi-Car never got past the prototype stage.

Specifications
Model G (1963 and earlier): with tow bar.
Model GA (1963 and earlier): less tow bar.

Model GE (1964 and later): electric start (less tow bar).

Wheelbase: 61 in.
Overall length: 100 in.
Overall width: 48 in.
Fuel tank: 3.4 U.S. gallons.
Oil tank: 3½ quarts.
Transmission: ¾ pint.
Engine: see specifications for DS 45 engine.
Battery: 12-volt, 60 amp-hr. capacity.
Circuit breaker points: .022 in.
Spark plugs, type: Harley-Davidson No. 3.
Size: 14 mm.
Gap: .025 to .030 in.
Spark timing: Retard 0 degrees (front piston top center); automatic advance 30 degrees (⁵/₁₆ in. before piston top center).
Transmission type: Constant mesh.
Speeds: Three forward, one reverse.
First gear: 14.4 to 1.
Second gear: 9.7 to 1.
Third gear: 5.85 to 1.
Reverse: 12.45 to 1.
Tire size (1968 and earlier): 5.00 × 16; 1969 and later: 5.10 × 16.

80 Cu. In. Side Valve Twin 1936–1945

The 80 cu. in. side valve twin, designated ULH and produced from 1937 through 1941, featured the Y-type intake manifold found on the more popular 45 and 74 cu. in. models, plus deeply finned heads and a new combustion chamber design shared with the smaller models. The factory especially recommended the 80, initially designated the ULH, for sidecar work. In 1937, the giant twin shared the circulating oil pump and dry sump lubrication with the 45 and 74. This was an entirely satisfactory bike in virtually every respect; the original four-speed transmission caused minor problems only the first year of production. The decision not to continue the side valve 80-incher following World War II probably was due to material shortages, and to the immense popularity of the Knucklehead.

Former H-D dealer Conrad Schlemmer points out that "considerable confusion" surrounds Harley-Davidson V-series and U-series engines. The V-series began in 1930 and ended with the 1936 model year and included the VL, VLD, VLH and others. The U-series, with the circulating oil system, began with the 1937 model year and includes the U, UL, ULH, etc. H-D advertised the bore on the 1930-36 74's and 80's as 3⁷/₁₆ in. but in reality it was a bit less than that. The standard bore on the V series was 3.422 in. and this was also the bore on the 1937 and later 80 cu. in. models.

Specifications
(From a 1936 dealer brochure)

Motor: Air-cooled four-stroke cycle, side by side valves, Ricardo cylinder heads. Lynite, cam-ground pistons. Cylinders straight honed, mirror finish. Linkert carburetor. Bore, 3.422 in.; stroke, 4¼ in.

Muffler: Burgess straight-through with gas-deflecting end.

Transmission: Three speed standard. Reverse gear available. Fourth speed available.

The 1931 VL. *Harley-Davidson, Inc.*

Lubrication: Throttle-controlled oil pump for motor with automatic front chain oiling. Transmission lubricated separately. All other bearings Alemite fitted.

Ignition: Harley-Davidson generator-battery.

Electric equipment: Large, 7-in. headlight with pre-focused double filament bulb. Dual beam control from handlebar. High output generator with automatic increase when headlight is in use. Twenty-two ampere-hour battery. Disc-type horn.

Handlebars: One piece, with double-acting twist-grip controls fully enclosed.

Frame: Extra low, strongly reinforced, seamless steel tubing, with drop forged fittings. Entire frame heat-treated. Theftproof lock.

Clutch: Multiple dry disc, foot-operated.

Front forks: Combination rigid and spring fork construction. Rigid fork drop-forged. Spring fork seamless steel tubing and drop-forging fitted with two sets helical cushion bumper and recoil springs.

Drive: Duplex extra heavy roller chain for front. Rear chain, extra heavy single roller.

Tires: Full balloon, 19 × 4.00 standard, 18 × 4.00 optional.

Wheels: Front and rear quickly demountable and interchangeable. Both wheels wire with drop-center rims.

Wheelbase: 60 in.

Overall length: 94 in.

Saddle height: 29½ in.

Tank: Saddle type, large capacity. Main gas tank, 21¾ pints (approximately three gallons); reserve tank, 8½ pints (approximately one gallon). Oil tank, 8¾ pints.

61, 74 Cu. In. Overhead Valve Models 1936–1947

As nice a guy as President Walter Davidson was, he'd run out of patience. The National Recovery Administration, a product of the Depression, prevented his engineers in 1934 from working overtime. The government body encouraged hiring more people rather than overworking people already on the payroll, and that's one of the reasons why the 61 cu. in. overhead valve model failed to make its debut until 1936 (and why just six variations, on two models, were offered in 1935). Despite the delay, the Knucklehead, as it came to be known, had a few initial problems. There seemed to be no way to regulate oil flow to the valves. Other parts received either too much or too little lubrication, so a crash lube improvement program began almost immediately and the new and usually reliable recirculating oil system of 1937 was the result.

The 74 cu. in. overhead valve model introduced for the 1941 model year was identical to the highly popular 61 cu. in. overhead valve model.

A 1936 74 cu. in. side valve, designated the VLD. The V series bikes were introduced disastrously in 1930 but evolved into dependable machines. *Harley-Davidson, Inc.*

According to the factory, the 74 was created by "a demand from a small number of riders for a model of this type of larger cubic inch capacity—a model that would handle a sidecar with ease and speed, and a solo motorcycle with performance far beyond ordinary requirements." Nice as that sounds, the 74 was instead an insurance policy to prevent speed-oriented H-D enthusiasts from being passed by an Indian. The biggest mechanical news within was a centrifugally controlled oil pump that at last solved the 61's problem of too much oil in some parts of the engine and not enough in others. A bypass valve, regulated by rpm, closed at high speed for maximum lubrication of the motor. At low speed, the valve opened to bypass the gear case and return to the supply tank. Vane-type pumps were installed in 1937 on the 45, 74 and 80 cu. in. side valve motors, with gear-driven pumps on the 61 and 74 OHV's.

The other major improvement on all models involved the clutch. Three steel discs, three friction (fiber) discs and a spring disc meant seven frictional surfaces on all big twins, instead of the five used in 1940. A total surface increase of 65 percent over the previous models made for smoother shifting, as did the new and larger clutch hub. Other niceties found on the new OHV and shared with other models included a larger and more effective air cleaner; larger rear brake on '37 and later models; better feel to the front brake lever, which was made of die-cast aluminum; a quieter muffler; a "new, airplane-style speedometer dial" featuring silver numerals on a black face with a white needle; and sturdier gearshift and foot clutch lever mechanisms. Unfortunately, all models also shared stainless steel styling strips on the gas tanks. These hunks of metal, viewed today, just don't come off as well as the decals on the mid-thirties Harley-Davidsons.

The 74 OHV was produced in extremely limited quantities during World War II and in only slightly larger batches in 1946 and 1947. Henry Koster, a long-time mechanic employed at Harley-Davidson of Bergen County in Rochelle Park, New Jersey, says the 1941 and '42 74's were the most efficient motors ever to come out of Milwaukee. His view is shared by James Lang, a former New England dealer who's familiar with every model H-D since 1924. And Mike Lange, a top restorer, says his '41 74 runs with and stays cooler than the hydraulic-lifter 74 cu. in. models that superseded the overhead valve machines in 1948.

Specifications (61 cu. in. model)
(From a 1936 brochure)

Motor: V-twin, overhead valve configuration, bore 3⁵/₁₆ in., stroke 3¹/₂ in., displacement 60.32 in., horsepower rating (NACC) 8.77.
Compression: EL (high compression, created by high piston), 7:1 without cylinder shims, 6.5:1 with cylinder shims. EL (low compression, created by low piston), 6:1 without cylinder shims, 5.6:1 with cylinder shims.
Horsepower: 40 at 4,800 rpm.
Gear ratios, motor sprocket: 23.
Clutch sprocket: 37.
Countershaft sprocket: 22.
Rear sprocket: 51.
Third-gear ratio: 4.57.
Fourth-gear ratio: 3.73.
Battery: Six volts.
Dry weight: 565 lbs.

Model S-125 1947–1952

The first new model after World War II was only new to these shores. The design was the work of prewar German DKW engineers, who had two strikes against them. First, losing the war meant losing all patent rights. Second, the DKW factory found itself behind the Iron Curtain. So BSA in Great Britain and H-D in America produced the two-stroke, single-cylinder machine. Returning soldiers were cycle hungry, but wanted more than this. William H. Davidson told directors that 10,000 were made and sold in the first seven months of 1947. However, the little bike never completely fulfilled the lightweight craving of H-D dealers, who have yet to spread the welcome mat for a two-cycle engine.

Specifications
(From a 1947 collateral piece)
Serial number: The engine (serial) number is stamped on the front end of the engine crankcase, on the left-hand side.
Wheelbase: 50 in.
Model designation: S.
Type of engine: Two cycle.
Number of cylinders: One.
Bore: 2¹/₁₆ in. (52.39 mm).
Stroke: 2⁹/₃₂ in. (57.94 mm).
Displacement: 7.6 cu. in. (124.87 cc).
Compression ratio: 6.6 to 1.
Horsepower (N.A.C.C. rating): 1.7.
Brake horsepower (approximate): 3.
Tire size: 3.25 × 19 in.
Gasoline tank, total: 1³/₄ gals.
Main supply: 1¹/₂ gals.
Reserve: 1 quart.
Transmission case: 1¹/₄ pints.
Low gear: 29.3 to 1.
Second gear: 15.4 to 1.
High gear: 8.45 to 1.

Model K, 45 and 55 Cu. In. V-Twin 1952–1956

The Harley-Davidson Model K, introduced in 1952, looked more like a contemporary cycle than anything produced by the company prior to that year. It featured rear suspension consisting of a swing arm and a sturdy pair of shocks, a revamped 45 cu. in. side valve motor and a combination foot shift and hand clutch. Unfortunately, problems plagued the sleek machine from its inception. Most worrisome from the corporation's point of view were some serious mechanical and performance problems, among them the breaking of gear teeth in the 1954 and '55 KH models. Art Kauper in the H-D experimental department noticed that there was a pattern to teeth breakage, but he could not initially tell why. On a visit to a steel supplier, however, he watched an ingot being rolled into flat stock and saw the corner outlines of the ingot in the finished steel. Those corners correlated with the teeth that were breaking. By going immediately to a forged gear, the problem was solved. But performance remained dismal, both in leaving a stoplight and attempting to reach a speed much in excess of 80. Boosting the motor to 55 cubes in 1954 helped some, but not enough.

Nevertheless, there was such a thing as a desirable K bike. Tom Lyman, now a Utah chiropractor, remembers getting a ride on a new K and trading his 1951 Hydra-Glide immediately for a KK model, in 1953. The KK featured hotter cams, less chrome and flatter bars and gave Lyman perfect service. Says he: "Where the KK was really great was out on the road, or blasting through a canyon. It cruised very nicely at 70 or 75 mph and had a top speed of 90 to 95 with the shorter gearing I had put on. All I can say is, it was smooth, leaned well into the twisties and was easy to take care of." Searching hard for a flaw, Lyman concedes that the ride might have been "mushy" by today's standards. But the bike was no lemon.

The K was a stopgap model, according to William H. Davidson, who reported that development time ran out on a radical, 60-degree V-twin called the KL. Unlike other H-D's, the KL featured connecting rods offset in side-by-side fashion. (In other models, the big end of one connecting rod fit within the big end of the other.) The aluminum high-cam motor sported dual carburetors and probably was the performance equal of the 1954 Golden Anniversary KH, with its 55 cu. in. motor and engine-transmission unit construction, a first for H-D.

Sure, it's a whimsical photo, but where do you think they got the idea for the Servi-Car? This arrangement, conceived on the West Coast and dubbed the Cycle Tow, allowed a bit of lateral movement. The wheels swung up and forward when not in tow. The late President William H. Davidson recalls that this creation was quite unstable, but inspired H-D to create the sturdy Servi-Car. *Harley-Davidson, Inc.*

Specifications
(From a brochure, printed in 1951)

45 cu. in. side valve motor—Air-cooled, four stroke, V-type twin cylinder. Removable aluminum alloy cylinder heads. Enclosed valve gear. Low-expansion, aluminum alloy, cam-ground, double slot pistons. Cylinder bores honed and parkerized. Deep cylinder fins extend around intake and exhaust ports for proper cooling. All main bearings retained roller type; double tapered Timken bearings on the sprocket side. Linkert carburetor. Motor develops approximately 30 horsepower. Bore, 2³/₄ inches. Stroke, 3¹³/₁₆ inches.

Transmission—Harley-Davidson four speed. Incorporated as an integral part of crankcase casting. Sliding dog clutches. Large, rugged gears for durability. Constant-mesh design. Foot shift, hand clutch.

Lubrication—Circulating lubrication system with gear-type pressure pump and gear-type scavenger pump with pressure feed direct to cylinder walls. Transmission and front chain lubricated by oil supply separate from engine. All other bearings Alemite-Zerk fitted.

Ignition—Two-brush shunt, voltage controlled generator, storage battery, spark coil, circuit breaker. Easy starting and waterproof.

Electric equipment—Large, sealed ray headlight with prefocused 32-32 candlepower, double filament bulb. Generator and oil pressure warning lights incorporated in the headlights. Electric, trumpet-type blast horn.

Clutch—Harley-Davidson multiple dry disc with bonded-on clutch facings. Left hand operated.

Drive—Motor to transmission by ³/₈-inch pitch triple chain running in oil bath and adjusted by Stellite-faced sliding shoe. ⁵/₈-inch pitch single-row roller chain to rear wheel. Engine has compensating sprocket.

Frame—Double loop, silver brazed tubular steel. Heat-treated steel head, seat post cluster, rear support arms and axle clips.

Rear suspension—Swing arm type sprung by means of two helical coil springs and controlled by means of two hydraulic, automotive type shock absorbers, all encased in royalite covers. Pivot point of swinging arm is supported by pre-loaded Timken bearings.

Front fork—Easy riding hydraulic fork. Load is transmitted by long helical springs supported and contained in main tubes, hydraulically dampened by oil of high viscosity index. Hydraulic stops are provided in both recoil and cushion positions.

Muffler—Designed to reduce back pressure and has resonating chamber to produce low note. Inner tube and end bells of heavy gauge steel. Chrome-plated finish.

Handlebars—Seamless steel tubing. Rubber mounted Buckhorn type. Neoprene twist-grip controls for throttle and spark, fully enclosed.

Wheels—Drop center rims. Cadmium plated spokes. Knock-out type axles. Ball bearing mounted.

Tires—Goodyear or Firestone, 3.25 by 19, four ply.

Brakes—Fully enclosed, front and rear brakes with molded anti-score lining. Cast iron rear brake drum. Front drum of steel. Front and rear brakes eight inches in diameter and one inch wide.

Tanks—Extra large, welded heavy gauge steel gas tank with center filling cap. Capacity: 4¹/₂ gallons, with reserve in addition. Reserve controlled by two-way gas valve with fuel strainer. Welded heavy gauge steel oil tank. Capacity: 3 quarts, with provision for filter. Oil tank has screw-down provision in cap.

Instrument panel—120-mph speedometer, ignition and light switch incorporated in the top part of the front fork cowling. Each switch incorporates a tumbler type lock.

Saddle—Suspended on two seat posts. Each part incorporating a helical coil spring. Form fitting, bucket type with foam-rubber padding, covered with soft, genuine leather.

Finish—All surfaces to be painted are treated to

An 80 cu. in. side valve machine, produced in 1936 and designated the VLH. These bikes greatly resemble the 45's of the same year; however, the heads are much larger, with deeper finning. This model currently is stored as part of H-D's collection of antique vehicles. *Harley-Davidson, Inc.*

resist rust and corrosion. Available in Persian Red, Rio Blue and Brilliant Black. Available at extra cost, Metallic Bronco Bronze. Chrome and stainless steel trim. Frame in black enamel.

XL Models 1957–1993

If the Model K was underwhelming, the Sportster, introduced in 1957, was successful beyond the wildest dreams of even the most optimistic engineer or designer. Larger by 10 cu. in. than the original K, the 55 cu. in. machine boasted overhead valves that produced twelve percent more horsepower, a claim no unsuspecting Triumph owner would contest. Now in their twenty-sixth year of production, the X models have proliferated into 61 cu. in. (1,000cc) corner straighteners that retain wads of torque and the deep thuds that bring joy to the ears of V-twin owners to this day.

The motor initially measured 53.9 cu. in. (883cc), producing 40 horsepower at 5,500 rpm. Introduced with a 7.5 to 1 compression ratio, the musclebike shared all of the assets and none of the liabilities associated with its predecessor: The engine and transmission were one unit, with transmission service accomplished via an easily removed cover. Automotive-style shocks (one of five shock types used from then to now) nestled beneath the seat, providing sufficient buffer for the bike to be touted originally as either an on- or off-road model. In only its second year of production, the fast got faster, thanks to higher compression through domed pistons, cleaner ports, larger valves and aluminum tappets. The stage was set for the awesome XLCH.

High pipes, a magneto-generator ignition, peanut gas tank and semi-knobby tires warned the timid away from the lightweight XLCH. Here was a case where Harley-Davidson slightly misjudged the market—and reaped the rewards. Riders everywhere passed up enduros for the highway with the XLCH (CH stood for "Competition Hot"). They quickly ran off or removed the knobbies to become the favorites in any asphalt game being played. Both XL's in 1959 received a horsepower hike via a high-lift intake cam and redesigned exhaust cams. Owners found ways of expending that power. . . .

John Heidt, formerly a top drag racer and now an H-D dealer in Fond du Lac, Wisconsin, believes the 1962 Sportster was the fastest of them all. "There were more fast '62's than any other year, though any '59–'65 Sportster with a stock Linkert carburetor would reach 115 mph in the quarter mile," he says. "I ran a 13.4-second quarter with a '59 Sportster without the muffler, which actually made the bike slower, due to insufficient back pressure. I ran 105–107 mph quarters Sunday

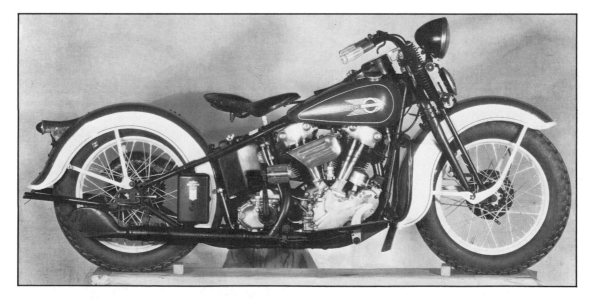

The 61 cu. in. 1936 overhead valve V-twin, designated the E model, was produced through 1947 and became popularly known as Knucklehead, due to the knuckle-like protrusions atop the head. *Harley-Davidson, Inc.*

after Sunday with a '62. The denser the air, the better it ran." Looking at reliability, Heidt says he frequently drag-raced two hours steady at the Union Grove, Wisconsin, strip without shutting the motor down. Not until a decade later was there a stock motorcycle that could stay with the Sportster.

Style became as important as speed. The staggered, shorty dual exhausts, first seen in 1962, have become classic Sportster equipment. A year earlier, H-D announced that all of the new Hi-Fi colors were available for either model, plus any color combination the prospective owner could conceive. That option lasted through 1971, when Sportster production reached such numbers under AMF that standardized hues were made mandatory. Nacelled headlights in various configurations appeared beginning in 1959 and lasted for more than a decade.

As the look changed, so too did the iron. The 1959 models started with a single-switch ignition, while in 1962 the speed-conscious engineers on Juneau Avenue converted such crucial items as fork brackets and motor mounts to aluminum. Full-width aluminum front wheel hubs, light but tough, were standard from 1964, as riders of all ages and sizes were stuffing H-D stroker kits into the machines for even better drag strip hole shots. The following year, the electricals were upgraded to a full 12-volt system, in anticipation of the 1967 electric starter. The XLH lost its kick starter in 1968, the year before the magneto ignition finale for the XLCH. Starting a magneto-equipped Sportster, by the way, taught a whole generation of riders how to use manual spark advance—and profanity. The battery system still in use employs a centrifugal advance with automatic retard. Riders who kick (no pun intended) about the lack of a

A 74 cu. in. 1942 Harley-Davidson overhead valve V-twin, as displayed by the Smithsonian Institution. *Smithsonian Institution photo by Rolfe Baggett*

manual starter never attempted to turn over a magneto-equipped XLCH.

The chassis continued to evolve, with a new front fork in 1968. The motor, a wonder in 1957, got better each year. Not even a "California" muffler, to control emissions, could prevent the V-twin in '68 from producing 58 horses at 6,800 rpm. Small wonder Michael Parks chose such a machine for *Then Came Bronson* the following year. For 1971, the timer was integrated into the cam cover, providing easier timing adjustment. A more important alteration was the switch that year from a dry to a wet clutch. The engineers were preparing the bike for the full 1,000cc treatment in 1972.

The megamotor combined with the reintroduction of the classic peanut tank and a low-profile seat to take advantage of the increasing interest in cruising bikes. Throughout the seventies, in fact, the Sportster became increasingly stylized as the feds descended upon H-D with a number of regulations. The pleasant "bread box" air cleaner of the late-sixties evolved into the infernal "ham can" in 1979. Side reflectors became mandatory in 1971, though stylists were able to work these shiny bits into elements already present on the bikes. About the only federal edict that made sense was the switch to a spring return and an external throttle cable in 1975.

Aware that a sound engine can look good with a number of chassis, the company in 1977 began to broaden the appeal of the XL's. Out came the XLCR Cafe Racer, a black-on-black, single-seat machine that proved Willie G.'s styling versatility and became an instant classic despite its two-year lifespan. The bikini-fairinged bike displayed siamesed exhausts and dual discs up front, the latter showing up on the XLH and XLCH from 1978. This bike is so highly regarded by those who know, that Willie G. and his two sons each own an XLCR. Finally, with an eye on the calendar, the Sportster has appeared in seventy-fifth company anniversary and twenty-fifth Sportster anniversary models, limited-production versions of everybody's favorite sports bike.

Other variations on the Sportster theme in 1979 were the Hugger, with its short shocks and low seating position, and the XLS Roadster with Low Rider styling and 16-in. rear tire. Two additions for 1983 were the no-frills XLX and the limited-production XR1000. Its heritage is evident in the dual Dell'Orto carbs and XR750-style pipes and aluminum heads and pistons from the racing bike. Horsepower, something H-D has recently downplayed, is 70.

All of these configurations now operate on the cutting edge of almost any rider's ability, thanks to 1982 introduction, at last, of a frame combining stamped and welded tubular construction. If you're unaware of the reception given fresh-framed Sportsters by the press, then you've really been out of touch—which is something no one will ever accuse the Sportster itself of being.

As late as the 1985 model year, the company was offering three variations on the Sportster theme—the XR-1000, the bargain-basement XLX and the Sportster itself—with the same 1000cc motor. All that changed in 1986, when the 883cc Evolution XLH replaced the XLX, and the Sportster 1100 XLH superseded its 1000cc brethren (sadly, the XR-1000 was dropped from the model line). Both of these motors showed the Evolution top end, complete with hydraulic lifters; new camshaft gear drive train; high-strength heads with new, oval combustion chambers; computer-designed camshafts; new rocker covers for easier servicing; three-piece flywheels; and revised intake and exhaust systems. Both machines run cooler than their elders, due mostly to superior oil flow.

By the 1993 model year, the company had expanded the Sportster line to five models: The basic XLH 883; the XLH 883 Hugger; the XLH 883 Deluxe; the XLH 1200; and an XLH 1200 90th Anniversary Edition! Sportsters have acquired a number of upgrades in the last five years. They include belt final drive, improved oil pumps, better generators and stronger top ends, and—best of all—the short-throw, five-speed transmission, which became standard in 1991. Late-breaking amenities on these popular bikes include redesigned, low-profile clutch and brake levers and a sight glass on the master brake cylinders for checking fluid levels. Standard 1993 colors include Vivid Black, Victory Red Sun-Glo, Bright Wineberry Sun-Glo, Two-Tone Victory Red Sun-Glo and Scarlet Red. The 90th Anniversary model is Two-Tone Silver/Charcoal Satin-Brite and features 90th Anniversary cloisonne fuel tank emblems and serialized nameplates.

Because the Sportster has evolved so completely, here are specs on the very first and very latest bikes. No list of parts and dimensions will convince you that the modern Sportster isn't the same hard-starting, filament-busting, frame-humming beast it once was. But a test ride most assuredly will.

Sportster H Specifications
(From a 1957 brochure)

Engine—55 cubic inch air-cooled four stroke, V-twin cylinder overhead valve engine. The size of the bore is 3 inches. The length of the stroke is $3^{13}/_{16}$ inches. Enclosed valve gear. Low expansion aluminum alloy, cam-ground pistons. Cylinder bores honed and parkerized. Deep cylinder fins extend around exhaust ports for proper cooling. All main bearings retained roller type; double tapered Timken bearings on the sprocket side; straight retained roller bearings on the gear side. Linkert carburetor. Includes cylinder heads with enlarged intake port openings, increased-size intake valves, light weight racing-type tappets, special 9-to-1 high dome pistons.

Transmission—Harley-Davidson four speed. Incorporated as an integral part of crankcase casting. Sliding dog clutches. Large, rugged gears for durability. Constant-mesh design. Foot shift, hand clutch.

Lubrication—Circulating lubrication system with gear-type pressure pump and gear-type scavenger pump. Transmission and front chain lubricated by oil supply separate from engine. All other bearings Alemite-Zerk fitted or prepacked.

Ignition—Two-brush shunt, voltage controlled generator, storage battery, spark coil, circuit breaker. Easy starting and water proof.

Clutch—Harley-Davidson multiple disc. One-piece clutch discs. Left hand operated.

Drive—Motor to transmission by $^3/_8$-inch pitch triple chain running in oil bath and sliding shoe tension control. $^5/_8$-inch pitch single-row roller chain to rear wheel.

Rear suspension—Swing-arm type sprung by means of two helical coil springs and controlled by means of two hydraulic, automotive type shock absorbers, all enclosed in chrome covers. Pivot point of swinging arm is supported by pre-loaded Timken bearings.

Front fork—Easy riding hydraulic fork. Load is transmitted by long helical springs supported and contained in main tubes, hydraulically damped by oil of high viscosity index. Hydraulic stops are provided in both recoil and cushion position.

Tires—Goodyear or Firestone, 3.50 by 18 inches.

Brakes—Fully enclosed, front and rear brakes with molded anti-score lining. Front and rear brakes 8 inches in diameter and 1 inch wide.

Tanks—Extra large welded heavy gauge steel tank with center filling cap. Capacity: 4.4 gallons including reserve in addition. Reserve controlled by two-way gas valve with fuel strainer. Welded heavy gauge steel oil tank. Capacity: 3 quarts, with provision for filter. Oil tank has secure, screw-down provision.

Special equipment—This model available with the Deluxe Group.

Finish—Harmonizing two-tone color styling: Black, Calypso Red, Skyline Blue, or Sabre-Grey Metallic with Birch White tank panel. (Other colors and combinations were available on special order through dealers.) Chrome and stainless steel trim.

1993 XLH Sportster 1200 Specifications
(From a company press kit)
Engine: OHV V Evolution.
Bore and stroke: 3.498 × 3.812 in (88.8 × 96.8 mm).
Displacement: 73.4 cu. in., 1200 cc.
Carburetion: 40mm constant-velocity with enricher and accelerator pump.
Ignition: Inductive, battery-powered, V Fire III electronic breakerless with solid-state dual stage advance.
Transmission: Five-speed, constant mesh.
Torque: 71 ft./lbs. at 4,000 rpm.
Length: 87.6 in. (222.5 cm).
Seat height: 29.0 in. (73.66 cm).
Wheelbase: 60.2 in. (152.9 cm).
Dry weight: 470 lbs.
Mileage: 45 mpg city, 52 mpg country.
Instruments: Tachometer, speedometer with odometer and resetable tripmeter.

A 1952 Model K. This sports bike employed the 45 cu. in. side valve motor. *David Wright*

61 and 74 Cu. In. Models 1948–1965

The Panhead motor began life in a hardtail frame, became the Hydra-Glide a year later, showed up as the Duo-Glide in 1958 and ended up in 1965 as the Electra Glide. Its eighteen years of dependable existence allowed the company to perfect non-motor aspects of its bikes.

The new overhead valve 61 and 74 cu. in. motors previewed in 1948 featured aluminum cylinder heads and used push-rod-type hydraulic lifters in the valve train. The rocker arms and cylinder heads were redesigned, with the latter the source for the eventual Panhead nickname. The new heads dissipated heat more rapidly than did the Knucklehead's, while the new lifters eliminated tappet noise. To accommodate the change in the length of the rocker arm fingers, a new camshaft was designed. Also new were the exhaust ports and pipes; the intake manifold was new and was fabricated from brazed tubing. Extensive work was done with oil flow and pressure. A new and larger pump delivered a reported twenty-five percent more oil to the overhead mechanism at 15 lbs. of pressure per square inch. From a cosmetic standpoint, the motor had no external oil pipes.

The cylinder heads were made of aluminum alloy, having aluminum-bronze valve seat inserts and steel valve guides. The lower portion of the rocker arm support was cast iron and the upper portion, or cap, of the rocker arm support was bronze. The cylinder heads were provided with steel inserts for the cylinder bolts and the spark plugs. The plugs themselves had a broader heat range, providing better performance at low speeds. The 74 cu. in. Panhead engine weighed eight pounds less than its Knucklehead counterpart, though horsepower was about the same.

Improvements outside the motor in 1948 included a steering head lock, a safety guard mounting plate on the frame and a more comfortable latex-filled saddle. Two forms of corrosion protection were applied to all body parts, including tanks. Forty-eight also was the first year for what may have been H-D's most startling color ever—Azure Blue.

In 1949, the year following the Panhead's premier, the company installed hydraulic front forks. These were an immense improvement over the rigid-spring forks known previously. Riders reported crossing railroads—even railroad ties—with ease. The forks were the single biggest improvement to date in terms of ride and handling and contributed to the touring reputation the 74 has passed on to the FLH and FLT. Today's touring rider might be put off by the 1949's low-speed handling: the uncanny balance of the big bikes was still several years down the road. Also found on the '49 was a front brake with a thirty-four-percent-larger drum. The Panhead transmission would be quite familiar to today's rider, since the harder it was shifted, the better it changed gears. The hand shift and foot clutch, by the way, showed a pattern change earlier, in 1947. From the rider's view, first gear was closest to him and fourth closest to the steering head. Prior to '47, riders pulled rather than pushed when they shifted up.

Porting work produced ten more horses for 1950, while '51 models boasted 55 horsepower and combined the serrated exhaust headers (seen on the 74 through 1973) with a chromed lower exhaust system. With an eye on traditional riders, Harley-Davidson continued to offer hand shift after 1952, the year of the first foot-shift Panhead. Competing for sales with such long-gone makes as Delfino, James, Panther and Sunbeam, 1952 was the swan song for the 61 cu. in. motor. The '52's sported wide tanks and 5.00×16 in. tires, whereas 1953 models are most easily identified by the speedometer, which read 1, 2, 3, rather than 10, 20, 30.

There was no mistaking the '53 models, since all H-D's that year displayed a $2\frac{1}{2}$-in. gold medallion on the front fender. A "trumpet blast" Jubilee air horn was standard, and plastic saddlebags were optional. A chrome medallion with "V" replaced gold the following year, together with a streamlined front chain guard and rubber-mounted, horizontal tail lamps. Not until '56 did the trusty Panhead motor need attention; high-lift cams and a freer air cleaner produced a reported twelve percent power hike. A lower seating position combined with the ever-plush saddle to provide an adequate ride, even with the solid rear. But that was about to change.

Ever hear of a fit too perfect on a motorcycle? That was the only initial problem with the Duo-Glide, offered from 1958 through 1964 and still seen in large numbers on the highway. A series of prototypes was built of the machine, some nearly a decade before production. All of the prototypes were afflicted with a fork damping problem, according to Art Kauper, who worked at the time with engineers assigned to the project. "We went into production at the absolute eleventh hour," he reports. The problem was solved when it was discovered, during the first few months, that the rubber seals on the fork legs actually rubbed the legs to a mirror finish, creating a perfect fit. This left no room for oil, which was forced past the seals as the forks worked up and down. The solution proved to be a new seal with slightly looser tolerance and a slightly rougher finish on the fork legs.

The only other malady surfaced following delivery of a sizeable Duo-Glide order to the California Highway Patrol. Officers experienced instability at or above the legal limit. John Nowak, service school dean and a troubleshooter for years with the company, was dispatched to the West Coast to attempt to solve the problem. "The police took a ride and wanted the solid rear ends back," says Nowak, who tried a number of fancy stunts before discovering that the head bearing was too tight. "Service Bulletin No. 510 tells dealers how to set the bearing. All the other stuff suggested is baloney." Proof that H-D could solve suspension problems was made evident a year or so later, when airplane manufacturers consulted the factory before developing their landing gears.

The FL's and FLH's in 1958 also showed a gold, silver and black tank insignia and enjoyed larger cylinder head fins for improved cooling. The insignia took on an arrow shape the following year, and there was now a neutral indicator light. The Duo-Glide by 1960 featured the same style headlight nacelle seen on the Sportster. Other early-sixties modifications included a larger rear chain, a new chain oiler and external oil lines to the overhead valve gear in '63; and full-width, finned, aluminum front brake drums in 1964. The stage was set for a new idea that fostered a new name for the FL and FLH.

The Electra Glide was one of three new Harley-Davidson models for 1965, yet its 12-volt electrics, push-button start, sealed and enclosed primary chain and five-gallon "turnpike" tank made riders forget the Sprint Scrambler and the M-50. H-D had for years preached that the 74 cu. in. bike was the ultimate highway cycle, and the Electra Glide certainly backed that claim. Instant starting

A 1962 Super CH Sportster. "CH" is said to have stood for "Competition Hot," while the "H" model was intended for the highway. *Harley-Davidson, Inc.*

proved to be the final tribute to the Panhead motor, a V-twin that began life as a postwar improvement on the Knuckler and ended with a reliability record roughly equivalent to the path of the sun. "H" stood for highway and was an indication that the model carried extras for touring; but any of the 74's would roll all day down any road to anywhere.

Specifications
(From a 1949 magazine road test)

Motor: V-type two-cylinder four-stroke engine, $3^{7}/_{16}$ in. bore, $3^{31}/_{32}$ in. stroke, 74 cu. in. displacement (also offered with 61 cu. in. motor). Dry sump lubrication, battery ignition, Schebler $1^{5}/_{16}$ in. carburetor, 50 horsepower (estimated) at 4,800 rpm.

Transmission: Four speeds, hand gear change, foot clutch, oil capacity one quart, primary chain drive, secondary chain drive.

Frame, running gear: Double loop seamless steel frame, Hydra-Glide forks, rigid rear suspension, $59^{1}/_{2}$ in. wheelbase. Oil tank capacity, 4 quarts, gasoline tank capacity, $3^{3}/_{4}$ gallons. Brakes, 8 in. front, 8 in. rear. Tire size, front and rear, 5.00×16 in. Dry weight, 560 lbs.

Model B, Hummer 1959–1960

Just a glance at the specs will reveal that the Hummer evolved from the 125cc DKW copy. Bore, stroke and dimensions were either the same or too close to call. The motorbike-like conveyance lasted only two years, due to the importation of the small Aermacchi/Harley-Davidsons.

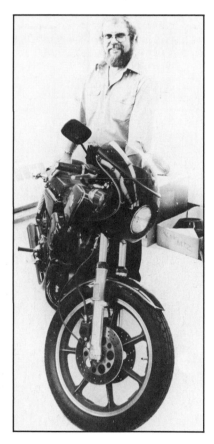

Willie G. Davidson with his cafe racer, the first XLCR produced. The vice president of styling has personalized his machine by adding pinstriping, trading the original Goodyear tires for Continentals and porcelainizing the exhausts. *David Wright*

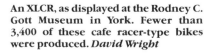

An XLCR, as displayed at the Rodney C. Gott Museum in York. Fewer than 3,400 of these cafe racer-type bikes were produced. *David Wright*

73

Serial number: The engine (serial) number is stamped on the front end of the engine crankcase, on the left-hand side.

Wheelbase: 51½ in.
Model designation: Hummer.
Type of engine: Two cycle.
Number of cylinders: One.
Bore: 2¹/₁₆ in. (52.39 mm).
Stroke: 2⁹/₃₂ in. (57.94 mm).
Displacement: 7.6 cu. in. (124.87 cc).
Compression ratio: 6.6 to 1.
Horsepower (NACC rating): 1.7.
Brake horsepower (approximate): 3.
Tire size: 3.50 × 18 in.
Gasoline tank, total: 1⅞ gals.
Main supply: 1½ gals.
Reserve: 1½ quarts.
Transmission case: 1¼ pints.
Low gear: 26.5 to 1.
Second gear: 15.4 to 1.

Topper Scooter 1960–1965

How many Harley-Davidsons can you name that had a parking brake? Or a starting system that involved neither kicking nor any kind of electrics? Or a buddy seat wherein there was room for a six-pack? Or belt drive? Sound like your kind of bike? Sorry to report that it was no one's kind of bike, but rather was the 165cc Topper scooter. Sold from 1960 through 1965, the Topper was H-D's answer to the brief popularity of the Italian Vespa and Lambretta scooters seen on college campuses and other strange places during the Eisenhower years. Among its features was a front brake lever on the left handlebar that could, via locking a cam, also serve to brake the bike when parked. The cam slid into the gap created when the front brake was squeezed; it wedged itself between the brake lever and the bracket that held the lever to the bar. Nothing tricky, but it worked; why a scooter needed a parking brake at all was a question best left unasked. Anyone who ever started a mower or a snowblower will be familiar with the Topper's hand recoil method. It worked, too. And while the factory recommended carrying surplus two-stroke oil beneath the buddy seat for mixing at

The 1978 25th Anniversary Sportster, a special edition model that includes paperwork proving its ancestry, signed by Chairman Vaughn Beals, President Charlie Thompson and Styling Vice President Willie G. Davidson. *Harley-Davidson, Inc.*

fuel stops, the space frequently was devoted to school books or contraband.

The scooter fad peaked right about the time the Topper was introduced, which was unfortunate, because the Topper seems to have used its original engine design to good advantage. The only complaint voiced by more than an occasional owner concerned the transmission. The unit automatically changed the driving ratio by varying the diameter of front and rear driving flanges on which the belt drive ran. Engine speeds caused balls operating on cams to move together, altering the diameter of the flanges. Negligent owners or those who ran the machines in muck quickly learned that the belt slipped on—and off—the flanges. Final drive was by a conventional chain. Both the 5- and 9-horsepower models sold for $445 in 1962 (the smaller horsepower model could be driven in some states without an operator's license).

Specifications

Serial number: The engine (serial) number is stamped on the engine crankcase.

Wheelbase: 51.5 in.
Model designation letter: A and AU.
Type of engine: Two cycle.
Number of cylinders: One, horizontal.
Bore: 2.375 in. (60.325 mm).
Stroke: 2.281 in. (57.937 mm).
Piston displacement: 10 cu. in. (165 cc).

Compression ratio: 6.6 to 1.
Horsepower (N.A.C.C. rating): 2.26.
Spark plug type: Harley-Davidson No. 4.
Size: 14 mm.
Gap: .025 to .030 in.
Circuit breaker point gap: .018 in.
Ignition timing: $5/_{64}$ in. (.078 mm) to 7.64 in. (.110 mm) before piston top center.
Fuel tank: 1.7 U.S. gallons, with .5 U.S. pint reserve.
Number of sprocket teeth: Transmission drive 14; rear wheel 63.
Overall ratio: Maximum 18.0; minimum 5.9.
Tire size: 4.00 × 12.

Bobcat, Ranger, Pacer, Scat, 175cc 1962–1966

These U.S.-designed and constructed bikes were aimed at riders not yet ready for the 250cc Sprint or Sprint H Aermacchi/Harley-Davidsons being imported at the time. They sold well, in one form or another, for five years. The 175cc two-stroke "would go just fast enough to get you hurt," according to one veteran dealer, who said he preferred selling kids the larger though less peaky four-strokes. Others contend these bikes were quite easy to ride, though with three-speed transmissions it took some skill to keep the machines in their power bands.

The only sort of problem involved the electrical system. Off-road riders frequently experienced shorts of various kinds, while road runners found

The left side of the XR-1000 is dominated by the XR750-derived exhaust system.
Harley-Davidson, Inc.

75

flickering headlights the norm as often as the exception. Full-size H-D riders also could not get used to some of the most unyielding upholstery known to man. No wonder the off-road guys stayed up on the pegs.

The machines were introduced with solid rear ends. The Ranger, a trail bike without lights, was sold only in 1962, while the surviving (street) Pacer and (on- or off-road) Scat received swing arms and shocks in '63. The Bobcat, offered either as a road or trail model, displayed an attractive, one-piece body in 1966, its only year of production.

Specifications
(From a 1966 Bobcat owners manual)
    Wheelbase: 52 in.
    Overall length: 79 in.
    Overall width: 30.5 in.
    Fuel tank: 1.87 U.S. gallons.
    Transmission: 1.25 pints.
    Model designation: BTH.
    Type: Two cycle, single cylinder.
    Bore: 2.375 in.
    Stroke: 2.406 in.
    Displacement: 10.7 cu. in. (175cc).
    Compression ratio: 7.5:1.
    Ignition timing: $7/32$ in. before piston top center.
    Circuit break point gap: .018 in.
    Spark plug type: H-D No. 4.

    Size: 14mm.
    Gap: .040 to .045 in.
    Transmission type: Constant mesh.
    Speeds: Three forward.
    Engine sprocket teeth: 15 standard, 15 trail model.
    Clutch sprocket teeth: 31 standard, 31 trail model.
    Countershaft sprocket teeth: 15 standard, 12 trail model.
    Rear wheel sprocket teeth: 49 standard, 84 trail model.
    Tire size: 3.50×18 in.

250cc, 350cc Sprint Four-Stroke Singles 1961–1974

The first Aermacchi/Harley-Davidson effort was single-cylinder machines that sold like, well, like Hondas during the first few years of importation into the U.S. However, the superior Italian-American styling could not overcome an inferior wiring system and a price tag that seemed to climb as the Japanese competition, such as the 305cc Honda Super Hawk and Scrambler, stayed cheap and got fast.

A Sprint H could compete on a regional racing level with most other machines; accomplished scrambles riders such as Alabama's Phil Scarborough made their presence known. But then along came the two-strokes and that blew the four-strokes, Italian and Japanese, out of the water.

The 1993 XLH Sportster 883. *Harley-Davidson, Inc.*

Part of the Aermacchi problem was that it made hardly anything except the engine, which was reliable. H-D supervisors on the scene fought constant quality battles with suppliers. Often, they lost. Still, the Sprint would, with dry points, give reliable service.

The motor was hung from a single-strut frame, plenty substantial for the H model, introduced in 1962. More popular than its street counterpart, the H scrambler ran bobbed fenders, high exhausts and semi-knobby tires, yet had a street-legal lighting system. By '63, both bikes more

The V2 Evolution 883cc XLH Sportster engine was new in 1986 and featured hydraulic lifters plus improved piston, cylinder, cylinder head and crankshaft components. This smaller-displacement Evolution machine was priced at $3,995. *Harley-Davidson, Inc.*

The Evolution also was offered in an 1100cc Sportster configuration for 1986: the XLH in a variety of colors. Both Sportsters retained the traditional four-speed transmission. *Harley-Davidson, Inc.*

closely resembled their big brethren cosmetically, while the H glistened with a new and large chrome air cleaner together with the largest air-hose-cartridge system ever on a non-racing H-D. Dubbed the Scrambler the following year, power was boosted via a 27mm Dell'Orto carburetor, 9.5-1 compression ratio and a megaphone to 25 horses at 8,700 rpm.

The capacity stayed the same but the iron cylinder and aluminum head took on a shorter stroke and a larger bore for 1966. Little else changed until the '69 model year, when the street model, now called the SS, showed up with a 350cc motor and dual exhausts. The Scrambler received the new motor and a new designation, the SX, in 1972.

Sprint Specifications
(From a 1961 owner's manual)
Serial numbers: The engine (serial) number is stamped on a pad on the engine crankcase, below the cylinder. The frame serial number is located on the right side of the steering head.
Wheelbase: 52.0 in. (Sprint); 53.3 in. (Sprint H).
Overall length: 78.5 in. (Sprint); 81 in. (Sprint H).
Overall width: 28.5 in. (Sprint); 28.8 in. (Sprint H).
Fuel tank (total capacity): 4 U.S. gallons (Sprint); 2.64 U.S. gallons (Sprint H).
Reserve: Two quarts (Sprint); 0.62 quarts (Sprint H).
Crankcase oil: Two quarts.
Model designation letter: C (Sprint); H (Sprint H).
Number of cylinders: One.
Type: Four cycle.
Bore: 2.598 in. (66 mm).

Stroke: 2.835 in. (72 mm).
Piston displacement: 15 cu. in. (246.2 cc).
Compression ratio: 8.5 to 1 (Sprint); 9.2 to 1 (Sprint H).
Horsepower: 18 at 7,500 rpm (Sprint); 19.5 at 6,700 rpm (Sprint H).
Horsepower (N.A.C.C. rating): 2.7.
Valve tappet clearance (cold): .004 in. (Sprint); intake, .003 in., exhaust, .005 in. (Sprint H).
Ignition timing: Retard 21 degrees (7/64-in.) BTC, automatic advance 41 degrees (13/32-in.) BTC (Sprint); retard 1 degree BTC, automatic advance 41 degrees (13/32-in.) BTC (Sprint H).
Circuit breaker points, gap: .018 in.
Spark plug type: Harley-Davidson No. 7.
Size: 14 mm.
Gap: .020 in.
Transmission type: Constant mesh.
Speeds: Four forward.
Drive pinion gear teeth: 26.
Clutch ring gear teeth: 65.
Transmission internal ratios: 1st, 2.91; 2nd, 1.76; 3rd, 1.27; 4th, 1.00.
Transmission sprocket: 16 (Sprint); 15 (Sprint H).
Rear wheel sprocket: 38.
First gear: 17.28 to 1 (Sprint); 18.44 to 1 (Sprint H).
Second gear: 10.45 to 1 (Sprint); 11.15 to 1 (Sprint H).
Third gear: 7.54 to 1 (Sprint); 8.09 to 1 (Sprint H).
Fourth gear: 6.33 to 1 (Sprint); 5.94 to 1 (Sprint H).
Tire, front: 3.00 × 17 (Sprint); 3.00 × 18 (Sprint H).
Tire, rear: 3.00 × 17 (Sprint); 3.50 × 18 (Sprint H).

M-50, M-50 Sport, M-65, M-65 Sport, Shortster 1965–1968

"A menace."

That's how a retired Harley-Davidson engineer describes the M-50 and M-50 Sport motor-driven

The Panhead motor, first produced for the 1948 model year. It superseded the Knucklehead and offered the advantages of better oil passage and lighter weight (the Knucklehead was all iron, whereas the Panhead, produced through 1965, had numerous aluminum upper end parts). *David Wright*

cycles, constructed in Italy by Aermacchi/Harley-Davidson and offered in the U.S. in 1965 and 1966. The 50cc, two-stroke bikes were handsomely finished in Holiday Red with White panels. The M-50, displayed in ads with females aboard, followed traditional motorbike lines and was available both years; the Sport model featured a racing-style gas tank and a flat, competition-look seat to entice riders of both genders. It was offered only in 1966. All of this was of little consolation to the rider who found himself short of acceleration as a Freightliner bore down on Route 66.

Essentially the same machines, enlarged to 65cc capacity, were offered beginning in 1967. "Sudden disinterest" in 1966 resulted in 4,000 M-50's in inventory. They were sold well below the $225 suggested retail price. (The Sport model was offered in 1966 for $275.) The M-65 and M-65 Sport went for $230 and $265, respectively. Strangely enough, such tiny transportation is still around. Honda, for example, currently sells the MB5, a 49cc bike with cafe racer styling. In contrast to the M-50's 1966 sticker price, the Honda retails for $798. That's about $266 per cubic inch.

The 1948 FL, introductory year for the hydraulic lifter motor that came to be known as the Panhead. *Harley-Davidson, Inc.*

Specifications

Wheelbase: 44.1 in.
Overall length: 71.4 in. (M), 67.8 in. (MS).
Overall width: 25.6 in. (M), 24.0 in. (MS).
Ground clearance: 4.3 in.
Fuel tank: 1.6 U.S. gallons (M), 2.5 U.S. gallons (MS).
Transmission: 1 pint.
Model designation letter: M, MS.
Type: 2 cycle, single cylinder.
Bore: 1.527 in. (38.8 mm).
Stroke: 1.654 in. (42.0 mm).
Piston displacement: 3.03 cu. in. (49.66 cc).
Taxable horsepower: .93.
Compression ratio: 10 to 1.
Circuit breaker point gap: .018 in.
Spark plug type: Harley-Davidson No. 7.
Size: 14 mm.
Gap: .025 to .030 in.
Ignition timing: 27 degrees (0.115) BTC.
Transmission type: Constant mesh.
Speeds: 3 forward.
Drive pinion gear teeth: 13.
Clutch ring gear teeth: 59.
Transmission internal ratios: 1st—3.18, 2nd—1.78, 3rd—1.17.
Transmission sprocket: 13.
Rear wheel sprocket: 27.
Low (first) gear: 29.85 to 1.
Second gear: 16.76 to 1.
Third gear: 11.06 to 1.
Tire size: 2.00 × 17 front, 2.00 × 17 rear.

Rapido Model 1968–1977

The Rapido and its successors, the TX (1973), the SX (1974) and the SXT (1975) were offered to the public during Aermacchi/Harley-Davidson's final decade. Though price competitive with the Japanese, they suffered in dealerships not used to catering to off-road riders, even young ones. All of the assets and liabilities associated with the Italian line were present here, though a four-speed transmission made the engine more flexible than previous play racers.

Specifications
(From a 1970 Rapido owners manual)
Overall length: 76.6 in.
Overall width: 32.7 in.
Wheelbase: 48.9 in.
Ground clearance: 6.7 in.
Fuel tank: 2.4 U.S. gallons (1 quart reserve).
Transmission: 1 pint.
Model designation: MLS.
Type: Two cycle, single cylinder.
Bore: 2.21 in.
Stroke: 1.97 in.
Displacement: 7.53 in. (123.5 cc).
Taxable horsepower: 1.95.
Compression ratio: 7.65:1.
Circuit breaker point gap: .016 in.
Spark plug type: H-D No. 6 or 5-6.
Size: 14 mm.

The 1949 Hydra-Glide, so named for the new telescopic front forks. *Harley-Davidson, Inc.*

Gap: .025 to .030 in.
Ignition timing: 20 degrees (0.073) BTC.
Transmission type: Constant mesh.
Speeds: Four forward.
Drive pinion gear teeth: 19.
Clutch ring gear teeth: 61.
Transmission internal ratios: 1st—2.50, 2nd—1.40, 3rd—.92, 4th—.72.
Transmission sprocket: 14.
Rear wheel sprocket (standard): 50.
Rear wheel sprocket (trail): 62.
First gear: 28.7:1 standard, 35.5:1 trail.
Second gear: 16.1:1 standard, 19.9:1 trail.
Third gear: 10.6:1 standard, 13.1:1 trail.
Fourth gear: 8.3:1 standard, 10.3:1 trail.
Tire size: 3.00 × 18 in. front, 3.50 × 18 in. rear.

Baja, SR 100 1970–1974

Bike magazines lavished high praise on the Baja after a class win in the Greenhorn Enduro. But over its five-year lifespan under two names, it failed to improve while the Japanese off-road bikes made major technological advances. Not even a lighting option in 1972 or automatic gas-oil mix, available on the SR 100 in 1973, could keep it in the fore of race-minded youngsters.

Specifications
(From a 1970 owners manual)
Wheelbase: 52 in.
Overall length: 78.5 in.
Overall width: 34 in.
Ground clearance: 10.8 in.
Fuel tank: 2.5 U.S. gallons (1 quart reserve).
Transmission: 1.3 pints.
Model designation: MSR.
Type: 2 cycle, single cylinder.
Bore: 1.97 in.
Stroke: 1.97 in.
Displacement: 5.98 cu. in. (98.1cc).
Taxable horsepower: 1.55.
Compression ratio: 9.5:1.
Circuit breaker point gap: .016 in.
Spark plug type: H-D No. 7.
Size: 14 mm.
Gap: .025 to .030 in.
Ignition timing: 20 degrees (0.073) BTC.
Transmission type: Constant mesh.
Speeds: Five forward.
Drive pinion gear teeth: 19.
Clutch ring gear teeth: 61.
Transmission internal ratios: 1st—2.06, 2nd—1.33, 3rd—.92, 4th—.75, 5th—.58.
Transmission sprocket teeth: 12, 13, 14, 15.
Rear wheel sprocket: 72.
Tire size: 3.00 × 21 in. front, 3.50 × 18 in. rear.

The Snowmobile 1971–1975

Repeatedly throughout its history, Harley-Davidson attempted to diversify. Except for golf cars, such attempts have largely been thwarted. One of the most recent examples was the H-D snowmobile, produced from 1971 through 1975. Snowmobiles, pioneered by Bombardier Ltd. in Quebec, appeared in the mid-sixties to be a real blessing for snow belt motorcycle dealers. Here was a machine that could be sold to riders who were putting their bikes away for the winter. Instead of hibernating, dealer and rider alike could remain active year-round.

That sort of thinking proved valid until the first glitch in the seventies' economy. Riders realized that snowmobiles were much less functional than bikes, frequently requiring trailering to a desirable trail, plus mounds of clothing, provisions, etc. Dozens of makes sprang up in Minnesota, Wisconsin and Michigan garages, only to disappear. Like pleasure boats, snowmobiles were a novelty most people could do without. Today, only four makes survive, and most of them are either partially or exclusively of Japanese manufacture.

The H-D snowmobiles differed only insignificantly from most other kinds, though the engines were manufactured by the company. With a pair of skis up front and a tread in the rear, they offered a choice of two-cylinder, two-cycle engines (24.29 cu. in. and 26.42 cu. in.), manual or electric start, chain drive and automatic transmission. The sleds actually competed briefly with AMF's Skidaddler before the H-D engine was placed in the AMF frame and the parent company's snowmobile disappeared.

SS/SX-175, SS/SX-250 Two-Cycle Singles 1974–1978

The off-road SX-175 was introduced in 1974, the streetgoing SS- and off-road SX-250 in 1975 and the street SS-175 in 1976. Timing could not have been worse, since the Environmental Protection Agency and the Department of Transportation were looking askance at two-cycle engines and since public acceptance of the ringading sound continued to decline.

These motors were copies of the Yamaha DT-1, the force in motocross in the seventies. Although the two-strokes were as trouble-free as their four-cycle Aermacchi counterparts, they contributed to the demise of the Italian lightweights. Folks just didn't like the sound. The 250 enjoyed some off-road competition success, notably in the hands of Californian Don Ogilvie.

Specifications
(From a 1976 dealer brochure)
Wheelbase: 56 in.

Overall length: 86 in.
Overall width: 31 in. (SS), 35 in. (SX).
Ground clearance: 7 in.
Fuel tank: 2.8 gals.
Reserve: 1.2 quarts.
Transmission: 2.5 pints.
Oil tank: 3.3 pints.
Type: Two cycle, single cylinder.
Model designation: SS/SX-175, SS/SX-250.
Bore: 175, 2.40 in. (61 mm); 250, 2.84 in. (72 mm).
Stroke: 2.35 in. (59.6 mm).
Displacement: 175, 10.63 in. (174.1 cc); 250, 14.80 in. (242.6 cc).
Taxable horsepower: 175, 2.3; 250, 3.22.
Compression ratio: 175, 10.6 to 1; 250, 10.3 to 1.
Spark plug type: 175, Harley-Davidson No. 7–8; 250, Harley-Davidson No. 7.
Size: 14 mm.
Gap: .025 in.
Ignition timing: 21 degrees (.100 in.) BTC.
Ignition timing pickup tap: .012 to .016 in.
Transmission type: Constant mesh.
Speeds: Five forward.
Drive pinion gear teeth: 20.
Clutch ring gear teeth: 56.
Transmission internal ratios: 1st, 2.53; 2nd, 1.79; 3rd, 1.30; 4th, 1.0; 5th, .80.
Transmission sprocket teeth: SX-175, 13; SS-175, 14; SS/SX-250, 15.
Rear wheel sprocket teeth: SX-175, 49; SS-175, 50; SX-250, 50; SS-250, 49.
Gear ratios, SX-175: First gear, 26.8; second gear, 18.6; third gear, 13.6; fourth gear, 10.6; fifth gear, 8.5.
Gear ratios, SS-175: First gear, 25.4; second gear, 17.6; third gear, 12.8; fourth gear, 10.0; fifth gear, 8.0.
Gear ratios, SX-250: First gear, 23.7; second gear, 16.5; third gear, 12.0; fourth gear, 9.3; fifth gear, 7.5.
Gear ratios, SS-250: First gear, 23.2; second gear, 16.1; third gear, 11.7; fourth gear, 9.1; fifth gear, 7.4.
Tire size: SS-175, 3.25 × 19 in. front, 4.00 × 18 in. rear; SX-175, 3.00 × 19 in. front, 4.00 × 18 in. rear; SS-250, 3.25 × 19 in. front, 4.00 × 18 in. rear; SX-250, 3.00 × 21 in. front, 4.00 × 18 in. rear.

74, 80 Cu. In. V-Twin 1966–1993

The name disappeared from the front fenders in 1983, but the effect the Electra Glide had on contemporary Harley-Davidson motorcycles lingers on.

Electric starting was introduced in 1965, with the motor now known as the Shovelhead making its debut in 1966. A Tillotson diaphragm carburetor combined with a new "power pac" head design to produce 60 horses, 5 more than the Panhead offered. That extra power came in handy as a higher percentage of riders were going the "Dresser" route—thanks to Harley-Davidson's numerous quality touring accessories. The motor itself evidenced less vibration than did its predecessor, emitting only a slight rhumba beat under

deceleration. The FLH, with higher compression, produced 60 horses, versus 54 for the FL. Soft, oversize handgrips, by this time an H-D trademark, neutralized any other commotion.

Contemporary road tests indicated that the FL's and FLH's remained the touring machines by which other bikes were judged. The H-D's were faulted only for inadequate brakes and the external presence of oil. The latter may have been a cheap shot, since those unfamiliar with the big V-twin frequently mistook the drip of the rear chain oiler for a lack of close tolerances.

Immediately following its introduction, evolutionary improvements began. In 1967, the bikes received a push-pull choke that allowed for infinite adjustment. Also added to the line was a pleated seat that made the already comfy H-D bench even more so. A new oil pump and warning lights for oil, generator and ignition were added in '68, followed by the unveiling in 1969 of the classic, bar-mounted FLH fairing. This piece, produced by H-D in the Tomahawk fiber-glass plant, was offered initially only in white, as were matching fiber-glass saddle bags. The most noticeable change for 1970 was the disappearance of serrated headers. The Shovelhead spat out its exhaust via chrome headers that looked infinitely better and worked as well as the parts they replaced.

Meanwhile, customizers were casting admiring glances at the Shovelhead motor in the FL frame, in part because 150,000 riders in 1970 were left with money in hand but no bikes—demand created in part by the war-time economy was that strong. Formerly content with modifying Sportsters, the would-be cruisers were cutting off the formidable Electra Glide forks and installing wild aftermarket front ends. These bits and pieces varied from dainty to dangerous, as West Coast extension forks kept pushing the front wheel farther from the motor. Fortunately, Willie G. was able to head the trend off with a design that has become a true watershed in U.S. riding: the Super Glide.

"Is the American motorcyclist ready to ride around on someone else's expression of personal, radical tastes?" *Cycle* magazine asked before testing the new '71 Super Glide. The publication put the bike through its paces and concluded that the machine "will succeed in this country like no machine Harley-Davidson has ever made or dreamed of making."

Davidson is characteristically modest about his first major design under the auspices of AMF: "AMF never knew quite what to make of this department [styling], so they just let us alone."

The handsome Sprint H, offered from 1961 through 1968, was a popular short-track mount. *Harley-Davidson, Inc.*

The first joint effort between H-D and Aeronautica Macchi was this 250cc (15 cu. in.), single-cylinder, Sprint road bike. Introduced in 1961, it was well finished and sold briskly. Full-size Harley riders expressed amazement at the time concerning the size of the fuel tank, which was larger than the single-cylinder head. *David Wright*

Willie G. grafted the Sportster's handsome—and stable—aluminum front forks onto the massive frame, compensating for their stock appearance by making the Super Glide graphically exciting. The boat-tail Sportster seat worked surprisingly well on the initial batch of Super Glides, which still carried the FLH designation on the timing cover.

The FX, as the Super Glide was designated, was significant for the following reasons:

—It was the first factory custom. Prior to 1971, no company had ever listened so closely to owners of its products. Until then, riders bought what was offered and set about individualizing as best they could.

—It combined traditional parts of one motorcycle with traditional parts of another to come away with an entirely new look. This alone endeared it to the Electra Glide and Sportster faithful, who could identify with the FX even if they did not intend to buy it.

—It was the first cruiser, the first bike to make so personal a statement about a whole new kind of rider who had never before had an acceptable, showroom-stock bike offered him. Harley-Davidson dealers were talking to a new kind of customer about a new kind of machine.

—It was a seed that sprouted everything from the Fat Bob to the Wide Glide to the Super Glide II. Thanks to this machine, no Harley owner has any excuse for owning a bike exactly like anyone else's.

And it was a good bike. It kick-started easily, the transmission was traditionally bulletproof, the clutch action was "the best in motorcycling," said a magazine, and in practice it handled much better than anyone could imagine. Slimmer by 70 pounds than an FL, the FX rocketed away from stoplights, yet would chug willingly through town all day. Drum brakes front and rear prevented the Super Glide from state-of-the-art stops, but that would be remedied quite soon. With an optional red, white and blue color scheme, the Super Glide was the perfect bike at the perfect time. Somehow, Willie G. had created something that was as outrageous as a Yippee and as conservative as an Orange County cop in one master stroke.

At this time, the feds began their descent upon manufacturers of transportation; their well-intentioned regulations were designed to make cars, trucks, buses and cycles safer. Harley-Davidson, thanks to AMF and healthy sales, had more development dollars than ever. Because of the federal edicts, however, most of those bucks went into safety rather than higher performance or new product design.

For example, left-hand foot shift became mandatory in 1972 and turn signals were the rule in 1973. Besides jacking up consumer prices, the regs meant that H-D had to divert time, money and manpower to find new suppliers, conduct safety testing and so on. Except for development of the "King of the Road" tour package in 1973, no significant modifications were made to the FL's through 1975. Lamented one employee: "We wanted magazines to conduct road tests on our bikes at a time when we had nothing new to show them."

Nevertheless, H-D soldiered on. Disc brakes showed up in 1973, silencing the major complaint

A 1961 250cc Sprint motor. Not really comparable to the full-size Harley-Davidsons, the Aermacchi/H-D's nevertheless brought cycling to a large number of beginning riders. *David Wright*

voiced about the company's products in postwar years. The Super Glide received optional electric starting to become the FXE in 1974. And in 1976, the company created a stylized eagle and five "Liberty Edition" versions of the V-twin.

In cruised the FXS Low Rider in 1977, a contrast to another new model, the Sportster-inspired XLCR Cafe Racer. The FXS deposited the low rider just 27 in. above the ground, featured highway pegs as standard equipment and displayed a Fat Bob (split) gas tank. It also bore, in its second year of production, the "ham can" air box, a unit shared with all other V-twins in hopes of appeasing Uncle Sam's noise and emissions savants.

The 1978 Electra Glide received the optional, enlarged 80 cu. in. motor, just in time for the company's diamond (seventy-fifth) anniversary. The less ornate FL was dropped in 1979 as the FLH was offered with more standard equipment than

any motorcycle ever: fairing/windshield, saddle bags with safety guards, luggage rack, passing lights, safety bars and running boards. At this time, owners of virtually all heavyweight cycles began to notice that their bikes did not run worth a damn on the lower-octane gasoline that, in leaded or unleaded form, was crowding premium fuel off the pumps. The 1930's vintage flywheel medallion on the handsome FLH tank reminded riders that the old bikes stuttered less because there were fewer federal impediments. Dealers leaned out the carburetion under the direction of a factory service bulletin, sold lots of octane additive and hoped for the best.

Harley-Davidson countered in 1980 with four entirely new models, the most significant being the FLT Tour Glide. Most evident was the dual-headlight, frame-mounted fairing, a slick answer to the aftermarket wind slicers. Less noticeable

A Harley-Davidson 440cc, two-cycle snowmobile, as seen in the Rodney C. Gott Museum storage facility in York. *David Wright*

The MX-250, produced only for the 1977 and 1978 model years, may be among the most competitive single-cylinder motocross bikes ever constructed. *David Wright*

but of more significance was Harley-Davidson's first five-speed gearbox. The unit made two-up riding with the standard TourPak especially effortless, while a new frame and the patented positioning of the steering head in front of the fork crowns created excellent low-speed stability.

The FLT's vibration-isolated motor, which used elastomer mounts to intercept vibes transmitted to the drive train swing arm or frame, received high marks from heavyweight riders. So did the V-Fire (1980) and V-Five II (1981) ignitions, which created a hotter spark without points. An enclosed secondary chain, five-gallon fuel tank, triple disc brakes, styled wheels and every conceivable touring amenity standard made the Tour Glide complete.

If the FLT was the ultimate tourer, the new Sturgis was the ultimate cruiser. One of three new-for-1980 offspring of the Super Glide, the FXB (for belt) was a study in black trimmed lightly in orange. Technically, the bike broke new ground with its 1⅛ in. primary and 1½ in. secondary drives accomplished with Aramid fibers from the

Gates Rubber Company. But the machine was so stylish that few owners cared if the driveline was quieter, lasted twice as long as a chain and required neither lubrication nor adjustment. They had to notice, however, that a compensating sprocket on the primary drive all but eliminated the lash characteristic of all chain-driven bikes. Drag bars with risers, a Fat Bob tank, a seat only 27 in. off the ground, the Bar and Shield adorning the tank—the Willie G.-designed machine may be the most handsome Harley-Davidson in the company's eighty years.

Joining the Sturgis were the FXWG Wide Glide and the FXEF Fat Bob (the latter and one 1980 FLH being the final evidence of the 74 cu. in. motor). The Wide Glide sported a 21 in. tire up front, a low seating position (26¼ in.), the pullback bars that had become common on H-D's and spoke wheels. The Fat Bob was so named because of its bobbed rear fender and five-gallon fuel tank. (Speaking of gasoline, the 1982 bikes ran just fine, thanks, on regular. That's due to lowered compression.)

The pinnacle of Harley-Davidson achievement

The original Super Glide with optional red, white and blue decor. This bike wed the F-series motor and chassis to a modified X-series front end. The success enjoyed by this Willie G. Davidson design spawned everything from the Low Rider to the Fat Bob to the Super Glide II. *Harley-Davidson, Inc.*

for 1983 was the FXR/FXRS, both termed Super Glide II. Recipients in 1982 of the five-speed transmission and a new frame that used FLT-type mounts to isolate the motor, these models were judged "Harley-Davidson's Great Leap Forward" by *Cycle World.* Besides cosmetic differences, the FXR ran traditional spoke wheels while the FXRS possessed mag-type wheels. There was even a less expensive Super Glide, the FXE, sans the five-speed or the elastomer-mount frame.

Improvements continue to evolve. The FXRT Sport Glide, introduced in 1986, showed a wind tunnel-tested fairing and a look that successfully linked touring and sports riding. In 1988 came the FXSTS or 85th Anniversary Springer Softail, a bike with more than four inches of front suspension travel. The Springer looked positively retro, though H-D engineers had subjected the front end to all sorts of computer-aided and road testing. The Ultra Classics rolled up in 1989 with electronically mounted cruise control, a new intercom and a sound system packing 80 watts of power. The 1990 Low Rider Convertible displayed nylon saddlebags cunningly designed to look leathery soft while they kept their shape at any and all speeds. All the '91s featured the self-canceling turn signals. And 1992 saw the introduction of the Dyna Glide chassis, which mixed the look of the

original, rigid-mounted H-D Lower Rider cycles of the late 1970s with the handling and rubber-isolated ride of today's Low Riders. Meanwhile, the Dressers were being fine-tuned with amenities such as a better 40 mm carburetor for cold-morning starts, continuously vented gas tanks and surer brakes. What's left to do?

For 1993 there are a slew of 90th Anniversary models. Every one has the distinctive cloisonne (chrome and fired enamel) fuel tank emblems and all feature serialized nameplates and custom two-tone silver/charcoal satin-brite decor. There are also three brand-new motorcycles, the FXDWG Dyna Wide Glide, the FXDL Dyna Low Rider and the FLSTN Heritage Softail Nostalgia. The new Dyna Wide Glide has Factory Ape Hanger handlebars, a sculpted, bobtail rear fender with tucked-in tail light and air-foil directionals, a one-piece Fat Bob fuel tank, a wide front fork, a 21-in. (53.34 cm) laced front wheel and a specially designed pillow-soft seat.

The Dyna Low Rider combines the look of the original from the 1970s with the handling and rubber-isolated ride of today's Low Riders. There's a two-piece seat with removable passenger pillion, dual front disc brakes and a black-and-chrome power train. Detailing includes a custom

The 1986¹/₂ FLST Heritage Softail is described in its press kit as the "re-creation of a classic style of motorcycle . . . built on a foundation of solid 1980's engineering." The model mimics 1949 Hydra-Glide styling. *Harley-Davidson, Inc.*

headlight shell, fender support and battery cover, all in chrome.

The FLSTN Heritage Softail Nostalgia was previewed in March 1992, in Daytona Beach. The bike features wide whitewall tires with laced wheels, natural cowhide inserts on the custom seat and saddlebags (hence the nickname, "Moo Glide"), a unique black-and-white paint scheme and cloisonne fuel tank emblems. The FXSTS Springer Softail receives a "floating" front fender that eliminates the gap between front fender and the tire, while the touring bikes picked up a number of detailed improvements: an automotive-style oil pan (for quicker oil changes and a lower center of gravity), battery repositioned below the driver's seat and roomier saddlebags. All the '93's have improved clutch and brake levers.

FL, FLH Specifications
(From a 1965 owners manual)
 Wheelbase: 60 in.
 Overall length: 92 in.
 Overall width: 35 in.
 Fuel tank total: 5 or 3³/₄ gals.
 Reserve: 1 or 1¹/₄ gals.
 Oil tank: 4 quarts.
 Transmission: 1¹/₂ pints.
 Model designation: FL, FLH.
 Number of cylinders: Two.

 Type: 45-degree V type.
 Horsepower: FLH, 60 horsepower at 5,400 rpm; FL, 55 horsepower at 5,400 rpm.
 Taxable horsepower: 9.44.
 Bore: 3⁷/₁₆ in. (87.3 mm).
 Stroke: 3³¹/₃₂ in. (100.8 mm).
 Displacement: 73.66 cu. in. (1,207 cc).
 Torque: FLH, 65 lb.-ft. at 3,200 rpm; FL, 62 lb.-ft. at 3,200 rpm.
 Compression ratio: FLH, 8 to 1; FL, 7.25 to 1.
 The engine (serial) number of your Harley-Davidson is stamped on the left side of the engine crankcase.
 Circuit breaker point gap: .022 in.
 Spark plugs, size: 14 mm.
 Gap: .025 to .030 in.
 Heat range for average use: No. 3-4.
 Spark timing: Retard 5 degrees BTC.
 Automatic advance: 35 degrees BTC.
 Transmission type: Constant mesh.
 Speeds: Four forward (foot shift or hand shift). Three forward and one reverse optional.
 Clutch sprocket teeth: 37.
 Transmission sprocket teeth: 22.
 Rear wheel sprocket teeth: 51.
 Engine sprocket (four-speed transmission): FL, 23; FLH, 24.
 Engine sprocket (three-speed transmission): FL, 23; FLH, 24.
 High gear ratio (four-speed transmission): FL, 3.73; FLH, 3.57.
 High gear ratio (three-speed transmission): FL, 3.73, FLH, 3.57.
 Tire sizes: 4.00 × 18 in., 4.50 × 18 in., 5.00 × 16 in.

The Wide Glide FXWG was offered with kick start, a rigid engine and a four-speed transmission. *Harley-Davidson, Inc.*

The FLHT Electra Glide also was offered for 1986 in a Liberty promotional edition. The bike has the Evolution engine and five speeds. *Harley-Davidson, Inc.*

The FXR (left) featured new seven-spoke cast-aluminum wheels for '87. The FXRS Low Rider (right) was offered in a Sport version for '87. *Harley-Davidson, Inc.*

One of the most visible differences between the FXST and FXSTC Custom was the latter's solid rear wheel. The Softail Custom FXSTC has unique scroll graphics, a central rear monoshock and the Evolution engine with five-speed transmission. *Harley-Davidson, Inc.*

The Sport Glide FXRT offered in 1986 continued to bridge the sport-touring gap. Highway mileage was 55 mpg, which the factory attributes in part to the wind-tunnel-tested fairing. *Harley-Davidson, Inc.*

Daytona Beach visitors admire the Evolution engine and final belt drive, displayed in a cutaway frame. *David Wright*

1993 FLSTN Heritage Softail Nostalgia Specifications
Engine: OHV V2 Evolution.
Bore and stroke: 3.498 × 4.250 in. (88.8 × 108 mm).
Displacement: 80 cu. in. (1,340cc).
Carburetion: 40mm constant velocity with enricher and accelerator pump.
Ignition: Inductive, battery-powered V Fire III electronic breakerless with solid-state dual stage advance.
Transmission: Five-speed, constant mesh.

Torque: 77 ft./lbs. at 3,600 rpm.
Length: 93.8 in. (238.8 cm).
Dry weight: 710 lbs. (359.9 kg).
Wheelbase: 64.2 in. (158.75 cm).
Seat height: 27.25 in. (67.31 cm).
Mileage: 42 mpg city, 51 mpg country.
Instruments: Speedometer with odometer and resetable tripmeter.

The 1993 FXDWG Dyna Wide Glide. *Harley-Davidson, Inc.*

The 1993 FXSTS Springer Softail. *Harley-Davidson, Inc.*

The 1993 FXSTC Softail Custom. *Harley-Davidson, Inc.*

The 1993 FLSTC Heritage Softail Classic. *Harley-Davidson, Inc.*

The 1993 FLSTF Fat Boy. *Harley-Davidson, Inc.*

The 1993 FLHTC Electra Glide Classic. *Harley-Davidson, Inc.*

Chapter 4

Uniforms

No one on a Harley-Davidson ever caught up with Pancho Villa. But neither did any of the National Guardsmen on horses, in cars or on foot during the "punitive expedition" in northern Mexico in the spring of 1916. From the military point of view, the foray south of the border to nab Villa and fellow banditos was a bust. For H-D fans, however, the raid stands out as the first use of the product in a combat situation.

The Harleys taken south were owned by the Army's First Aero Squadron. They were equipped with sidecar-mounted machine guns and were sufficiently impressive to warrant two additional orders for machines, on March 16 and March 27. Credit for mating machine gun and motorcycle was given jointly to the New Mexico Military Institute, the Springfield (Massachusetts) Armory and H-D engineers, according to a 1916 copy of *The Enthusiast.* "When machine guns were carried on mules in the old way, from two to four minutes were required to set up and begin firing. The motorcycle machine gun permits of [sic] instant firing from the sidecar and when it is desired to set up separately, firing can be started within 50 seconds from the command to halt when the rate of fire is 480 shots per minute," *The Enthusiast* enthused. At least twenty-two such machines saw service.

Other folks in uniform were experimenting with cycles and sidecars. In Spain at about the same time, the militia staged raids on the homes of alleged revolutionaries, confiscating "a lot of seditious papers" and hauling them off in an H-D sidecar outfit. The same issue reported the McKeesport, Pennsylvania, Police Department's conversion to Harleys from another make, indicating that motorcycles were becoming accepted

transportation for the law. Even earlier, in 1909, Pittsburgh's first motorized police vehicle turned out to be a Harley-Davidson. From the mid-teens through the sixties, *The Enthusiast* dutifully reported every city, county and state police department astride H-D's. And while there were few service problems associated with use of the cycles by police, that futile pursuit of the bandits in Mexico pointed out the need for in-field service and maintenance. Yes, Harley riders have Pancho Villa to thank for inception of the service school.

But, beginning in July 1917, H-D dealer personnel were no longer admitted to the school. Instead, groups of thirty enlisted men spent three weeks in Milwaukee, learning how to maintain the thousands of Harleys seeing service in France and to greater extent at Army camps throughout the U.S. More than 300 enlisted repairmen were put through the service school in the sixteen months before the World War I armistice was signed in November 1918. Most of the instant mechanics never made it to France, primarily because the United States was not fully mobilized when peace came.

The first glimpse of Harley-Davidsons by World War I soldiers may have been the line of bikes that gave rides to the wounded at various hospitals in England prior to U.S. entry into the war. This country was strongly supportive of the English and French months before American involvement. Once war was declared, the cycles were shipped with all other vehicles, though they were used primarily for messenger service rather than in actual combat. It is reasonable to assume that as many as 7,000 Harley-Davidsons found their way to France. War Department records show that 26,486 H-D's were ordered through November 1,

1918, and that a total of 20,007 Indians and Harley-Davidsons were shipped overseas. The most noteworthy was a sidecar rig ridden boldly—and inadvertently—into Germany.

"The first Yank to enter Germany" actually shows a doughboy riding a Harley-Davidson with sidecar and heading west, *out* of Germany, as the Kaiser's forces retreat. The picture, reproduced worldwide, was shot by a resident of a town near the Rhine River. It was taken on November 11, 1918, the very day the Germans surrendered. But who was the Allied soldier? What were the circumstances? More than twenty-five years would elapse before the rider's identity became known.

In 1944, an electrical contractor name Roy Holtz, from Chippewa Falls, Wisconsin, showed up at Juneau Avenue to obtain a copy of his picture. Puzzled, the editors of *The Enthusiast* learned that Holtz was the unidentified soldier in the famous World War I photo. "I didn't even remember when the picture was taken," Holtz said. "It appeared first in American newspapers and magazines. . . . But there's nothing exciting about the incident."

Under questioning, Holtz provided this account: On the night of November 8, 1918, Holtz left a forward position in northern Belgium with his captain in the sidecar. A heavy rain disoriented the officer, who insisted that Holtz steer his H-D

east, into Germany. When the two stopped at a farmhouse to ask directions, they were taken prisoner by German officers from a Bavarian division. Holtz, a corporal who could speak fluent German, was treated to shots of potent potato whiskey while his inept superior sat soaking in his uniform. The two were imprisoned until the morning of the armistice, November 11, then freed to return to Allied lines.

Because both were in unfamiliar territory, they drove farther into Germany, then became separated. At one time as much as sixty miles east of his own unit, Holtz rode westward, through retreating Germans, to meet the Allied advance. Not only was he the first Yank into Germany, but he was there nearly seventy-two hours ahead of his comrades.

At war's end, Harley-Davidson did not need to convert to peacetime production—the cycles it had furnished the military were no different from the H-D's available in approximately 1,000 dealerships throughout the United States. The most visible indication that H-D had been to war was the olive paint job, which lasted with minor variations into the thirties.

Since, by 1919, Henry Ford's assembly line was only beginning to make a low-priced car a reality, municipalities bought motorcycles in sizeable numbers. Many of the bikes found their way into the hands of the police, who could use the

An early H-D single and a shotgun-carrying prison guard somewhere in the South prior to World War I. *Harley-Davidson, Inc.*

machines in metropolitan areas to ease their way through traffic. Briefly, before the Great War, Harley-Davidson even offered a sidecar unit with fire extinguishers and first-aid equipment. They and at least a small number of public officials reasoned that two firefighters on a cycle could reach a blaze and haul out victims while a cumbersome truck was stuck in what was becoming a familiar phenomenon—rush hour.

By 1925, more than 2,500 city and county police units used Harley-Davidsons. As American salaries rose and the prices of cars created by mass production fell, more and more four-wheelers were on the roads. The twenties may have been roaring in part because there were few speed limits outside towns and those rural limits were hardly ever enforced. Consequently, highway fatalities rose at an alarming rate and states responded with troopers, highway patrols and police. "Harley-Davidson will curb this tragic traffic slaughter," trumpeted a 1926 company publication, and a special office for fleet sales to law enforcement agencies was established. With

each large order, *The Enthusiast* would report that another state was covering its major highways with H-D's. By the mid-thirties, the cartoon showing a motorcycle cop hiding behind a billboard had become a cliche.

In other countries, law enforcement, frequently indistinguishable from the military, was employing the Harley-Davidson. Movietone newsreels, *Life* magazine and daily papers commonly showed at least half a dozen Guatemalans forming a human pyramid atop a police-style H-D that is somehow still in motion. Such stunts made Americans forget that Latin lawmen were probably using the bikes to keep their fellow citizens subservient. In fact, police in the U.S. had their own drill teams. Such cities as Detroit and Washington, D.C., turned out dozens of precision police riders. They did much to maintain interest in law enforcement by performing close-order drill on wheels in parades and in competition. The Miami Beach Police Department, today among the most besieged in the country, won a national drill team competition, staged by the American Legion, in

This 1929 advertisement touted the use of H-D's by the police. It appeared in *The Enthusiast*, which devoted an entire issue each year in the late-twenties and the thirties to law enforcement. *Harley-Davidson, Inc.*

The California Highway Patrol's first batch of Harley-Davidsons, 1930 VL models, delivered at Frank Murray's Sacramento dealership. *Armando Magri collection*

Seventeen new 1930 VL's delivered to Buffalo, New York, police. Young William H. Davidson, second from left in the far group, was sent to Buffalo to remedy matters when the police reported disappointment with speed. The first one serviced by Davidson reached a speed of 90 miles an hour, he stated. *William H. Davidson collection.*

1955. Police drill teams exist even today. Perhaps the most accomplished is the twelve-man Louisville H-D force.

By 1930, police models differed from street Harleys in several ways. The most evident to the populace was the one-way radio, with volume on high, that was the motorcycle cop's only link with headquarters. Not until 1948 were two-way radios introduced by H-D. The first two-way, delivered on a Servi-Car to Oshkosh, Wisconsin, dealer Joe Robl's shop, was a Motorola FM unit. It featured a 152,000-kilocycle frequency that eliminated most of the "dead spots" found on earlier rolling radios. Installed just to the rear of the driver's left hip, the unit was cushion-mounted and proved to be successful virtually from the start. State police, using even higher frequencies, reported a range of seventy-five miles with their Motorolas.

What was being a motorized police officer like in the thirties? William J. Lally, a retired trooper with the New York State Police, reports that the H-D's were ridden each year from about May 1 through October 15, enforcing speed limits that changed several times during his years in the saddle. In 1937, New York law stated, "A speed of over 50 miles an hour for a distance of over a quarter of a mile is considered operating a vehicle in a manner not careful and prudent." (The heavily populated Northeast has always had slower speed limits than other parts of the U.S.—Nevada, for example, posted speed limits only within city limits until 1974.) Happily for the officers, the Harleys were more than a match for passenger

William S. Harley, left, and President Walter Davidson, right, pose with a U.S. Army inspector about to take delivery of 1932 45 cu. in. R models. *Harley-Davidson, Inc.*

cars of that era. "In the years I rode [1937–41 and 1946–48], I never had anyone with any make of automobile get away from me," says Lally.

Working out of the Oneida barracks, Officer Lally and fellow troopers in the early and mid-thirties were provided with bikes devoid of the paraphernalia usually associated with law enforcement. "They were taken out of the crates 'bare' and assigned to the troopers," he remembers. "Any red lights, sirens, mirrors or windshields had to be purchased by the troopers. Not until 1938 or 1939 were sirens and radios installed [by the State Police]. . . . If you didn't have some sort of makeshift arrangements, you carried all your reports and papers in your pockets. And as far as rain protection was concerned, you simply strapped a plain, everyday black raincoat over the back fender. If you got caught in a bad storm you would drive in some farmer's barn and call the station. They would send a car out to pick you up—or tell you to ride back to the station." Still a rider today at age sixty-eight, Lally says a New York cycle trooper not only enforced speed limits but performed all tasks normally associated with police work—homicide investigation, aid at the scene of an accident, directing dragging operations in connection with a drowning, etc. In contrast, states such as Wisconsin limited state officers to traffic control or to involvement in an investigation only if the crime actually took place on a state highway.

While mounted officers patrolled Depression-era highways, war clouds were gathering again in Europe. Nazis and Communists used Spain during the period 1936–39 as a location for testing the weapons they were to fire in Poland, over Great Britain, in North Africa and elsewhere. It was from the conflict in Spain that one of the classic stories about Harley-Davidson turns up. . . . Some 500 soldiers and civilians took refuge during fighting in Toledo inside the Alcazar—the fortress-like Spanish military academy. As the foe lay siege to the structure, food supplies dwindled. At night, the defenders stole out to nearby fields and gathered whatever grain they could find. Returning, they hooked one of two Harley-Davidsons via a belt to a small hammer mill. The mill ground the grain into a coarse flour, used in bread that fed the inhabitants of the old stone fortress. The H-D, despite being run in a stationary position for two

Trooper W. J. Lally on his 1936 H-D 74 cu. in. police bike. "The red light and the mirror were mine," says Lally, now retired. "The saddlebags I borrowed from my horse—no foolin'." *W. J. Lally collection*

Sgt. Carmen R. Sicilia works on a New York State Police cycle in the mid-thirties. Frequently, municipalities turn to the selling dealer to service their motorcycles. *W. J. Lally collection*

months, did not falter. And the Alcazar did not fall.

Other garrisons, towns, even countries were falling beginning in August 1939, more than two years before Pearl Harbor. United States industry, including Harley-Davidson, was put on a war footing. "That war was planned," John Nowak, former dean of the service school, believes. "The Army came in in 1937 to look over the civilian service school and equipment, making sure everything was ready." John was ready, too, traveling to every Army encampment east of the Mississippi to ensure that the fifty service school mechanics turned out in Milwaukee every four weeks were doing things by the books. In four years, he logged an incredible 200,000 miles on a 61 cu. in. EL with sidecar.

A total of 88,000 motorcycles (plus spare parts for an additional 30,000) was produced by H-D during World War II, following some unique tests conducted at Fort Knox and in Louisiana by Nowak, under the direction of founder Bill Harley. "We were told our cycles had to ford a stream sixteen inches deep," Nowak recalls. "So we stuck the oil breather tube up toward the gas tank. If we hadn't done that, the circulating oil systems would have sucked water into the crankcases through

An extremely rare bike—a shaft-drive Knucklehead Servi-Car. The Army designated these Motor-Tricycles and ordered sixteen of the prototypes constructed. The Jeep, however, soon made three-wheelers obsolete. *David Wright*

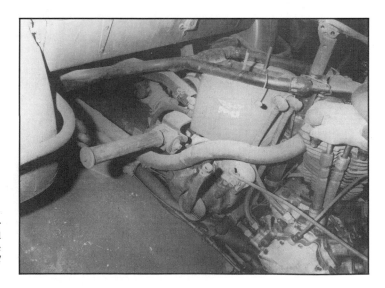

A closeup of the same three-wheeler shows a universal joint just below and to the right of the hinge visible in the upper left portion of the photo. *David Wright*

the breather. The spark plugs were above water, but any speed over three miles an hour would splash them and drown out the bike."

The Model 42XA-Solo motorcycle built by Harley-Davidson for the U.S. Army from late 1941 into 1943 looked more familiar to German prisoners of war than it did to GI's. The twin-cylinder, L-head bike with a carburetor for each cylinder and shaft drive was copied from the BMW used by the Axis early in the war. H-D engineers converted the various measurements from centimeters to inches and began to tool up for production. Just 1,000 of the XA's were built, due to the fact that the Germans had, by 1942, been chased successfully across the Sahara.

"Somebody in the Army—who should have been shot—got the idea for a shaft drive. Why have two completely different sets of parts (the WLA and the XA)? That should have been the question from the beginning." So states Wilbur Petri, a retired mechanical engineer whose assignments included everything from plant layout to post-war liaison with the Aermacchi factory. He confirms William H. Davidson's belief that the XA's cost the Army slightly less than $1 million, or $1,000 per machine. Those figures include design,

tooling, development, etc. "We practically gave it to them," Davidson said.

The consumer got no closer to the XA (which featured a four-speed transmission, hand clutch and both hand and foot shift) than isolated photos of cyclists in training at Fort Knox. *The Enthusiast* pointed out as early as mid-1942 that this bike was experimental and that H-D riders would be told when—and if—it was offered to the public. Plans to produce the XA in civilian form were explored to the point that a prototype with an overhead valve engine and hydraulic forks was created and ridden extensively in 1946. Petri rode the XA and says it was smoother than the V-twin, since the vibrations in opposed-engine cylinders tend to be self-canceling. The usual shaft drive quirks, including the feeling of levitation when the throttle was cracked open, were present, too.

XA Specifications
(Issued February 1, 1942)
    Type of engine: Twin cylinder, opposed, L-head.
    Bore: 3 1/16 in.
    Stroke: 3 1/16 in.
    Displacement: 45.038 cu. in.
    Compression ratio: 5.7 to 1.
    Horsepower: 7.5.
    Wheelbase: 59 1/2 in.
    High gear ratio: 4.70 to 1.

A Colt machine gun and an attempt at armor plate adorned this 1940 experimental model. *Harley-Davidson, Inc.*

Tire size: 4.00 × 18.
Crankcase capacity: 2 quarts.
Transmission capacity: 2 quarts.
Rear drive housing: 4½ ounces.
Left gasoline tank: (slightly more than) 2 gallons.
Right gasoline tank: (slightly more than) 2 gallons.
Includes ½ gallon reserve supply.

If the Army should indeed have shot the officials who gave the nod for the XA, then they should have staged a parade for the honchos on the WLA project. Instead of drawing up specs on a clean sheet of paper, the bureaucrats wisely took a look at the proven H-D WL, added some military adornments and went off to war. Although the WLA varied minutely from one defense contract to another, it generally differed from the civilian machine in only these ways:

—A more substantial luggage rack was installed.

—A scabbard for a Thompson machine gun or a rifle ran parallel to the right front fork.

—Blackout lights front and rear were standard.

—Oil, spark plug and speed recommendations were listed on a metal plate attached to the gasoline tank, between the instruments and the seat.

—A skid plate was attached to the crankcase.

The XA motor. With upswept exhaust and shaft drive, the XA was less likely to bog down in mud or water. *David Wright*

The XA featured a BMW-type horizontally opposed two-cylinder engine and shaft drive. Just 1,000 were constructed early in the war. *David Wright*

Anyone who ever rode or serviced a WLA reports staggering abuse without any sort of non-repairable breakdown. Standard procedure for riders included throwing the bikes down whenever the enemy was nearby. The WLA's slid without complaint on their tanks in several continents, since every armored division listed 540 cycles in its complement of vehicles. Nor were U.S. armored divisions the only units lucky enough to have the trusty 45's. Approximately 20,000 WLC's, the Canadian version of the 45 and almost one-quarter of wartime production, were shipped northward. The Canadian bikes featured the clutch on the right, brake on the left, right foot shift and the horn atop the headlight rather than beneath it. The metal luggage rack, mounted on the rear fender of the WLA only, was designed to carry a forty-pound radio the Army never quite managed to affix to the bike in quantity. The Canadians did have an "auxiliary box" atop the front fender, and were less concerned about being followed: The WLC was shipped without a rear-view mirror.

W. T. Basore, who now lives in Tulsa, recalls his introduction to the WLA, on a remote island off Burma, in the Bay of Bengal. Stationed there as a private first class in late 1944, Basore used the machine to take him to his swing-shift assignment on the other side of the island. "I generally made the return trip each night about midnight, traveling 20 to 30 mph with the lights off." Unlike the ballyhooed riders trained at Fort Knox and elsewhere, Basore had never ridden a cycle. "Due to a severe shortage of fuel [all air-lifted in], two or three Harleys had been brought in to make best possible use of the fuel we had," he reports. Basore learned the rudiments of riding, failing to encounter anything more hostile than an occasional jackal or a cow on his midnight rides. "I found that blipping the ignition switch would cause a racket not unlike a high-powered rifle," he says, adding that the 45 never let him down.

WLA Specifications
(Training manual no. TM 9-879, no issue date listed)
Type of engine: Two-cylinder, V-type L-head, air cooled.
Cylinder bore: 2³/₄ in.
Stroke: 3¹³/₁₆ in.
Engine (serial) number left side engine base, below front cylinder.
Wheelbase: 59¹/₂ in.
Length, overall: 88 in.
Width, overall (handle bars): 41 in.
Wheel size: 18 in.
Tire size: 4.00 × 18 in.
Tire type: drop center.
Weight, without rider or armament: 540 lb.
Ground clearance (skid plate): 4 in.
Fuel: 72 octane or higher gasoline.

An XA with sidecar, designated the XS, 1942. *Harley-Davidson, Inc.*

High gear ratio: 4.59:1.
Engine sprocket: 31-tooth.
Countershaft sprocket: 17-tooth.
Rear wheel sprocket: 41-tooth.
Maximum allowable speed: 65 mph.
Miles per gallon (hard surface): 35.
Cruising range: 100 miles.
Fording depth (carburetor): 18 in.
Fuel capacity (left tank): 3³/₈ gals.
Oil capacity (right rank): 1¹/₈ gals. Transmission capacity: ³/₄ pint.

While the WLA and the XA were addressing armed forces needs, the H-D factory chased several wild geese in an effort to win the war. Somehow, in 1941, sidecar-equipped Indians wound up in Louisiana for a series of tests in swampy, tropical conditions. The inability of these machines to function hastened development of another all-terrain vehicle, the Jeep. Shortly after the Jeep was in production, Harley-Davidson provided Willys with XA-type, opposed-twin motors intended for airborne mini-Jeeps. But the Toledo, Ohio, firm was so busy cranking out full-size models that the junior version never got past the Willys experimental experts. Some 5,000 motor generators, based on the XA engine, were ordered; but the war ended before these units could be produced. And H-D's most closely held wartime secret—mating two V-twin engines for

The Harley-Davidson WLA, which belongs to the factory, has just nine miles on the odometer. Note the shift pattern, which was turned around after WW II. The twin almond shapes just below the speedometer housed warning lights on the civilian bikes but were virtually invisible on military models. *David Wright*

A 1942 WLA. This particular bike was used from year to year by H-D photographers throughout the war. The WLA was produced from September, 1941, through July, 1945. *Harley-Davidson, Inc.*

installation in a Canadian mini-tank—also failed to materialize. By war's end, H-D was creating such things as telescope equipment under sub-contract to Bell & Howell and Argus.

The fortunate few who received new Harley-Davidsons during the war years included civilian police, of course, and those who could demonstrate a legitimate need. Mounted, armed guards patrolled the sprawling munitions plant operated by the Olin Company outside Baraboo, Wisconsin, keeping it safe from saboteurs. Other strategic installations also featured routine civilian and military cycle patrols. Of less importance were such quasi-police units as the Dayton (Ohio) Funeral Escort Service, which led processions through the city on H-D's bearing the only civilian paint job available—gray. Cyclists who, for one reason or another, were not drafted kept their thirties machines together as best they could, riding on rationed rubber and gasoline.

John Nowak pinpoints the rationing rationale: "We had plenty of gasoline throughout the war, but we didn't have much rubber. I guess the government figured that the best way to preserve tires was to keep people off the roads. They did that by restricting the sale of fuel."

Harley-Davidson's fortunes with the military may have diminished since World War II, but police worldwide are riding the bikes as never before. The U.S. Army and Navy use a few motorcycles for military police and shore patrols, whereas more than 800 state, provincial, county and local law-enforcement departments ride Harley-Davidsons here, in Canada and Mexico and worldwide.

Police sales now are a part of the company's business development. H-D often enters a foreign market first with law-enforcement units, then follows with civilian bikes. An example is Taiwan, where the national police and city of Taipei officers ride more than 300 Harley-Davidsons. The distributor there is solid, having opened shops around the island to service the bikes. When and if the country's displacement limit on motorcycles is lifted, Harley-Davidson will have a dealer network in place. Jon S. Syverson, H-D's manager/police and fleet sales, calls Taiwan's web of service "a building block for pleasure sales."

Back home, the list of officers riding Harley-Davidsons is long and growing. Since 1990, many departments have been added, from Long Beach, California, to Brantford, Ontario, to Harnette County, North Carolina. Private services ranging from Alabama's Serenity Funeral Escort to Con-

A World War II WLA, as displayed at Daytona Beach in 1982. *David Wright*

necticut's Yale University campus police also have chosen American-made machines. Little of this increased market share has happened by accident.

The company really does cater to law enforcement, producing a semi-annual magazine, *The Mounted Officer,* just for bike cops, and offering two different models from which government bodies can choose. Also available through H-D are police strobe lights, sirens and more, made by Whelen Engineering Co. From time to time, H-D also creates special police-only civilian models, aimed exclusively at riders who can show a badge. "Good guys ride Harleys—even when they're off duty," says the company. The Peace Officer series is available at the moment as FLHTC Electra Glide Classic and as an FLHTC Electra Glide Ultra Classic.

More important, H-D and the Northwestern University Traffic Institute offer several police motorcycle operations courses. Graduates of a five-day operations session can then be taught to instruct. In this way, a single mounted officer from, say, Tulsa, can take both courses and ultimately return to his home town to teach fellow police riders. In contrast, Eastside Harley-Davidson in Kirkland, Washington, reports the existence of a tricked-up FXRP Pursuit Glide. Seattle police call it the "DARE 911," and it's billed as the world's fastest police motorcycle. The machine, with a special 1290cc motor, has run 158 miles an hour at Bonneville! And in yet another market, the Shriners each year purchase about 200 full-dress machines for parades and conventions.

1993 FLHTP Electra Glide Specifications
  Engine type: 1340cc/80 cu. in. Evolution OHV vibration-isolated V-Twin.
  Bore and stroke: 3.498 × 4.25 in.
  Carburetion: 40 mm.
  Compression ratio: 8.5 to 1.
  Electrical: 12 volt, 20 amp-hour battery.

Francis Blake, sidecar restoration specialist, poses in his U model with sidecar. "SP" stands for Shore Patrol, the Navy's military police.

A 44-U (U indicating a medium-compression 74 cu. in. flathead motor) with sidecar chassis. A reported 136 such machines were delivered, painted gray. *Harley-Davidson, Inc.*

Ignition switch: Exclusive design permits operation with or without key. Contains integral fork lock.

Torque: 82.5 ft./lbs. at 4,000 rpm.

Clutch: Wet multiplate.

Clutch starter lockout: Requires clutch disengagement for starter motor operation.

Drive train: Final belt drive, Gates Kevlar-reinforced belt.

Exhaust system: Crossover dual exhaust.

Transmission: Five forward speeds, constant mesh.

Brakes: Dual front, drilled discs; single rear disc.

Wheels: Sixteen spoke cast.

Front tire: MT 90 × 16T tubeless blackwall.

Rear tire: MT 90 × 16 tubeless blackwall.

Frame: Steel tube, heavy-duty double loop, fully gussetted.

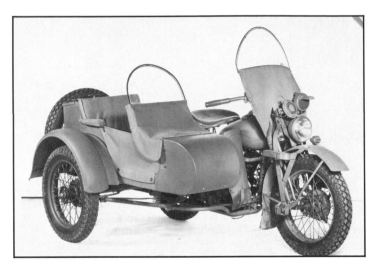

This prototype, labeled the WSR, apparently was designed to be used on the Russian front. Created in 1944, after thousands of WLA's were sent to the Soviets, this machine never left Milwaukee. The late William H. Davidson believed the WSR to have been a very minor project, because "the Army never told us where shipments were going." *Harley-Davidson, Inc.*

This experimental engine, consisting of two 61 cu. in. overhead valve motors, was designed in 1944 to power a Canadian mini-tank. *Harley-Davidson, Inc.*

Fuel tank capacity: Five U.S. gallons with reserve; locking gas cover.

Headlamp: Quartz halogen.

Oil tank capacity: 4.0 quarts.

Overall height: 61 in.

Overall length: 94.2 in.

Ground clearance: 5.12 in.

Solo saddle: Deluxe, air suspension.

Saddle height: 31 in.

Wheelbase: 62.9 in.

Weight, dry: 712 lbs.

Front suspension: Telescopic fork, air suspension with anti-drive system.

Rear suspension: Air-adjustable rear shocks.

1993 FXRP Pursuit Glide Specifications

Engine type: 1340cc/80 cu. in. Evolution OHV V-Twin.

Bore and stroke: 3.498 × 4.25 in.

Carburetion: 40 mm.

Compression ratio: 8.5 to 1.

Electrical: 12 volt, 19 amp-hour battery.

Ignition system: Coil electronic V-Fire III.

Torque: 80.4 ft./lbs. at 4,000 rpm.

Clutch: Wet multiplate.

Clutch starter lockout: Requires clutch disengagement for starter motor operation.

Drive train: Final belt drive, Gates Kevlar-reinforced belt.

Exhaust system: Staggered shorty duals or optional high-performance crossover dual exhaust.

Transmission: Five forward speeds, constant mesh.

Front tire: MM 90 × 19 Dunlop tubeless blackwall.

Rear tire: MT 90 × 16 Dunlop tubeless blackwall.

Fender extender: Rear inner fender extender to reduce wheel splash.

Frame: Steel tube, heavy duty.

Fuel tank capacity: 4.2 gallons.

Oshkosh, Wisconsin, dealer Joe Robl, seated, and William H. Davidson check out the new two-way radio installation on the first Servi-Car so equipped. *William H. Davidson collection*

At H-D's Milwaukee headquarters, Chicago police take delivery of 16 Servi-Cars— either during or immediately after World War II. *William H. Davidson collection*

1963 Sportsters, designated XLA, were procured by the U.S. Army. *Harley-Davidson, Inc.*

The 1983 FLHT Police bike.

Headlamp: Quartz halogen.
Oil tank capacity: 3.5 quarts.
Overall height: 59 in.
Overall length: 94.2 in.
Saddle height: 30 in.
Wheelbase: 64.7 in.
Wheels: Cast.
Weight, dry: 630 lbs.
Front suspension: Telescopic fork (39 mm).

Rear suspension: Five-position adjustable shocks.

Both bikes have a number of standard features, including a red and blue pursuit light on either side of the headlight, radio carrier, engine guard, four-way flashers and floorboards. The standard color is Birch White, with special colors available. Options include electronic siren, microphone kit and strobe light.

The California Highway Patrol ordered 131 of these FXRP police H-D's for 1984, following with a 161-bike order in 1985. Though Kawasaki won the 1986 CHP order, H-D's are in use by such prominent law-enforcement bodies as Milwaukee, Indianapolis, Boston, Pittsburgh, Montreal, Toronto and Vancouver. *Harley-Davidson, Inc.*

Montgomery County, Maryland, police show a sizeable Harley-Davidson fleet.

The United States Park Police are based in Washington, D.C. Their duties include escoring the President.

Deputy Jerry Lawrence of the Ventura (California) County Sheriff's Department. This is one of many departments that recently decided to purchase H-D's.

A State of Maryland trooper poses with his bike near the U.S. Capitol.

Trooper Robert Benefiel of the Colorado State Police sharpens his skills aboard his Harley-Davidson.

Chapter 5

Dealing

Arthur Davidson was quick to realize the potential of the motorcycle. So, immediately following 1907 incorporation, he set off on a dealer recruiting odyssey that began in New England and spread south and westward. Ten years later, on the eve of America's entry into World War I, Arthur had almost singlehandedly signed up Harley-Davidson dealers in every one of the forty-eight states—more than 800 total. Records are scarce on who these cycling pioneers were, but it's safe to guess that they were already involved in transportation (car and bicycle dealers) or a manual trade (blacksmiths, mechanics), or were riders who saw a way to mix business and pleasure. Wisely, Arthur shied away from offering his cycles to competing dealers.

The very first Harley-Davidson dealer sought out the tiny shed on Milwaukee's west side to see if the Davidsons and William Harley were serious about producing motorcycles. C. H. Lang of Chicago sold all the H-D's produced in 1904—three machines. He quickly set up an office on the fifth floor of a Windy City office building and by 1912 was selling 800 machines a year, without a showroom or even a demonstrator model. A highly successful businessman, Lang by 1916 was the nation's leading motorcycle dealer. He told a cycle magazine at the time that his brisk trade was due to constant distribution of "direct literature" via a 3,000-name mailing list and to a time payment plan of his own making.

Lang moved his business into showroom quarters after World War I, where 300–400 cycles were sold each year until the Depression. The pioneering dealer attributed the leveling off of sales in the twenties to the failure of city fathers to maintain roads and to the harebrained drivers of automobiles. Lang himself had earlier been "run down by a flivver driver and crippled in one leg ever since."

Meanwhile, fellow H-D dealers were prospering elsewhere. In 1907, a fourteen-year-old Californian named Dudley Perkins straddled a Reading Standard cycle and became not only an enthusiast but a racer as well. A mechanic by trade, he worked for Excelsior, Merkel and Indian dealers in the Bay Area before joining Al Maggini to open a Jefferson and DeLuxe dealership in 1913. Perkins realized that racing was a solid way of promoting his dealership and parlayed his flat-track success into floor traffic and sales. Arthur Davidson was recruiting dealers on the West Coast at the time and quickly convinced Perkins of the superiority of the H-D twins and singles. In January 1914, Maggini and Perkins opened their Harley-Davidson dealership at 626 Market St. in San Francisco.

A booming business and a new bride who considered racing dangerous ended Perkins' racing career in 1915—more or less. The soft-spoken fellow turned to hillclimbs, winning hundreds of "slant meets" up and down the coast through 1936. His reputation established, Perkins bought out Maggini and moved into larger quarters. Throughout the twenties, he sold not only hundreds of road bikes, but commercial vehicles as well. By 1928, Perkins' knowledge of municipal and private business needs had made him the largest Package Truck dealer in the country.

Like other pioneering dealers—Bruce Walters in Peoria, Illinois, and Bill Cleary in Savannah, Georgia—the economic woes of the thirties did very little good for Perkins' bank account. Cycle enthusiasts were penniless until around 1940, when the U.S. military buildup was under way. Since most riders were young and able-bodied, they were drafted before they could so much as renew acquaintance with their local dealer. Those who remained behind during World War II had a ravenous appetite for new bikes that only an extremely enterprising dealer like Dudley Perkins could feed. By 1944, Perkins realized that the Allies would emerge victorious and that many of the 80,000-plus machines produced by Harley-Davidson for the military were still in crates. So the San Francisco dealer located the bikes, purchased them from the government, repainted them and peddled hundreds of new 45 cu. in. WLA's to civilians. It's no coincidence that parts for 45's are still plentiful in northern California.

Dealers without such resources frequently found World War II to be more of a hardship than the Depression. Overnight, they went from down-at-the-heels idleness to manic activity. Harry Molenaar, a dealer in Hammond, Indiana, since 1933, says he kept alive during World War II by selling nothing and servicing everything. Mo-lenaar held service contracts for a dozen police departments and was on call to keep running a number of Harley-Davidson two- and three-wheelers in use in the Gary-Hammond-East Chicago steel mills. Rathbun Chambless of Montgomery, Alabama, recalled his wartime activities to *American Motorcyclist* magazine in 1949:

"When the war came along, the picture was not too bright. No new motorcycles, no parts, practically no help. . . . We [Chambless and two mechanics] worked on motorcycles during the day, making what parts we couldn't buy. From five in the afternoon till midnight or later, we ran three lathes, making axle spindles for [Army] tanks—a subcontract. About the middle of the war, my next-to-last mechanic was drafted. We [two] made it through the war by working eighteen hours a day."

A dealer who was an enthusiast and a good businessman, too, could count on recognition. Dudley Perkins was named to the American Motorcycle Association competition committee in 1932 and served the AMA until his retirement.

Dudley Perkins Company, the world's oldest Harley-Davidson dealership, is in San Francisco. Begun in 1914 as Maggini and Perkins, the dealership is now operated by Dudley Perkins, Jr., son of the founder. *David Wright*

A fixture at dirt-track national races on the West Coast until his death in 1978, Perkins also sponsored a number of great riders, including 1969 AMA champ Mert Lawwill. The Perkins organization, now run by Dudley, Jr., and his two sons, is still in San Francisco and is billed as the world's oldest Harley-Davidson dealership.

More than 200 dealerships were thriving by 1912, allowing Arthur Davidson to pay attention to the related chores of advertising and sales promotion. He retained a Milwaukee advertising agency and created a barrage of printed assistance to combat Indian, Thor, Excelsior plus other brands either established earlier than H-D or with strong followings in a particular state or region. By 1919, just sixteen years after the first Harley-Davidson was constructed, the world's largest motorcycle manufacturer was providing dealers with:

—Service bulletins, issued whenever a problem surfaced. Those who wonder how things got done before product recalls have only to look at such fliers.

—Motorcycle manuals, now called owners manuals, issued with each machine. Dealers were advised to keep additional copies on hand, since they were "particularly complete and comprehensive."

—Motor repair manuals, covering the most practical methods of fixing the bikes. Harley-Davidson also provided schools and libraries with this sort of repair information.

—Engine and transmission blueprints, "suitable for framing" but intended primarily for reference.

—"Standards of Practice" manuals, designed to be used by the dealer when he held seminars for his buyers on operation and maintenance. This piece contained 410 questions and answers and was developed initially for training World War I soldiers.

Other publications included electrical repair manuals, lubrication charts, a hint-filled flier on service topics, actual cutaway motors and tables of standard bearing sizes and clearances. These in-shop guides were supplemented by *The Enthusiast*, which in 1919 was about to be published

Dudley Perkins, Sr. *James Perkins collection*

Dudley Perkins, Sr., tilts his hill-climber skyward for a publicity shot. *James Perkins collection*

monthly; posters that boasted of H-D accomplishments on the racetrack; even form letters that taught mechanics how to bill a customer.

All of the above contributed to uniformity, making H-D dealerships in Oregon resemble H-D dealerships in New Jersey. At the time, there were too many Mom 'n' Pop storefronts or even sheds where the motorcycle was peddled. Today, except for size and location, dealerships greatly resemble one another. But there are a few exceptions, frequently made to accommodate the local market. In Littleton, Colorado, for example, a rider will find an authorized shop with its own tattoo facility and a distinct skull-and-crossbones look. Vinnie, the proprietor, says he gets no heat from the factory because he's one of the nation's top ten dealers and "I pay my bills on time." Maybe Vinnie really knows his market. And maybe a little individuality is a good thing. The company's continuing challenge is to turn enthusiasts—individualists and conformists—into good businessmen.

"Harley-Davidson is successful because of its dealers. And remember, that's the opinion of someone who was a factory engineer." So says Wilbur Petri, jointly responsible for some of H-D's better designs over the years and the man who helped the H-D lightweight factory in Italy turn a profit during the period 1969–76.

In the beginning, Harley-Davidson demanded—and received—total brand loyalty. In return, a dealer could count on a finely tuned marketing force that could lead the inexperienced or greatly assist the established. The company today is attempting to expand its 500-dealer network at a time when it's tough to deal in any kind of vehicle. A large inventory, for example, means a dealer is more likely to have the model a customer wants; but excessive inventory means that dealer is paying 1.5 percent interest monthly on every unsold bike. Several months of interest eat at the profit of each unsold machine. And since twenty-three percent of all H-D outlets sell other makes, Milwaukee machines frequently compete for floor

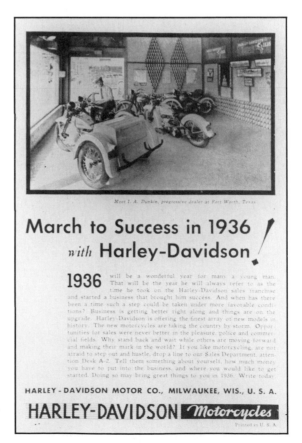

A dealer recruitment ad, from the back cover of *The Enthusiast. Harley-Davidson, Inc.*

space. Meanwhile, Harley-Davidson parts and accessories are up against aftermarket products such as Drag Specialties, Jammer, Gary Bang and so on. So long as the factory believes the big twins are receiving their share of the dealer's time and floor space, little can be said.

The two dealers we're about to meet have little in common. In fact, they share only one trait—success. The first is a lifelong Midwest resident, while the other fled Lake Erie winters for better weather and increased opportunity. Here's a look at each. . . .

Older brothers can get you involved in all sorts of things. For Wayne Wiebler, growing up in Illinois, his brother bought a motorcycle and Wayne became addicted to bikes. He started work

as a mechanic at Walters Harley-Davidson in Peoria in 1951 at the age of 14. He was still in school. Among other things, he figured out how someone his size, weighing only 130 pounds at the time, could kick over a huge V-twin. He also learned to ride: In 1959, he placed fourth in the 100-mile National at Daytona in the final race run on the old beach course. When he wasn't wrenching he spent long days riding off road with friends such as former Daytona winner Roger Reiman, from nearby Kewanee, IL.

Wiebler had good teachers in the Walters brothers, who opened their first dealership up the road in Galesburg in 1921. Bob Walters stayed in Galesburg, while Bruce and Gladys Walters opened the Peoria store in 1931, hiring Wayne 20

Wayne Wiebler's shop in downtown Peoria is spacious and modern. *David Wright*

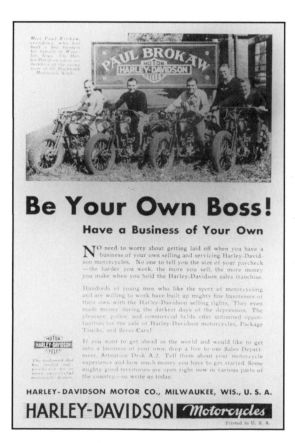

"They even made money during the darkest days of the depression," claims this late-thirties dealer-recruitment ad. The dealer featured is Paul Brokaw, Waterloo, Iowa. *Harley-Davidson, Inc.*

North Dakotans Louis (left) and Arnold Hoffman with their 1939 61 cu. in. overhead valve demonstrator. The Hoffmans ran their dealership out of their farmstead and were typical of rural dealers at the time. *Arnold Hoffman collection*

Harley-Davidsons were represented in London, England, by the Warr dealership, shown here in late 1958. *Harley-Davidson, Inc.*

Sacramento, California, dealer Frank Murray escorts his wife in an early sidecar.
Armando Magri collection

Frank Murray, pioneer dealer in Sacramento, California, stands in front of his
store with four mounted policemen. *Armando Magri collection*

years later. By 1971 Wayne was the manager and by 1980 he was the owner of Walter Brothers in downtown Peoria. To this day, he admires the perseverance of the Walters family through some very lean years. "I've seen the early books," Wiebler says. "There was one amazing year when they made only $3,200."

The newer owner has done much better, moving from gross annual sales of $500,000 to $2 million in the last dozen or so years. He also has helped a son and a nephew open Wiebler Harley-Davidson, to the west in Bettendorf, Iowa. Wiebler and his shop have a reputation that is statewide at the very least; this has happened because the owner was and is a strong supporter of motorcycling activities. (Wayne modestly attributes much of his success to the incredible array of parts and accessories he now carries and displays.)

It's tough to think of the Illinois resident and his modern shop as representing traditional dealers—he still strikes a visitor as a young and energetic guy. But if you ask the right questions, he may haul out a couple of dusty photo albums that pretty much cover the history of motorcycling in Mid America. Wiebler also is involved as race director with the very best AMA Grand National there is, the Springfield Mile, sponsored by the Illinois Harley-Davidson Dealers Association. He formerly served as race director for the Peoria TT before that event went political, and he puts on everything from a July 4 fish fry and an annual fall pig roast to a number of local H.O.G. events.

Wiebler has been a consistent H-D supporter, noting that the only difference between the old days and now is that dealers worked more often

Murray's shop. Lack of doors indicates this may have been on the second floor. *Armando Magri collection*

Murray's original showroom in his Sacramento storefront. *Armando Magri collection*

The resplendent showroom of Rossiter's Harley-Davidson in Sarasota, Florida.

Mr. and Mrs. Eric Rossiter with Eric's personal machine. "The pipes," he says, "are almost legal." *David Wright*

123

with individuals at the factory back then. When the company urged the retailers to modernize their showrooms and expand the parts and accessories business, the Peorian simply got ahold of riders who were plumbers and carpenters and electricians and the work was completed quickly and very well.

At the moment, there are more people who want to be dealers than there are dealerships available. That's because established dealers can't get enough bikes to sell, so why spread production even thinner by opening up more stores? Wiebler sold all he was allotted in '92. So did Eric Rossiter, a new dealer in Sarasota, FL.

Rossiter's Harley-Davidson looks like Jukebox Saturday Night. "I had to put in a Designer Showroom, which is a tremendous investment," he says. Besides everything you'd expect in terms of bikes, clothing, parts and accessories, there's an old-time Seeburg jukebox playing 45's and a 10-

cent Coke machine. All this in a town that had seen half a dozen H-D dealers come and go. Fortunately, Eric Rossiter was different.

"I'm a businessperson, not a mechanic," he says. "I was national vice president of sales and marketing for a Cleveland company that made mattresses. I'd been there 15 years, so I was vested. I dreamt of relocating to Florida, retiring from the business I was in and opening a Harley-Davidson dealership. There were 100 applicants for this dealership. I think Harley-Davidson is looking for people with business backgrounds, because what I'm really doing is running a retail store."

Rossiter opened in September 1990. He sold 53 bikes the first year and 87 the second. Both these figures are far beyond his allocation. He found machines by beating his telephone to death, then driving as far as Vermont or Massachusetts to pick up a dealer's unsold Sportster or Softail. The rookie dealer was featured on ABC-TV's *20/20*

Here's one way a dealer can make the connection between the track and his dealership. H-D has a kit for personal appearances by riders at dealerships in the vicinity of an AMA national race. This "slick" is designed for newspaper advertising. *Harley-Davidson, Inc.*

Some dealers prefer their own logos, as this Littleton, Colorado, example proves. *Vinnie*

after he sold a dentist and the dentist's family a total of five new machines. With more than 50 kinds of T-shirts alone on display, grandmothers invaded his store to buy shirts for their children and grandchildren up north. The Sarasota market, he says, is double what he and Harley-Davidson had projected.

"Buyers are a real cross section. There's a good income level here and a number of bike buyers are white-collar people. The average dealership is supposed to net four percent of gross sales. At the moment, my net is 12 percent. I'm beginning to realize that there's the economy and there's the 'Harley economy.' If a person wants a H-D bad enough, the unemployment rate or rate of inflation or cost to borrow just won't matter."

Do you have what it takes to be a dealer? The company has a short list of franchises for sale and you're welcome to inquire. With Harley-Davidson revitalized, they're more choosey than ever. Bring a business background, a fat wallet and loyalty if you apply.

Thanks to a thorough canvassing of all U.S. cycle registrations, the company can provide an applicant a very educated guess on how many bikes he will sell in a given territory. H-D will then be able to tell whether the new dealer can make money in his or another chosen location.

Dealers are divided into four groups, based on population. Obviously, a dealership in a small town costs less to buy or start up than does a metropolitan outlet. The average age of a Harley-Davidson dealership is less than ten years, since a major expansion of the network occurred during the cycle boom in the late-sixties and early-seventies. Recently, fifty to sixty dealerships a year have turned over. A company spokesman attributes this to interest rates, energy costs and the stabilizing of the market. It's also likely that many of the men who returned from World War II with a little cash and the urge to sell Harleys are of retirement age. The company will help those veteran dealers find successors by running newspaper advertisements and urging competent applicants in one geographic area to move to a lucrative franchise elsewhere.

Some guys will do anything to qualify. A fellow by the name of Barry Matteson, up Anchorage, Alaska, way, was determined to sell H-D's. In 1971, he went into business for himself as Barry's Custom Cycles—in his one-car garage. He created "lots of choppers and go-fast Harleys" before moving up the economic ladder in 1973 to a larger shop. The property was bought out from under him in '76, so Barry found a gutted house, converted it into his "showroom" and took on the H-D lightweight line, followed soon by the V-twins. Able to show just five bikes in his new quarters, he added a twelve-by-twenty-four-foot modular building nearby, shrugging off Alaska's weather while running between showroom and shop. In 1981, due to the large number of North Slope construction workers with "wads of money," Barry peddled more than 100 bikes. That

Harley-Davidsons were popular raffle prizes even back in the 1930s, as this photo from Walters Brothers H-D in Peoria, Illinois, attests. *Wayne Wiebler collection*

year enabled him to cut a deal on a larger dealership, under one roof, where he can now show thirty bikes on a major road between downtown Anchorage and the city's airport. A knack for bike work has evolved into a sophisticated operation, with attractive "House of Harley" stationery and all of the trappings of the biggest and best outlets.

Patience is required, though today's very low interest rates make for an attractive buying atmosphere, both for prospective dealers and riders. In the wake of double-digit inflation of a few years ago, H-D proprietors deserve low rates. Things were bad at the time but even worse in the thirties. Back then, many dealers purchased a demonstrator, then found they had so little money left that they had to sell the demonstrator before ordering any other bike. In 1932, an average of 100 Harley-Davidsons was sold in each state. In 1981, by contrast, the average H-D dealer in the U.S. was able to move nearly seventy bikes. With unemployment in 1982 the highest since the thirties, sales declined. The results were lower production and a month-long shutdown of the York and Capitol Drive plants in the spring. The decision to temporarily close the engine and assembly plants was influenced by the company's retail sale and warranty registration (RSWR) system, in place since 1978. This monthly report shows what each dealer has sold and what he has in inventory. It reports sales by district, region and nation, enabling H-D either to build the right models at the right time or adjust its inventory by any of several means, including a brief layoff to work off unsold units.

The key person between the dealer and the company is the district manager. He helps the dealer get the bikes he wants when he wants them, provides the factory with a slew of reports on the dealers' well-being in his geographic area and ensures that neither his dealers nor the company is excessively tardy in mailing money to each other. The DM's, as the thirty-one H-D field people are known, "have to walk the fence," according to one dealer, pleasing both the company and its 593 contacts with the public. Usual grousing aside, Harley-Davidson and those who analyze the industry believe H-D dealers get the fairest shake of all. An informal survey conducted in connection with this book contacted every U.S. Harley dealer by letter. Of the 350 replies received (amazing in itself), just one dealer voiced total disagreement with company policies.

Assuming an applicant meets the financial and other criteria and finds a dealership he'd like to call his own, he's thoroughly indoctrinated at the plant on Juneau Avenue. Nothing appears to be held back. He's shown the supersecret styling studio and research and development, then given a cram course in management. Down through the years, Harley-Davidson has said, "We do not serve the public, we serve our dealers." The new dealer comes away from his visit to headquarters with that belief sinking in. But that's not the last time

Two Peoria, IL, riders in front of the Walters Brothers dealership sometime in the 1950s. *Wayne Wiebler collection*

he'll call on Milwaukee. Each year, dealers gather there or at some more exotic location to preview the new models. There's the predictable hoopla, to include earnest speeches on the future from the brass. More meaningful meetings take place at other times of the year and include workshops on such things as office practices and procedures and on service. Collectively, this has been known since the spring of 1992 as Harley-Davidson University. The school covers every conceivable aspect of running a modern dealership.

Bastions of Harley-Davidson strength are found in California, Texas and throughout the snowbelt states, from Massachusetts through Minnesota, according to registration information provided by the company. Frank Cimermancic, director of market research, points out that strong dealerships in a state can make a big difference; Minnesota recently moved into the top ten in registrations, due largely to three strong dealers in the greater Twin Cities area. With their large populations and extended riding seasons, California and Texas are the top two states in registrations. And while the list changes each year, other strong states include Michigan, Ohio, Pennsylvania and, of course, Wisconsin.

Chapter 6

Restoration

Down Florida way, there's this sand dune, see. A local resident, not given to exaggeration, says he's sure there are hundreds of Harley-Davidson XA's buried in the dune. An overeager Army captain celebrated the end of World War II by off-loading the bikes from a train so that he could fill the cars with citrus and make a pile of cash. There are several holes in this story, not the least being that the last XA was created in 1942, three years before hostilities ceased. But maybe they're WLA's, instead. And maybe, with a metal detector and a couple of weeks vacation. . . .

If that's too far-fetched, try this: In an extremely rural area of Missouri is an old fellow with several quonset huts filled with H-D's. Depending on his mood, he's apt to sell you a bike just so you'll quit pestering him. This story is from an Oregon Harley dealer who's actually seen all of the allegedly well-preserved iron. . . .

Finally, perhaps you're aware of motorcycle mountain. Another quonset hut, this one filled not only with Harleys but with Vincents, BSA's, etc., was in the way of a Colorado construction project. The old man who owned the place, a former H-D dealer, was too apathetic to move bikes and building; so the construction guys

H-D museum bikes on display at the Ocean Center in Daytona Beach. *David Wright*

either piled earth on everything or it was hit by a land or mud slide (take your pick). In any event, this place really exists and a guy named Vinnie in Littleton is allowed on the property once in a while to rescue the mud-encrusted machines.

Let's return to earth, shall we? If you want a restored or restorable Harley-Davidson, the best thing to do is buy it or trade for it with a known restorer. That's the advice of Connie Schlemmer and his friend, Louis Bartley, both of whom have a reputation for not only restoring bikes but for offering solid advice to the restorer-to-be. Here's more sobering news: Frequently, the restorer will not set a price on a vintage bike, but will insist that the buyer trade him one or more motorcycles or motorcycle pieces that he can use in future restoration work. Yes, there are times when not even money works! What, then, can someone who wants to restore or own a restored Harley-

Davidson do? Let's pin down a trio of restorers, who worked on three vastly different bikes, to learn how they did it.

Mike Lange, who lives west of Milwaukee, attributes the finding of his 1924 two-cam racer to the guy who stole his car. Lange was driving down an alley, on the way to test-drive a car to replace the one taken from in front of his home. "I saw those Castle springs sticking out from under a blanket in a garage, so I stopped," he relates. Lange offered the owner $2,000 cash on the spot for what turned out to be a 1924 JD, but the owner decided to make things a little more difficult. He insisted that he would trade the grotty, old bike only for a new 3500cc, four-cylinder Honda. Lange ordered the Honda—and the JD owner reneged. Finally, the deal was consummated for $1,500.

"I bought the two-cam because I needed valve

Banker Greg Duray shows one of two XR750s he has restored. One member of his racing-bike registry owns "16 or 17" of the legendary XR750s! *David Wright*

springs for the JD," he says. Said valve springs were located in Louisiana, along with a two-cam motor the owner offered for sale but refused to ship. So Lange drove to Louisiana, picking up the valve springs, the two-cam motor, the front end and a keystone frame, all for $750. Restoration on the racer was begun immediately. Lange is a machinist in the prototype department of a large job shop and so has skill and access to lathes, and so on. He began to restore both bikes simultaneously. The results speak for themselves, though he has since dismantled the JD to fix a couple of things that annoy him. Except for a crack in the lower rear portion of the frame (which Lange will fix in the

Michael Lange's 1950 WR. This yellow color was offered in 1950, but not for the WR. So Lange is repainting the machine an authentic WR color, ruby red. *David Wright*

Lange's 1941 Knucklehead. *David Wright*

job shop), the two-cam is as tidy as it was nearly sixty years ago, when the serial number 24FHAC577 was banged into the engine case.

"I made a chopper before I came to my senses," says Lange, who also has restored a 1941 74 cu. in. Knucklehead and sidecar, plus a WLDR racer. Unlike many restorers, he has driven the two-cam at speeds. One such junket almost cost him damage to the bike and himself. "There's no transmission and it's geared for a mile track," he reports. "It doesn't even start to breathe till 70–90 miles an hour, and I'm guessing the top speed is 140." On a seldom-traveled portion of road, Lange recently opened 'er up, running at least 80 miles

This 45 cu. in. model, from 1929, is being restored by Norwegian Ola Jonassen.

This restored 1937 45 cu. in. V-twin belongs to Norwegian restorer Ola Jonassen. Parts for the 45 motor continue to be available in the U.S. and throughout Europe.

This 30.50 cu. in. CAC cinder-track or speedway machine from early 1934 belongs to restorer Dan Pugens of Milwaukee. Not more than a dozen of the overhead valve machines, which featured direct drive and weighed 265 pounds, were made. Most such bikes were sold on the East Coast or in California. This example may have been run by East Coast star Goldy Restall. *David Wright*

Dan Pugens of Milwaukee also has restored this 1931 500cc (28.4 cu. in.) speedway racer, a twin-port single with lower end modified to accept a Bosch magneto. Stock 1926–31 H-D singles frames were modified at the factory for these bikes, which were assembled by hand. Handmade items include push rods, cylinders, J.A.P.-style forks, handlebars and steering damper. Bore was $3^3/_{32}$ in., stroke was 4 in. *David Wright*

an hour. The rear Universal tire, never intended for anything much past idle, flew off the rim, wrapping itself around the axle. Somehow, the brakeless machine and rider managed to stop without incident.

Glenn Harding's 1941 restored 61 cu. in. EL had been reduced to just one part—the rear cylinder head—when he got ahold of it in 1962. The former Harley-Davidson dealer, who now teaches at Patrick Henry Community College in Martinsville, Virginia, spent the following nineteen years acquiring parts here and there for what may be the nicest Knucklehead in existence. The son of an engineer-machinist, Harding began working in a cycle shop at the age of twelve and from 1939 to 1962 ran a combination H-D/lawn mower/small engine dealership. Only after he sold the business did he begin to long intensely for an EL. The cylinder head was snagged from a fenced-in area apparently filled with junk parts at his former dealership.

"As luck would have it, I began to pick up old parts and was given others—first the engine, then a transmission, then a frame," he says. The frame itself was created from parts of three choppers; Harding paid heed to old books and manuals for proper dimensions. "Every part I managed to find was worn out or discarded. If someone has a valuable part these days, money won't work—you have to trade him something he wants more than that part." The motor on the bike carries serial number 41EL2394 and is entirely stock except for minor internal refinements. Harding modified the

valve gear for quiet, more endurable running. The paint, he admits, is a compromise. The black is authentic DuPont enamel, whereas the red is DuPont lacquer. "Originally, it was all enamel, but the more you rub lacquer, the better it looks."

The saddlebags aren't stock, but they can be considered authentic, since Harding sold similar units out of his shop. "I went to Daytona right after the war and saw these great looking square leather saddlebags. So I came home and designed them to sell in my shop." The bags were made by hand carving wood to the proper shape, then applying a thin layer of foam rubber and stretching the leather over the wooden mold. The hand-tooled bags and seat skirt were sold in quantity at the dealership and Harding was able to recall how he created them. The original bags, incidentally, continued to sell well until 1957, when swinging arms and plastic conspired to make rigid bags more practical and capable of matching the color of the bike.

"I was forced to use a non-authentic seat rail," he admits, pointing out that the small rim of bright metal did not come out until the fifties. And since no one he knew performed cadmium plating, Harding found a shop in another part of the state that imparts a cadmium look in their plating process. It is, he says, a different appearance than chrome.

No attempt was made to run the bike until it was entirely together. On June 15, 1981, the EL started on the first kick. Only a toolbox and Eagle fender tips have been added since these photos

Restorer Francis Blake recently was given this pre-World War II 45 with sidecar—if he would renovate a similar model. Both were recovered by an American visiting Egypt. *Francis Blake*

were taken. The machine, says its proud owner, is a joy to operate. "It's very easy to handle, since it has a low center of gravity. It honestly feels like a 150- or 200-pound minibike. The ride is harsh by today's standards, but vibration is negligible. If you had significant vibrations, you had a problem with these bikes, though it was my experience that Harley-Davidson was never as critical as they should have been with engine balancing. The bike just doesn't have any brakes compared to the new ones. And the front spring has just 1½ in. of travel. This model had ride control, which consisted of two plates and a friction disc. The disc, mounted on the rigid fork, tightened steering."

Harding doesn't ride the bike excessively or at high speeds, and it isn't set up for parades, which

Harding says he has eliminated much of the motor's inherent vibration by balancing the original parts. *Luther Oehlbeck*

Glenn Harding's 1941 61 cu. in. overhead valve model. His restoration project began with only a rear cylinder. The saddlebags and skirt are similar to ones offered by Harding when he was an H-D dealer. The seat rail is similar to that found on postwar models. *Luther Oehlbeck*

requires more cooling than the motor gets at long periods near idle. It's more to be admired than anything else, as is the owner's next project. He's restoring a 1934 Seafoam Blue VLD, which he says has "bushels of power." Check with him in nineteen years or so.

The paint is wrong, the shift arm is missing, the head was borrowed from an Excelsior and many small items are elsewhere. So what is Bill McMahon's 1914 magneto single doing in a chapter on restorations? First, his bike is in running order, something many antique H-D owners may never accomplish due to missing parts. Second, the Wisconsin Rapids, Wisconsin, owner rides the darned thing at regular intervals. An antique Ford buff, McMahon noticed in a newspaper in 1972 that a "1915 motorcycle fram [sic]" was among

contents of an old farmstead coming up for auction. "My partner in old car parts and I bought the contents of five sheds at that auction," he says. "I bought the frame for $15."

Attached to the frame were a front wheel, dangling from broken front forks, plus rusted tanks, both fenders and bent handlebars. In one of the sheds McMahon uncovered a motor, extra handlebars, fenders, running boards, linkage, another gas tank and miscellaneous parts that appeared to be from the magneto, fuel lines, etc. He then purchased those pieces from his partner for $35 and had "what I thought was a fairly complete pile of parts. Little did I know. . . ." Once in his basement, McMahon discovered that he'd purchased a 1914 Model 10C, serial number D7807. The bike appeared rust colored but underneath

Here's a rider's-eye view of LaFerrera's machine. The speedometer was an option in 1928. *David Wright*

Salvatore LaFerrera of San Francisco rides this 1928 V-twin daily. He says the bike's performance is entirely adequate—except for the brakes. Front brakes were introduced on H-D's in '28. *David Wright*

showed faint flecks of gray paint. He spent the next seven years following parts leads, shopping swap meets and contacting the factory. Failing to receive any company information, McMahon snooped around the factory in Milwaukee, met a man on a loading dock who identified himself only as "a Harley friend" and eventually provided him with photos and a copy of a 1914 owners manual.

Purchasing the only new parts available—tires, tubes, decals and rubber mats—McMahon brought the motor to life for the first time in 1979. "As soon as I got it running, everybody wanted to buy it," he says, despite the fact that running condition was more important to him than 100-percent faithful restoration or checks of $3,000 or more. In addition to the parts already mentioned, the bike is missing a shift crank, which prevents the rider from using top gear in the two-speed, hub-mounted transmission. Also missing are the primary chain guard, the muffler cutout and the original nickel plating. A manual H-D klaxon horn is affixed, while the carbide lamp and kerosene tail lamp were borrowed from a long-forgotten motorcycle or bicycle.

"It isn't restored perfect. That's why I let a lot of people ride it and why I ride it a lot," says McMahon. The 1914 cycles were the first year of the step starter; starting, says the owner, is easy. "You start the oil to drip to the motor at about thirty drops a minute, then fill the carb with gasoline using the tickle valve," he reports. "Bring it up to compression and step down hard with either pedal. One or two kicks is all it needs. It idles like a new Harley. You know—thumpa, thumpa."

McMahon allows the bike to warm up for about two minutes before jumping aboard, easing out the clutch and riding off. "I locked it in low gear and that's fast enough," he says. "I can go between 35 and 40 miles an hour. If I could shift it, it should go 60 to 70 miles an hour. That's too fast for 2½ in. tires and a sixty-eight-year-old machine." Nevertheless, you'll see McMahon—and other folks he trusts—aboard the milky gray machine in local parades, at a big antique car show in Iola, Wisconsin, each summer and at an occasional antique meet. "It has chipped paint, but it's a runner. I like to drive my antique vehicles, not look at them."

Now that your appetite is whetted, where can

Bill McMahon adjusts the gravity oil feed to his restored 1914 single. *David Wright*

you see old-time Harley-Davidsons? The premier place is H-D's own Gott Museum in York, or in the company's traveling display somewhere like Daytona. If that isn't convenient, the following list indicates there's at least one historic H-D being shown within a long day's ride of virtually every American biker. Rather than speed finding out if that's true, remember the location nearest you and stop the next time you tour.

American Police Museum and Hall of Fame
3801 Biscayne Blvd.
Miami, FL 33137
305/891-1700

A 1960 Duo-Glide police solo stands tall here. Motorcyclists may find it ironic that there's a police museum in one of the more lawless towns around. Admission is $3 for adults, $1.50 for kids and seniors. Open 10 a.m.-5:30 p.m., seven days a week. Lock your bike.

Henry Ford Museum
Greenfield Village
Dearborn, Michigan 48121
1-800/835-2246 ext. 218

Willie G. himself noted the absence of any worthwhile motorcycles in 1956 while working for Ford's Lincoln division. A year later, he and Walter C. Davidson remedied the situation by presenting the museum with an authentically restored 1907 single, complete with belt drive. The machine was found in mediocre shape somewhere in Milwaukee and restored to original condition at the H-D factory. There's now a 1941 Fleet Red, 74 cu. in. Knucklehead with sidecar, too, restored by Don Montgomery. Open 9 am to 5 pm, admission charged.

Rodney C. Gott Museum
Harley-Davidson York
1425 Eden Road
York, Pennsylvania 17403
717/848-1177

This immaculate 1926 JD showed up at Sturgis in 1982 with California restorer John Cameron aboard. Much of the bike appears to be original, though the cloth oil-line braiding is an old aftermarket item. *Richard Creed*

If you don't see the particular Harley-Davidson model you want at the H-D museum, come back in a few months. There are approximately 100 bikes stored in a barn on factory property that are periodically exchanged with bikes on display. Obviously, this is the most complete collection of Harley-Davidsons anywhere. Following a tour of the old bikes, visitors receive an up-close view of the assembly line in action. Both tours are free, neither given on holidays.

Indianapolis Motor Speedway Hall of Fame Museum
4790 W. 16th St.
Speedway, Indiana 46224
317/241-2501

There are more than twenty-five Indy-winning cars on display, but that's not why we're here. A fairly authentic reproduction of a 1935 Joe Petrali "Peashooter," restored with the help of Harry Molenaar and presented by Harley-Davidson, was admitted to the speedway several years ago. Admission charged.

Museum of Science and Industry
57th Street and Lake Shore Drive
Chicago, Illinois 60637

This place is huge, but it's so interesting you may not mind searching in coal mines and caves, Gay Nineties streets and space-shuttle settings for the lone H-D on exhibit. The bike is a 1922 horizontally opposed 37 cu. in. Sport Twin. The label on the bike says the company "was a leading manufacturer of early motorcycles," but makes up for that slur by pointing out that a similar machine once set the cross-country speed record.

The National Museum of American History
Smithsonian Institution
14th St. and Constitution Ave. N.W.
Washington, D.C. 20560

A pair of Harley-Davidsons graces the Smithsonian. On display are a 1913 Model 9-B single and a 1942 74 cu. in. overhead valve model. Both are in super shape and are worth visiting if only because a visit here puts Harley-Davidson into excellent perspective in two-wheel history. 10 am to 5:30 pm daily, no admission.

Kersting's Cycle Center, Inc.
P.O. Box 186
North Judson, IN 46366
219/896-2974

This dealership has on display a 1925 V-twin, a JD of indeterminate age and a recently purchased 1910 single. In business 30 years, the establishment is a bit hard to find because the street address is Rural Route 3, Winnemac. Closed Sundays and Mondays.

Motorcycle Heritage Museum
33 College View Rd.
Westerville, OH 43081
614/891-2425

Many of the great bikes carefully restored by the Antique Motorcycle Club of America are on display here. As you can tell by the address and phone, this museum is courtesy of the American Motorcyclist Association. There's no charge and hours are 9 a.m. to 5 p.m. Monday-Friday, 10 a.m. to 4 p.m. Saturday and noon to 4 p.m. Sunday.

George Kragel, now retired, formerly conducted tours of the Rodney C. Gott Museum at the York, Pennsylvania, H-D assembly plant. *Harley-David-son, Inc.*

National Motorcycle Museum and Hall of Fame
2438 Junction Ave.
Sturgis, SD 57785
605/347-4875

There's no shortage of Harley-Davidsons here! Latest count is nine, and they're surrounded by lesser machines and neat memorabilia. Open since May of 1990, the museum charges $2 for adults, with kids under 12 admitted free. Hours Memorial Day-Labor Day are 8 a.m. to 5 p.m. weekdays, 10 a.m.-4 p.m. Saturdays. Hours are Monday-Friday 9 a.m.-5 p.m. the rest of the year.

San Diego Hall of Champions
1649 El Prado, Balboa Park
San Diego, CA 92101
619/234-2544

Brad Andres, who was fast and my wife says good lookin', has his 750cc side valve on display here. Andres was a Daytona winner and a Grand National champion. Donation requested.

Sundays Only Cycle Museum
P.O. Box 1135
Hawthorne, FL 32640
904/481-3758

Herb Dickey shows visitors around his extensive (seventy-five or so Harley-Davidsons) collection from noon to five on the Sabbath. His only complaints are those who "demand I show the motorcycles at other times" and "so-called big spenders from Europe and South America who will take anything free and then complain."

A couple of notes of caution: museums come and go,

The Harley-Davidsons are thick as flies at the Sunday Only Motorcycle Museum in Hawthorne, FL.

change and move. For example, Harrah's National Automobile Museum, in Reno, no longer displays motorcycles. The bikes were sold when the corporation changed hands. Other things you might consider are the facts that small museums keep erratic hours and big museums often rotate their displays in and out of storage. A telephone call could save aggravation.

Restoration, like museum visitation, can be shot through with disappointment. You may find the original cylinder head for your 1926 Single, only to learn that money won't buy it. The person who owns the head will insist on your providing him or her with, say, a gas tank from a 1920 Sport model in trade. In other words, some parts are worth more than money, and bartering is the rule. Virtually all of the folks on the list that follows will accept money for the precious parts they peddle. Some have catalogs, while others report that their parts come and go too quickly to put anything on paper. Frequently, they are so busy searching for and salvaging parts that they can't write a lot down. Please accept the descriptions for what they are—groundwork you may not have to cover in bringing that VL or ULH back to showroom shape. Happy hunting!

Antique Cycle Supply
Route 1
Cedar Springs, MI 49319
616/636-8200

Now in its 18th year, Antique has a sumptuous, hefty, 208-page catalog that contains many, many authentic and remanufactured parts, accessories and literature from down through the years. The strength of the catalog lies in the number of large, easy-to-understand exploded drawings of carburetors, generators, cases, covers, motors, tanks and more. Terms remain the same, COD or prepaid, no credit cards honored.

Antique Harley Works
P.O. Box 2063
Seffner, FL 33584

Bruce Palmer should be kickstarting this business once again. He and Francis Blake, the dashing chap in the photo on page 110, are cousins.

Bill's Custom Cycles
7145 New Berwick Highway
Bloomsburg, PA 17815
717/759-9613

Bill's shop is about two hours north of York, just off Interstate Highway 80. "We have just bought nine semi-loads of obsolete and late original factory Harley parts," says his catalog, which also contains custom stuff and current, officially licensed products. The shop itself is a real treat, overflowing as it does with old bikes, old parts and memorabilia such as a collection of 60 H-D kidney belts from days of yore. Bill accepts MasterCard or Visa.

Charleston Custom Cycle
211 Washington St.
Charleston, IL 61920
217/345-2577

New old stock parts for American- and Italian-made H-D lightweights, from 1948 through 1978, are the specialties here. The fellows accept MasterCard or Visa and they will ship via UPS.

Coker Tire Co.
1317 Chestnut St.
Chattanooga, TN 37402
800/251-6336

A toll-free number beats money from home, and that's what the Coker people offer. They also offer a large number of vintage bike tires carrying the Coker brand name. Coker folks seem especially friendly and

More than 100 bikes are stabled in a barn to the east of the York assembly facility, awaiting their turn to be shown in the museum. Museum displays are rotated on a regular basis. *David Wright*

willing to work with restorers—perhaps because Corky Coker owns a '47 Knucklehead. It and lots of tires are shown in the company's color catalog, which now runs 20 pages. The piece also shows tubes, flaps, valves and more and is free. The company accepts virtually every credit card known.

Competition Harley Network
1355 Kingsdale
Hoffman Estates, IL 60194
708/884-6033

If you own an XR or XRTT and want to be included in this registry, send two bucks. A total of twelve bucks will get you the network's primo newsletter, which includes profiles of bikes and owners, answers to tech questions, ads and names and phone numbers of owners of the mighty 750s, plus CRs, KRs, MXs, RRs, WRs and a Buell or two. This noble project is handled by Gregory E. Duray, who by day is a banker and by night is a restorer of great race bikes.

H.D. 45 Restoration Co.
P.O. Box 12843
Albany, NY 12212
518/459-5012

These restorers make about 130 different pieces. The rest they obtain from various small suppliers. A 48-page illustrated catalog, with more than 1,400 parts, also is available. So is a catalog of specifically designed, dealer-like tools. A spokesperson said their fill rate is about 96 percent. In business 20 years, the orders are processed quickly on an Apple Macintosh. This is a mail-order operation only and there's a separate catalog covering UL models.

Harbor Vintage Motor Co.
Box 248, Route 2
Jonesville, VT 05466
802/434-4040

In business 15 years, Mike Herbert and Dave ("Rat") Scherk buy out dealerships and restore obsolete and antique American bikes. At the moment they're redoing a 1934 VL, a 1936 Knucklehead and a 1934 Crocker speedway racer. "Parts go out of here so quickly, it's impossible to put together a catalog," Mike says. "We do a brisk mail-order business because we'd die if we depended on walk-in traffic." Look on the map near Burlington.

Harley Hummer Club
GMF Suburban MD 20898-7294

Introduced as a 125cc machine in 1955, the Hummer lightweight has a following, as this nonprofit club would indicate. The organization puts out a very professional quarterly newsletter, well written and carefully desk-top-published. The illustrations show bikes that are handsome enough to line up alongside the classic single-cylinder bikes of the '20s and early '30s. The last domestic lightweight was the 1966 Bobcat. Dues are $10/year.

Chris Haynes
P.O. Box 922620
Sylmar, CA 91392-2620

Chris warned readers in an earlier edition to beware of restoration-business profiteers. We're pleased to report he ain't one. The former Oregon Harley-Davidson dealer restores bikes and sells American-made reproduction parts. His favorite bike is the '36 Knucklehead, but he can talk 1930-1969 Big Twins, too.

"Indian" Joe Martin's Antique Motorcycle Parts
P.O. Box 3156
Chattanooga, TN 37404

The late "Indian" Joe Martin was a real collector and a true gentleman and his son, David Joe, preserves the

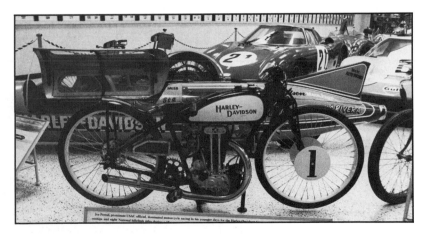

Joe Petrali's dirt-track bike is in the foreground; in the back is the Cal Rayborn Bonneville record-breaker. The former was donated to the Indianapolis Speedway museum by H-D and was restored with the aid of Hammond, Indiana, dealer Harry Molenaar. *Indianapolis Motor Speedway*

141

good name of his father and the business. Don't let the name fool you—many of the $3 catalog's new old stock, army surplus and reproduction parts are for Harley-Davidsons. The 22-year-old company specializes in parts for the years 1920 through 1973 and prefers to service a finite number of customers well.

Motorcycles Only
127 W. 54th St.
Gardena, CA 90248
310/323-6264

This outfit, run by the Ross family in greater Los Angeles, specializes in ground-up restorations, in the restoration of JD to Shovelhead engines and transmissions, plus frame straightening, finding and straightening early handlebars and forks and generally digging up and selling used obsolete H-D parts. They've been in business since 1964.

Conrad F. Schlemmer
1218 Wedgewood Drive
Council Bluffs, IA 51503

Here's your singles source, old-time Harley fans. Connie Schlemmer, former hillclimber and Red Oak, IA, H-D dealer, specializes in the 1926-1935 singles, selling parts and serving as a dispenser of extremely accurate information. Conrad rides and displays his factory-built, 21 cu. in. OHV hillclimber, "which still does well at shows," plus a 1932 45 cu. in. RL he likes. "If a person is sincere and needs some help, I'll be happy to assist him." Look for Mr. Schlemmer on his 45 at national road runs in Canada or in the Rockies each summer.

Universal Tire Company
987 Stone Battery Rd.
Lancaster, PA 17601
800/233-3827; Canada: 800/321-1934

Your Rand-McNally reveals that Universal is down the road from York, where we understand motorcycles are assembled. Universal has a new address and two new toll-free lines, which will access you to many an antique bike tire, particularly sizes for cycles built 1903-1930. "We also carry an extensive line of tubes," says a spokesperson, "which means we can accommodate the short, 1¼ in. motorcycle brass stem, which was also original and authentic for many restorations of early motorcycles." Nice to know you're dealing with those who understand bits and pieces. Like Coker, most Universal business is automobile related, but don't let that impede your progress. Their color catalog is free and they take American Express, MasterCard and Visa.

Walneck's Classic Cycle Trader
7923 Janes Ave.
Woodridge, IL 60517
708/985-4995

Our favorite restoration newspaper has become a monthly magazine. Walneck's turned 101 issues in June of 1992 and is 100 pages of antique and vintage ads, primarily British and American. This is where to find a '77 XLCR Cafe Racer, an '83 XR1000 with only 1,500 miles, or a '57 Sportster with no miles since its ground-up restoration. Every ad includes a photo of the bike, with some in color. Twelve issues are $24 from Buzz Walneck and family.

This 1930 21 cu. in. hillclimber has been restored by Conrad Schlemmer. He has owned the machine, believed to have been ridden by racer Herb Reiber, since 1943 and restored it in 1977.

This 30.50 cu. in. single was constructed out of parts by Conrad Schlemmer of Council Bluffs, Iowa. The exhaust and fenders were built by hand when Schlemmer could not find originals.

Conrad Schlemmer astride his 1932 45 cu. in. model. The paint is original delft blue and turquoise.

Sacramento dealer Armando Magri displays restored bikes on his showroom floor. *Armando Magri collection*

This Panhead sidecar outfit graces Magri's showroom window. *David Wright*

Seven of the dozens of original motor-cycles owned by Hammond, Indiana, dealer Harry Molenaar. The bike in the foreground is a 250cc Aermacchi/Har-ley-Davidson road racer equipped with a front disc brake. *David Wright*

This 1928 Single, an overhead valve 350 cubic centimeter BA model, proves that overseas restorers are active. The owner is Olle Ridelius, a Swede. Scandinavian sales of H-D's prior to the Depression were high.

Chapter 7

Adornments

Jerry Wilke, vice president for motorcycles parts and accessories marketing, has no trouble recalling the low point in his 18 years with Harley-Davidson. It was 1983 or so, shortly after a two-year salary freeze which had taken place following a nine percent salary reduction. "A friend called me who had been among the 40 percent of employees we had to terminate," Wilke recalls. "He said, 'I can get you a job at my new place. You'd better move now—Harley's going to fold.' Staying with the company was one of the tough personal decisions a lot of us had to make."

If it was tough, it also proved to be correct. If the demand for the cycles is high and ongoing, so is the demand for clothing, collectibles, parts and accessories. That's because, Wilke says, "We have a different marketing philosophy. The sale of the product is just the beginning of the relationship. We actually spend more marketing dollars to reach people after the sale than before. That makes us different from the other companies and from Detroit."

Not one buyback member conceived the importance of parts and accessories on that ride from York back to Milwaukee in 1981. During the company's desperate early '80s years, however, someone (it may have been Jeff Bleustein) realized there were big bucks to be made on aftermarket items. Not only is the money there, but the potential continues to expand. H-D now markets several kinds of parts: Genuine, which as the name implies, are factory replacements for current bikes; Eagle Iron, reasonably priced parts for non-current models; and Screamin' Eagle, high-performance parts for today's modern bikes.

The bolt-ons and kits and shims and stuff

compete very capably at the dealership with Custom Chrome, Drag Specialties, Arlen Ness and many others. (It's worth noting that, if the item says Harley-Davidson or carries any of the H-D trademarks, the product is made under license to the company, which gets a percentage of each piece sold.) A Midwest dealer says his business grossed no more than $600,000 a year before H-D restyled dealerships and went after the aftermarket. This same dealer grossed $2 million for 1991—in a city where the largest employer endured a long and gut-wrenching strike.

Ersatz parts were a problem very early, and Arthur Davidson warned dealers that the company would not tolerate affixing aftermarket parts on H-D bikes. He knew he was addressing many people who had attended only the Baling Wire School of Motorcycle Maintenance, and that insisting on genuine parts and accessories would maintain the company's reputation. The very first parts and accessories to carry the H-D trademark were aimed at the rider rather than the bike. The initial issue of *The Enthusiast* in 1916 shows several wool-lined leather gloves and mittens, designed for operating the bikes in cold weather (it should be remembered that cycles were competing for sales with automobiles at that time, and that bikes were virtually as warm as cars in the winter). Those trusty mittens, which retailed for up to $2.50, were fondly recalled by the late former H-D President William H. Davidson. "The styles may change, but cold-weather gear either keeps you warm or it doesn't."

A separate parts and accessories department was actually formed in 1912, indicating just how early Harley and the Davidsons realized the

"BROWN LEADER" IS FINEST JACKET

The "Brown Leader" jacket is made up to our own specifications, and is everything that we think a motorcycle jacket should be. It is designed to take care of all sorts of conditions under which you would wear it, and when you get one you will agree that it is the ideal jacket.

This extra fine jacket is made from rich, brown horsehide leather, that will not scuff or scar in the hardest kind of service. It is lined throughout with a good brown moleskin cloth that has excellent wearing qualities. The collar is leather, and so are the cuffs and waist band. Cuffs can be buttoned tight to keep the wind out, and two take-up straps at the waist band assure a good fit. The two pocket flaps button down. Has a genuine Talon zipper.

This jacket, being full grain horsehide, is shower proof and absolutely windproof. It is soft and flexible and can be doubled up and stowed away in a saddle bag without damage. Fully guaranteed. Sizes 34 to 46 are standard.

Code
11067-34—Brown Leader Jacket .... $11.85 bytuj

FINE LOOKING RIDING BREECHES

This 1934 line of riding breeches is an even better assortment to choose from than we have shown in previous years. Careful purchasing in large quantities has enabled us to maintain prices at very low figures. Every number has been carefully selected as the best available at anywhere near the price.

Good riding breeches are a very good investment, as they are comfortable, very good looking, and wear for a long time. They are particularly well adapted to motorcycle riding.

The sizes available from our stock are as follows:

11093-34 In standard lengths only—28, 30, 32, 34, 36, 38 waist measures.

Other numbers—
Sizes 28, 30, 32, 34, 36, 38, 40 in standard lengths
Sizes 30, 32, 34, 36, 38 in extra longs
Sizes 28, 30, 32 in extra shorts

These sizes should fit nearly everyone. Where special sizes are needed, they can be supplied at an extra charge.

English Military Style Breeches

Cavalry Style Tan Breeches

Full peg top as shown, with double knees and seat. A very good looking tan mixture, of great wearing quality. Five roomy, turned and stitched pockets. No special sizes.

Code
11093-34—Tan whipcord breeches .... $2.95 byize

Polo Style Dark Oxford Breeches

Extra wide peg top, with safety pockets, double knees and seat. Very dressy. Extra good grade of Oxford Whipcord. A really excellent breech for any service—many worn by Police.

Code
11097-34—Oxford Whipcord Breeches .... $3.95 bakah

Polo Style Tan Whipcord Breeches

These are the same style as described above, with button top safety pockets, leather knee facings, double seat, and full peg. The material in these breeches is made from a double twisted yarn that insures extra long wear. Color is a light brown or tan mixture that will not soil easily. Very smart appearing.

Code
11098-X .... $4.75 bakfo

English Military Style Breeches

These are very high grade, part wool breeches, that anyone would be proud to wear. The English Military Style is very attractive, as you can see from the picture. Full grain leather facings are used on the knees. Button top safety pockets are fitted. These breeches will please the most particular.

Code
11099-X .... $7.75 bajox

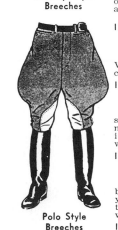

Cavalry Style Breeches

Polo Style Breeches

"Styles may have changed, but motorcycle clothing either keeps you warm or it doesn't," said William H. Davidson, the late retired H-D president. This is a page from the 1934 accessories catalog.

importance of these items. Down through the years, the company has tried to accommodate an incredible variety of interests, from the highly successful molded plastic saddlebags introduced for the 1954 model K to the hunting-fishing (trail-riding) kit for the 1963 Aermacchi-H-D Scat. And while the vast majority of accessories ideas came from within (the first safety bars were an option with the 1935 models), occasional aftermarket firms preceded H-D thinking (such as the B&H foot-shift conversion kit, offered in 1947).

It can be argued that custom bikes originated the moment the first rider pried off a fender or replaced the first factory part with an aftermarket trinket. But consistent custom evidence surfaced initially in California in the thirties. Destitute riders, aching for new bikes but unable to afford them, took to bobbing fenders and repainting their machines to make the Harleys and lesser makes look new and different. It is a credit to H-D that owners were largely content to leave the engines and transmissions alone prior to World War II. After that global conflict, riders found themselves in exactly the opposite situation: They oozed money but were able to buy only designs that had been formulated in the late thirties. So they began to toy with performance.

Numerous Harley-Davidson dealers have been sources of performance parts, since they fielded Class C American Motorcycle Association racers as early as the mid-thirties. The most successful ever was Tom Sifton, owner of the H-D franchise in San Jose, California. Prior to WW II, Sifton's reputation was earned for the porting work he performed on his own racing machines. As GI's returned to civilian life, Sifton offered them cams and related hardware that propelled Milwaukee iron to unheard-of speeds on the California dry lakes, at Bonneville, on drag strips and on flat tracks. Both the factory and independent speed shops responded. Today, there are more speed parts for Harley-Davidson motorcycles than for any other two-wheeled vehicle.

The introduction of the overhead valve Sportster in 1957 appeased most performance buffs, so riders took a page from the thirties and, again, began modifying the looks of their bikes. The factory declined to see who could produce the most outrageously extended forks, but bikes designed by such Californians as Ed "Big Daddy" Roth, Von Dutch and others became less and less transportation and more and more artistic statements. In the last few years, the customizers have retreated from the radical chopper look, in part because "Choppers won't pass state vehicle inspections, at least not in the East," says long-time

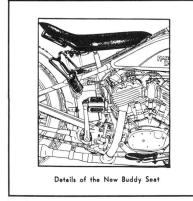

Details of the New Buddy Seat

Here's how Harley-Davidson riders took a friend along before twin seating became standard equipment. This illustration is from H-D's 1934 accessories catalog. The first such edition was produced about 1915.

New Jersey dealer Eddy Mills. Today, modified bikes fill the used cycle ads as the company produces designs that satisfy the customizer, the speed freak, the cruiser and the tourist.

Harley-Davidson is more than the last American motorcycle. It's the last (in fact, the *only*) production custom motorcycle. With the parts, accessories and paint options available, today's H-D owner

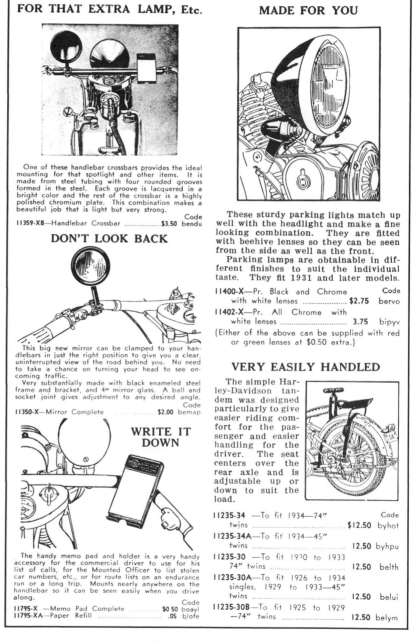

FOR THAT EXTRA LAMP, Etc.

One of these handlebar crossbars provides the ideal mounting for that spotlight and other items. It is made from steel tubing with four rounded grooves formed in the steel. Each groove is lacquered in a bright color and the rest of the crossbar is a highly polished chromium plate. This combination makes a beautiful job that is light but very strong.

Code
11359-XB—Handlebar Crossbar .... $3.50 bendu

DON'T LOOK BACK

This big new mirror can be clamped to your handlebars in just the right position to give you a clear, uninterrupted view of the road behind you. No need to take a chance on turning your head to see oncoming traffic.
Very substantially made with black enameled steel frame and bracket, and 4" mirror glass. A ball and socket joint gives adjustment to any desired angle.

Code
11350-X—Mirror Complete .... $2.00 bemap

WRITE IT DOWN

The handy memo pad and holder is a very handy accessory for the commercial driver to use for his list of calls, for the Mounted Officer to list stolen car numbers, etc., or for route lists on an endurance run or a long trip. Mounts nearly anywhere on the handlebar so it can be seen easily when you drive along.

Code
11795-X —Memo Pad Complete .... $0.50 boayl
11795-XA—Paper Refill .... .05 blofe

MADE FOR YOU

These sturdy parking lights match up well with the headlight and make a fine looking combination. They are fitted with beehive lenses so they can be seen from the side as well as the front.
Parking lamps are obtainable in different finishes to suit the individual taste. They fit 1931 and later models.

Code
11400-X—Pr. Black and Chrome
with white lenses .... $2.75 bervo
11402-X—Pr. All Chrome with
white lenses .... 3.75 bipyv
(Either of the above can be supplied with red or green lenses at $0.50 extra.)

VERY EASILY HANDLED

The simple Harley-Davidson tandem was designed particularly to give easier riding comfort for the passenger and easier handling for the driver. The seat centers over the rear axle and is adjustable up or down to suit the load.

		Code
11235-34 —To fit 1934—74" twins		$12.50 byhot
11235-34A—To fit 1934—45" twins		12.50 byhpu
11235-30 —To fit 1930 to 1933 74" twins		12.50 belth
11235-30A—To fit 1926 to 1934 singles, 1929 to 1933—45" twins		12.50 belui
11235-30B—To fit 1925 to 1929 —74" twins		12.50 belym

Mirrors were an option in 1934, as this page from that year's catalogue shows. The notepad indicates that numerous Harley-Davidsons continued to be used for deliveries.

149

has no excuse for possessing a machine that looks like anyone else's. Earl Widman, who sells H-D's and Suzukis in St. Louis, defines the difference between his two kinds of buyers and the feelings they have toward their machines. "A Harley owner will customize his bike, whereas a Suzuki owner won't even replace a damaged tank or fender. They're content to buy the bike and just ride." With that in mind, let's examine a few H-D's to learn what individuality is all about. . . .

If your Harley-Davidson looks exactly like any other Harley-Davidson, pick up a factory catalog. There are two Motorclothes and Collectible catalogs each year, along with the annual parts and accessories book and the yearly Eagle Iron catalog. The factory these days rolls 1,000 variations (if you count color) off the assembly line. From

that point, you can further modify your machine via the dealer's official custom-paint program, with parts and accessories from H-D or elsewhere, or you can design and build it yourself.

Gary Best of Hartland, WI, took several routes in individualizing his motorcycle. Best's bike originally was a black 1992 Sportster with the 2.2-gallon peanut tank. He opted for a Low Rider custom tank, sending tank and fenders off for Caliber custom paint through his dealer, Van Beek Cycle in nearby West Bend. While tank and fenders were receiving a black and golden-orange finish, the tool and die maker went to work individualizing every nut, bolt, bracket and gusset.

"I strive for perfection and settle for excellence," Best says. Immediately after purchasing

This candy-apple custom is the work of Hall's Harley-Davidson in Chico, California. Besides being an important source of income, custom work allows dealers who so choose to show their design talents.

the bike, he began to machine and fabricate parts. The engine remains stock internally, but since Best has a very understanding employer, he had access to million-dollar machines, computers and software to craft his cycle. Virtually every nut has been replaced by a nut made by hand. The oil tank ribs are silver soldered. The exhaust heat shields, which work well, were made with a die. The rocker boxes were machined so that the letters on them stand out. They read "Born in the USA" and "Simply the Best." Best found that the air cleaner was .030 in. thick and so he machined everything down around a portrait of the American flag. The flag stands about .015 in. above the new surface.

"The better you know a new Sportster, the better you can appreciate this bike," he says. He estimates that he has 700 hours—or 100 days of staying at his job an extra seven hours—in the bike. The Screamin' Eagle exhaust system he chose for the renovated Sportster is, in his words, "street illegal but not as loud as you might think."

Speaking of the street, Best rides the leather-trimmed custom cycle all over the place. He's getting 51.7 miles per gallon on an Evolution motor that isn't yet broken in. "I try not to ride in the rain," he says, adding that he plans to enter the creation in a show or two in the future. We may as well tell you that Best is a H-D employee, by day creating engines identical to his Sportster. This project, he says, was undertaken because, as a young man he didn't have the time to ride or to customize a bike. He is amazed at the civility of

Safety guards, currently a controversial accessory, were popular in the thirties, as this 1935 45 cu. in. model indicates. The bike is part of the H-D collection in York. *David Wright*

This sumptuous fiber-glass trailer shows what "Boss Hawg" uses when his Dresser becomes overloaded. The bike and trailer were seen at Daytona in 1982. *David Wright*

Gary Best is a tool and die maker at the Capitol Drive plant and an exacting creator of this custom '92 Sportster. *David Wright*

Gary Best's bike throbs with chrome and incredible detail. *David Wright*

West Bend, WI, dealer Jim Dricken helped Gary Best bring his dream bike to life by steering him to the custom paint program. *David Wright*

Audrey Xydas of Hyattsville, Maryland, created this Knucklehead-powered three wheeler. *David Wright*

Best's modified Sportster includes
leather trim. *David Wright*

Here's a popular modification—Panhead cylinders and heads atop a Sportster
bottom end. This example, dubbed a PanSter, was seen at Daytona in 1982. *David
Wright*

the new Sportsters. As for his own stunning machine, the project "was meant to be a relief but it didn't turn out that way."

Best got his bike together much quicker than did Audrey Xydas of Hyattsville, Maryland. She bought the motor for her 1946 Knucklehead three wheeler as a basket case, then spent a few hours now and then tearing it down and rebuilding it, chroming as she progressed. The frame and the transmission were sold to her by a fellow with a wooden leg who said he wanted to try two-wheel cycling once again.

"I got my ideas by going to different shows and looking around," she says. The trike's stubby appearance she attributes to the Springer front end. A bit later she acquired a handsome set of pipes that have only one failing—they hit the pavement when she rides over large bumps. The little seat in the back was crafted by a friend who is a carpenter. The deep blue bike with Freebird on the tank was completed to Audrey's satisfaction, and with her own money, in 1988.

So far, she's entered four shows, two in the Baltimore area and two in Daytona Beach, and has four trophies to display. "There are two trike classes," she says, "one for auto engines and one for cycle engines. I didn't do anything really outrageous to the bike, but I change a few things from one year to the next."

She rides on an irregular basis for one good reason: The Knucklehead is tough to kick over, so if she stalls in traffic there's not much she can do. A large male friend in Florida who is an expert in such things can consistently kick over her V-twin with one stomp. But Audrey is content to show more than ride the three wheeler, which has been featured in a magazine in France. "An American magazine wanted to do a story on it, but they backed out when I refused to show my tits in a photo. I don't need that."

"I never had a bike as a kid," confesses Arlen Ness, king of the aftermarket motorcycle designers and a Californian with a neatly trimmed mustache and goatee. Highly respected by H-D personnel, he is one of hundreds of financial successes associated with the motorcycle and the

Here's a well-turned-out FLH Classic. The owner is Ken Smance of Manchester, New Hampshire, a member of the International Northeast Harley-Davidson Dresser Association. The sidecar features a convertible top and a television set.

aftermarket products made for it. "I married young, and neither my dad, my mother nor my wife wanted me to have a motorcycle."

Surprisingly, the man who spent his first twelve years in Minnesota didn't own his own machine until the ripe old age of twenty-seven. To get the money, he had to save winnings he realized as a professional bowler. His "half-trick," used Knucklehead pleased him, but not so much that he was content to leave it alone. The stunts he pulled on that used bike soon turned up on bikes belonging to friends—they'd seen his machine and wanted him to work the molding and customizing magic that suddenly made their H-D's look less exotic than Arlen's old Knucklehead. A truck driver at the time, Ness switched to carpentry; the four-and-one-half-day workweek for San Leandro carpenters gave him a bit more time to work out of his home. "My house became a place to hang out," he says.

Arlen rented a store, set it up for painting, then began to design the dramatic parts that have become his signature. He created ram horn bars,

welded frames and more. Along the way, he began to farm out the work to those he could trust: racing car builders who knew materials and how to form those materials into a finished product from a Ness drawing. "Long front ends looked unsafe to me, so I lowered the bike all around, like a drag bike. The look worked well. After that, I designed a series of sleek tanks, then clamps, brackets, etc. The last three years, I haven't been able to make stuff fast enough." At present, more than 400 dealers, Harley-Davidson and otherwise, carry Ness aftermarket products. Like H-D, he is plagued with imitators. And unlike many aftermarket wheeler-dealers, Ness scrupulously avoids using the H-D trademark. His products sell without it.

To meet the demand a few years ago, he opened two additional stores and a machine shop. But they complicated his life excessively and he reverted to a single store and to a catalog that generates nearly half of his present business. With three employees, plus his wife and himself, and that catalog, Ness can find time to turn out new

Arlen Ness, acknowledged by many at Harley-Davidson to be a seminal figure in custom motorcycles. *David Wright*

A Ness-equipped 1973 Sportster owned by Andrew Oberle of New York. *David Wright* designs and to take on freelance design assignments. He also has the time now to conduct an Associated Press writer and photographer through his business, or to answer questions for a network television interviewer. And he's hot on the rebuying trail for some of his most memorable creations, since there's talk of a syndicated Arlen Ness Custom Show and of a museum. Modestly, he says: "I'm lucky. I can look at something and it will fall into place. Somehow, I can foresee good lines on a bike."

Those who customize XL's and those who customize FLT's really should communicate more. While their tastes differ, the amount of labor and degree of devotion to the machines are the same. A case in point is the well-dressed Dresser of Joseph and Alice Espada of Mount Vernon, New York. The Espadas, members of the International Northeastern Harley-Davidson Dresser and Touring Association, Inc., took their Electra Glide to Modern Cycle Works in their hometown; the results speak ornately for themselves. Here, courtesy of the builder, is a list of the adornments on what may be the ultimate attention getter:

1. Scrolled and chained front bumper, front fender, rear crash bars, bag guards, transmission cover, battery cover, oil tank cover, front crash bars, gas tank and hooded "peace" light.
2. Front fender with built-in running light.
3. Chained axle stars.
4. Custom turn signals built into fairing.
5. Air-scoop-mounted "six gun."
6. Air-cleaner-mounted "six gun."
7. Chrome engine, chrome Mikuni carburetors.
8. Chained floorboards with fore and aft air vents.
9. Passenger pegs replaced with illuminated, stained glass, scroll-paneled running boards.
10. Stock seat rail replaced with highback scrolled and chain "Bird of Paradise" rail.
11. Padded dashboard features built-in television set, quartz LED clock, cylinder head temperature gauge, battery-generator gauge, map light, cigarette lighter, accessory switches, indicator lights.
12. TourPak is lined with white mink fur.
13. Within the padded and chrome-plated TourPak is an electric clock, FM quad stereo with concealed antenna and eight-track cassette.
14. Padded saddlebags feature scroll and rhinestone trim and carry stereo quad speakers.
15. Custom light mount carries nine chained and hooded lights.
16. The custom rear pan is topped with a staggered-step rear bumper.
17. "Star-tipped" Hollywood mufflers.
18. Fairing, front and rear fenders painted royal blue metal flake with twenty-four coats of clear lacquer.
19. All else except tires and upholstery is chrome plated.

One look at the Espadas' cycle indicates that anything added to this chapter would be anti-climactic.

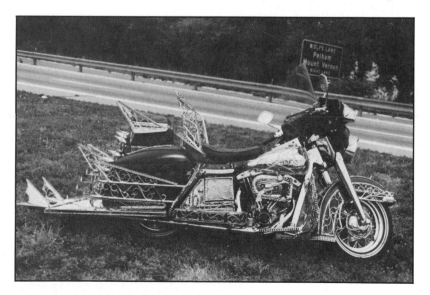

This six-gun encrusted Dresser was created for a Texan (who else?) by the Modern Cycle Works in Mount Vernon, New York. Several owners of such creations belong to the International Northeast H-D Dresser Association. *Joseph Espada*

A custom bike prepared by Hall's Harley-Davidson, Chico, California, for former drag racer and Bonneville runner Les Waterman. This machine began as a 1977 XLH Sportster. In addition to a completely high-performance motor, the creation has a handling package and is capable of turning in the high ten-seconds in the quarter miles. It's valued at $14,000! Fabrication and paint are by Ron Hall, one of the West Coast's top H-D customizers.

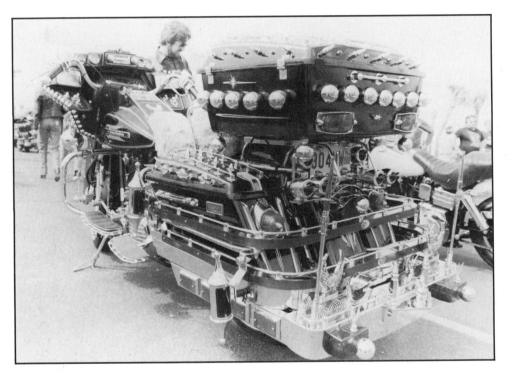

Ornately yours, from Daytona Beach. *David Wright*

Chapter 8

Racing

The late Charlie Thompson, president of Harley-Davidson, saw his first motorcycle race in 1966 at the Springfield, Illinois, mile. "Two kids got killed there and I thought, 'Jesus, if that happens at every race, this is the last one I'm going to attend.' Since then, I've been to hundreds of races and only seen one other death." Former football coach Thompson understood the analogy between racing and the Woody Hayes belief that, when you throw a forward pass, three things can happen and two are bad. In racing, that's also true. A rider can race and be maimed or killed, he can race and end up broke, or he can race and finish without a completely empty wallet or chronic aches, pains—or worse.

Since the early teens, when H-D began fielding racing bikes, not much has changed. The riders still flirt with dismemberment, they live from one meager payoff to the next, the majority never make it as expert riders—and they will be racing as long as there are wheeled vehicles. Among those vehicles will be Harley-Davidsons, so long as numerous dealers and key employees believe racing is of benefit to the company.

There are at least five kinds of motorcycle racing and, over the years, Harley-Davidson has played a prominent part in each of them. They include:

—Flat track. This is the familiar half-mile or mile horse track, where riders stay on the gas, off the brakes (if there are any) and pitch the bikes sideways to scrub off enough speed to make it around the two 180-degree bends. There has yet to be a national dirt-track event without a Harley-Davidson in the field, which gives an indication of the part the machines have played over the years

in U.S. racing. Virtually all of the approximately sixteen events on the current AMA/Camel Pro Series national circuit are flat tracks, so it's a foregone conclusion that the rider who carries off the No. 1 plate must be able to win on the dirt. This kind of competition evolved from dirt roads in the teens and banked tracks constructed of two-by-fours laid on their sides in the teens and twenties. Variations include the TT courses, which are ovals punctuated by one or more jumps and a couple of right turns; short track, usually quarter-mile tracks for smaller-displacement bikes; and an occasional banked track.

—Off-road racing. This can be anything from a neighborhood scrambles track to the run down the Baja Peninsula to the Jack Pine Enduro. Before bikes became excessively specialized, H-D's capable of legal operation on the highway proved their durability by slogging through swamps and being pounded across deserts. These forms of racing have spawned many of the top flat-track riders, such as former factory team man and ex-national champ Randy Goss.

—Road racing. This includes left turns, right turns, elevation changes, blind corners—in short, all the situations except oncoming traffic that a rider is likely to encounter on a twisting, two-lane blacktop. The amazing thing about road racing is the number of incredibly good riders this country has produced, considering that road racing has been less popular in America than either flat-track or off-road competition. Harley-Davidson provided the power for much of that glory through 1973, when the company ceased to be competitive against the multicylinder two-stroke bikes from Japan. At the moment, H-D road-racing laurels are upheld by the AMA's virtually stock 883 series for Sportsters and by several V-Twin Buells.

—Drag racing. Road riders were cracking the throttle open long before the California drag bikers took to the dry lakes shortly after World War II. Like most things motorcycling, Harley-Davidsons were popular mounts in the beginning and continue to star in quarter-mile showdowns. This is the last bastion of those who believe you should run what you brung; for every double-engine fueler, there are hundreds of box-stock H-D's at drag strips each weekend.

—Hillclimbs. Due to the popularity of other kinds of off-road events and alleged damage to the environment, this fascinating form of entertainment has decreased in popularity. U.S. hillclimbs are run off-road, whereas Europeans climb hills on paved roads. Both feature individual riders against the clock.

With an eye on the various uses of a racing

H-D's were ridden in races every-where, as this 1925 post card from Italy indicates. Exact date and location are unknown, but the gentlemen are named Orlandi and Gantarini.

Gordon (left) and William Davidson following two days on the Jack Pine trail in 1931. H-D-ridden machines captured ten consecutive Jack Pine contests. *William H. Davidson collection*

motorcycle, let's look at some of the mechanical stars of the shows through the years. If details are lacking, it's because H-D has not always been as willing as it is today to divulge specifications of what propelled its machines into the winner's circle. If your personal favorite is missing, see Chapter III. Many racing machines were little more than street models with the lights pried off.

Early Racers—The 8-Valve, The Two-Cam

Harley-Davidson's first model built exclusively for competition was the 61 cu. in. (999cc) eight-valve V-twin, created just prior to World War I for the group of racers that came to be known as the Wrecking Crew—Hepburn, Parkhurst, Davis, Weishaar and others. The first of the three-speed bikes was constructed in 1916 in three versions: one lubricated by hand, one with an oil pump and one that featured both a mechanical pump and a plunger. To prevent dilettantes from dabbling with their eight-valves, Harley-Davidson priced the machines at $1,500 apiece (compared to $350 for a new Indian racer). Unfortunately, verifiable specifications on these neat bikes no longer exist. That's true, too, of the two-cam racing models,

Who says you can't drag-race a Duo-Glide? Jeff Mowry, Patterson, New Jersey, took top stock eliminator honors at Atco Dragway in 1968 on this A/Stock Harley-Davidson. His elapsed time was 14.96 seconds, with a speed of 82.56 miles per hour. *National Hot Rod Association*

Joe Smith on his double-engine Harley-Davidson smokes off the line during a 1976 meet. Smith broke the nine-second quarter-mile barrier on this machine. *National Hot Rod Association*

which at 65 cu. in. had a top speed approaching 120 miles an hour. Both machines had wheelbases of about 50 in., 28 × 2½ in. tires, forty-spoke, soldered wheels, a magneto cutout switch on the handlebars that served as the only means of braking for a turn and direct drive. With their very high compression, the bikes frequently needed to be pushed by two or three men or pulled by an automobile in order to start.

JH, JDH "Two-Cam" 1928–1929

The two-cam was billed as "The Fastest Model Ever offered by Harley-Davidson," and it was indeed that. Independent cam action was provided for each valve by two big, broad-faced cams on the gears. The results were better timing, higher compressions and more rpm. The appearance was striking, too, since the tall engine protruded into the lower edge of the gas tank to accommodate the valve stems, valve springs and pushrods. The JDH 74 in. model, "particularly recommended by our engineers for greatest speed and maximum performance," was $370, fob Milwaukee. The JH 61 in. cost $360, certainly a strong temptation to spend $10 more.

Harley-Davidson enthusiasts at the time were quite familiar with the two-cam, since it had been winning races for several years prior to its public offering. On July 4, 1925, Joe Petrali became the first two-cam rider to exceed 100 mph in a broad-track race when he averaged 100.36 in winning at the Altoona, Pennsylvania, speedway. The machine, with its increased horsepower, retained a broad power band; hillclimbers, particularly in the East and Mideast, hauled home lots of silver, courtesy of the two-cam.

A 1920 61 cu. in. racing bike. The plunger in the middle of the separate gas and oil tanks was used periodically during high speeds to supplement the gravity-feed lubrication system. Early racers were direct drive; that is, there was no transmission. They were tough to push-start, they had no brakes and they could easily exceed 100 miles per hour. Note the American Bosch magneto, used on many H-D models well into the 1920s. *Harley-Davidson, Inc.*

Why, then, were these classic bikes offered for just two years? As attractive as the prices appear today, they were considered excessive in the late twenties. Americans were buying automobiles by the hundreds of thousands, but were unwilling to purchase more than 19,911 H-D's in the prosperous year of 1927. These were superbikes in the contemporary sense of the word; the racing-type adornments (special tank and handlebars, solo seat) were standard rather than optional. The 1930 VL models could at least be called new and inexpensive, even if they offered less power.

Specifications

(From a 1928 brochure. The following figures are for the road bikes, since specs on the racing bikes are much less complete.)

Motor—Two cam, twin-cylinder, V-type, air-cooled, four-stroke cycle. Fitted with Dow metal pistons. 74 cu. in. model—bore 3$\frac{7}{16}$ inches, stroke 4 inches, piston displacement 74 cubic inches. 61 cu. in. model—bore 3$\frac{5}{16}$ inches, stroke 3$\frac{1}{2}$ inches, piston displacement 60.34 cubic inches.

Carburetor—Schebler DeLuxe with air cleaner.

Transmission—Harley-Davidson three-speed progressive sliding gear with positive gear shifter locking device.

Lubrication—Harley-Davidson throttle controlled motor oiler provides proper lubrication at all motor speeds. Transmission lubricated separately. Twenty Alemite fittings.

Ignition—Harley-Davidson generator-battery.

Electric equipment—Harley-Davidson generator, weather and waterproof coil, timer, 22 ampere hour storage battery, motor driven horn, two-bulb headlight, standard tail light, switch panel. Relay cutout in generator-battery circuit.

Starter—Harley-Davidson rear stroke on right side.

Clutch—Harley-Davidson multiple dry disc, foot operated.

Handlebars—Roadster type, one piece, one inch tubular, double stem with closed end grips. Regular style handlebars optional.

Frame—Strongly reinforced heavy gauge high carbon, seamless tubular steel with wide trussed loop. Drop forged steel head.

Controls—Grip, double-acting wire controls enclosed in handlebars and cables. Toe operated compression relief.

Brakes—Harley-Davidson foot controlled contracting rear brake and built-in hand controlled expanding front wheel brake.

Driving chains—Roller, $\frac{5}{8}$ in. pitch and $\frac{3}{8}$ in. width.

Saddle—Large, roomy form-fitting Mesinger. Harley-Davidson adjustable spring seat post.

Tires—Full balloon, 25 × 3.85 inches. Standard 27 × 3.85 inch size optional.

Wheelbase—60 inches.

Tanks—Narrow saddle type. Gasoline capacity 2$\frac{1}{2}$ gallons. Reserve gasoline tank, 1$\frac{1}{4}$ gallons. Lubricating oil tank, 1 gallon. Wide, standard capacity tank optional.

Footboards—Harley-Davidson folding.

Tool equipment—Complete tool and tire repair kit.

Finish—Harley-Davidson Olive Green with maroon stripe with gold center and edged in black.

WR, WR-TT 1940–1951

As ungainly as they look today, the rigid-tail WR's gave a good account of themselves in the

A 1928 JDH "two-cam." *Harley-Davidson, Inc.*

controversial years when the AMA allowed 750cc capacity for side valve machines, but just 500cc for overhead valve (i.e., foreign) bikes. The WR was characterized by a low compression ratio, another criterion used by the Harley-Davidson-dominated sanctioning body to keep the English vertical twins out of the winner's circle. The WR put out about 40 horsepower; modest by modern standards but, when combined with the sheer numbers of Harleys on the track, quite enough. Hot shoes such as Paul Goldsmith and Jimmy Chann gave the WR a good ride while youngsters such as Joe Leonard and Everett Brashear cut their racing teeth on bikes like these. The WR's also

A twin-cam hillclimber from about 1925. The motor featured an overhead inlet valve and a side exhaust valve on each cylinder. *Harley-Davidson, Inc.*

The 1928 21 cu. in. overhead valve Peashooter, ridden successfully in professional races by Joe Petrali and others. *Harley-Davidson, Inc.*

were the overwhelming favorite of TT riders, who found that the frames were as reliable as the motors.

Specifications
(From a 1951 brochure)

Engine: 45 cu. in. side valve; bore, 2³/₄ in.; stroke, 3¹³/₁₆ in.; Dow metal or aluminum pistons. Wico vertical magneto, mounted on side of engine; or Wico horizontal magneto, mounted in front.

Frame: Special light frame, chrome molybdenum tubing (WR); Standard WL (WR-TT).

Tanks: Narrow, rubber mounted. Capacity, 1³/₄ gallons of gasoline and 1³/₄ gallons of oil (WR); large, rubber mounted tanks for long distance racing. Each side holds 2¹/₂ gallons of gasoline, can only be used with aluminum oil tank, part No. R 3501-41. Narrow rubber mounted tanks; hold 1³/₄ gallons of gasoline and 1³/₄ gallons of oil (tank choice on WR-TT).

Handlebar: Speedster bars, solid or rubber mounted.

This one-of-a-kind 45 cu. in. overhead valve twin was exported in 1930 for racing in Europe. It featured two exhaust pipes per cylinder (note exhaust on opposite side of machine, positioned to allow kick starting), front and rear drum brakes and a three-speed transmission. Such an extravagance was probably cut short by the Depression. *Harley-Davidson, Inc.*

A 1950 WR model, the standard 45 cu. in. racer. *Harley-Davidson, Inc.*

Wheels: Special ball bearing hubs, no brake, 18 in. or 19 in. rim optional, Firestone tires, 4.00 × 18 or 3.25 × 19 (WR). Standard WL with brakes; 18 in. or 19 in. rims optional, Firestone tires, 4.00 × 18 or 3.25 × 19.

Transmission: 3/8-in. pitch clutch sprocket, standard or close ratio gears (WR). 3/8-in. or 1/2-in. pitch clutch sprocket, standard or close ratio gears; 1/2-in. pitch recommended for long distance racing only (WR-TT).

Front mudguard: Not supplied on track models (WR). Special front mudguard (WR-TT).

Rear mudguard: Special WR, special WR-TT.

Footpegs: Footpegs and Servi-Car-type clutch (WR). Footboards and side bars, standard WL (WR-TT).

Saddle: Special, no seat bar or seat post (WR). Special WR with standard WL seat bar and post (WR-TT).

Front chain guard: 1940 type outer, standard WL inner.

Tank pad: Furnished with large tanks only (WR-TT).

Gear ratio: 3/8-in. pitch front chain; 22, engine; 59, clutch; 17, countershaft; 39, rear wheel equals 6.15 to 1 (WR). 3/8-in. pitch front chain; 30, engine; 59, clutch; 17, countershaft; 41, rear wheel, equals 4.74 to 1 (WR-TT). 36, 37 and 38 tooth rear wheel sprockets furnished with WR. Other sprockets available as follows: 17 to 33 tooth 3/8-in. pitch engine sprockets and 15 and 16 tooth countershaft sprockets (WR). 1/2-in. pitch front chain; 24, engine; 45, clutch; 17, countershaft; 41, rear wheel, equals 4.52 to 1 (WR-TT). Other sprockets for WR-TT available as follows: 17 to 33 tooth 3/8-in. pitch engine sprockets; 14 to 25 tooth 1/2-in. pitch engine sprockets; 15 and 16 tooth countershaft sprockets; 42 tooth rear wheel sprocket and brake shell assembly.

Colors: Brilliant black, ruby red and riviera blue at no extra cost. Available at extra cost: metallic green, flight red, azure blue, white.

KR, KR-TT 1952–1969

The KR is the bike all the experts tried, year after year, to bury. And year after year, riders such as Carroll Resweber, Bart Markel, Mert Lawwill and others continued to win on the supposedly outmoded side valve machine. The specs indicate that the KR's were 750cc machines. That wasn't the case. As delivered to the customer ($1,320 for the dirt-tracker, $1,425 for the road-racer, in 1966), the motor measured 744cc. Following 200 miles of break-in, however, the cylinder barrels distorted and had to be rebored. The AMA permitted racers to be 0.045 in. oversize, so the eventual size of the engine was 767cc.

The AMA also was responsible for the demise of the bike, since it ruled in 1969 that European bikes no longer had either a compression or a displacement limitation. Prior to 1970, the KR 750 side valve competed against the 500cc overhead valve Triumph, BSA, Matchless and Norton, as had its predecessor, the WR. In addition to producing almost twice as many horses per cube, the English bikes handled infinitely better, particularly on TT and road courses.

A 1952 K model racer. *Harley-Davidson, Inc.*

The differences between Harley-Davidson's TT-designated road racer and the flat-track bike were few but significant: The road racer ran inert gas shocks as opposed to a solid rear end, it showed up with a six-gallon gas tank and its pavement wheels and tires were daintier than the broadsliding KR. Top speed of the bike at its peak exceeded 150 miles an hour, as clocked on the high banks of Daytona International Speedway. That held up until about 1967, when the British bikes ran with and then away from the H-D team on the straights. The English riders had an even greater advantage on the several tight road courses—Laconia, Marlboro (Maryland), Nelson Ledges (Ohio)—where Nationals were held. No one ever merely flicked a KR-TT from side to side in an S-turn. The large, heavy machine was a chore to ride. After breaking-in on KR's, Cal Rayborn was able to handle the new XR with ease. Still, this bike won national championships for the factory for twelve of its seventeen years. Not bad for an "obsolete" machine.

Specifications

Motor: 744cc side-valve V-twin, bore 2.747 in., stroke 3.8125 in., compression ratio 9:1, horsepower 48 at 7,000 rpm. Torque, 50 lbs./ft. at 5,000 rpm. Linkert carburetor with 1.312 in. bore.

Frame: Chrome moly seamless steel tubing, 1 in. outside diameter, .062 in. wall. Duplex cradle.

Wheelbase: 56 in.

Suspension: Telescopic front forks; inert gas shock absorbers (KR-TT only).

Ignition: Fairbanks-Morse magneto.

Brakes: 8 in. × 1½ in., front and rear, 50.3 sq. in. braking surface (no brakes on KR).

Weight: 385 lbs. (KR-TT) 377 lbs. (KR)

XR750 1970–

A leading cycle magazine has called the XR750 the most successful dirt-track racer of the decade. As time passes, that becomes an understatement. Nineteen eighty-seven marked the eighteenth year that riders, independent as well as factory-sponsored, have chosen the very narrow bike with the destroked 880cc Sportster engine for battle on the Grand National tracks.

Introduced in 1970 with iron barrels, the XR suffered through that season and the next before aluminum cylinders and cylinder heads were perfected and installed. Since then, except for a brief period when Yamaha proved that there could be a bike created that was too dangerous to race, the XR750 has been the overdog on everything but pavement. In the hands of Cal Rayborn, the machine even chalked up significant road racing victories, notably at Daytona and London, before being edged out by the peaky, Oriental, water-cooled two-strokes. The similarities and differences between the iron-barreled and aluminum-barreled machines deserve closer scrutiny.

The most obvious difference, from a distance,

The KR in road racing trim, 1966. *Harley-Davidson, Inc.*

concerns the exhausts. The earlier model featured a pair of straight pipes painted silver that exited right. The new model sports flat-black megaphones carried high on the left side of the machine to avoid contact with the dirt on mile, half-mile and TT tracks.

Both bikes are equipped with Ceriani forks and Girling racing shocks, proof that this selection was correct from the start. The suspension is hooked to identical frames of welded, tubular 4130 steel. (The first 100 XR frames, incidentally, were furnished by an outside supplier from St. Louis.) Both display aluminum rims and spoked wheels. The earlier model was delivered with a Pirelli tread on the front wheel and a Goodyear on the back. Recent thinking favored Goodyear on both ends.

Internally, valves, pistons and cams are polished and valve stems are chrome plated on both machines. The later version carries an enlarged flywheel, probably because the motor turns out approximately 90 horsepower, versus 70 for the iron-heads.

Pieter Zylstra, product designer for the racing department, notes that another major difference is the compression ratios. "We had to run very low compression—about 8 to 1—for the [iron-head] engine to stay together. The motor had a shorter

stroke and larger valves than the aluminum motor. It was fast but not reliable." Compression for the aluminum engine is 10.5 to 1.

What's riding an XR 750 like? The first clue after straddling the machine is provided by the bike's size—or rather its lack of size. The XR750 is by far the smallest Harley-Davidson currently in production. The second hint is the utter lack of any sort of starting mechanism. Run-and-bump starting is the order of the day. As soon as the engine thumps to life, the rider realizes his right hand is much more lethal than usual. That's because the throttle goes from nothing to everything with only one-quarter turn. There's a rear disc brake, but engine compression is more frequently used to scrub off speed on the way toward a corner. The power band is as wide as any bike in existence; the XR pulls strongly from 2000 rpm on up. Since it produces 90 horsepower, you'll have to ask a racer what it's like flat out.

Specifications

Engine type: OHV V-twin.
Carburetion: Dual 36mm Mikuni carburetors.
Exhaust system: Tuned dual exhausts with reverse-cone megaphones.
Bore and stroke, inches: 3.125 × 2.983.
Displacement: 45 cu. in. (750cc).
Clutch type: Multi-plate, dry.

The XR750, dominant on dirt for more than a decade. *Harley-Davidson, Inc.*

Primary drive: 25-tooth motor sprocket, 59-tooth clutch, triple row roller chain.

Rear drive: 16-tooth transmission sprocket, 40-tooth rear wheel sprocket.

Drive ratio, overall: 5.90:1.

Transmission: Constant mesh, four-speed.

Transmission ratio: 1st, 2.091:1; 2nd, 1.51; 3rd, 1.14; 4th, 1.00.

Weight: 290 lbs.

Tire size, front and rear: 4.00 × 19.

Gas capacity, gallons: 2½.

Oil capacity, quarts: 3.

Electrical equipment: Fairbanks-Morse magneto.

Color: Jet Fire Orange.

Aermacchi/Harley-Davidson RR-250, RR-350 1971–1976

The Aermacchi/Harley-Davidson RR-250 and RR-350, in the hands of Walter Villa, proved to be world beaters. Like most front-running Italian bikes, they featured bits and pieces from all over—Dunlop tires and Girling forks from England, Mikuni carburetors from Japan and Ceriani forks, Borrani rims and Dansi ignition from around the block. The bikes' only drawback, in air- or water-cooled configuration, proved to be the brakes. Initially, the drums were very good, but drums nevertheless, at a time when discs were seen on most competing 250's. Like many things associated with Italian machinery, there was a reason for the drums: The maker paid A/H-D to use them.

Villa overcame early braking points to win three 250 world championships, in 1974, 1975 and 1976, on board the machine. The following year, he snagged the 350 world title. All that is quite a feat for a company that built its first-ever two-cycle engine in 1967. The bike enjoyed some success stateside, too, ridden by Cal Rayborn, Gary Scott and others. But U.S. racers and fans showed a preference for bigger-bore equipment, despite 58 horsepower at 12,000 rpm for the 250 and 70 horses at 11,400 for the 350. Since these bikes were all constructed by hand, specs differed from one machine to the next. The switch to disc brakes up front took place prior to the 1976 season.

Specifications (250cc dated 1972)

Engine type: Two-cycle, liquid cooled twin.

Bore: 2.213 in.

Stroke: 1.968 in.

Displacement: 15 cu. in. (248.06 cc.).

Compression ratio: 11.33:1.

Clutch type: Multi plate, dry.

Primary drive: Helical gear, 2.438:1.

Final drive: Chain.

Transmission gear: 16 teeth.

Rear wheel gear: 46 teeth.

Drive ratio: 6.427:1.

The mighty XR750, as displayed at York. *David Wright*

Transmission: Six-speed, constant mesh.
Transmission ratio: 1st, 2.00:1; 2nd, 1.527; 3rd, 1.286; 4th, 1.087; 5th, 0.958; 6th, 0.917.
Front suspension: Ceriani forks.
Rear suspension: Girling 3-position shock absorbers.
Front brake: Twin double leading shoe.
Rear brake: Double leading shoe.
Carburetor: Twin 34 mm Mikuni.
Tire size, front: 3.00/18 in. Dunlop.
Tire size, rear: 3.00/3.25/18 in. Dunlop.
Dry weight: 230 lbs.
Fuel capacity: Six gallons (pre-mix).
Oil capacity: Two quarts.
Ignition: Dansi or CDI.

Color: Jet fire orange and black w/ white number plaques.

Aermacchi/Harley-Davidson MX-250 1977–1978

The Aermacchi/Harley-Davidson, manufactured in 1977 and 1978, remains a potent motocross or dirt-track machine in the hands of a good rider. Jay Springsteen showed how good he and a bike with an MX-based motor were in 1982 when he won the short-track event to kick off the season's AMA/Winston Pro Series in the Houston Astrodome. It should be remembered that, for

Aermacchi/H-D produced a potent motocrosser, the MX-250. Rex Staten rode for the factory team in 1977. *Harley-Davidson, Inc.*

Jay Springsteen was a capable road racer. He finished sixth on this out-gunned Aermacchi/H-D in the 1978 250cc Daytona 100-miler. *Harley-Davidson, Inc.*

170

every MX bike raced, there were dozens of the four-stroke Sprints on short tracks and in scrambles, proving once again how prone street-stock H-D's—even foreign models—were to racing.

Specifications MX-250, MX-250 Dirt Tracker
Overall length: 83.6 in. (212.5 cm).
Handlebar width: 34.2 in. (87 cm.).
Ground clearance: 12 in. (30.5 cm).
Wheelbase: 57.3 in. (145.5 cm).
Dry weight: 233 lbs. (105 Kg).
Steering angle: 45 degrees.
Rake: 30 degrees.
Trail: 5.5 in. (140 mm).

Front suspension: Telescopic oil dampened, 8.9 in. (225 mm) travel.
Rear suspension: Swinging arm, coil spring, oil dampened.
Front wheel tire: 3.00 × 21 in.
Rear wheel tire: 4.50 × 18 in.
Front brake: Internal expanding, single leading shoe type, inside diameter 140 mm.
Rear brake: Internal expanding, single leading shoe type, inside diameter 140 mm.
Rims: Akront, shoulderless light alloy.
Spokes: 36 per wheel, 4 mm diameter.
Transmission: 2⅛ pints (1,000cc). Fuel tank: 2.2 gals. (8.5 liters).
Front forks: 7 oz. (wet) each side (210cc).
Model designation: MX.

Team H-D motocross rider Don Kudalski. *Harley-Davidson, Inc.*

Jay Springsteen ate up the competition, winning the 1983 Daytona Battle of the Twins race with top speeds of 167 mph. *Harley-Davidson, Inc.*

171

Type: Two cycle, single cylinder.
Bore: 2.835 in. (72 mm).
Stroke: 2.346 in. (59.6 mm).
Displacement: 14.81 in. (242.6cc).
Compression ratio: 11.8 to 1.
Lubrication system: Fuel and oil mixture, 20:1.

Starter system: Primary kick starter.
Type: Capacitor discharge Dansi or CDI Motoplat.
Ignition timing: .080 in. (18 degrees, 2 mm) before TDC.
Trigger air gap: (Dansi) .012-.016 in. (.30-.40 mm).
Spark plug: Champion N59G.

Oscar Lenz, seen here at a New Jersey endurance run, won the Jack Pine event six times and tied a seventh between 1923 and 1936. **Harley-Davidson, Inc.**

The original Harley-Davidson Wrecking Crew, a group of racers who over-whelmed the competition in the late teens. *Harley-Davidson, Inc.*

172

Plug gap: .020 in. (.5 mm).
Dell'Orto carburetor (not included) type: PHB E 38.
Venturi diameter: 1.496 in. (38 mm).
Main jet: 170.
Low speed jet: 70.
Mikuni carburetor (not included) type: Vm-38.
Venturi diameter: 1.496 in. (38 mm).
Main jet: 320.
Needle (middle position): 6CF1.
Needle jet: Q0.
Slide: 2.0.
Needle valve: 3.3.
Air jet: 1.0.
Pilot jet: No. 45.
Clutch: Wet, multi plate.
Primary drive pinion gear: 22 teeth.
Primary drive clutch gear: 60 teeth.
Primary ratio: 2.73.
Gear ratios: 1st, 14/27; 2nd, 18/28; 3rd, 21/26; 4th, 21/21; 5th, 23/19.
Gearshift pattern: One down, four up.
Transmission sprocket: 13-, 14-, 15-, 16-tooth supplied.

Chain type: ⅝ × ⅜ in.
Fuel-oil recommendation: SAE 30 viscosity racing oil, mixed one part oil to twenty parts high-octane, leaded gasoline.

XR1000 1983–1984

Whenever enthusiasts believe they've seen all the tricks in the Juneau Avenue bag, along comes a machine such as the XR1000. This XR750-inspired, XL-based street bike and AMA Battle of the Twins road racer was developed in just sixty days in the fall of 1982, allowing H-D to meet AMA rules by producing 200 such bikes in time for the 1983 racing season.

The $6,800 bike boasts 70.6 horsepower at 5,600 rpm (versus 56 on a stock XL). Peak torque is 71.4 ft.-lb. (versus 58 for the XL). And with high-performance kit parts from the factory, 90 horses becomes a reality. Power emanates from XR

East Coast speedway star Goldy Restall on the cinder-track CAC model. Just ten of these machines were made, in late 1933 and early 1934, for combat with highly specialized English bikes, according to company records. *Harley-Davidson, Inc.*

Another view of the 1934 CAC model. *Harley-Davidson, Inc.*

Petrali leads Indian-mounted Lou Balinski during the 1935 three-mile national at Reading, Pennsylvania. This was one of Petrali's 13 consecutive victories. *Harley-Davidson, Inc.*

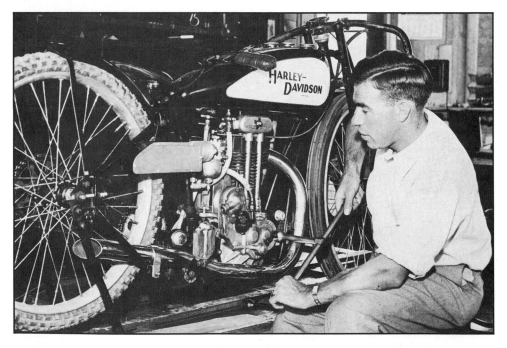

Joe Petrali readies his motor at the factory for the Milwaukee races in 1936. Taped iron bar protruding from in front of seat served as a thigh brace for riders on the rough dirt tracks. *Harley-Davidson, Inc.*

aluminum heads and rocker boxes, high-compression (9:1) aluminum XR pistons, Branch Flowmetrics heads, a redesigned combustion chamber and port area, plus dual Dell'Orto slide carburetors and XR-style megaphone exhausts.

The frame is 100 percent XL, though a number of performance adornments have been added. Dunlop K291 Sport Elite tires, dual front 11½ in. disc brakes up front, an 11½ in. rear disc, flat-track bars and 2.5-gallon fuel tank add up to a dry weight of just 480 pounds. Performance options include higher compression ratio pistons, special cams and special exhausts.

Dick O'Brien, former racing director, oversaw the quick, quality work. The bike in the hands of Jay Springsteen handily won the Battle of the Twins contest at Daytona in March 1983.

Specifications
Wheelbase: 60.0 in.
Seat height: 29.0 in.
Tire size, front: MM90V-19* (100/90V-1)
Rake: 29.7 degrees
Overall length: 87.7 in.
Ground clearance: 6.8 in.
Tire size, rear: MT90V-16* (130/90V-1)
Trail: 4.5 in.
Engine type: OHV V-Twin
Bore & Stroke: 3.189 × 3.812 in.
Oil capacity: 2.5 qt.
Carburetion: Dual 36mm slide Dell'Orto
Ignition: V-Fire III electronic breakerless
Clutch: Multiplate oil bath
Primary drive: Triple chain
Gear ratios, overall: 1st, 10.02; 2nd, 7.25; 3rd, 5.49; 4th, 3.97
Brake, front diameter × width (x2): 11.5 × .20 in.
Front brake swept area: 99.5 in.

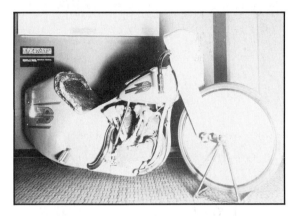

Joe Petrali's 1936 Knucklehead record breaker, as displayed in the Rodney C. Gott Museum, York. The "fairing" was constructed from a gasoline tank. The machine is painted an unusual color —light blue. *David Wright*

"Windy" Lindstrom, a top thirties hill-climber. *Harley-Davidson, Inc.*

Braking distance @ 60 mph: 145 ft.
Suspension travel, front: 6.9 in.; rear: 3.25 in.
Dry weight: 480 lbs.
Wheels: 9-spoke cast aluminum
Headlamp: Quartz Halogen, 50-watt high beam
Color options: Slate gray/silver striping
Electrical system: 12-volt battery, 19-amp-hour, generator-13 amp, coil, regulator, headlight, tail light, turn signals, stoplight, horn; entire system meets or exceeds all state and federal regulations for lighting, electric start.
Displacement: 1000cc/61 CID
Compression ratio: 9.0:1

Fuel capacity: 2.25 gals., reserve: .25 gals.
Exhaust system: Left-side, high megaphone dual
Cam: Q cam
Transmission: 4-speed, constant mesh
Final drive: Single chain
Primary drive ratio: 1.74
Final drive ratio: 2.29
Torque: 71.4 ft/lbs @ 5600 rpm
Brake, rear diameter × width: 11.5 × .23 in.
Total brake swept area: 198.5 sq. in.
Lean angles (SAE J1168)
Right: 37 degrees
Left: 36 degrees

Petrali goes up . . . and over the Hornell, New York, hill during a 1938 climb. He's on a 45 cu. in. twin. *William H. Davidson collection*

Herb Reiber, center, considered by many to have been underrated, powers around the Langhorne, Pennsylvania, track in a 1939 Class C race. Reiber also was a skilled hillclimber and TT rider. *Harley-Davidson, Inc.*

Optional equipment: 18 inches mag rear wheel; 3.3-gal. gas tank
GVWR: 900 lbs.

What kinds of people race motorcycles? Few have ever gone racing for the money; it simply isn't there. Fewer still have any conscious desire for fame or glory, though fame and glory are the assets and can be the liabilities of winning. Not one racer in anyone's memory ever thought he would end up in the ambulance, so death wishes can be ruled out. What's left is the rush riders receive from competition, from playing a game made fast far beyond human power by means of an internal combustion motor. The first group of riders to race Harley-Davidsons with major success was The Wrecking Crew. That included, at various times, factory riders Eddie Brinck, Jim Davis, Walter Higley, Ralph Hepburn, Irving Jahnke, Maldwyn Jones, Fred Ludlow, "Red" Parkhurst,

Arthur "Babe" Tancrede, a successful Class C competitor, poses prior to a 1940 race in Richmond, Virginia. *Harley-Davidson, Inc.*

Jack Piners ford a stream in 1946. *Harley-Davidson, Inc.*

Otto Walker and Ray Weishaar. Created following a poor showing by Harley-Davidson in the 1914 Dodge City, Kansas, road race, The Wrecking Crew all but owned the dusty road courses until 1921, when H-D opted out of racing for economic reasons.

Far from being motorcycle bums, these riders frequently possessed an advanced degree of mechanical knowledge and held full-time jobs off the track. Typical was Eddie Brinck, the Dayton, Ohio, native who raced for fifteen years while a foreman with the U.S. government motor testing department at McCook Aviation Field. Brinck applied what he learned on the job (internal combustion engines were still relatively new) to his cycles. In addition to scoring significant victories here, he took the single-cylinder H-D Peashooter to Australia in 1926 and recorded several wins. A family man, he died August 13, 1927, when a tire blew in

the first lap of a Springfield, Massachusetts, event.

Brinck was one of numerous brilliant riders discovered by Bill Ottoway, an engineer recruited from the Thor motorcycle company by Harley-Davidson in 1913. Ottoway was a capable engineer, a shrewd assessor of talent and, according to contemporaries, as trusting as he was honest. On one occasion, when Gene Walker's Indian ran suspiciously fast to sweep a series of events, Ottoway was asked by race officials if he wanted the competing motor torn down. "If Indian says the motor is OK, it's OK," he replied. One indication of H-D's stability is that just three men—Ottoway, Hank Syvertson and Dick O'Brien—have run the racing department in the company's seventy years of competition.

Ottoway watched a number of his riders come and go, including Otto Walker and Ralph Hepburn. Both Wrecking Crew members, the pair ran

National champ Jimmy Chann, seen here at Springfield in 1952. *Harley-Davidson, Inc.*

Joe Leonard is greeted by his wife after a dirt-track win. *Harley-Davidson, Inc.*

board and horse tracks as factory riders and as independents. Walker capped a stunning career in 1921 by winning a fifty-mile race at the San Joaquin, California, speedway in 29 minutes, 34.6 seconds (101.43 mph) and posting one lap in excess of 109. All this was accomplished on a 61 cu. in. machine. In contrast to Walker, who retired to the safety of a charter fishing boat, Hepburn competed until 1948 when, at the age of fifty-one, he died at the wheel of the infamous Novi racer at the Indianapolis Motor Speedway.

Sadly, death was common in the early years, as riders donned cloth caps at worst and gauze-and-airplane dope helmets at best for 100-plus-mile-an-hour competition. Besides Brinck, racing has claimed H-D riders Walter Stoddard, Tommy Hayes, Billy Huber, Dick Ince, Cal Rayborn, Renzo Pasolini and most recently, Willie Crabbe, among many others. Automobiles, through the years, have also taken a toll, off the track (Fred Nix) and on (Hepburn and David "Swede" Savage). Joe Leonard, first of the modern national champs, was disabled after a successful career on four wheels. Still, racing seems almost natural.

H-D recorded victories all over the world in the twenties, in the hands of U.S. and foreign riders alike. In England, D. H. Davidson (not related to the company) exceeded 100 miles an hour as early as 1920 in a speed run, and Fred Dixon won numerous solo and sidecar races. Grass tracks were popular in Australia and New Zealand, and Harley-Davidson scored well there. Yet another surface, ice, was favored in Scandinavia by little-known but highly talented Erik Westerberg. He averaged an incredible 87.561 miles an hour in winning a 1923 ice race aboard his eight-valve machine. And in 1930, Olle Virgin captured a dirt-track series run in Sweden and Denmark by posting average speeds as high as 111.78 miles an hour on an overhead valve 45 cu. in. machine. Clearly, the world's largest manufacturer was well-represented on the world's starting lines.

While Harley-Davidsons were winning speed contests, they were faring equally well in various endurance runs. Less than a decade after Walter Davidson's Long Island endurance win, Alan Bedel ran 1,000 miles nonstop at Ascot Park. He averaged 48.3 mph for nearly twenty-one hours, a

San Diego's Brad Andres, national champion in 1955. *Harley-Davidson, Inc.*

Scott Parker. *Harley-Davidson, Inc.*

creditable speed for 1917. History failed to record the kind of H-D beneath Bedell, but notes that he also set a twenty-four-hour mark (48.1 mph), a 500-mile world record (50.1 mph) and a record for 12 hours (49.5 mph). Almost simultaneously, C. F. Bruschi and Walter House set a 1,000-mile record for sidecars, pushing their H-D to an average speed of 48.42 mph in less than twenty-

As U.S. roads improved, riders began to challenge each other from one point to another. Walter Hadfield repeatedly lowered the elapsed time from Vancouver to Tiajuana in what became known as the Three Flags Run. Hap Sherer, aboard a Sport Twin, rode from Denver to Chicago in 1920 in about 48 hours (averaging 26.4 mph). And while racer Otto Walker was posting flying-mile world records at 112-plus mph, Canadian H-D distributor Fred Deeley and friends were setting a world economy record; they rode from Vancouver to Tiajuana in 1926 averaging 104.67 miles per gallon of fuel and 1,234.7 per gallon of oil. But the king and queen of the endurance riders were Earl and Dot Robinson.

The Michigan Harley-Davidson dealer twice lowered the time and upped the speed needed to run between Los Angeles and New York. Earl toured the 3,000 or so miles solo in 77 hrs. 53 min. in 1935, then teamed with Dot to cover the same wide-open space in a sidecar in 86 hrs. 55 min.

Following World War II, time trials and drag racing became popular, with Bonneville producing records year after year. Privateers who did well in Utah included Jack Dale, who in 1951 ran 123.52 mph on a 45 cu. in. side-valve H-D; and Jack Heller, who took a 55 cu. in. Sportster to a speed of 134.881 mph on the salt in 1958. And by 1971, several drag racers on single-engine H-D's had broken the nine-second barrier for the quarter mile.

No one aboard a Harley-Davidson attracted more attention during the period 1925–50 than Windy Lindstrom. The Californian won more than 300 hillclimbs at a time when climbs attracted large crowds at the foot of virtually any hill worthy of the name. While less successful "slant artists" played games with elongated frames, Lindstrom stuck with standard 45 or 74 cu. in. H-D

Chris Carr.

Kevin Atherton.

hillclimbers with special gearing, a rear-wheel chain and a kill button. He attributed his success to using the same throttle opening all the way up the hill, tapping the kill button for a split second whenever the front end of his machine threatened to head where it came from.

Movietone newsreels showed Lindstrom and others astride their bucking bikes, a strip of leather running from the right wrist to the spark plug contact points in the electrical circuit. Lindstrom rarely departed his bike anywhere but at the end of his run; but when he did, the leather strip was yanked from between the points, grounding out the motor. Such a precaution prevented a riderless bike from veering into the crowd that lined the hill.

There were good riders aplenty in the thirties, though the economy and lack of national news coverage might have indicated otherwise. East Coast honors were upheld by Arthur "Babe" Tancrede and Ben Campanele, who were superb on road courses such as Laconia and Daytona Beach, and Goldie Restall, who did battle on cinder-track speedways. Out West, Lindstrom, Sam Arena, "Sprouts" Elder, Jack Cottrell, Joe Herb and Milton Iverson starred in hillclimbs, TT's and flat tracks, with Arena winning from 1934 until after 1950 in one of the most versatile careers of all time. Midwesterners Herb Reiber and Paul Goldsmith were joined after World War II by Roger Soderstrom and Leo Anthony, while down south such names as June McCall, Herman Dahlke and Buck Brigance were to be reckoned with. These and others seldom made the sports section but were seen regularly in faithful racing coverage by *The Enthusiast.*

Not even H-D's owner magazine covered the so-called outlaw races in the thirties, though H-D

Start of the annual Daytona 200-mile race on the beach. The date is believed to be 1958. *Harley-Davidson, Inc.*

frequently was the most common machine on the track. Bob Holder, now retired and living in Lincoln, California, reports that "you could ride whatever you wanted at outlaw tracks, so long as the size of the engine was legal—45 cu. in. for side valves and 30.5 cu. in. for overhead valves. . . . We used to take a 1929 Harley 61 cu. in. bike and remove one cylinder and rebalance the rest. We had a 30.5 cu. in. bike with one overhead valve. I was riding one of these at Santa Ana one Sunday and just before I crossed the finish line the crankpin broke, causing parts of the engine to fly

Gene Church. *Harley-Davidson, Inc.*

Bart Markel. *Harley-Davidson, Inc.*

Carroll Resweber holds trophies at the Santa Fe (Illinois) short-track meet in 1961. In the middle is Bart Markel, on the right is Joe Leonard. The trio won a total of ten national championships. *Harley-Davidson, Inc.*

up between my legs. When I got the checkered flag, I didn't have an engine in the frame."

Things were more organized, and not much more expensive, under AMA sanction. Ed Rusk, who competed throughout the South in the forties and fifties, was a good rider and a meticu-

Leo Payne ran a 9.71-second quarter mile, turning 152.38 miles an hour in 1967 at Connecticut Dragway. *Brian King*

Drag Racer Ron Fringer poses with wife, children, trophy girl, trophy and Top Gas Eliminator H-D. Fringer, seen at Beech Bend (Kentucky) International Raceway, had just posted a 10.09-second time and a 133.72-mile-an-hour speed during a 1971 meet. The Woodstock, Illinois, racer was one of numerous Midwesterners who did especially well in the sixties and early seventies using Sportster motors. *National Hot Rod Association*

lous record keeper. In 1947, for example, he ran twenty-seven TT and flat-track races from Jacksonville to as far north as Peoria. He picked up six trophies and more than $2,100 in prize money, paying out $335 for expenses and just $260 for repairs to his 45 and 80 cu. in. motors. After doling out $12(!) to a Columbus, Georgia, hospital following a spill, he still had enough cash for a new motor ($600) at season's end. Purses have been stagnant since then, but expenses have taken a quantum leap, with $120 tires and $1.50-a-gallon gasoline the rule rather than the exception. Small wonder that flat-track riders live from paycheck to paycheck to (meager) payoff.

The invasion of the U.S. by English machines following World War II meant more registrations. As registrations increased, so did the number of top-flight racers, many of whom were able to give H-D some competition at last. And although Indian was on its last legs, ageless Ed Kretz and Bobby Hill won just often enough to make things interesting. Throughout the fifties and sixties, Triumphs and BSA's tormented Milwaukee bikes on dirt and pavement, all but going broke in the process. Meanwhile, hundreds of talented riders who would never see a No. 1 plate were competing regionally and nationally on Harley-Davidsons. They included Paul Albrecht, Rex Beauchamp, Ernie Beckman, Everett Brashear, Scott Brelsford, Duane Buchanan, Charles Carey, Babe DeMay,

Darrel Dovel, Chet Dykgraaf, Harry Fearey, Walt Fulton, John Gibson, Dick Hammer, Bill Huber, Corky Keener, Troy Lee, Bill Miller, Tony Murguia, Ronnie Rall, Roger Reiman, George Roeder, Greg Sassaman, Larry Schafer, Dave Sehl, Bob Tindall, Joe Weatherly, Ralph White and many, many other riders.

Drag racing and motocross gained popularity as hillclimbs and the inclination to try for a land speed record at Bonneville declined. The Utah site saw H-D's run with great frequency, from Jack Dale's Class C record of 123.52 miles an hour on a 45 cu. in. side valve in 1951 through Les Waterman's 164.89-mph effort with a pair of 80 cu. in. motors in 1962 to factory-backed efforts. George Roeder, a superb racer, drove a missile-shaped bike with a Sprint engine to a speed of 177.255 mph in 1965, while Cal Rayborn posted a speed of 265.492 inside an 89 cu. in. engined, fuel-burning Sportster streamliner five years later. Motocross was forced on H-D by its acquisition of Aermacchi and by the herd of Japanese two-strokes that first gained popularity on the West Coast.

Despite factory support in the late seventies, the Aermacchi riders found themselves the victims of an old Harley stunt—they were beaten simply because they were greatly outnumbered. The money saved when Aermacchi was sold went into drag racing, belatedly. Marion Owens and a

The Sprint in road racing trim, 1966. *Harley-Davidson, Inc.*

Driver Dave Campos with the recordbreaking Harley-Davidson streamliner sponsored by *Easyriders* magazine. *Harley-Davidson, Inc.*

The company has been known to advertise its victories.

H.O.G. is a sponsor of the factory team, as this ad indicates.

few others campaigned against megabuck Japanese multicylinder machines, with varying degrees of success in 1979 and 1980. Harley-Davidson is still represented in road racing in The Battle of the Twins, an AMA-sanctioned event limited to two-cylinder cycles. Gene Church has come to dominate this series on a H.O.G.-sponsored bike. More about both later.

Dealers such as Robison, plus Earl Widman, Leonard Andres, Dudley Perkins, Hank Reiman, Wayne Wiebler, Lawrence Smith and Flint, Michigan's renowned Bert Cummings have contributed disproportionately over the years to H-D's racing success. Willing to experiment with racing motors, they are part of the reason the nonfactory Harley rider can count on running with Springsteen, Goss and Parker if he has the talent. Another source of speed is the independent tuner, best exemplified today by "Tex" Peel, also from Michigan. An employee of GM's Buick assembly plant by day, Peel works nights and weekends making the XR as fast as, or faster than, the factory machines. Peel's diligence, combined with Ricky Graham's skill and Dick O'Brien's sharing of speed secrets, propelled Graham to the Winston Pro Series national championship in 1982.

Dick O'Brien, former H-D racing director. *Harley-Davidson, Inc.*

An early-seventies flat-track event. From left are Mike Kidd (72); Rex Beauchamp (31); Dave Sehl (16); Greg Sassaman (80); and young Jay Springsteen (65). *Harley-Davidson, Inc.*

There just isn't room to list all of today's great racers. But there are plenty out there, mostly young, scratching for cash but running up front on any track you'd care to name. Here's a quick glance at four of today's top racers, all of whom ride for the factory. It's fortunate that there are factory-backed riders today because, on the retirement in 1983 of Dick O'Brien, the company cut back its sponsorship. But money, technical expertise and occasional production of new

Not only was Mert Lawwill a national champ, he was the subject of a successful movie, *On Any Sunday*. *Harley-Davidson, Inc.*

An 883cc Sportster awaits its rider in the Daytona Beach infield. *David Wright*

H-D dealer Don Tilley leads the AMA 883cc series with this bike and rider Scott Zampach. *David Wright*

H-D dealer Don Tilley says a rider can make an 883 raceworthy for $7,000, which includes the cost of the new bike. That's the approximate cost of a Formula 1 bike's crankshaft. *David Wright*

XR750 motors continue from Milwaukee today, under the engineering department. Steve Schiebe is the engineer who passes along what the factory knows, keeping the bar and shield far forward. . . .

Scott Parker. Another in the seemingly endless list of Michigan riders, Scott has forty-eight Grand National wins as this is being written and is closing in on a record fifth consecutive title. No one else has statistics like the man with the current No. 1 plate, who once won six consecutive mile events and was AMA's Rookie of the Year in 1979 at the age of 18. The resident of Swartz Creek, MI, has a total of 30 wins on mile tracks, also a record. Parker has been a member of the Harley-Davidson factory team for eleven years.

With credentials like these, astride a bike built and tuned by H-D's legendary Bill Werner, you might think Parker would be uppity. Not a chance. He is sincere, down to earth, patient, smart and all the other good things required of heroes. If you crave controversy, look elsewhere. The strongest thing Scott says about his fellow racers is that he's more comfortable alongside some guys than others as they orbit a mile track, hub to hub, at speeds in excess of 100 mph.

Chris Carr. When Parker walks away from racing, here's the guy who will take his place. It won't be much of an upward step for Carr—he had the points lead throughout the '91 season and lost on a tie-breaker to Parker at season's end. Just

Cal Rayborn in 1973. *Cycle News, Inc.*

Cal Rayborn takes the checker at a road-racing national. Those who said the KR's and XR's weren't road-racing bikes never saw Cal Rayborn on one. *Harley-Davidson, Inc.*

25 in 1992, the Californian has been runnerup to Scott for three years and was the AMA's 600cc champion four years in a row. Carr was named AMA Rookie of the Year at the age of 18 in 1985 and joined the factory team a year later. Astride his Kenny Tolbert-tuned H-D, the small blond rider may be the most competitive person in the sport at the moment.

Kevin Atherton. Kevin was only 21 in 1992, yet he had been a member of Harley-Davidson Racing since 1989. His biggest win came at the Pomona Mile in 1991 on his Al Stangler-tuned factory bike. A resident of White Pigeon, MI, Kevin made a one-two-three factory finish at any AMA Grand National event a distinct possibility. For '93, he has gone road racing.

Scott Zampach. This is the hot guy in the AMA's Harley Twin Sport Series, having taken the championship in 1991. Running the Don Tilley-tuned (and H.O.G.- and Screamin' Eagle-sponsored) Sportster, Scott scored a big win at Daytona in 1992, only to be deprived of the victory after officials disqualified the first three riders for bikes with illegally shaved cylinder heads. A 27-year-old from Milwaukee, Zampach is a veteran road racer who has given the young 883cc series excitement and respect.

Harley-Davidson is the only motorcycle that has shown sustained support of AMA dirt-track events. Since we all age at the same rate, the names of the riders will change. But the faces in the infield will be familiar because, once you've run and won, it's hard to stay away.

There are others out there beyond the flow of the Camel Pro Series or the Stroh's Miles, running bull-ring regionals where 120 riders may vie for a total purse of $1,200. Some will slide almost unnoticed into the Expert ranks, picking off today's stars. Many will be aboard Harley-Davidsons, since, despite Honda's recent brilliance, H-D is the only make that shows sustained interest in AMA competition.

The MX-250 with the extra headlight successfully ran the Baja in 1975. *Harley-Davidson, Inc.*

Randy Goss, No. 1 as a team rider in 1980, is another in a seemingly never-ending procession of Michigan dirt-track riders. *Harley-Davidson, Inc.*

Speaking of winners, here's a look at some of the great names associated with Harley-Davidson and racing. . . . The first guy we should mention was the third—and apparently final—head of the racing department in company history. His eyes rest behind two thick slabs of glass, perhaps the result of too many blindingly sun-filled afternoons in a swirling infield. A hearing aid is graphic evidence of excess time near the rough bark of an unmuffled V-twin. Neither the glasses nor the hearing device is an indication of age or infirmity, at least not on Dick O'Brien. The former head of Harley-Davidson's racing department is as likeably foul-mouthed and honest as he was in 1936, when

Marion Owens smokes the tire at a Dragbike meet. *Harley-Davidson, Inc.*

Drag racer Danny Johnson leaves the line with his double-engined H-D. *Harley-Davidson, Inc.*

he began working on H-D motors at Puckett's shop in Orlando, Florida. In those days, O'Brien raced sprint cars and stockers with some success, finishing tenth in a stock car race on the old Daytona beach course. When war broke out, the angular Floridian climbed aboard his bike and rode nonstop, without eye protection, to Tennessee to sign up for pilot training. The marathon ride left his vision temporarily blurred, so O'Brien spent the war on the ground as a civilian machinist for the Navy and as a senior aircraft mechanic with the Army Air Corps. Among his duties was dissecting captured enemy aircraft. "You think racing teams are secretive? The Army wouldn't even allow cameras on the base," he says.

O'Brien returned to the H-D shop service manager's position he left in 1941. For more than a decade he and friends raced, built and rebuilt Harleys, producing speed parts that were tested at Daytona Beach and on tracks throughout the Southeast. On June 3, 1957, he joined the factory as assistant to racing director Hank Syvertson. Three months later, Syvertson retired and O'Brien stepped in. In his twenty-six years on tour with the factory team, the man with the shock of white hair did battle with Norton, Indian, Triumph, BSA, Matchless, Yamaha, Suzuki, Honda, Kawasaki and many brands that have come and gone. One mark of his maturity is the credit he is willing to give riders who consistently took on—and occasionally beat—the factory H-D's and the swarm of independents who favored the V-twin. Among the opposition he's willing to praise are Dick Mann, Kenny Roberts and Mike Hailwood.

Of Mann, O'Brien expresses admiration, both for his sure riding style and his David-and-Goliath effort as tuner and racer to take two No. 1 plates. He still wonders how Roberts stayed aboard the treacherous, blindingly fast TZ-750 dirt tracker that day in 1975, when Kenny won the Indianapolis mile. And he believes Mike Hailwood was as good a road racer as anyone is likely to see. But his special insights are reserved for the H-D factory riders, whom he got to know as he and his men readied their machines for combat.

O'Brien also will talk, though a bit reluctantly, about the dark side of racing—the injuries, the disfigurement, the deaths. Mark Brelsford, who today is ranching in Alaska, broke some bones in a fiery Daytona crash while trying to defend his

Scott Pearson (42) ahead of a falling rider at the Astrodome in 1977. *Harley-Davidson, Inc.*

national championship. On the comeback trail, Brelsford ran the 1973 Charity Newsies flat-track event in Columbus, falling in the wrong turn at the wrong time. "He almost died twice that night in the hospital," says O'Brien, explaining that the youthful Californian had bone marrow in his blood stream. Carroll Resweber, who we'll meet a bit later, was a constant reminder of the dangers of the track. The four-time national champion went down in a multibike pileup during a 1962 flat-track event in Illinois. Resweber still favors his left arm and left leg, which is a bit shorter than the right. But he is luckier than Jack Gholson, who died in the mishap, and virtually as lucky as Dick Klamfoth, who initially was believed to have broken his back.

Harley-Davidson came close to fielding no factory team in 1982, primarily due to the cost of the program. It has been estimated that the racing program is a $300,000-a-year proposition, fairly small by auto racing standards but awesome to a company with a history of relatively low profits. However, a number of long-time H-D dealers appealed successfully and the two-bike team became three (Scott Parker came on board, thanks in part to sponsorship from Pabst Brewing Company). O'Brien believes that racing, especially to the older dealers and employees at the factory, is vital to morale. "It gives them something to be proud of," he says. Pride showed through in the mid 1980s as Honda launched another offensive with Bubba Shobert and other

Springsteen with Lyn Griffis, Miss Winston, celebrates a victory. *Harley-Davidson, Inc.*

Jay Springsteen. *Harley-Davidson, Inc.*

Springsteen arrives at the Peoria TT. *Harley-Davidson, Inc.*

great riders. But as the 1990s progress, with people like Ronnie Jones moving from Honda to H-D, Milwaukee visits to the winner's circle continue.

Despite his racing commitment, O'Brien maintains other interests. Recently remarried, he enjoys Indy-type auto racing and is a long-time friend of Bobby Unser. When time permits, O'Brien climbs on his own bike, a Low Rider. He's converted his new mate to riding the bike, but only after she attended a riding course at a local technical college.

O'Brien has seen it all—the high banks of Daytona; the long-defunct, washboard Pennsylvania bull rings; the sweet, swift Springfield cushion. He's watched a pushy parent ruin a young factory rider's chance of being rehired. He's observed riders lose their touch to the ravages of age by either charging harder to make up for reflex loss, or slowing imperceptibly with each season. And he's seen Harley-Davidson racing bikes evolve from solid-tail snorters to machines lightened

with space-age metal and tuned to the individual rider.

When O'Brien retired after '83, the H-D racing program existed briefly on its own before being moved into engineering. An era ended, but the great machines, in the hands of the riders described below, will live on in fans' memories.

What's more unbelievable, winning every national event during an entire cycling season, capturing five nationals in one day, or being Howard Hughes' engineer aboard the only flight of the Hughes Spruce Goose? Joe Petrali, among the most successful racers ever to straddle a Harley-Davidson, performed those feats and some others, living a swashbuckling sort of life that had to be seen to be believed. Born in 1904, two years prior to the earthquake in San Francisco, Petrali grew up in Sacramento. By the age of thirteen he owned a beater bike, and by the age of sixteen he was winning races on treacherous board tracks. As good a mechanic as he was a rider, Petrali earned a job in Kansas City and a place on the

Bill Werner, tuner for Springsteen. *Harley-Davidson, Inc.*

Springer on a roll. Note the tearaway plastic, layered and alternatively tabbed so that the rider can rip it off during the race, thereby improving his view. *Harley-Davidson, Inc.*

then-prestigious Indian factory team. He raced and wrenched for several years.

Alliances were rather loose in those days, so when Joe showed up at the Altoona, Pennsylvania, board track in 1925 without a ride, Ralph Hepburn noticed. Hepburn had broken his hand in a practice spill and offered the youngster his Harley-Davidson factory mount. Joe orbited the track a few times, experimented with a new additive known as tetraethyl, then left the field in a cloud of dust. The 100-mile race ended just 59 minutes, 47.2 seconds later; that's right, Petrali had averaged more than 100 miles an hour on the 61 cu. in. H-D. The factory bowed out of competition briefly during the period 1926–30, so Petrali successfully entered the new 350cc class on an Excelsior. He returned to Harley-Davidson to ride the Milwaukee version of the 350 class, an overhead valve single dubbed the Peashooter. From then until his voluntary retirement in 1938, Petrali mowed down every other professional racer on every other kind of bike. In 1935, he won all thirteen events on the national calendar, in-

cluding five nationals in a single day on the Syracuse, New York, track. And in 1937, he set a speed record of 136.183 miles an hour on a new 61 cu. in. overhead valve Knucklehead at Daytona Beach.

Some will say the demise of Class A (350cc) professional racing after 1937 was due to the economy. Others may well blame Petrali, who dominated the series as no rider has ever dominated any series before or since. When the rules changed for the '38 season to 750cc Class C road bikes, Petrali opted to run only a few hillclimbs, another area in which he excelled. For all of his experience, Joe hardly ever crashed. He once cracked ribs when his mount fell on him at a hillclimb, and he crashed heavily on the dirt once when another competitor's bike lay in his path. "He was tough," said the late former H-D President William H. Davidson. "He was a nice guy, but he wouldn't give an inch on the track." Contemporary riders who come upon the spindly racing bikes of the twenties wonder how any man could muster the courage to climb on the gearless,

An auspicious moment, Daytona 1984: Dave McClure (left) wins Battle of the Twins heavyweight modified class; Gene Church (center) wins grand prix class; and Will Roeder wins stock class, all on XR-1000's in various states of tune. *Harley-Davidson, Inc.*

Three-time Battle of the Twins GP champ Gene Church at Daytona, 1986. *Harley-Davidson, Inc.*

The 883 Sportster of Randy Texter of New Providence, PA, in the pits at Daytona, 1991. Note the steering damper and the dual front disc brakes. *David Wright*

Scott Zampach rode the rapid Tilley H-D Buell in the Pro Twins event at Daytona in 1991. *David Wright*

brakeless machines. Petrali got on and stayed on for twenty years.

Happily, Joe did well after his racing retirement. He worked for Hughes, worked for a brake lining company and served as an official for the United States Auto Club. Petrali appeared regularly at the Bonneville (Utah) Salt Flats, sanctioning the speeds turned in by many riders and drivers, including those on Harley-Davidsons. The man with forth-eight national wins to his credit died of natural causes in 1972.

Two soldiers, one from Indiana and one from Wisconsin, were sharing a bunker one night in 1967 at the Ninth Infantry Division base camp in Vietnam. The Hoosier, who had attended the Charity Newsies event in Columbus, Ohio, a couple of times, said he thought Dick Mann was the best rider he'd ever seen. "That's because," said the Wisconsin native, a few years older, "you never saw Carroll Resweber."

Resweber caused that kind of comment from the time he first climbed on his old Knucklehead in Port Arthur, Texas, challenging his friends to race on and off the Gulf Coast area roads. Everett Brashear, an expert rider from nearby Beaumont, was sufficiently impressed with Resweber to take the novice rider north on the dirt-track trail. Carroll had been promised a ride on a Paul Goldsmith machine, arriving in Illinois only to find that Goldsmith had bent the bike in a crash. So Resweber rode what he could find in three Wisconsin junior events, winning all three and making an impression on independent tuner Ralph Berndt. Berndt worked for H-D but put together his own bikes, since there were no true factory riders in those days. By 1956 Resweber was an expert; by 1957 he finished ahead of Brashear in the point standings; and by 1958 he displayed the No. 1 plate.

Resweber won sixteen nationals in his four-consecutive-year reign as the national racing champion. And he did it while working a forty-hour week for Mercury Marine in Cedarburg, Wisconsin, the only village ever to fete a cycle champ by holding a "Carroll Resweber Day." The slim Texas native would no doubt have earned a fifth consecutive title in 1962, but for a tragic evening spent in Lincoln, Illinois. . . . You may hear tales of that half-mile track, about how the dust was so thick that Resweber ran into fallen Jack Gholson and Dick Klamfoth because his eyes were closed. The champ suffered a broken neck in the spill, an incident of which he has no recall. "I remember looking over to Ralph [Berndt], who was timing other riders, and I remember leaving the pits. That's all," he said recently. "I'm told that I wasn't breathing when they picked me off the track in a sheet—they'd run out of stretchers. But

Flat-track action at Barberville, a bowl in Florida that opens just before Daytona.
David Wright

an ambulance attendant gave me mouth-to-mouth."

Ironically, 1962 was to have been Carroll's last year on two wheels; he had an offer to race stock cars. He lay unconscious nine days, then spent two years being told by medical experts that his left arm was useless. Today, he has more than eighty-percent use of the arm, which would have been enough to climb on and ride the stylized street bike he crafted while a fabricator and machinist in Dick O'Brien's race shop.

"I loved to win," he said a few years ago. "On equal equipment, I believed I could beat the other guys. That's the way I felt inside." Known for running a precise groove lap after lap, Resweber was said to have psyched Bart Markel, the high-road, low-road, anywhere-between competitor. "If Bart would have slowed down, he would have beaten me," Resweber said with a smile. His records on 50-horsepower bikes withstood the onslaught of today's 90-plus horsepower machines until two or three years ago—that's how fast he was. At the Springfield Mile in 1962, Resweber lapped the entire field in the 50-mile main event before running out of fuel.

The old guys, the ones who've been around racetracks for years, smile slyly when Bart Markel is brought up. His name causes them to flash on something they saw at a race Bart ran during his very long professional career, which stretched from 1957 through 1979. In those twenty-two grueling years, the stubby AC Delco tool-and-die machinist from Flint, Michigan, bounced off hay bales, guardrails and other competitors in winning twenty-eight dirt-track nationals and three No. 1 plates, in 1962, 1965 and 1966.

A high-cushion rider, Markel was best on the half-mile tracks, where the bikes and the action were the thickest. As one of his admirers once said, he'd win every race through a room filled with coat hangers. He was once suspended, accused by the AMA of rough riding and thereby earning his nickname, "Black Bart." Few who know him believe he's ever intentionally run anyone into the fence (except maybe Sammy Tanner, who did it to Bart several weeks before Bart did it to him). Rather, Markel is probably the most extreme example of a rider who violated all of the laws of gravity and still won. He raced as if he were allergic to the groove, in contrast to his old nemesis, Resweber.

Dick O'Brien doesn't wonder why Bart was a less-than-successful road racer. "He refused to slow down for the turns," O'Brien recalls. While other asphalt competitors rode with clip-on bars and fairings, Markel's machine sported wide, dirt-track bars; he sat bolt upright, waiting impatiently for the opportunity to pitch the bike into a slide, an opportunity that usually came along in the worst possible way. Photos in the Harley-Davidson archives show him in every turn, foot in the outrigger position, waiting for the cushion to

Dave Feazell leaves the line during the AMRA Harley Homecoming National in Union Grove, WI, in 1988. Feazell won the pro stock class, setting two national records. Later, he turned 8.99 seconds for the quarter mile, the fastest time ever recorded by an Evolution-engine Sportster. *Jerry Cummings*

Dave Feazell churns up the Anamosa, IA, hill during a meet on his 750 KR. Besides hillclimbing and drag racing, Feazell has his own motorcycle shop. He also holds a Bonneville Salt Flats record, set in 1991. *Dave Feazell collection*

propel him ahead of half-a-dozen riders. Ironically, Markel seldom suffered any lasting injury, though he might show up for a national with his left leg supported by a bungee cord tied around his waist. The fact that he kept himself in superb physical condition, even as age caught up with him, probably helped Bart overcome aches and pains that would have sidelined lesser riders. Today, he can be seen at an occasional half-mile or mile race, a quiet, unassuming man with glasses. Markel's legacy is still on the track in the form of virtually every Michigan rider competing for national points. The fact that Michigan seems to produce more flat-trackers than automobiles is a tribute to the rider they called "Black Bart." But they didn't call him that to his face.

"Cal Rayborn never played out his string," says one veteran dealer, who turns his shop over to H-D factory bikes and independents alike each year when the big national show comes to town. Indeed, Rayborn's star seemed to be ascending when he reluctantly left H-D at the end of the '73 season. The XR750 had at last been eclipsed by

the two-strokes on pavement, and the lanky resident of Spring Valley, near San Diego, signed up with Suzuki. Rayborn had acquired a Chevy-engined racing car, deciding to take the machine to Australia to sell it—at a handsome price. "I told him before he left not to ride any junk," says Dick O'Brien. But the temptation to climb on an Aussie dealer's bike—with a reputation for seizing—was too much. The machine locked up, throwing Rayborn violently into a trackside steel barrier. He died shortly afterward.

Cal's career began with a severe injury, a broken back suffered in a road race on the then-new Riverside, California, course in 1958. The eighteen-year-old recovered, began to ride scrambles, then was taken under dealer Leonard Andres' wing. Andres' son, Brad, had won one national title and was a superior road racer himself. So Andres senior knew what to look for. Fighting perennially weak brakes, Rayborn almost overnight emerged in front of a pack of very, very talented road racers: Dick Mann, Gary Nixon, Dick Hammer—and Brad Andres. He won Daytona with ease, he once

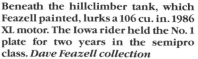

Beneath the hillclimber tank, which Feazell painted, lurks a 106 cu. in. 1986 XL motor. The Iowa rider held the No. 1 plate for two years in the semipro class. *Dave Feazell collection*

ran a streak of six straight pavement wins and he passed Roger Reiman in an Indianapolis Raceway Park turn by sliding his bike sideways for nearly 100 feet. Yet Rayborn never mastered the dirt, which prevented him from affixing the No. 1 to the fairing of his XR. A loner and, in O'Brien's words, "a constant bitcher," Rayborn scuffed the cases, the pegs, the fairing and more—no matter how far up and in the factory mechanics moved whatever protruded. He then complained about the quality of help he was receiving. "Anybody can take the fast turns," according to O'Brien, "but Calvin and Mike Hailwood were the only two I ever saw who mastered the slow ones. Calvin and Mike—now that would have been a race."

Jay Springsteen was luckier than either Carroll Resweber or Cal Rayborn. The Michigan resident has won on every kind of dirt—short track, TT, half mile and mile. Springer also was an able road racer, having finished sixth in the 1978 250cc 100-miler at Daytona on a vastly underpowered machine. The wiry kid who loves to race but hates the publicity hoopla attached to racing is an avid hunter and fisherman. He lives in the small town of Lapeer, Michigan, where he has to do little more than walk out his back door to be in ideal out-of-doors surroundings. Only a chronic stomach problem that defied control for years kept Springer from rolling up more than his forty wins and four AMA Grand National titles.

The ailment surfaced repeatedly throughout the 1980s. Jay would show up with the factory team, watch tuner Bill Werner set up his bike, turn qualifying laps and then, before or during the heats he would be in agony. Dieting helped. He stayed away from the deplorable food most racers thrive on. Medication helped. He was diagnosed as having a rare form of diabetes and was dosed accordingly. But the shy, quiet man with the No. 1 plate had to sit frequently and watch others run for his title. "I think it all may be in my head," he said recently, though tests he has undergone indicate his stomach produces two-and-one-half times the normal amount of digestive acids. He may be right, since Werner usually was given back a bike that was totally wrung out by a seemingly emotionless Jay Springsteen. One gauge of his skill, as if a gauge were needed, is that he has taken thirteen of his forty victories on mile tracks, the most demanding of all AMA venues.

Incidentally, the world's fastest motorcycle is a Harley-Davidson. The two-wheel land speed record was set on July 14, 1990, by Albuquerque's Joe Campos in a twin-engine streamliner at the Bonneville, Utah, salt flats. The effort was sponsored by *Easyriders* magazine and several aftermarket companies (and by 10,000 individuals whose names adorned the shell of the machine). The story is harrowing—the rocket-shaped motorcycle was plagued by everything from crosswinds to tires that tended to swell and come apart. Nevertheless, the world's record, 322.15 miles an hour, was achieved in the dwindling light of a big, warm western sky. The liner may be capable of even higher speeds, since it has a nitrous oxide boost system that was never activated.

Chapter 9

Scenes

There's a dirty little secret about Cycle Week in Daytona Beach. This is it: The places and the people probably are less dangerous than your neighborhood—no matter how upscale you happen to be. Yes, riders, it used to take guts, gristle and a good rainsuit to show up on a bike on the east coast of Florida in March. Now all it takes is money. Just don't tell everybody the whole truth about Daytona Beach. We should keep the fun to ourselves.

Fun at Daytona means heading first and foremost for the Ocean Center convention hall, where Harley-Davidson holds forth with all its newest models, as well as bikes hauled down from the museum, factory executives, team riders, special greetin' and eatin' for H.O.G. members only, Muscular Dystrophy Association fund-raising efforts and more. Many visitors don't know it, but the folks running the show are the same Milwaukee people who exerted themselves to turn the company around after the buyout. Admission fees go to MDA and the leatherclad line of riders queues at the door all four days, rain or shine. Harley-Davidson formerly held its show at the Hilton, a few miles south. But the blindingly white and cavernous Ocean Center is the only building in town now large enough for all of H-D's doings.

There's a bigger place on the western outskirts of Daytona Beach, namely, the speedway. But the races lost some of their cachet for H-D fans when the road-racing XR750 was withdrawn from competition way back in 1973. The track never was intended for motorcycles, anyway. Unlike Loudon or Elkhart Lake, Daytona International Speedway may be the world's least scenic place to race. Still, quite a few Harley-Davidsons, particularly vintage racers and Sportsters in the American Motorcyclist Association's new 883 class, roll in to tussle with the 3.87-mile combination of high bank and infield road course. Those who care about racing can view the back straight from the Harley Heaven bleachers.

"I'm not sure how Cycle Week became synonymous with Harley-Davidson," says one of a legion of Juneau Avenue employees who migrates here to entertain anyone who rides, fixes or gets off on company products. It may be one of motorcycling's all-time public relations coups that riders of all brands of bikes think Harley-Davidson when they think Daytona. The more cycles H-D sells, the less likely that is to change.

Riders drift in early in the week for the short-track races north of the speedway at Municipal Stadium. This quarter-mile venue is limited to 600cc bikes, but many of today's top riders square off for five nights over decent prize money on the limestone and marl surface. Since many of the veteran Harley-Davidson folks cut their teeth on fairgrounds dirt tracks, it's old-home week for those whose old homes were motorcycle dealerships. Even some Shriners show up and profile, by night at the track and by day on the street.

By the time H-D's Ocean Center extravaganza opens on Wednesday, everybody knows everybody else. The factory always has something up its sleeve, whether it's Willie G.'s introduction of a Moo-Glide with cowhide seat in 1992, a chance to test-drive the official Harley-Davidson pinball machine or the opportunity to chat with Peter Fonda. No one notices that, each year, stomachs stress black T-shirts a little more. Hey—who cares?

For lots of riders, the best thing after the H-D exhibit is The Rat Hole's Custom Bike Show, held all day long on Saturday. Big Daddy Rat is no fool—he surrounds himself with Miss Easyriders, Miss Rat Hole, Miss Custom Bike and other bikini'd women with sashes and titles. There are 300 custom bikes for viewing and the $3 admission lets you stick around for the 5 p.m. drawing for the Easter Seal Heritage Softail Classic. With money going toward helping disabled people, Dad Rat (real name: Karl Smith) can be forgiven for his chauvinistic little show, which really does include

H-D's Cuban dealer, Del Campo (center, with camera), brought several family members and race fans to Daytona in the late forties. That's William H. Davidson in the light shirt, beneath the banner. *William H. Davidson collection*

The street alongside Robison Harley-Davidson becomes so packed during race week that Daytona city fathers turn it into a one-way thoroughfare. *David Wright*

many of the top custom cycles in the eastern half of the U.S., a number of them Harley-Davidsons.

There's no escaping H-D influence. Riding west to get away from beachfront gridlock puts you in Volusia County. There's a bar out there that gives free coffee to "anyone who needs it," and a swap meet at the county fairgrounds with some parts still warm from a previous evening's caper in a motel parking lot. Mechanics at Meyer's Motorcycles in DeLand have a 24-hour emergency number for Harleys and they give 10 percent off to members of ABATE. And at Sopotnik's Tavern on Tomoka Farms Road, patrons can fracture a furrin bike with sledge hammers.

Daytona Beach, downtown. *David Wright*

Visitors check out a Buell at the Harley-Davidson show in the Daytona Beach Ocean Center. Buells are Harley-engined, limited-production machines crafted by former H-D engineer Eric Buell. *David Wright*

Once you've wandered around the country, slide back into metro Daytona for Friday's Leather & Lace open house, a chance to hear the Charlie Daniels Band, an exhibit of H-D photos at the city Culture Center and the obligatory visit to the local dealership, Robison Harley-Davidson Sales on Volusia Avenue, a block or two west of Highway A1A. Come Sunday morning, you're apt to get your motorcycle blessed before you get in a line of bikes that stretches from the beach to the speedway. After you've done it all once, do it again. Like Sturgis, it only happens once a year.

"You know what makes Sturgis better than Daytona?"

Wait a minute—is this a trick question? The guy doing the asking is perched on his Low Rider with

A passenger attacks a dangling, mustard-dipped hot dog in one of several contests conducted by the company in "Harley Heaven" at the Daytona Beach International Speedway. *David Wright*

How to arrive at Daytona Beach warm, dry and in style—in a Cadillac with Dresser attached. *David Wright*

its Florida plates on the outskirts of Sturgis, South Dakota.

"I'll tell you," the Floridian volunteers. "At Daytona, you walk around or sit in traffic. Out here," he says, sucking in cubic inches of Western air, "you can really *ride!*"

The Black Hills rally and races began in 1938 under AMA sanction. The Jackpine Gypsies Motorcycle Club got things started by posting a purse of $300 and the event grew, despite incomplete Depression recovery and the thunder in the distance that became World War II. Riders who showed up at Sturgis each year demanded even more riding, in the form of tours that featured the

A finalist in the "King Kicker" contest finds out how many times he can kick over his bike in one minute, when it really counts. Five of the most skilled survive earlier elimination before the "finals" in front of the Harley Heaven grandstand on the morning of the Daytona 200 race. *David Wright*

Boot Hill Saloon, a popular watering hole during Cycle Week in Daytona Beach, Florida. *David Wright*

small farming town as a jumping-off point. There are now five full days of tours during the week in mid-August set aside for the event.

The late J. C. "Pappy" Hoel formed the Jackpine Gypsies Motorcycle Club in 1936. The perseverance of Pappy and fellow club members put Sturgis on motorcycling's map, despite gaining and then losing national sanction of their racing event (it's still an AMA regional). "We have never had any serious problems with the 'outlaw' group," said the founder a few years back. "We have their cooperation as long as we do not hassle them. We have a few motorcycles stolen, but that is normal when you consider that we have an estimated 15,000 motorcycles in a town of 5,000 people. There is nothing quite like it anywhere in the world and reservations, even months early, are hard to get."

The first day is devoted largely to signing in, being seen and checking out the iron and occupants arriving in streams from the East and West (Interstate Highway 90) and the North and South (U.S. Highway 85). Because Sturgis is more or less in the middle of the continent (900 miles west of Chicago, 1,500 miles east of San Francisco), and because the weather in August in South Dakota is as warm as it ever gets, the rally-races are a meeting of the Heartland Harleys and the West Coast wonderbikes.

Campgrounds outside fill up early with the mirthful. Here is where you're likely to get your first look at a female chest unencumbered by bra or T-shirt, where you'll inhale the first of many whiffs of marijuana, where beards are so common it looks like a tree farm. It's not really difficult to tell the good guys from the bad guys; most of the latter tend to go off by themselves. Unfortunately, in recent years, the nearby town of Deadwood has assumed that everyone who looks nasty, is; such unreasonable regulations as banning biker's wallets and prohibiting cycles on many city streets show among other things that Deadwood isn't the wide-open drinking and whoring town it likes to promote (such lusty institutions as Pam's Purple Door are, sad to say, shut down). The road tours themselves are enough to make a Dresser devotee cringe. Clapped-out, reworked and underdone Harleys from years long gone take to the road, not with a TourPak but with a six pack, showing one and all that the rider, if no one else, has confidence in his machine. No one is left stranded. And those who tire of touring can attend an aftermarket show in the armory or go to four nights and an afternoon of flat-track competition. Leather goods, ersatz accessories, T-shirts and more are peddled by the dozens of the visitors.

The locals, at least the ones who have overcome their fear of rolling thunder, also make a lot of money off the bikers. The United Presbyterian women turn out great hot cakes each morning, while the gals at Grace Lutheran Church offer lunch all day long. The Bear Butte Cafe (honest!) sells enough Grain Belt beer to irrigate the U.S. wheat crop, while Mr. Al's Main Street concession stand just keeps the hot dogs coming. Those who take a pass on one of the tours test their bravery on

H-D Chairman Vaughn Beals addresses a press conference at the Harley-Davidson show in the Daytona Beach Hilton. *David Wright*

the infamous Rainbow Curve, out on the highway toward Deadwood. There are three days of swap meet and two nights of sanctioned Dragbike racing.

Speaking of racing, Pappy Hoel conceived an illuminated Lucite memorial to White Plate Flat Trackers, that select group of riders who ran the AMA professional expert class at one time or another. He's put together a monument to motorcycling, complete with names of many of the greats. In the unlikely event that you have money to spare in Sturgis, this is a chance to contribute. It's not tax deductible or anything, but Pappy will furnish contributors a T-shirt and the feeling that you have a piece of his rock.

Meanwhile, the brotherhood all week is thick as new paint. And malice—except for shenanigans associated with excessive consumption of booze and thousands of traffic violations—is as scarce as a conventional handshake. It's a much more homogenous crowd than Daytona, making up for long hours in the saddle on the interstate highways. If Willie G. attends with regularity, is it all bad?

The third stop on our tour is Milwaukee—and virtually everywhere else in North America. It only took one national homecoming celebration, Harley-Davidson's 85th anniversary, to realize that the ride had to become a regular event. If you missed the first get-together celebrating the resurgence of H-D in 1988, the 90th anniversary ride is set for June 1993. Here's how it will work: Ten routes around North America's perimeter have been selected, with a company officer leading a parade from places like Kitty Hawk, NC, or Vancouver, BC, to Milwaukee for a party. The cross-country trek is a fund-raising ride (for the Muscular Dystrophy Association).

A friend who did the '88 homecoming says the ride isn't your average poker run. "You stop in every town along the way with a Harley dealership and have a party there. So by the time you hit Milwaukee, you know how to have a good time!" Once everyone shows up in H-D's hometown, there'll be a daylong party at the lakefront, where riders meet Milwaukeeans and everyone else, to the tune of top entertainment, good food and bike displays. The reunion will coincide with the annual three-day H.O.G. rally June 9-11.

"We hope everyone, regardless of what brand

Dayton, Ohio's Bill Kirmec hand stripes more than 40 bikes behind Robison Harley-Davidson each year, more than paying for his trip to Florida. *David Wright*

Carroll Resweber, four-time national champion and currently a member of H-D's racing department, owns this FXRS. The motor has been brought up to XR specs. It was one of numerous employee-owned machines shown in 1982 at Daytona. *David Wright*

motorcycle they ride, or if they ride at all, will join us in this event to celebrate our 90 years as a family and to raise money for MDA," says Richard Teerlink, the company's president and chief executive officer. Teerlink and other VIPs will have roared in with H-D owners from all over. Ask any of the 30,000 or so who were there five years ago—it goes beyond a good time. To participate, donate $25 to MDA at your local dealership. And be sure to ask the boss for some vacation time in early to mid June.

There are other rallies, of course, from Americade to Ruidoso to H.O.G. and club rides and activities almost year round. Some even contribute to the Muscular Dystrophy Association, which over the years has received $11 million from Harley-Davidson as a corporate sponsor. So while you're having fun, your donation will be doing a lot of good.

Not all Harley-Davidson riders have been to Daytona or Sturgis or Milwaukee. As H-D oriented

as these events may be, they aren't representative of the majority of those who own the V-twins. What *is* representative? If the company's marketing research is accurate, the most common scene on a contemporary Harley is *cruising*. The term means different things to different riders, but H-D ad copy sees it as enjoyable jaunts in the open, away from wife, kids, jobs, cares, conformity, unemployment and inflation. Exemplified by the FXR, the cruise bike has an ample (3.8-gallon) tank, rubber-isolated engine, premium Dunlop tires, a supersoft seat and the 80-in. motor that turns just 2,400 rpm at 55 miles an hour. This machine and its stablemate, the Super Glide, are engineered to separate the rider from the conscious exertion of a sports bike while reminding him that he's aboard a leaner, hungrier machine than an FLH or FLT. The bike also will idle around town most of the day without complaint on regular gasoline. Designed for the nontouring, habitual rider, the cruiser represents mainstream

Main Street, Sturgis, South Dakota. Close examination will show which make of machine is favored by those in attendance. *Richard Creed*

motorcycling to Harley-Davidson.

Cruising riders may think a got-up touring bike resembles a tipped-over juke box. Touring riders could not care less. They're a large minority in the H-D scheme of things, buying the big-buck, big-size, fat-wheeled machines that have transported generations of riders from one coast to the other and, more importantly, back. Despite such recent Japanese attempts to out-Harley Harley-Davidson with the Honda Aspencade and others, nothing quite approaches touring on an FLT or an FLH. The current Tour Glide Classic, for example, can carry the frame-mounted fairing, the saddlebags and an amazing 455 pounds on the frame-mounted seat and in all those compartments. Small wonder veteran H-D riders can't get used to the gusty instability of a lesser touring machine. Like the cruiser, the touring rider tends to travel with one or more of his own kind, frequently two up. By now you get the idea—no matter how you want to ride, there's a model for you in the 25-bike lineup.

If you're not into creating your own scene, here are several clubs that are national or international, either have a strong H-D orientation or welcome Harley-Davidson owners. They gather at more or less regular intervals at Daytona, Sturgis or at functions of their own.

American Motorcyclist Association
P.O. Box 6114
Westerville, OH 43081-6114
800/262-5646

This is the oldest and largest motorcycling organization in the country. The association has evolved from being a shill for manufacturers in the 1920s to today's diverse group of tourers, competitors, dealers and more. In addition to sanctioning racing activity, AMA personnel staff an effective lobby in Washington. In 1987, for example, the organization headed off a federal attempt to ban large-displacement motorcycles in the U.S. The AMA also puts out *American Motorcyclist,* a nice national monthly magazine, and stages a variety of

This is the machine Willie G. Davidson rode to Sturgis in 1982. It's a prototype belt-drive Wide Glide. *David Wright*

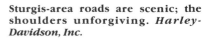

Sturgis-area roads are scenic; the shoulders unforgiving. *Harley-Davidson, Inc.*

racing and nonracing events. Annual membership is $20, which gives the member voting rights on club issues, a break on insurance, discounts on everything from eyewear to motorhome rentals and more. Discover, MasterCard or Visa accepted for phoned-in membership.

Dick Winger
Antique Motorcycle Club of America
Box 333
Sweetser, IN 46987

There are about 5,000 members in this, the largest cycle restoration club. Membership is $20 in the U.S.— write for membership details if you're outside the country. AMCA is 38 years old and holds eight major meets each year from March to September in Florida, Iowa, New Jersey, New York, Ohio and Pennsylvania. It also offers a nice quarterly magazine that details the national meets and profiles top restorers. Many of the AMA museum's display bikes belong to AMCA members. Your bike must be 35 years old to be considered an antique. That means the very first Sportster became eligible in 1992.

Harley Owners Group (H.O.G.)
c/o Harley-Davidson, Inc.
P.O. Box 653
Milwaukee, WI 53201

This is the only official Harley-Davidson club, backed as it is by the corporation. There are more than 100,000 members and membership the first year is free with the purchase of a new bike. H.O.G. is sort of like an automobile club, only better. Benefits include emergency pickup service, Fly & Ride deals, insurance, a

A Knucklehead and a tent are all you need to fit in at the Sturgis campground. *Richard Creed*

toll-free line, copies of *Hog Tales* and *The Enthusiast,* a travel center that books airline flights and hotel rooms and more. But here's why it beats a car club—there are H.O.G. social and riding activities going on all over the country, all the time. Once your H-D reaches its first birthday, you can choose full membership, life membership or associate membership. (Membership fees are priced to support the organization in different countries and, therefore, vary.) Female members also are eligible for Ladies of Harley, which is operated by H.O.G. administrators. And in a very recent development, H.O.G. has a European office—the first such administrative arm outside H-D's Juneau Avenue home.

International Northeast Harley-Davidson Dresser and Touring Association, Inc.
c/o Bobby Reeves
Rt. 1, Box 152-A
Gloucester, VA 23061

Dresser News, the INHDDTA's monthly publication, is just one of the benefits you'll derive from membership in this touring and social organization. Most chapters are in the eastern half of the U.S., but there are members in Canada, much of Europe and Japan. All ride full-dress touring bikes, as the name would imply. Models that make you eligible include the FLH, FLT, FLHT, FLTC, FLHTC, FLHS and the FLSTC, but *not* the

FLSTF. Membership is $30 for a couple or $25 single, and decorum is important at the club's three major rallies each year. The INHDDTA's annual international rally is the place to be for the well-known "Million Dollar Dresser Show."

Motor Maids
P.O. Box 443
Chardon, OH 44024

Founded in 1940, this female-only club is made up of women who own or ride. The organization goes way back with Harley-Davidson, since the first president was Dot Robinson, wife of the late cross-country record-setter and former H-D dealer, Earl Robinson. The club has an annual, nationwide convention and state chapters meet one weekend a year, frequently at an AMA dirt-track national. Motor Maids in formation prior to the drop of the flag is a popular addition to a promoter's schedule. Members are expelled if they're caught towing their bikes to a Motor Maids event! Dues are $10 a year.

Women in the Wind
P.O. Box 8392
Toledo, OH 43605

Founded in October 1985, this women-only organization has 35 chapters including five in Canada and one in

This V-twin's authenticity is betrayed by the disc brake up front. Other giveaways include the headlight, turn signals, tires and mirror. The motor is from the J series. This machine, seen at Sturgis, is one of hundreds of "blend" bikes ridden to South Dakota each year for the festivities. *Richard Creed*

England. The club is open to any female rider with any kind of bike; president Becky Brown says the most popular machines are Harley-Davidsons. Dues are $12/year for full membership and $6/year for associate. Activities include poker runs, picnics, meetings and mutual support from H-D and from *Harley Women* magazine. The winter '93 national meeting is set for Milwaukee, with the summer '93 confab scheduled for the Denver area.

This list does not include organizations that aren't much into mainstream membership or have initiation or membership requirements they would rather not discuss. Such a bunch is the Hell's Angels, the subject of much fawning by the news media in the sixties and a group that is, unfortunately, associated with Harley-Davidson.

The Angels were just one of dozens of California bike gangs until immortalized on film and in print in *Life* magazine photos and in a Hunter Thompson book that, from a cycling enthusiast's point of view, was heavy on sociology but weak on mechanicals. Somewhere along the line, the Angels began to believe their clippings and performed some genuinely outrageous, antisocial acts. It all seemed bearable—runs into the California outback to suck wine and smoke dope,

This photo proves, if nothing else, that a few bikes showed up for Aspencade events without TourPaks. *Harley-Davidson, Inc.*

Ruidoso was Mecca for touring riders of all ages. *Harley-Davidson, Inc.*

Members of a Corpus Christi, Texas, motorcycle club; photo believed to have been shot in the mid-forties. *Harley-Davidson, Inc.*

Harley Owners Group (H.O.G.) logo. *Harley-Davidson, Inc.*

Riding to an AMA national, somewhere in Pennsylvania in the mid-fifties. *Harley-Davidson, Inc.*

volunteering to take their bikes to Vietnam to clean up the Vietcong, showing what they thought of peace and civil rights in Berkeley—until they became entwined in the drug trade. Local, state and federal authorities began to take them seriously, once guns and drugs were being moved in earnest by the Oakland, California-based, group. While other gangs nationwide were dealing in (relatively) harmless stolen motorcycle parts, the Angels were snuffing and being snuffed on a regular basis. Even their leader at the time, Sonny Barger, had to park his Harley to serve time in prison.

The Oakland Police Department reported recently that the gang is still active, though there have been no problems in three or four years. The most recent police/Angel run-in occurred in front of the gang's national headquarters on Foothill Boulevard in 1978. Following a number of arrests just outside, the confrontation spilled into the Angel building. When the dust settled, it was discovered that four Oakland policemen had conspired to trash the building. "The four were dismissed and one was later reinstated through civil service," says Sgt. Dan Krause, who keeps an eye on bike gangs from the office of the Oakland chief of police. That's been it, save for sporadic,

individual arrests and occasional raids on suspected Hell's Angels' drug laboratories, according to Krause, who says there's no indication that the Angels, or any other California gang, is either growing or dying out. "They [the Angels] still ride Harley-Davidsons and you can still see forty or fifty Harleys parked in front of their clubhouse every Friday or Saturday night." But that's true, too, of a lot of legitimate clubs and associations, not only in California but throughout North America.

Incidentally, there's absolutely no evidence to indicate that Harley-Davidson, Inc. ever had any dealing with or condoned the actions of local or national motorcycle gangs. In fact, an incident in 1973 shows that at least one gang treats H-D as shabbily as it treats everyone else. The first hint of the factory's problem came from an authorized—and very reputable—dealer in California. The dealer had been approached by a Milwaukee-area biker, who offered to sell him 10,000 Harley-Davidson spark plugs at fifty percent of the cost of manufacture. Shrugging off the easy money, the dealer notified the company. Employees discovered a total of 29,000 spark plugs missing, then notified the FBI.

Motor Maids in convention, 1967, Pennsylvania.

Agents obtained a court order and placed a tap on the home telephone of John Buschman, who had been an H-D employee for less than three months, in late 1965 and early 1966, before being dismissed for excessive absenteeism. Buschman lived in Mequon, an exclusive suburb north of Milwaukee, without readily evident means of support. The monitored phone conversations, the Bureau reported, indicated that "Buschman was a captain in a local chapter of a nationwide motorcycle gang called the 'Outlaws.'" His long-distance calls amounted to orders for parts. In cahoots with another former employee, a then-current employee and one or more truck drivers, Buschman managed to help steal hundreds of thousands of dollars in parts, selling them to dealers and bike shops as far away as the West Coast and Florida. One United Parcel shipment from Buschman's home to California was valued at $24,609.

"Their primary income is their old ladies and stolen Harleys," reported a cycle mechanic in

A California priest offers a prayer prior to a club ride in the fifties. Note the saddlebag purse carried by the lady closest to camera. *James Perkins collection*

More than 100 riders depart the Capitol Drive plant in May 1982, headed for Madison to protest use of Kawasakis by Wisconsin State Police. The ride was organized by union members, many of whom were laid off at the time. *David Wright*

A rider goes for a putt on the H-D pinball machine, introduced at Daytona in 1991. *David Wright*

Members of a club organized at the Hagerstown, Maryland, Mack Truck assembly plant, during a recent visit to the H-D museum at York. Note that 28 of the 32 bikes are Harleys. *Harley-Davidson, Inc.*

Florida who had been approached by an Outlaw peddling new factory parts. He, too, was suspicious, primarily because he was used to buying only *used* stolen parts from the gang. More court paperwork was obtained by the FBI and a raid was staged on Buschman's residence early in 1974. The agents found hundreds of Harley parts and "an arsenal of weapons" at the Buschman home and in a barn Buschman rented. Trial testimony indicated that parts were moving out of the plant in quantity in trucks and vans, and piecemeal via a few dishonest employees. Buschman was sent to prison, but his caper has left its mark on even the most casual plant visitor. Whether tattooed or tuxedoed, persons leaving the premises must to this day open packages, briefcases and lunch pails for inspection by guards.

A radical custom greets the crowd at the H-D show in Daytona Beach, 1991. *David Wright*

Becky Brown, founder and head of Women in the Wind.

There's a Harley-Davidson under there somewhere. This unusual specimen was shown recently at Daytona Beach. *David Wright*

A H.O.G. member searches the club's Daytona message board for familiar names. *David Wright*

Chapter 10

Image

"The average H-D buyer is age 18–70 and ranges from bankers to low-class motorcycle clubs."—Kentucky dealer.

"Customers represent all walks of life; young, old, rich, poor (not *too* poor)."—Connecticut dealer.

"Average Harley-Davidson riders are between twenty and thirty, blue collar workers of macho status."—California dealer.

"Our customers are fifty percent white collar, fifty percent blue collar."—Pennsylvania dealer.

"A lot of our buyers turn their bikes into customs."—Missouri dealer.

"Custom bikes have been dead for several years."—New York dealer.

"Average buyer? Harley-Davidson buyers are *not* average."—Washington dealer.

"Many of our customers are getting or have just gotten a divorce."—Illinois dealer.

Clearly, Harley-Davidson riders were (and are) a diverse audience and the trick was to reach the many kinds of riders.

The first ad to appear in any sort of non-company publication may have been a simple piece extolling the virtues of the 1914 models. That half-page example appeared in *Western Bicyclist & Motorcyclist,* a monthly magazine aimed at dealers as much as at riders. A third audience, business-government, attracted the majority of Harley-Davidson lineage well into the twenties. In fact, the company expended a large sum of ad money in 1915 to obtain approval for the use of motorcycles in the then-new U.S. Post Office Rural Free Delivery (RFD) system. Once cycles were given the federal OK, Harley-Davidson not only used them in print ads but based an entire campaign on the high number of miles and low cents-per-mile rates recorded by the rural postal service workers. One ad, produced shortly after World War I, "proved" that a Harley-Davidson was cheaper than shoe leather!

Meanwhile, consumers were reached primarily through dealers, with a dealer and direct mail campaign outlining innumerable advantages for the young factory worker who could depart the gloomy city and head for the countryside, with or without a female acquaintance in a sidecar. Since most H-D's were sold with sidehacks well into the twenties, hauling a friend was a snap. Harley-Davidson's incredible racing results during this period were not used to attract first-time buyers, but were instead posted regularly in *The Enthusiast* and in a few trade magazines. Marketing experts then and marketing experts now see no link between success on the track and luring the new rider. And while the thirties were hub-deep in wonderful H-D models, sales were so weak that the company had to strain to produce *The Enthusiast* each month.

Following World War II, the company continued with Milwaukee's Klau-Van Pietersom-Dunlap, the only ad agency used until the sixties. Print ads were inserted in such national magazines as *Mechanix Illustrated* and *Popular Science;* magazines such as *Boy's Life* were used to advance the Topper scooter and other small machines. Throughout the fifties, the company continued to devote more than half its national print budget to motorcycling magazines. Those ads alternated between street model previews and racing results. Naturally, when something as stupendous as H-D's 1960 sweep of the first fourteen places in the Daytona race occurred, extra ad funds were expended.

The cycling boom that began around 1965 pretty much terminated racing ads, as the company sought the thousands of would-be riders who identified most closely with street and trail machines.

Successful ads link the product to the reader. Lately, Harley-Davidson has conveyed the feeling a rider gets on a Harley, a feeling the ads say can't be had on any other kind of machine. Like the bikes, the ads frequently are plagiarized by agencies selling foreign bikes. The company hopes and believes the consumer can tell the difference.

There are approximately 500 Harley-Davidson dealers, and no two serve precisely the same kind of rider. With that in mind, the advertising department is expected to entice *every* kind of customer. That's a big-league problem, according to Bill Dutcher, former AMF motorcycle products group public relations director.

"A 1977 study commissioned by Harley-David-

Each September issue of *The Enthusiast* during the thirties and forties was devoted to new models. Here is the 1940 customer's first look at the newest Knucklehead. *David Wright*

Harley-Davidson toys have been around a long time, as this 1929 ad in *The Enthusiast* attests. Either a parcel car or a sidecar was available; both made "a noise like the exhaust when pulled along." The metal models featured authentic paint, rubber tires and removable drivers. *David Wright*

son indicated that there are three types of motorcycle riders: custom/performance, touring and sport," Dutcher relates. "H-D has a sizeable share of the custom market, is strong in the touring market and is absolutely nowhere with the sport rider. So there are two kinds of Harley riders—the bikers and the tourers. If I can, let me call them the left and right wing, but not in any political sense. It's just that they're on opposite sides of virtually every issue. So if you run an ad that appeals to one, you're automatically turning off the other. Ruidoso doesn't mean anything to a guy on a chopper, and seeing guys with bandanas in H-D ads won't win you touring riders. And without any models that can stay with the current crop of Japanese superbikes, H-D isn't likely to corner the sport market."

Harley-Davidson evidently viewed the market

in a similar way until 1982. In addition to offering the usual custom (FXRS, Sturgis, Low Rider, Wide Glide) and touring (Electra Glides, Tour Glide, FXR) bikes, the company produced a pair of sport bikes (Sportster, Roadster) that met with critical acclaim from cycle magazines and from riders who get off on being able to flick a cycle through a series of sharp turns, then come to a safe, sure stop. Harley-Davidson still makes performance motorcycles. The challenge was to spread the word.

The three kinds of bikes were segregated by types into different brochures. A dealer, the thinking properly went, can tell what kind of potential customer he has after a brief conversation. Said dealer then lays on the customer a brochure tailored to the kind of riding the customer intends to pursue. No bandanas with Elec-

Direct mail, 1939. Post cards such as these were provided to dealers to announce new models. H-D currently conducts cycling's most effective mail advertising campaign, using the names of owners of 700cc-and-up bikes registered with each state.

This 1952 advertisement for the Hydra-Glide was run in magazines such as *Popular Science.* Were the saddle bags meant to conceal the lack of rear suspension, common on the K model and on English bikes? *Harley-Davidson, Inc.*

tra Glides, no choppers mixed in with the fiber glass, no sport bikes with riders who look like they're members of the Booze Fighters M.C. This sounds simpler than it really was, since the enthusiast publications weren't about to give an H-D high marks in a road test, just to benefit a marketing plan. Were the bikes in fact better, or have such quality magazines as *Cycle World* succumbed to Harley propaganda? "The product is greatly improved," says a member of the H-D national advertising program. That makes advertising much easier.

Advertising has never really been easy for H-D, particularly since the company labored throughout the teens, twenties and early thirties under a delusion. "We tried for a long time to convince people that motorcycles had some utility value," said William H. Davidson, the late former presi-

Another Hydra-Glide national ad. Compare this to the current four-color offerings in cycle publications. *Harley-Davidson, Inc.*

dent. "Motorcycles have never been anything but pleasure." His assessment coincided with a styling change made for 1933, wherein the bikes dropped the utility look—and olive drab paint— in favor of a rainbow of colors and ads peopled with models who looked more like cycle club members and less like delivery boys. Today, the last thing you'll find in a Harley ad is a bike carrying a stack of pizzas or a bundle of dry cleaning.

The role of those involved with advertising also has changed. The first person concerned with spreading the word was Lacy Crolius, whose photo is easiest to find in the Harley-Davidson racing archives. Crolius, and Walter Davidson, for that matter, took time off from their duties as ad manager and president, respectively, to enter endurance runs in the very early years. Later came W. E. Kleimenhagen, a more polished man but one who would argue the merits of the Crocker

motorcycle with a dealer as readily as any rider. During Kleimenhagen's thirty-year tenure, there is an almost exact correlation between how attractive the ads were and how well the cycles were received by the public. The early-thirties and early-fifties print material has a somewhat listless appearance, while the later-thirties and fifties ads, brochures and posters carry a snap that makes the reader believe the company knew what it was doing. In fact, H-D had a better understanding of its role than did its acquirer, AMF.

AMF in 1976 hired Benton & Bowles, a prestigious Chicago ad agency, for all of the conglomerate's recreational lines. Harley-Davidson received a rigid set of guidelines as to format and appearance of all advertising and collateral (dealer) material. AMF believed, with some validity, that the polished firm would bring needed marketing expertise to its large subsidiary. Thus began a battle that did not end until just prior to

Harley-Davidson has always made the most of racing wins, as these dealer posters indicate. *Harley-Davidson, Inc.*

the buyback. "Benton & Bowles tried to apply package goods techniques to motorcycle marketing," says Clyde Fessler, director of marketing services. "They were nonenthusiasts trying to appeal to enthusiasts."

Other suspicions also upset H-D personnel. Since Benton & Bowles had been retained by AMF, there was the feeling that B&B was most interested in satisfying the Connecticut parent rather than the folks in Milwaukee. And since AMF believed itself to be highly visible and therefore vulnerable to attack from all sides, an individual ad had to pass through five levels of corporate approval.

Harley-Davidson remained in charge of its own sales promotion, and so hired another agency to create brochures, literature, point-of-purchase displays and related collateral. And since B&B was responsible only for national (primarily print) advertising, H-D marketers hired a third agency to create radio and television spots; H-D paid for production and the dealers then had an opportunity to run the radio and TV spots locally, splitting the cost with Harley on a cooperative basis. As time went on, H-D spent more on those segments of advertising under their control and less on national print. The tail was wagging the hog, so to speak, even though H-D was obeying AMF advertising edicts.

Harley-Davidson continued to run this devious pattern until the spring of 1978. Responding to numerous dealer requests, H-D saw to it that a full-page ad was placed in *Easyriders*, the largest-circulation outlaw-type sex/bike monthly. AMF

This late seventies ad is significant. It allows H-D to take a shot at government, it mentions celebrities (race car drivers Al and Bobby Unser) and it peddles an important accessory. Ironically, the company realizes that a smaller percentage of H-D riders than average wear helmets. *Harley-Davidson, Inc.*

This 1927 JD was restored by Andy Batsleer of New Smyrna Beach, Florida. Numerous unobtainable parts were hand-crafted by Batsleer. The bike looks authentic. *David Wright*

A 1948 Panhead, the first year for this engine with hydraulic valves, as shown in Harley-Davidson's Rodney C. Gott Museum in York, Pennsylvania. *David Wright*

The first Hydra-Glide, produced in 1949, also on museum display. *David Wright*

The **1952 Model K, as displayed at H-D's Gott Museum.** *David Wright*

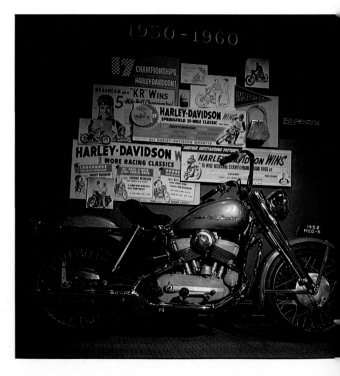

The first Sportster, produced in 1957, is displayed in H-D's Gott Museum. *David Wright*

The Duo-Glide, offered in 1958, provided an alternative to a solid rear end for riders of the big Harley-Davidsons. *David Wright*

Bill McMahon, Wisconsin Rapids, Wisconsin, adjusts, fires up, then rides his 1914 Harley-Davidson. Although his restoration isn't exact, he probably puts more miles on his antique H-D than most. *David Wright*

A 1971 Electra Glide, ready for touring or display, is shown in the Daytona Beach Hilton lot. *David Wright*

The immaculately restored two-cam racer of Michael Lange, Oconomowoc, Wisconsin. The motor was first created in 1916 and was made through 1929. Lange's bike is a 1924 model. The motor in this bike was bored and stroked to 80 cu. in., probably for hillclimbing purposes. Lange points out that displacement for the track racers such as his were 61 cu. in. *David Wright*

Joe Petrali's 1936 Knucklehead record breaker exceeded 136mph on the sands of Daytona Beach. Here it's displayed in the H-D museum. *David Wright*

From left, Cal Rayborn's XR, Walter Villa's 250cc Aermacchi and a replica of the Baja-winning motocross 250. All are on display from time to time in the Rodney C. Gott Museum. *David Wright*

Beautiful artwork and printing were featured on H-D brochures in the teens. *David Wright*

A contemporary example of H-D national print advertising. The hog is now offered as a piggy bank through dealers. *Harley-Davidson, Inc.*

OG?

some, the term "Hog" is as mud. But to the thousands of avidson owners who affec- refer to their motorcycles there is no confusion. Harley-Davidson is not fat. t eat you out of house and nd it's definitely not a gas h its incredible resale value, money in the bank. t's take it point by point. First, -Davidson is not fat. Throw over one and see. Harley's er, lower and leaner than any

other big bike on the road.
A Harley-Davidson is not overweight either. Don't compare a Harley with some little lightweight bike; there is a world of difference and we'd like to keep it that way. The key is balance. A Harley has the power to match the weight. When you're off the scales and on the highway, that weight translates into stability. And that's exactly what you need in this age of 18 wheelers and gusty Interstate highways.
A Harley-Davidson is not a gas hog.

To begin with, all Harleys burn less expensive regular gas. And they burn less of it than you'd imagine. On average, our motorcycles get between 47 and 54 MPG on the highway*. Compared with engines of similar displacement, our 1000cc and 1340cc V-Twins, by design, are a couple of the most efficient internal combustion engines made.
A Harley-Davidson won't eat you out of house and home after you buy it. Simplicity of design is the best way to insure durability, dependability and

serviceability. So Harley's aren't loaded down with high-tech complexity. For instance, we use only one carburetor. You don't pay for four and the hassles later. In fact, many of the routine maintenance tasks can be performed by the rider.
Harley-Davidson is the best grade of motorcycle you can buy. Actually as the quality of many products is going down, the quality of Harley-Davidson motorcycles is going up. Because we don't turn out motorcycles like popcorn. There's

a lot of careful hand work. A lot of meticulous assembly and constant quality control. The result. This year, our motorcycles are the best handling, the best all around performance motorcycles we've ever built.
Harley-Davidson motorcycles are not cheap. We don't build them that way, so it stands to reason we can't sell them that way. We put more into a Harley. So you get more out of your Harley. You get more every time you ride down the street. And you get more down the road, when it comes

time to sell. Just check the want ads in your paper. You'll see. A Harley may be called a Hog. But don't be confused. There's no better place to put your money.

**MOTORCYCLES.
BY THE PEOPLE.
FOR THE PEOPLE.**

ur own test results. Your mileage may vary depending on your personal driving habits, weather conditions and trip length.

Customs line the boardwalk each Saturday morning during Daytona Beach Speed Week. This stunning white creation is from South Carolina. *David Wright*

A 1981 FLH Heritage model on display in the Rodney C. Gott Museum, York, Pennsylvania. This is said to be the first bike off the assembly line following the buyback from AMF. *David Wright*

was mortified that one of its subsidiaries was a part of the "Swastika" set and ordered H-D not to run future ads in such a prurient publication. Lou (Spider) Kimzey, the force behind *Easyriders*, filled the page meant for the H-D ad with a Surgeon General's-type warning that the motorcycle manufacturer had determined *Easyriders* was injurious to its image. The black page with the small, rectangular block of type was a stroke of genius: Letters displaying various degrees of literacy and outrage poured in to the magazine, the motor company and the conglomerate. Both H-D's Clyde Fessler and AMF's Bill Dutcher acted to pacify everyone. Dutcher put on his shabbiest clothes and went west to meet Kimzey personally. Kimzey got himself up in a three-piece suit for the occasion. They nearly missed meeting at a restaurant as a result. Fessler worked a deal wherein the AMF logo was exorcised from the ads, to be replaced by a line crediting the ad to the H-D

dealer network. An individual dealer placed and paid for the ad, then was reimbursed by Harley-Davidson. Somehow, everyone was pacified, since the money for the ads was taken from the dealer coop program. But that led to other corporate shenanigans.

The dealer coop program grew from $200,000 in 1976 to $2 million in 1978. There followed numerous heated meetings between AMFers and H-D personnel, since the conglomerate had a deal with B&B wherein the agency was paid a flat annual fee and all ad commissions were rebated to AMF. The large and independent sum being spent by Harley-Davidson was preventing AMF from getting any sort of rebate on H-D advertising. Like a parent who runs out of patience, AMF ordered Harley-Davidson in the spring of 1980 to run its cooperative ad program through Benton & Bowles. At about that time the economy began to sour, so H-D abandoned more expensive advertis-

Harley-Davidson still uses racing results to draw customers, as this 1978 flier featuring Marion Owens attests.

233

ing for the direct mail approach. Again, this resulted in no revenue being rebated to AMF, since a Minneapolis agency prepared the creative work and a Chicago agency was retained for other dealer coop programs. The parent firm capitulated in January 1981, stating that all recreational subsidiaries could select their own agencies effective June 10. The point was moot, since both sides were aware that soon the motorcycle company would be independent once again.

Today, two distinct things are happening in motorcycle advertising, according to Mike Keefe, H-D ad manager. The Japanese, after years of trying to broaden the market by advertising in the mass media, are cutting back their motorcycle programs and, consequently, their advertising. That's a reaction to a flat or declining cycle market. But H-D continues to do what it's been doing: "We don't use the mass media," Keefe states. "Instead, we try to reach those already on bikes through an aggressive direct-mail program and by advertising in the buff books." The last major push to broaden the market was Honda's $5 million television and print campaign to get first-time riders on their 250cc Rebel.

Nevertheless, Keefe continues, there are some interesting things going on in the market. "Do scooter buyers become motorcyclists? No one knows. But the entry-level vehicle theory here has been revised with the introduction in 1986 of the 883. Before, a used bike was the most common introduction to H-D. We're finding some other interesting things—like the unusually high number of people who already own a Harley who are buying the 883. Or the success of the 1100, which is a dressed-up, punched-out 883.

"Another pleasant surprise has been the success of the demo program. This was the best way to show riders how nice the new Evolution machines really were. Based on successful demos in Daytona, we have a demo fleet semi truck that goes to rallies and has given 5-6,000 rides per year, in addition to Daytona.

Keefe also believes that the belated creation of giant V-twins by Suzuki and others merely serves

Appealing to a specific kind of biker, H-D in 1979 introduced the Low Rider in the kind of bold advertising the Japanese are now copying. *Harley-Davidson, Inc.*

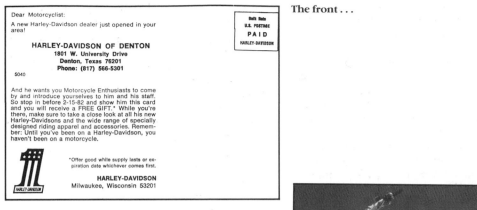

The front . . .

. . . and back of a direct-mail piece, aimed at Texas riders of motorcycles over 750cc in the Denton area. H-D uses direct mail frequently and effectively.

SHOULD YOUR POLICE DEPARTMENT'S PUBLIC IMAGE BE RIDING ON FOREIGN MOTORCYCLES?

A pointed message currently provided municipalities as part of the sales effort for police bikes. *Harley-Davidson, Inc.*

to focus on what has become a born-again configuration for bike engines.

Does the company have an overall ad strategy? Here's Keefe again: "We're starting to sell the entire Harley-Davidson experience. With the establishment of local H.O.G. chapters, everything you need to enjoy the sport is at your H-D dealer. We offer the whole environment, something no other bikemaker can match." Keefe admits there's no cafe racer in the Harley lineup at the moment, but points out that current manufacturing techniques lend themselves to short-run, specialty models. If the market demands it, the company may well produce it.

Savvy marketing is good, but having a mystique about its products is even better. Larger companies than H-D have spent millions trying to create a similar devotion, only to fail. How did Harley do it? They're not sure themselves. (Why do you think it's called a mystique?) Eyeing the aura that surrounds the bikes, Clyde Fessler sizes it up this way: "It's like a fire. You can pull and use a color from the fire, but if you just try to grab the whole thing, you're going to get burned." That analogy cuts several ways. On a personal basis, at least one H-D president during the AMF years got so caught up in the mystique that he is said to have committed a stunt with a biker's old lady in full view of Daytona Beach Hilton guests. On a marketing basis, it appears that Japanese manufacturers are attempting to grab the fire rather than the colors.

Mystique also means simultaneously serving cruisers, touring riders and sporting riders. The latter are younger people who see in the Sportster a moderately priced bike with a mile-wide power band and handling that holds a corner with its sticky Dunlops as well as any production motorcycle. And since H-D people have always been the backbone of any flat-track crowd, the company continues to sponsor Camel Pro Series AMA racing on ESPN, the cable-television sports network. MotorClothes and parts and accessories are offered in two different TV spots for 10 events, which range from San Jose to Syracuse and back to Pomona, and Springfield twice.

Advertising no longer has to make apologies for inferior quality. Empowered workers in York, Wauwatosa and Tomahawk (plus a host of suppliers) now combine to offer machines with world-class quality, service and support. Warranty claims have decreased, oil-puddle jokes are drying up and first-time owners, who may or may not be lifelong H-D people, are proud of their purchases. No wonder the new bikes will be gone by March.

With all that in mind, who is today's typical H-D buyer? About five percent are female, but the usual rider is predominantly male, age 38.5, usually married, earning more than $40,000 or more a year. Two-thirds have some college or trade school training or are college grads or post graduates. Says H-D's Ken Schmidt: "These are people who have been in the workforce a while and can afford to own a piece of machinery like this. Our riders today are really no different than the people next door. In fact, they usually *are* the people next door."

Chapter 11

Celebrities

Harry Taintor knew how to attract attention, all right. The Seattle Harley-Davidson dealer found out one day in 1918 that something called Trixie Friganza, The Vaudeville Queen, was in town. He called the theater, asked Trixie if he could show her the sights of the city in his H-D V-twin sidecar and she consented. Harry eased his three-wheeler to the curb under the marquee and was greeted by Miss Friganza, all 250-or-so pounds of her. Never one to miss a publicity opportunity, Harry alerted the local newspaper and then took the plump young actress up the steep hills of his hometown. Since he couldn't convince the photographer that this was a cheesecake assignment, he managed to relate that the trip around town indicated how powerful the H-D with sidecar really was. If it could haul Trixie, it could haul anything.

Since then, Harley-Davidson has been associated with an incredible number of celebrities, who either proved they'd made it by buying one or more Harleys, or were conned into posing for some kind of publicity shot with an H-D occupying center stage. Sylvester Stallone, an H-D owner, may have said it all in *Rocky II*. Heavyweight boxing hopeful Rocky Balboa is asked by the press why he wants a return match after the beating administered by the champ. Rocky's only audible reason is that the money won in the fight will enable him to buy a motorcycle. Muhammad Ali warned Joe Frazier several years ago that "Motorcycles is for crazy people." Today, Ali owns a Harley-Davidson.

Perhaps H-D ownership among the stars provides the same kind of rush it gives everyone who has ever owned or ridden a Harley. It's also one of the only ways the most famous actors, singers and athletes can assume a little welcome anonymity. Pulling on a full-face helmet, they can ride among their adoring public without fear of being recognized. A few years ago, however, a fellow from Montana inverted the equation. He used a motorcycle to escape anonymity, becoming the most famous cycling celebrity of all time. His name—Evel Knievel.

Robert Knievel grew up like a lot of us—he played a good game of high school football and hockey, tried his hand at rodeo, held an AMA amateur competition license, chased a lot of women and caught a few, sold insurance, even worked as a private detective. But success seemed beyond his grasp until he hit on the idea of jumping objects—cars, trucks, fountains, canyons, you name it—on a motorcycle. Evel, as he came to be known, worked the West Coast in the beginning, accruing cash in direct proportion to the size or number of the objects a track promoter or county fair director wanted him to leap. By 1968, he'd cleared most possible obstacles and, despite multitudinous broken bones, may have thought himself indestructible. So he announced that he would leap the Grand Canyon. An Indian tribe and the federal government prevented Evel from performing this 1$^1/_2$-mile jump (or plunge), so he continued to thrill crowds while he waited for another ultimate trick to come along.

Millions of dollars were paid by the public to watch Evel clear twenty-one cars at the Ontario (California) Speedway, sail over another large number of vehicles before crashing into a wall in the Astrodome and fly above the Caesar's Palace fountain. The Las Vegas stunt, next to the assassination of John F. Kennedy, may be the most commonly run strip of film in history. It shows Evel taking off, landing wrong, tumbling off cars and going end-over-end, seemingly forever, across the hotel parking lot. Bones snap and poke his leathers and skin singes on the asphalt as speed rips at man and riderless machine. Following numerous stays in the hospital, Evel would emerge, believing more strongly in his invincibility and in the righteousness of his cause (whatever that was).

Harley-Davidson entered the picture in 1970, providing Evel with a modest fee, technical expertise and, what he wanted most, an All-American machine. It's more than coincidence that Evel and the entire line of H-D's took on the stars-and-stripes motif simultaneously and in earnest. The deal garnered reams of publicity for the company, since Evel's likeness and his bike were being reproduced by everybody from T-shirt peddlers to toymakers. The company even made sure that the AMF logo was on board Knievel's jet-powered machine as it sailed off for a test run in 1973 and fizzled during the real Snake River Canyon jump attempt in 1974. Diplomatically, Harley-Davidson and Evel parted company after he was convicted of beating a former business associate with a baseball bat. Sheldon Saltman had cowritten a book on Evel that poked holes in the Knievel legend. Saltman suffered a broken left arm and right wrist, small change for a daredevil but of sufficient concern to Saltman that he successfully sued Evel.

Today, Knievel lives modestly, dividing his time between painting—he's a decent artist—and launching his son's stunt-riding career. The late H-D President Charlie Thompson pointed out that, despite his reputation, Evel abided by every

Robert (Evel) Knievel.

One of Knievel's XR's. The bike, along with a car and Evel paraphernalia, is on display in a suburban Chicago auto museum.

Cycle World columnist and contributing editor Peter Egan owns a pair of H-Ds—
a Sportster and a Dresser. *David Wright*

**Knievel's career following the Snake River Canyon stunt approximated the
trajectory of his missile.** *Harley-Davidson, Inc.*

agreement he made with the company.

Evel Knievel isn't the only fellow out there who has ridden motorcycles to fame, if not fortune. Back in the twenties and thirties, a brief and nutty fad involved running one's bike into and—the rider hoped—through a wall of wood. The participants performed at county fairs and were looked on much like the barnstormers in their rickety airplanes at about the same time. The first documented board bash on a Harley-Davidson was performed in Texas in 1932 by a Texas Tech student named Daisy May Hendrich. He proved life's not easy for a boy named Daisy May by slamming his H-D repeatedly through inch-thick boards constructed in a six-by-six foot wall. Adam

Beyer of Fond du Lac, Wisconsin, also H-D mounted, was entertaining folks farther north in a similar vein. But J. R. Bruce of Wooster, Ohio, outdid both Hendrich and Beyer by setting the wooden wall aflame before he rammed successfully through it. And while Putt Mossman was running up and down a ladder mounted to his H-D as it traveled at forty miles an hour, a resident of Valparaiso, Chile, *really* upped the ante. Juan Maliu climbed aboard his Milwaukee-made machine and pleased a crowd by roaring (intentionally) through a wall of plate glass. Prudently, most U.S. stunt riders settled for flaming wood.

Among them was Harry Molenaar, now retired after fifty years as a Harley-Davidson dealer in

George Hamilton portrayed Evel Knievel in a successful telling of the stunt man's life. *Harley-Davidson, Inc.*

Seven-year-old Jimmie Hinds may not have been the first to smash through a flaming wood wall, but he was among the youngest, as this 1940 photo indicates. *Harley-Davidson, Inc.*

Hammond, Indiana, outside Chicago. Molenaar and a friend performed flaming wall crashes in the thirties as part of a thrill show featured throughout northern Indiana. On one particular evening, following a day of rain, the grandstand was packed as Harry and his cohort lined up to do their promised side-by-side simultaneous crash through a pair of flaming walls. The friend noticed that *two-by-fours* were being used and that the boards were so rain-soaked they weren't turning into ashes, which had been the key to their success so far. He told Harry that he felt ill and that the show must go on without him. Molenaar promised the throng that he would eliminate both burning walls, kicked over his bike and aimed for wall No. 1. "I hit it and it knocked me cold. But I stayed on the bike and woke up half way round the track," he recalls. He got the bike lined up once again and roared down the muddy straightaway toward wall No. 2. That collision gave him a concussion but, he says, the crowd loved it.

Not all tricks with a motorcycle are so dangerous. Those who have seen a cadre of Shriners perform on their Hogs realize that speed isn't necessary for a good show. "The Masons do the work and the Shriners have the fun," explains Freddy Ephrem of Jacksonville, Florida, a Shriner who has been involved for years with Harleys.

Chicago's Medinah Temple Shrine features this 13-man team.

Not all drill teams are Shriners, as this photo proves. The Schuylkill County Pennsylvania MC Drill Team favors dissimilar H-D's and similar white shirts with black vests.

241

Ephrem says the southeastern U.S. is the most active area in the country for motorized Shrine drill teams, adding that the most impressive unit may come out of Nashville. That city's Al Menah Shrine has sixteen members aboard special H-D Shrine bikes (similar in appearance to police bikes, minus sirens, red lights and radios). Two years following its creation in 1960, the Al Menah Motor Corps began winning awards and hasn't stopped since. Temple member Jim Hester relates

A Mexican stunt man entertains the crowd at the 1948 Peoria Tourist Trophy races. *Harley-Davidson, Inc.*

Tony Hulman (right), millionaire owner of the Indianapolis Motor Speedway, accepts the restored Peashooter racer for his museum from Willie G. and William H. Davidson in 1964. Hulman rode an H-D while a student at Yale. *Indianapolis Motor Speedway*

that Al Menah has won one or more first, second or third place trophies in every southeastern or international competition each year. The "finals" for such competition include rigid inspection for cleanliness and uniformity by no less than the Marines. Routines are worked out in long, arduous hours on a drill field. Any organization that can pass military muster must find the numerous parades and other civic festivities easy by comparison.

If thousands have seen the Shriners, millions have watched Harley-Davidsons as they were put through their paces in the movies. It's no coincidence that the biker image was spread by overly dramatic films and television, all too ready to show a fringe element of motorcycling that may never have existed in the numbers or the ways Hollywood believed. H-D's first recorded appearance on the silver screen was in 1926, when

Christy Comedy star Bill Dooley cantered along on a JD in a silent, slapstick film with a long-forgotten title. California's Highway Patrol acquired motorcycles in 1930, and Columbia Pictures responded in 1933 with a movie entitled *State Trooper*. A less-than-memorable production starring Bob Artman, the picture nevertheless was viewed by thousands, since films were the primary entertainment of the Depression. A bit later, Movietone newsreels began to deliver brief, well-filmed news capsules, among the "selected short subjects" that accompanied a feature. The Movietoners knew that a strip of film was worth 1,000 words; all of them seem to contain, between views of Franklin Delano Roosevelt or Hitler or Churchill, sports action scenes. These seemed to be either some poor soul jumping barrels on ice skates, jumping from an airplane or jumping off a hillclimbing Harley-Davidson as the front wheel kicked upward.

Elvis himself owned and rode H-D's. This KH model was said to have cost Presley $3,000. *Harley-Davidson, Inc.*

Former race-car driver Bob Bondurant gets around his California driving school on a Sportster. *Buzz Buzzelli*

H-D's have escorted politicians for years. This is the Shah of Iran, riding in a Rolls-Royce and accompanied by Electra Glides. The year is not known, but the place is Iran. *Harley-Davidson, Inc.*

Movie actor Victor McLaglen formed a precision drill team in 1937. The group has performed off and on ever since, on the screen and in person. At about the same time, an enterprising *Photoplay* magazine photographer named Hyman Fink began furnishing *The Enthusiast* with snapshots of movie stars and starlets on one or more H-D's. Jimmy Durante, Ward Bond, Robert Taylor, Robert Young, Clark Gable, Tyrone Power, Preston Foster, Gene Tierney, Van Johnson, Keenan Wynn, Marlene Dietrich, Andy Devine—riders and nonriders alike were snared by Fink's lens. Captions showing the actresses made no bones about the fact that the accompanying photos were publicity ploys. But the actors were said to be doing things

like saving World War II-rationed gasoline or memorizing lines for a movie as they rode. Many actors, such as Keenan Wynn, actually were avid cyclists. A Hollywood group, the Three Point Motorcycle Club, founded the Big Bear enduro, in 1941.

Use of H-D's in films following World War II began slowly but built up momentum. Unfortunately, numerous Harley-Davidsons could be seen in Stanley Kubrick's *The Wild One*, starring Marlon Brando. Though the company was silent about this fairly accurate portrayal of the sacking of Hollister, California, in 1947 by a motorcycle gang, dealers to this day blame the movie for cycling's lingering poor image. Ironically, Brando

Country singer Tanya Tucker is one of numerous current celebrity owners. *Ian Vaughan*

Doobie Brothers Pat Simmons (seated) and (from left) Keith Knudson, Chet McCracken and Bobby LaKind. *Harley-Davidson, Inc.*

245

rode a Triumph in the film. But to the average American, a bike was a bike—something nice people stayed off. An MGM movie at about the same time, *Code Two*, with Keenan Wynn, Ralph Meeker and Robert Horton, failed to make a counterbalancing positive impression. The three portrayed cycle cops with less verve, apparently, than the superstar Brando in his role as the leader of a pack. Rank-and-file cyclists tried to counter the negative image in several ways. The Lexington (Kentucky) Eagles Motorcycle Club put on a ride in 1957 for the March of Dimes and several clubs staged "a blessing of the motorcycles" before taking off on a tour. But the damage had been done before millions of moviegoers.

Many of the Harley-Davidsons seen in the movies (such as the early twin ridden by James Stewart in the Lindbergh story, *The Spirit of St. Louis*) came from Bud Ekins. The former desert rider and a friend of the late Steve McQueen has provided bikes for films and for such television series as *Nichols*, which starred James Garner astride an H-D single. But most of the cycles seen in sixties films were straight from the factory.

They included everything from Edd (Kooky) Byrnes' 1960 Topper scooter to Robert (*Baretta*) Blake's Electra Glide as late as 1973. The latter may be the only bike ever to have a movie named after it, since the story of the Arizona state patrolman was titled *Electra Glide in Blue.* Meanwhile, the success of *Easy Rider*, the 1969 Peter Fonda/ Dennis Hopper low-budget film that became a blockbuster, spawned a succession of cheap imitations. American-International pumped out a slew of forgettable flicks with titles such as *The Wild Angels* and *Run, Angel, Run.* Drive-in screens across the country were filled with the thunder of choppers and the biker lifestyle.

Fortunately, a pair of Hollywood productions counterbalanced the American-International films. *On Any Sunday*, a documentary covering most aspects of motorcycle competition, featured a modest, swarthily handsome young man new to the screen, one Mert Lawwill. H-D's top factory rider at the time (1970), Lawwill was highlighted throughout an entire AMA season, riding at Daytona, riding at San Jose, riding in his van from one track to the next. Though the production was a

Dan Aykroyd, John Belushi and others gather beneath a Milwaukee freeway overpass during filming of *The Blues Brothers*. Aykroyd later led Belushi's funeral procession on an H-D. *Harley-Davidson, Inc.*

246

success because motorcyclists saw it numerous times, the image it projected had nothing whatsoever to do with outlaws. An effort with even more positive impact was *Then Came Bronson*, starring Michael Parks. Once a week in 1969 and 1970, the televised roar of a Sportster echoed in living rooms across the land. A sweet-tempered drifter coped with life on the road and the series was successful enough to survive the ratings war for seventy-eight episodes. Cyclists were quick to point out that the lead character more closely resembled the average rider than did any previous effort from Tinseltown.

Even Evel Knievel got in the act, initially with George Hamilton playing the role of the infamous stunt man, then in Evel's own production. Evel modestly titled his film, *Viva Knievel.* While the acting isn't memorable, the picture—and Lauren Hutton—are visual treats to this day on late-night TV.

All of the films on earth have had less impact than television, which increasingly shapes the points of view of many Americans. Television, for a while, anyway, somehow saw a link between riding a motorcycle and behavior that might shame Charles Manson. The portrayals were aired, riders complained to the network and little else occurred. Fortunately, most Americans today know that there is no absolute correlation between riding a bike and hunger for preteen children or road-killed game. With that in mind, here's the best list available of famous folks who, at one time or another, owned a Harley-Davidson.

Kareem Abdul-Jabbar
Aerosmith
Muhammad Ali
Paul Anderson
Ann-Margret
Dan Aykroyd
BoDeans

Michael Parks aboard his Sportster during filming of the 1969–70 TV series, *Then Came Bronson*.

Bob Bondurant
Sonny Bono
Terry Bradshaw
James Caan
Earl Campbell
Sir Malcolm Campbell
Bobby Caradine
Kim Catrell
Cheap Whiskey Band
Cher
Eric Clapton
Roy Clark
Wayne Cochran
David Allan Coe
David Copperfield
Dave Cowans
Loch David Crane
David Crosby
"Wild Bill" Cummings
Glenn Curtis
Charlie Daniels Band
Phil Delta
Jack Dempsey
Desert Rose Band
Andy Devine
Neil Diamond
Doobie Brothers
Buster Douglas
James Drury
Fred Dryer
Bob Dylan
Clint Eastwood
Foghat
Peter Fonda
Malcolm Forbes
Harrison Ford
Preston Foster
Russ Francis
Daniel Frohman
Clark Gable
John Gardner
Leif Garrett
Bobby Goldsboro
Barry Goldwater, Jr.

Grateful Dead
Nick Halaris
Goldie Hawn
Isaac Hayes
Howard Hessman
Hulk Hogan
Larry Holmes
Tony Hulman
James Hylton
INXS
Billy Idol
Michael Jackson
Reggie Jackson
Lew Jenkins
Bruce Jenner
Billy Joel
Don Johnson
Alan Jones
Steve Jones
Jack Kelly
Lorenzo Lamas
Jay Leno
Charles Lindberg
Howie Long
Victor McLaglen
Barbara McQueen
Al McGuire
John Mellenkamp
George Michael
Bill Mitchell
Motley Crue
Willie Nelson
Olivia Newton-John
Ken Norton
Crown Prince Olaf
Roy Orbison
Michael Parks
Dan Pastorini
John Payne
David Pearson
Steve Perry
Joe Piscopo
Robert Plant
Poison

Tyrone Power
Elvis Presley
Priscilla Presley
Wade Preston
Peter Reckell
Lou Reed
Burt Reynolds
Roy Rogers
Mickey Rourke
Kurt Russell
Charles Russell
Neal Schon
Arnold Schwarzenegger
Brian Setzer
Charlie Sexton
Wilbur Shaw
Roger Smith
Tommy Smothers
Bruce Springsteen
Ken Stabler
Robert Stafford
Sylvester Stallone
Starship
Steppenwolf
Andrew Stevens
Gil Stratton, Jr.
Stray Cats
Barbra Streisand
Liz Taylor
Robert Taylor
Fabulous Thunderbirds
Tanya Tucker
U2
Eddie Van Halen
Stevie Ray Vaughn
Visa
Hershel Walker
Mike Weaver
White Lion
Hank Williams, Jr.
Paul Winchell
Keenan Wynn
Robert Young

Chapter 12

Buyback and Beyond

Motorcycling suffered an immense loss in the late spring of 1992 with the death of William H. Davidson. To his neighbors in the Milwaukee suburb of Elm Grove he was another retired industrialist who gave time, money and wise counsel to a trust fund and to benevolent organizations. But to cyclists, he was the mortar that held the Harley-Davidson Motor Company together in good times and bad for several decades. In fact, William H. was the connection between the past and the present. . . .

Davidson signed on with the company just prior to the Depression, in 1928. In part because literally everyone at Harley-Davidson started at the bottom, he paid his dues on loading docks, in warehouses and on assembly lines. It became evident that he was not only a skilled rider but an excellent administrator, as well. Not one employee wondered at the directors' decision in 1931 to elect him to the board, less than five years after graduation from the University of Wisconsin. William H. began to matter increasingly as H-D fortunes followed American industry downward in the early thirties. Named a vice president in 1937, he was the driving force behind the company's crucial government contracts; the engineers and assemblers got the glory and William H. saw to it that corporate promises were kept to Uncle Sam. When President Walter Davidson died in 1942, the board knew William A.'s son was most capable of guiding company fortunes. He was elected without a dissenting vote.

The milestones in Davidson's career include continuing to meet Defense Department needs; returning Harley-Davidson to a prosperous, stable, peacetime footing; doing battle with the

imports while making the right decisions on evolution of the product line each year; deciding to sell H-D stock publicly; and, then, steering shareholders in the public company away from the jaws of predators and into the waiting arms of AMF. Looking back, William H. saw no mystery about why Harley-Davidson opted to sell stock to anyone with the money in 1965. "There were a number of shareholders in the privately owned company who wanted to pursue other interests." Rather than attempting to keep track of private stock in 326 hands, and to create capital for the coming cycle boom, the directors made their first public offering in 1965.

Several chances to buy H-D stock took place during the period 1965–69, with more than 1.3 million shares ultimately made available. The company seemed to be a good investment, despite the fact that Harley-Davidson had just twelve to sixteen percent of the total motorcycle market: Accessories were blossoming, riders were queued up with money in hand at the dealerships and H-D had a reputation for being soundly managed. In addition to attracting individual investors, the company was noticed by such firms as AMF, Bangor Punta, Chrysler, International Harvester and White Motor. These and other corporations made at least informal inquiries about purchasing the company—lock, stock and barrel. All were politely turned down.

Meanwhile, Harley-Davidson could do very little about the sales of foreign bikes, but it was able for several years to prevent British machines from becoming too uppity on America's flat tracks and road racing courses. Until 1969, H-D personnel and allies on the American Motorcycle Association's competition committee preserved the 750cc flathead side valve by permitting overhead valve engines with a maximum displacement of just 500cc. Earlier, the committee had further thwarted efforts of Triumph and BSA by limiting compression ratios; the trusty flathead would run at relatively low compression, say 7.5:1, while the British vertical twins could not pull the higher rpm they needed to pass the Harleys without a ratio of 9.5:1 or higher.

The late Floyd Clymer, a pioneer racer, Indian dealer, cycling entrepreneur and publisher, reported in 1956 on an AMA competition committee meeting that was orchestrated by H-D's favorite AMA official, E. C. Smith. Sensing that the compression ratio rule was in trouble, AMA officials waited until a proponent of British bikes angrily left the room to take the compression vote. It failed by a single ballot.

An increasing number of racers, however, were voting for foreign machines. Riders such as Dick Mann, Gary Nixon and, a bit later, Kenny Roberts, won national championships aboard Matchless, BSA, Triumph, Honda, Yamaha—anything but the Milwaukee bikes. Immediately after the rules were opened up in '69, the Triumps and BSA's temporarily blew the iron-head XR's into the hay bales, spending themselves toward financial oblivion when they should have been casting a nervous eye at the thousands of little Hondas that were spawning wickedly quick Suzuki X-6 Hustlers that

in turn gestated vile-handling but fast Kawasakis and the milestone Honda 750cc four-cylinder.

Coincidentally, Harley-Davidson worked with the transverse-four configuration several years prior to the introduction of the bigger Honda. Very little is known about the machine, though photos of a non-running model still exist. The machine sports an engine that carries double overhead cams and is labeled the X1000. Many H-D employees with access to the archives are aware of the photos, but few seem to know why the mock-up was created. According to William H., it was only a styling exercise and never got into the metal stage.

Production on less esoteric models continued, supplemented by the many small machines that arrived from Italy with the H-D name. Merger mania was sweeping the country in the late sixties, as smaller companies by the hundreds were devoured by such conglomerates as Litton, TRW, LTV and others. There were, it seemed, just two kinds of corporations in Vietnam-era America: those doing the digesting and those about to be chewed. One of the corporations eager to grab a merger meal ticket was Bangor Punta, an East Coast firm with roots in the railroad business. A neighbor of H-D, the respected Waukesha Engine Company, was merged into B-P, which then cast a covetous eye at Harley-Davidson. Anxiety among H-D directors grew in direct proportion to the amount of Harley-Davidson stock the conglomer-

The Juneau Avenue home office, as it appears today. *David Wright*

ate was acquiring. Prompted in part by rumors that B-P had a reputation for exploiting its acquisitions, President William H. Davidson in 1968 reopened talks with AMF.

A bidding war for outstanding shares ensued, with H-D principals urging shareholders to peddle their stake to AMF. There were, William Davidson told shareholders, "substantial benefits to the stockholders of both companies. . . . The merger will be a tax-free reorganization and will give the stockholders of H-D participation in a large and more diversified enterprise with greater financial resources for further development and growth." Unfortunately, at least one H-D board member almost queered the deal by passing on to Bangor Punta some of Harley-Davidson's most private antimerger thoughts. Despite a lawsuit, Bangor Punta lost the bidding war for America's only motorcycle to American Machine & Foundry. Shareholders in H-D expressed their confidence in William H. by voting overwhelmingly to merge with AMF on December 18, 1968. For the record, 713,554 shares in H-D became 1,020,331 shares in AMF. Had it been a cash deal, the conglomerate would have paid something over $30 million for Harley-Davidson.

The more shareholders thought about it, the better they liked the AMF offer to purchase the company. One employee, who bought 100 shares of H-D stock at $7 per share in 1965, as it first went public, was confronted with the happy prospect of receiving 1.5 shares of AMF stock for each share in Harley-Davidson. At that time, AMF shares were selling for $28 per share. They moved rapidly to $35, allowing the shareholder, in less than five years, to realize $5,200 from his $700 investment. It did not take long for many Harley and Davidson relatives, who wanted more liquidity, to liquidate—much to their financial benefit.

Among the first to depart from within H-D was Walter C. Davidson, vice president of sales. He quickly became disenchanted with his position in the new scheme of things. William H. Davidson was named chairman in 1971, though he no longer had a board to chair. "They pulled my teeth," he complained to one of his employees. In a company characterized previously by stability, a succession of leaders came and went. William. H. Davidson, John H. O'Brien, John A. Davidson, Vaughn L. Beals, E. Gus Davis and Charles K. Thompson all took their turns in the president's chair—in a single decade. O'Brien departed after displeasing AMF personnel with some sort of tentative deal he had in mind in Europe. Davis left in less than eighteen months, a victim of his own bombast, according to those who were associated with him.

The York, Pennsylvania, assembly facility formerly housed munitions-making equipment for the U.S. Navy, which still pays H-D to store the armament machinery. *Harley-Davidson, Inc.*

And William H. and son John had the outrageous (to AMF) idea that the president of Harley-Davidson should make some of the decisions affecting the company.

Dealers nationwide still hear it: "Harley-Davidson didn't build any good motorcycles while they were owned by AMF." Not only is this statement not true, it is a cheap shot at a conglomerate that poured millions of developmental dollars into H-D, allowing it to produce such significant bikes of yesterday as the Super Glide and such monumental bikes of today as the FXLR Low Rider Custom. Harley-Davidson motorcycles would not be half as good as they are (and they are *very* good bikes) without AMF willingness to spend money.

AMF shareholders approved the merger on January 7, 1969. At the time, H-D was selling 15,475 domestically produced cycles. A dozen years later, on the eve of the buyback by company personnel, H-D would be selling more than 50,000 machines—all U.S.-made heavyweights. In addition to dollars, AMF descended upon Juneau Avenue with diverse engineering skills, modern management techniques and with marketing, advertising and promotional ideas that heightened recognition almost overnight. The red-white-and-blue No. 1 insignia, Michael Parks astride a Sportster in TV's *Then Came Bronson*, movie star

Robert Blake enforcing the law in *Electra Glide in Blue*, Evel Knievel's death-defying leaps—all were correctly calculated to make the public more aware of H-D during a period of incredible increases in U.S. cycling registrations.

Not all of the AMF decisions proved to be of long-range benefit. The company's massive York, Pennsylvania, defense and bowling equipment plant lay all but idle in 1972, just when H-D badly needed more assembly space and when Milwaukee's unionized assemblers were more militant than ever. The decision was made to refurbish the York facility, converting it to final assembly and relying on Capitol Drive only for production of engines and transmissions. Confirmed reports of sabotage of a few 1972 models at the Capitol Drive assembly line hastened the move, allowing the first bike produced in York to bob down the overhead conveyor line in February of 1973. Quality control problems afflicted some '73's, but that affliction was minute compared to a world news event the following year.

The Middle East War in October 1974 caused American drivers and riders to become aware of the price of gasoline and just how far a gallon of that precious fuel would allow them to travel. H-D and fellow bikemakers rejoiced—here at last was a prudent reason to buy a motorcycle. But the oil

The H-D test track, just east of the York assembly plant. The facility, on a gentle slope, also houses pillboxes formerly used to test weaponry. The track is now used primarily for the quality audit program. *Harley-Davidson, Inc.*

crisis was also a blow to AMF/H-D, because it greatly increased the cost of hauling engines and transmissions from Milwaukee to York, a distance of 700 miles, for final assembly. At a time when the price difference between a Harley-Davidson and a Japanese bike was already noticeable, this added expense was frightening. There was soon at least one indication that the parent company was concerned.

Q. Do you see more growth in the leisure area than in the industrial side of your business?

A. At this point, we intend to develop relatively more strength on the industrial side, which now accounts for about 36 percent of AMF's business. We would like to see closer to 50 percent of AMF's business come from industrial products and services.

The above question, answered by AMF President Rodney C. Gott in the company's 1975 annual report, is the first clue the public had that Gott and friends were less than enthralled with bicycles, sailboats, tennis rackets, skis, golf clubs, rubber balls—and motorcycles. Gott and company had

good reason to be disillusioned with H-D, since a strike in 1974 idled the Capitol Drive and York assembly lines. The 101-day strike, over cost of living allowance, cost the company fourteen weeks of production before AMF acceded to worker demands. Actually, the strike helped H-D work off an inventory created by a drop of twenty-five percent in U.S. cycle registrations, combined with intensified Japanese production of cycles with engines larger than 750cc. Readers of the company's financial statements noticed throughout AMF's tenure that motorcycle products were strong on sales but weak on profits. In 1978, for example, motorcycles and other travel vehicles accounted for seventeen percent of revenue but just one percent of profit, though that tiny figure is due to the large write-off related to the sale of Aermacchi rather than lack of demand for the heavyweights. Incentive to sell H-D was increased by the exceptional long-range potential of AMF products used in oil fields. Therefore, the question became not whether AMF would peddle H-D, but when.

Another view of the York plant. The Rodney C. Gott Museum, named for the former AMF chairman, is at the extreme left center of the photo. *Harley-Davidson, Inc.*

Asked a few years ago to assess the AMF years, William H. Davidson believed the conglomerate made only one major miscalculation. "They thought Harley-Davidson could become another Honda. That's ridiculous," he said, pulling out the latest Honda Motor Company annual report. "This states that Honda produced 3,518,000 units in the year ending February 28, 1982. No one can imagine Harley-Davidson ever producing one-tenth that many machines. We were never meant to be a high-production company."

AMF investment (such as $4.5 million for just one machine for Capitol Drive that makes the FLT's five-speed transmission) placed H-D in a difficult spot. The product was neither quite a hand-built, premium-priced, limited production item nor was it a "nifty, thrifty Honda 50," stamped out like cookies. While its unique position in the market accounted for the majority of sales then and now, this position caused concern —and a futile trip to Washington.

The charge of "dumping" initiated by AMF in April 1978 resulted in good news and bad news for Harley-Davidson. The good news was that the U.S. Treasury Department in August 1978 found three of the four major Japanese manufacturers guilty of selling their bikes at prices even lower than on the home (Japanese) market, as AMF had contended.

The bad news came three months later, when the nonpartisan International Trade Commission ruled that the dumping had not damaged sales of Harley-Davidson motorcycles.

"The law says dumping is selling products at less than fair market value," said John A. Davidson, then H-D's president. AMF picked him to lead the fight in Washington against the Japanese. "In the early seventies, when the motorcycle business was doing well worldwide, the Japanese established production schedules that were much higher than the mid-seventies demand for their products. We contended that they chose the U.S. to unload their excess production."

The charges were not based on manufacturers' costs, though consultants were hired by AMF to check the costs of Japanese cyclemaking. Rather, Davidson reports, those numbers were used as guidelines to compare U.S. selling prices with prices in Japan and were adjusted for such factors as shipping costs and value of the Japanese yen relative to the dollar. AMF decided to pursue matters with the Treasury after totaling all of the figures and coming up with what it believed to be less than fair market value. This conclusion led AMF to believe that federal antidumping statutes had been violated.

Davidson remembers that the case was unusu-

Vaughn L. Beals. *David Wright*

The Capitol Drive plant in Wauwatosa, a suburb immediately west of Milwaukee. The plywood on the sign covers the AMF insignia following the buyback. The sign later was replaced with a new Harley-Davidson Motor Company logo. *David Wright*

A very early rendering by Willie G., on the back of his father's company letterhead. *William H. Davidson collection*

Willie G. Davidson (standing), vice president of styling, discusses a design detail with Louis Netz. Stylist Netz was in large part responsible for the look of the lean, low-priced 1983 XLX. *David Wright*

Ex-President Charles Thompson (left) and former Chairman Vaughn Beals aboard the 1982 Tour Glides ridden from the Canadian Pacific to Florida to test the new oil control package. *David Wright*

ally complicated because no Japanese manufacturer is allowed to sell motorcycles larger than 750cc in Japan. Investigators thus had to look to other free-market economies such as France and Canada for model comparisons with big bikes offered in the U.S. The Japanese attempted to muddy the waters with minor model differences and designations, which made comparison difficult. Nevertheless, the weighted average dumping margins found for each of three Japanese manufacturers were: Honda, 2.9 percent; Kawasaki, 7.26 percent; and Yamaha, 1.98 percent. The fourth major Japanese bikemaker, Suzuki, was guilty of so tiny a margin that the Treasury dropped charges against it, Davidson said.

AMF and Harley-Davidson evidently looked at the percentages, realized they didn't appear that dramatic, and began to produce press releases commenting on the Treasury decision. Davidson is quoted as saying that "the dumping margins were very much higher on certain models. Some ranged as high as 54 percent." There is no indication which models are referred to. In any event, a finding equally favorable to H-D by the

independent International Trade Commission would have meant that the Japanese had the unenviable choice of either boosting U.S. prices or paying duty on the bikes they shipped to this country.

Late in 1978, the commission delivered the bad news: Although the Japanese had indeed dumped products on these shores, the practice had not injured Harley-Davidson. AMF and H-D employees not directly involved with the proceedings probably were stunned by the decision. But those who spent countless hours preparing the material sensed trouble when the commissioners requested and received permission to query Harley dealers about the problem. "We told our dealers to be frank with the commission, and that's where the case was lost," Davidson said. H-D dealers, plagued with real and imagined problems with the Aermacchis, told the commission that the smaller H-D's were obsolete and could not compete with the state-of-the-art Japanese bikes. "So they ruled that we injured ourselves by failing to keep our product up to date," said Davidson.

Despite the months of work without reward,

1985 and later H-D's bear the A.I.W./I.A.M. union label. Application of the label was agreed to between the company and the unions before contract talks opened. The label is on the right-hand downtube, near the steering head. *Harley-Davidson, Inc.*

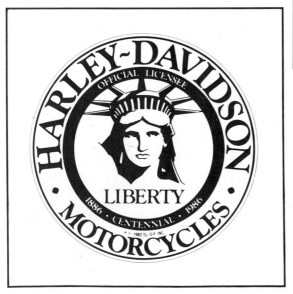

The 1986 Ride for Liberty invited owners of all bikes to join Vaughn Beals and Willie G. Davidson in a ride that raised $250,000 for restoration of the Statue of Liberty. The promotion introduced the Liberty edition H-D series. *Harley-Davidson, Inc.*

Davidson believed the whole process was worthwhile. "It stabilized prices and made everyone—us and the Japanese—take a close look at production." The big loser in the proceedings may well have been Yamaha. That company petitioned to have its case dropped, due to the small difference between its U.S. and Japanese prices. The Treasury Department agreed to drop the Yamaha matter—if Yamaha would permit it to monitor the company's pricing. "This drove Yamaha nuts," Davidson said. The other big loser was the troubled Aermacchi operation in Italy. If anyone at AMF or Harley-Davidson had any doubts about what dealers thought of the H-D lightweights, they knew after the commission recessed.

An AMF corporate employee who prefers anonymity believes pursuit of the Japanese was not only a waste of time, but was hideously expensive in terms of the number of well-paid executives who commuted between Milwaukee and Washington, D.C., on and off, for weeks at a time. "AMF's

bankroll was of great value to Harley-Davidson," he contends. "But the dumping thing proves that not all of the money was wisely spent."

All this is significant, as we'll see later on. . . .

Those who ran the country were affecting H-D in other, equally troublesome ways. California took action in the late-sixties to curb its awesome pollution problem, and the feds appropriated many of the emissions, noise—and safety—decrees created originally in Los Angeles County, which has more motorized vehicles than virtually any of the forty-nine other states. H-D recruited engineers from all fields in an eleventh-hour rush to meet increasingly stringent federal vehicle standards. Those standards were most evident in the enlarged air cleaners, constricted breathing and low-octane, unleaded fuel being foisted upon the 1978–80 models.

Harley-Davidson joined the growing chorus from the media and from auto manufacturers for relief from—or at least a holding action on—the

Exact date and location not known, but the company-produced caption says John Davidson (left) is discussing "plans for the new company and the 1982 model year" with (from Davidson's left) Dr. Jeff Bleustein, vice president engineering; Charles K. Thompson, president; and Vaughn L. Beals, chairman. Just weeks later, John opted out. *Harley-Davidson, Inc.*

regulations. The election of Ronald Reagan in 1980 meant that Joan Claybrook of the National Highway Transportation Safety Administration was out of office and that tougher requirements would be shelved. Eyeing the trusty V-twin and the federal edicts, Racing Director Dick O'Brien summed it up succinctly: "If it can't breathe and it can't fart, how do they expect it to live?"

O'Brien's XR750 bikes were not only living but dominating AMA dirt-track racing well into the 1980's. That domination began to unravel in 1984 as former H-D riders such as Ricky Graham and Bubba Shobert defected to Team Honda's V-twins. Despite lingering stomach problems, Jay Springsteen copped his fortieth national victory in 1986, a total exceeded only recently by Scott Parker.

Racing wins may be appreciated only by the dealers and by H-D employees. With that in mind, the company has for the last several years instantaneously created collateral material for dealers to

display in their shops. The posters, telegrams, etc., also adorn the Milwaukee and York facilities, where a new breed of manager is as interested in racing as in anything else that pertains to the company.

This new manager, reared in, or at least accustomed to, the AMF way of doing things, appreciates and believes in what the company tries to do; in the motorcycles themselves, with exciting new Low Rider, Wide Glide and Roadster models; in quality control, where employees are now convinced that premium quality is imperative if a premium price is on the tag; in a sense of history, whether understanding how real motorcycles evolve or staging a nationwide ride to raise money for the Statue of Liberty; and in an entrepreneurial urge that culminated in a dozen of the managers buying the company from AMF. How can just twelve men raise an estimated $75 million to purchase a company that had been in business

Pre-buyout executives prepare to depart Juneau Avenue in 1978 to celebrate H-D's 75th anniversary with a cross-country ride. Members of the buyback team in the photo include Chairman Vaughn Beals (front row, second from left); Styling Vice President Willie G. Davidson (front row, second from right); President Charles Thompson (behind Davidson); Engineering Vice President Jeff Bleustein (on Thompson's right); and Vice President Peter Profumo (behind and to the right of Beals). John A. Davidson, Willie G.'s younger brother and the former H-D president, is on the left in the front row. *Harley-Davidson, Inc.*

eighty years? By pooling their resources, finding bankers who share the dream and streamlining their new company as it's never been streamlined before. Before detailing the buyback, here's a glance at some of the men who put it all together. . . .

Vaughn L. Beals—Vaughn Beals is retired now, but the intelligence and drive he brought to Harley-Davidson was crucial to its success.

"Vaughn Beals didn't climb on a motorcycle till he was forty-five years old," says Bill Dutcher, who served AMF's motorcycle products group as public relations manager until the buyback. "Yet he's a natural rider, if I ever saw one." Dutcher, a former racer, is a good judge of talent—as sales manager for Bultaco until 1975, he signed up such rising stars as Mike Kidd and Freddy Spencer. If Dutcher was surprised at Beals' ability on a bike, the head

of Harley-Davidson had a few surprises in store for him when he moved to Milwaukee.

"I was talking to a mechanic attending service school when I noticed a series of numbers tattooed on his arm. I asked him what they were and he rolled up his sleeve to display a Harley-Davidson logo, with the numbers beneath it. This guy was wearing the serial number of every Harley-Davidson he'd owned. There were at least six or seven. Who else tattoos the name of a product on his arm but a Harley-Davidson fan?"

One of the subtle adornments Vaughn Beals carries about is a ring with a beaver on it, symbolizing the fact that he holds bachelor's and master's degrees from Massachusetts Institute of Technology, among the most prestigious technical colleges in the U.S. Beals, the son of a Nova Scotian, studied aeronautical engineering, then spent

These four H-D employees rode this 1984 FXRT Sport Glide 8,704 miles in seven days as part of the Cannonball One Lap of America contest. The lone motorcycle in the "high-performance rally" averaged 53 mph and got 55 mpg. *Harley-Davidson, Inc.*

more than fifteen years in aerospace industry research and technology. In 1965, he made the transition from technology to management when he joined Cummins, a maker of diesel engines. Beals managed worldwide diesel sales five years before striking out on his own, founding a company that manufactured logging and related equipment in Seattle. When tapped by AMF's Ray Tritten as vice president and group executive for the motorcycle products group, he was a consultant to several Pacific Northwest companies.

What was a person with credentials on the

Cutups Willie G. and John Davidson open the 1978 H-D exhibit at the Daytona Beach Hilton. *Harley-Davidson, Inc.*

The Capitol Drive plant, located between a multilane highway and numerous railroad tracks, now produces engines and transmissions. The plant is in the Milwaukee suburb of Wauwatosa. *Harley-Davidson, Inc.*

frontier of technology doing at the head of a company frequently accused of throwing away calendars after 1936? Beals was recruited more for his style of management than for his knowledge of ballistic missiles. A tall, balding, soft-spoken man, Beals comes off as exuding the type of authority in the board room that he displays in the saddle of his own Electra Glide or the company's FLT Tour Glide. Despite his reserve, he says he enjoys meeting and mingling with Harley-Davidson owners. In fact, the only drawback to the York-to-Milwaukee buyback ride in June of 1981 was the insistence by every H-D dealer en route that Mr. Beals consume a near-lethal first cutting of commemorative cake.

Beals and the buyback group succeeded because, "at Harley-Davidson, we're different. No one yet has successfully competed against us, though the Japanese are trying like hell. They're great engineers and great manufacturers, and we're feeling their V-twin push, but they don't understand the 'soft' areas. They do, however, learn fast."

Unlike Ray Tritten, who managed H-D capably but at a distance, Beals was involved in—and could talk knowledgeably about—any phase of the company. A detractor once complained that Vaughn Beals "has his nose in everything." But another former AMF employee said Beals' presence and grasp of the entire company reassured those who might have faltered during the lean days of the early 1980s.

Recently retired, Vaughn Beals (along with Richard F. Teerlink, chief executive officer) is responsible for the vibrant, progressive company Harley-Davidson, Inc., is today.

William G. Davidson—"I'll bring my crayons and be right down."

That was William ("Willie G.") Davidson's reaction when, on February 18, 1963, he was invited by his father, then President William H. Davidson, to sign on as H-D styling director. Unlike the proverbial much-maligned boss's son, Willie G. was experienced prior to being offered the styling position. Besides spending more than five years working for Brooks Stevens (designer-builder of the Excalibur sports car), Davidson had styled for Ford Motor Company's Continental Division. According to the senior Davidson, Willie G. owes it all to *The Saturday Evening Post.*

A transversely mounted, in-line-four mockup, created in 1966. This "idea bike" was on the minds of H-D three years before the first Honda four was introduced. This model progressed sufficiently to receive a designation, the X1000, but no engine or transmission work took place. *Harley-Davidson, Inc.*

Richard F. Teerlink. *Harley-Davidson, Inc.*

Among the ideas presented to H-D has been a gas turbine cycle. Details on this prototype are lacking, but it appears heavy and, unlike a Harley-Davidson, has a very wide engine.

"It was Christmas and Bill was home from the University of Wisconsin," William recalled. "He was in his junior year majoring in art and complained that he wasn't looking forward to a career teaching unwilling schoolkids how to draw in rural Wisconsin. He read about a kid who was doing well at The Art Center College of Design in Los Angeles and showed me the *Post* article. I checked with an ad agency artist, who gave the place high marks. Two weeks later, Bill was enrolled and on his way to California."

It's easy to conclude that many of the lush designs created by Willie G. were influenced by his Los Angeles stay. But there is little comparison between the customs in California in the middle fifties and the FXRS, for example. A lifetime of being in and around every department at the Juneau Avenue plant, plus the Art Center College of Design training, were much more likely to have left their marks on the former president's elder son. "I realized early I was a part of something unique. My dad rode a bike every day. It wasn't tough to tell that he was coming home on something none of the neighbors had," Willie states. "I hung around the experimental shop, I went to the races. I had the bug at an early age."

If California played only a small part in his designs, it has well influenced his lifestyle. In contrast to some fellow officers of Harley-Davidson, who favor traditional business attire, Davidson wears leather vests, jeans and the kinds of opulent personal accessories popular with many H-D owners. Since he rides to work year-round (his bike is equipped with a sidecar in the winter), the biker gear serves its purpose. He opted out of three-piece suits several years ago, leading one to believe that there are two sides to the man who

currently carries the title of vice president, styling. The serious side of Willie G. dutifully performed all Art Center assignments at the year-round school. The less serious side can be seen strolling Daytona's boardwalks each March.

Today, Willie G. also can be seen on his bike frequently leading a contingent of riders to Daytona and other events in order to raise money for the Muscular Dystrophy Association. He enjoys such outings. "I really like being around Harley-Davidson people. It's my hobby as well as theirs. They're a fun-loving group of people. And our motorcycle attracts a devotion, a dedication, that's total." Willie G's dedication occasionally shows through his clothing and the long hours he enjoys in the saddle. Returning from the annual Sturgis, South Dakota, rally a couple of years ago, he stopped in a Minnesota wayside with an idea. Rummaging in a trash receptacle, he found a fairly clean paper bag. Willie began to work frantically with a pencil, recalling what he'd seen and liked at Sturgis and what seemed possible for H-D stylists and engineers. That brief stop to sketch while sitting on a picnic bench resulted in the belt-drive Sturgis. Not bad for a guy who showed up a few years ago with a bunch of crayons.

Back in 1982, when smart money was staying away from America's only remaining motorcycle maker, someone asked a laid-off employee if Willie G. was good or bad for Harley-Davidson. The further into the future we get, the dumber that question becomes. Willie transcends mere ownership or family. The kind of person he is and the skills he displays each model year make him the very soul of this corporation's motorcycle division.

Jeffrey L. Bleustein—Jeff Bleustein had nu-

H-D may be getting into the toy business, but someone beat them to it. This HRD "Florida" is constructed in Italy with a two-stroke, 50cc motor and is imported to the U.S. in small numbers.

Mr. and Mrs. Willie G. lead the buyback team, plus wives and others, away from a gas stop during the ride from York back to Milwaukee in July 1981. *People*

The 1993 XLH Sportster 883 Hugger. *Harley-Davidson, Inc.*

merous occasions to become acquainted with Milwaukee before being named vice president of engineering in 1975. As a member of AMF's corporate research and engineering division, he made frequent trips to Harley-Davidson to iron-out technical problems associated with his mechanical engineering specialties. "One of my 'clients' was Harley-Davidson," he says. "A lot of neat things were going on out here." So it may have been easy for him to decide on joining the buyback team; he had a special interest in the company.

A native of greater New York City, Bleustein holds a PhD in mechanical engineering from Columbia University. Following completion of a NATO research grant that took him to England, he served as an instructor at Yale University's department of engineering and applied science. The theory of elasticity, dynamics, electro-mechanical interaction—Bleustein taught these and other courses before being recruited by AMF researchers in 1971. One of six specialists, he recalls

his early years for the company fondly: "We floated around the world with our attaché cases. Everyone assumed we were experts because we were called in from far away. And we worked on everything—skis, tobacco machinery, oil industry products, motorcycles. It was a good existence."

Bleustein was surprised at the Juneau Avenue staff. "There weren't many engineers," he recalls. "A lot of people in engineering were there because they loved Harley-Davidsons. So we began to bring in some engineers from several different industries—RV's, agriculture, diesels, trucks—people with good credentials who may not have known anything about motorcycles. We doubled the staff in two or three years and the new people are all assimilated." Bleustein says AMF had two goals in mind in the early seventies: first, to bring production up to meet demand, then to put more effort into product development. Veteran employees point to the FXRS as evidence of the infusion of AMF corporate dollars at that time.

York employees gather round the 10,000th Evolution 883cc Sportster to roll off the assembly line. The date is June 26, 1986. *Harley-Davidson, Inc.*

Bleustein also became an expert in turbulence during this period—that is, he and fellow H-D employees watched a succession of executives come and go at the head of the subsidiary. But the engineers were more concerned with a host of federal Environmental Protection Agency regulations that affected noise and emission levels on the bikes. "Some people here acted as if, by disregarding the regulations, they would go away. We made our products conform, but we came very, very close to the deadline." With those problems apparently behind him, Bleustein watched with pleasure as the buyback team took shape. "After all of the turnover and the EPA, this served as a unifying force," he says.

Today, Bleustein is the president and chief operating officer of Harley-Davidson, Inc.'s motorcycle division. He returned to cycling after looking after the entire corporation's operations as a vice president. Earlier, he left in place an engineering department not only capable of running the racing program but of creating constant, evolutionary product improvements. Of the transformation by the motorcycle company, he says, "We have to invest in quality. Only that would lead to success of the product, which led to success of the company. We've attracted a lot of attention, and there's a danger that we may spend too much time celebrating. But we can't stop improving if we want to remain competitive into the next century."

Asked if former Chairman Vaughn Beals recruited him, Bleustein laughs. "I was only 36 years old and had been here six months before Vaughn arrived. After he'd been here two or three months, he said, 'If it had been up to me, I wouldn't have hired you.' Fortunately, I stuck around a while longer."

Timothy K. Hoelter—Timothy K. Hoelter, vice president/general counsel, has an unusual ambition for an attorney: He wants to avoid representing his client in court whenever possible. The only man on the buyback team who was neither associated with AMF nor Harley-Davidson, Hoelter served H-D for eight years as a member of the Milwaukee law firm of Whyte & Hirschboeck S.C. He specialized in corporate law "by accident," being assigned to a hearing before the Wisconsin Department of Motor Vehicles that involved H-D just four months after graduation from Harvard Law School. A Milwaukee native who did his undergraduate work at the University of Wiscon-

The 1993 XLH Sportster 883 Deluxe. *Harley-Davidson, Inc.*

sin, Hoelter today is concerned with an incredible array of subjects where the company and the legal system meet: trade regulations (how Harley-Davidson treats dealers), warranties, antitrust matters, truth in advertising and promotion, the environment and more. He adheres to few rigid lines, but one to which he voices commitment is preserving the company trademark.

"The law doesn't distinguish between 'good infringement' [the logo on an attractive T-shirt or quality decal, for example] and 'bad infringement.' They tell you to protect your trademark against those who use it or give it up and let everyone use it. That doesn't give us much choice in prosecuting." Holding a file, he displays an example of what the company believes is "bad infringement." A catalog from Texas displays a Bat Wing Power Hitter, apparently a device to aid the marijuana smoker. Emblazoned thereon is the Harley-Davidson trademark. He can lay his hands on items the company finds equally offensive: cocaine spoons, swastikas and skull decals, various pins, bits of clothing, all bearing the bar and shield. "Are you going to control your promotional effort, or do you intend to leave it in the hands of third parties? That's the question. Unfortunately, we sometimes

have to give our answer in court, though a surprisingly large number of offenders cease and desist when we explain our position," Hoelter says. A California firm, Joe's MCN, that refused to cease the use of the H-D trademark recently was ordered to do so in court.

Fortunately, not all of the attorney's confrontations are hostile. As an officer in the company, one of his responsibilities is to improve relations with vendors. He's personally responsible for half-a-dozen vendors, making them feel that they're a part of the new effort, offering them a special program wherein they can receive a discount on the purchase of a machine, even inviting some of them to the annual unveiling of new models. He also keeps an eye on the way in which H-D treats its dealers. "A dealer today has a minimal obligation to the company. The current feeling here is that we don't want to force any of our dealers into a particular program. But if they choose to participate, then we want them to abide by the rules we've set forth." In view of some dealer complaints in the dim, distant past, that's a very enlightened attitude.

One more thing—Tim is now a rider. He led a contingent of H-D owners from Seattle to Mil-

The 1993 XLH Sportster 1200. *Harley-Davidson, Inc.*

waukee for the company's 85th anniversary celebration.

James Paterson—When we last checked with Jim, he had yet to ride his own Harley-Davidson. Since he led a contingent of bikes and riders all the way from Augusta, Maine, to Milwaukee for the 85th anniversary celebration, it's safe to conclude he now knows how. As executive vice president of the motorcycle division, he doesn't need an excuse to hit the starter and motor off.

From AMF's home turf in Connecticut, Paterson joined the conglomerate after college and following a stint with Kraft Foods in Chicago. As a sailing enthusiast, hooking up with AMF in January 1971 seemed to be the ideal job, first with the corporate staff and then with the conglomerate's motorcycle products group. Paterson and Vaughn Beals were caught up in structuring the financing for the leveraged buyout. Today, he is responsible for gauging the demand for every product in the company's mix—plus such staff functions as advertising and public and investor relations.

"AMF got rid of Harley-Davidson because of the extreme capital requirements and because it needed to use that capital in some of its other divisions," he believes. "Harley-Davidson contra-

dicted the corporate strategy, which was to deemphasize leisure products in favor of industrial and energy pursuits. One of the problems during the AMF years was the fact that the company went for a long while without a corporate strategy. I think Harley-Davidson is improving in that respect, it's becoming much more professional. However, H-D would not exist today, as we know it, without AMF. It probably would be in one location—perhaps Capitol Drive—making only 15,000 or so motorcycles a year."

Paterson intends to learn to ride. "Growing up, a lot of my friends had Harley-Davidsons. I've been to Daytona and I can understand the fascination. Watching the Bikers Fight MD parade at Daytona this year, I saw the Harleys go by and heard the thunder. Then, some Japanese bikes went by and they sounded tinny. The sound was anticlimactic."

Richard F. Teerlink—There are several heroes walking around Juneau Avenue, but none more important to the survival of the new company than this man. As chief financial officer and treasurer, Teerlink successfully returned the company to public ownership by offering two million shares of common stock and $70 million in high-yield notes in July 1986. The sale was necessitated

The 1993 XLH Sportster 1200 (90th Anniversary Edition). *Harley-Davidson, Inc.*

The 1993 FXDWG Dyna Wide Glide (90th Anniversary Edition). *Harley-Davidson, Inc.*

The 1993 FLHTC Electra Glide Ultra Classic (90th Anniversary Edition). *Harley-Davidson, Inc.*

by the fact that Citicorp, lead bank among the four lending the buyback team money, wanted out of the deal. Had Teerlink not devised a solid method of rounding up cash, the firm's future would have been a lot shakier than it is.

"We just got some breathing room," he says, pointing out that the $70 million in high-yield or "junk" bonds means that H-D should be prepared for a big payout in 1996. But "we decided that living the life of leveraged buyout was not how we wanted to exist." The common stock, listed on the New York Stock Exchange, supports the company's borrowing base. "Now," says the Chicago native, "a lender can't change our plans."

The buyback dudes, some of whom are retired, didn't do it alone. They had help from longtime employees like Tom Gelb, who now holds the title of vice president of continuous improvement and is as responsible for improved quality as anyone; Jerry Wilke, vice president of sales and marketing; Clyde Fessler, a vice president and in charge of Motorclothes marketing; Mark Tuttle, vice president of engineering; Ron Hutchinson, vice president of corporate services, and many, many others.

Notably absent among the buyback members

was John A. Davidson, former H-D president and a third-generation member of the founding family.

The AMF news releases weren't terribly informative where John A. was concerned. The February 27, 1981, announcement of the planned buyback listed the H-D board chairman and golf car division president as one of the prospective investors. Three months later, a brief news item reported that Willie G.'s younger brother had decided not to join Beals and associates in the newly independent company.

What did Davidson's decision do to those who were pondering being a part of the buyback? More than one came to him after learning that John would be leaving, he says. They wondered if he saw something in the plans they had not. "I didn't attempt to discourage any of them," he says. "I just told them not to do anything emotional."

All buyback principals will admit that their venture was a risk; it was a risk John Davidson did not want to take. Because of John's decision, he and his brother now travel different roads.

In a procession that followed signing over the company on June 23, 1981, buyback members, their wives and the press made a symbolic ride from York to Milwaukee. Along the way, the riders

The 1993 FLTC Tour Glide Ultra Classic (90th Anniversary Edition). *Harley-Davidson, Inc.*

The 1993 FXR Super Glide. *Harley-Davidson, Inc.*

The 1993 FXRS-Conv. Low Rider Convertible. *Harley-Davidson, Inc.*

were greeted by dealers and H-D enthusiasts with the kind of buoyancy last seen when the Allies liberated Paris. That attitude prevailed in Milwaukee into 1982, as the company did a lot of things right. It franchised the bar-and-shield symbol for added income, prosecuted those who used the H-D name illegally, aggressively searched for new dealers and exuded a "We're all in this together" sort of brotherhood. But a recession that threatened at the time of the buyback became reality. Coupled with stratospheric interest rates, things did not look good.

In August of 1982, Harley-Davidson went once again to Washington. As the sole remaining domestic motorcycle manufacturer, the company was seeking relief under the Trade Act of 1974. In papers filed with the same International Trade Commission that stifled them in 1978, H-D stated its belief that Japanese manufacturers were deliberately building abnormally high inventories of unsold motorcycles in the United States and that there was "a direct onslaught on Harley's markets by virtually copying our motorcycles' styling and components, as well as our marketing research." Unlike Chrysler Corporation, H-D is not seeking government funds. Rather, the company wants the Japanese to compete "in the real world," a world with less discretionary income.

Harley-Davidson had a strong case. The 1974 act under which it sought relief was created for U.S. industries seriously injured by imports. If 1982 sales of 12,000 Honda Aspencades didn't represent serious injury, what did? "We are running at only fifty-one percent of capacity, despite costly rebate and promotion campaigns," Beals said in testimony before the commission on November 30, 1982. "The company has suffered unprecedented financial losses, and our future is in the hands of our lenders."

The White House weighed the evidence, then surprised financial analysts and shocked Oriental bikemakers on April 1, 1983, by imposing sizeable tariffs on all Japanese cycles 700cc or larger. A tariff of forty-five percent was added to the regular tariff on heavyweights above 6,000 total (from all four major Japanese producers) brought into the country this year. The duty decreases to thirty-five percent after the first 7,000 cycles in 1984, twenty percent after the first 8,000 in 1985, fifteen percent after the first 9,000 in 1986 and ten

The 1993 FXRS-SP Low Rider Sport Edition. *Harley-Davidson, Inc.*

The 1993 FXLR Low Rider Custom. *Harley-Davidson, Inc.*

The 1993 FLHS Electra Glide Sport. *Harley-Davidson, Inc.*

percent after the first 10,000 in 1987. The tariff increase does not apply to bikes already in the U.S. but took effect quickly, on April 15.

The most exciting decade in company history has been the period since the 1983 tariff decision. The 90th year, 1993, looks especially attractive because:

—It appears that Harley-Davidson will, for the 1983 model year ship more motorcycles than ever. The record, set during the AMF year of 1973, is 70,903. Production in 1991 totaled 68,626 units. Of that total, 21,633, or 31.5 percent, were exported to riders in 30 different countries.

—As the figures indicate, Harley-Davidson is building world-class machines for a world market. The bikes all have five-speed transmissions and final belt drive. The chassis continue to evolve: The Dyna Wide Glide and the Dyna Low Rider have directionally controlled engine mounts made with a new compound for virtually total vibration control. "It's like the engine's running the bike from some distance away," said a test-rider at Sturgis in August, 1992.

—MotorClothes, plus Screamin' Eagle and Eagle Iron and Genuine parts have added to dealer income, helping the company to pacify the many retailers who could sell more bikes than they are allotted. Where once the search was on for dealers, Harley-Davidson now has more inquiries than dealerships available, here and abroad.

—They take the past and make it work like the future. Mark Tuttle, engineering vice president, says his biggest thrill so far has been presenting the Springer Softail to a chuckling motorcycle press. The writers rode the bike and were stunned by the precise handling evident in this unusual machine and its unconventional suspension. No one laughs at Harley-Davidson innovation these days.

—Shares of stock in Harley-Davidson, Inc., have climbed as high as $60 after being offered in 1986 for less than one-third of that figure. Even the people who bought a single share of stock for sentimental reasons, paying more for the transaction than for the stock itself, made money! Best of all, those who laid it on the line—the buyback guys—have prospered.

—Harley Owners Group (H.O.G.) has more than 100,000 members. The organization is the most vibrant in all of motorcycling at the

The 1993 FLHTC Electra Glide Ultra Classic. *Harley-Davidson, Inc.*

moment, running hundreds of neat events (rides, rallies, shows) and making the local dealership the year-round focus of leisure-time activities.

—Speaking of dealerships, they total about 500 in the U.S. and have become about as foreboding as the local Dairy Queen. Clothing and parts and accessories are now tastefully displayed, there's no rush to put down a visitor who just parked a Japanese bike out front and sales personnel wear pastel golf shirts, tidy jeans and H-D tennis shoes. One result is that your mother now shops there for Christmas. So do lots of other people.

—Given breathing room with a tariff by the White House, H-D asked in March 1987 that the tariff on Japanese bikes be lifted a year early. The company was ready to compete with anyone. President Ronald Reagan came to York to start the first 30th Anniversary Sportster and to praise "everyone from the board room to the factory."

Today, Harley-Davidson has almost two-thirds of the superheavyweight (850cc-plus) American market. Gaining market share in a mature market is a textbook sign that you are the strongest player in the game. *The New York Times* reported late in 1991 that total motorcycle registrations and sales are well below the peak year of 1984.

Armed with some of the money from the sale of its stock, the company in late 1986 purchased Holiday Rambler, a diversified manufacturer of recreational vehicles. RVs are popular with older people who are more into comfort than cyclists. It appears that this is a wise decision, particularly since Indiana-based Holiday Rambler has a successful statistical quality control program of its own.

All of which leaves Harley-Davidson, Inc., where? Has it abandoned traditional bikers for a shot at fat yuppy pocketbooks? Or have the new and different bikes lured a greater variety of rider? The answer to those questions comes from a pair of H-D owners who also happen to be members of the media. . . .

The first is Peter Egan, a *Cycle World* columnist and the owner of a pair of Harley-Davidsons. Egan and his wife climbed on an FLH more than ten years ago for a ride from Los Angeles to Seattle. That trip became an article called "Shooting the Coast." Egan's verdict on H-D after that trip? "I still admired them, I liked the look and the sound," he

The 1993 FLTC Tour Glide Ultra Classic. *Harley-Davidson, Inc.*

says. "They were fun to ride, but they just didn't hold up."

Today, two of Egan's five bikes are Harley-Davidsons. His '92 Sportster features a SuperTrapp exhaust system, the carburetor has been rejetted, the bike is fitted with a 1971 FX-E tank and there's a Screamin' Eagle ignition module and a Freeflow air cleaner. His next move will be a 1200cc conversion. The '92 FLH-Sport is 100 percent stock. "I just can't find anything on it I want to change," he says.

"Harley-Davidsons are just much, much better machines," reports the writer, adding that he paid full retail for both bikes so that "I could criticize them honestly without feeling bad about it."

Less objective, but equally important from the marketing point of view is Linda (Jo) Giovannoni, editor/publisher ("and janitor") of *Harley Women* magazine. Now in its seventh year and almost profitable, the semi-monthly has found a real audience among women who consider other bike mags too raw or too dull for their tastes.

"I didn't do any market research, I just plunged right in," Giovannoni recalls. The company has been supportive over the years, she says, pointing out that she pays a licensing fee for the use of the name on the masthead. Jo rides an '88 Heritage Softail and has owned seven other Harley-Davidsons. With more new buyers female, *Harley Women* is addressing a market that has flown below radar for several years but now seems almost mainstream.

As this tradition-rich company heads toward its 100th year, with sales and interest here and abroad increasing, the motorcycles could evolve into even more of a mainstream product than they are in 1993. We can't wait.

Linda (Jo) Giovannoni, editor/publisher of *Harley Women* magazine.

Vaughn L. Beals. *Carroll-Haig Studios*

Harley-Davidson Models 1908-1983

From Harley-Davidson factory archives, with assistance from retired H-D dealer Conrad Schlemmer. Please note that no similar printed information exists concerning the 1903–1907 models.

1908
Model 4: single cylinder, single-belt drive, 28 in. wheels, battery ignition, 3.9 horsepower, $3^1/_8$ in. bore, motor numbers under 2500.

1909
Model 5: single-cylinder, single-belt drive, 28 in. wheels, battery ignition, 4.34 horsepower, $3^5/_{16}$ in. bore, 4 in. stroke, 35 cu. in., motor numbers 2500–4200.
Model 5A: single-cylinder, single-belt drive, 28 in. wheels, magneto ignition, 4.34 horsepower, $3^5/_{16}$ in. bore, 4 in. stroke, 35 cu. in., motor numbers 2500–4200.
Model 5C: single-cylinder, single-belt drive, 26 in. wheels, magneto ignition, 4.34 horsepower, $3^5/_{16}$ in. bore, 4 in. stroke, 35 cu. in., motor numbers 2500–4200.
Model 5D: twin-cylinder, single-belt drive, 28 in. wheels, magneto ignition, $6^1/_2$ horsepower, 3 in. bore, $3^1/_2$ in. stroke, 49.48 cu. in., motor numbers 2500–4200.

1910
Model 6: single-cylinder, single-belt drive, 28 in. wheels, battery ignition, 4.34 horsepower, $3^5/_{16}$ in. bore, 4 in. stroke, 35 cu. in., motor numbers 4200–7600.
Model 6A: single-cylinder, single-belt drive, 28 in. wheels, magneto ignition, 4.34 horsepower, $3^5/_{16}$ in. bore, 4 in. stroke, 35 cu. in., motor numbers 4200–7600.
Model 6B: single-cylinder, single-belt drive, 26 in. wheels, battery ignition, 4.34 horsepower, $3^5/_{16}$ in. bore, 4 in. stroke, 35 cu. in., motor numbers 4200–7600.
Model 6C: single-cylinder, single-belt drive, 26 in. wheels, magneto ignition, 4.34 horsepower, $3^5/_{16}$ in. bore, 4 in. stroke, 35 cu. in., motor numbers 4200–7600.
Model 6D: twin-cylinder, single-belt drive, 28 in. wheels, magneto ignition, $6^1/_2$ horsepower, 3 in. bore, $3^1/_2$ in. stroke, 49.48 cu. in., motor numbers 4200–7600.

1911
Model 7: single-cylinder, single-belt drive, 28 in. wheels, battery ignition, 4.34 horsepower, $3^5/_{16}$ in. bore, 4 in. stroke, 35 cu. in., motor numbers 7600–10000, followed by letter A.
Model 7A: single-cylinder, single-belt drive, 28 in. wheels, magneto ignition, 4.34 horsepower, $3^5/_{16}$ in. bore, 4 in. stroke, 35 cu. in., motor numbers 7600–10000, followed by letter A.
Model 7B: single-cylinder, single-belt drive, 26 in. wheels, battery ignition, 4.34 horsepower, $3^5/_{16}$ in. bore, 4 in. stroke, 35 cu. in., motor numbers 7600–10000, followed by letter A.

Model 7C: single-cylinder, single-belt drive, 26 in. wheels, magneto ignition, 4.34 horsepower, $3^5/_{16}$ in. bore, 4 in. stroke, 35 cu. in., motor numbers 7600–10000, followed by letter A.
Model 7D: twin-cylinder, single-belt drive, 28 in. wheels, magneto ignition, $6^1/_2$ horsepower, 3 in. bore, $3^1/_2$ in. stroke, 49.48 cu. in., motor numbers 7600–10000, followed by letter A.

1912
Model 8: single-cylinder, single-belt drive, 28 in. wheels, battery ignition, 4.34 horsepower, $3^5/_{16}$ in. bore, 4 in. stroke, 35 cu. in., motor numbers followed by letters AB, BA or B.
Model X8: single-cylinder, single-belt drive, 28 in. wheels, battery ignition, free-wheel control (clutch), 4.34 horsepower, $3^5/_{16}$ in. bore, 4 in. stroke, 35 cu. in., motor numbers followed by letters AB, BA or B.
Model 8A: single-cylinder, single-belt drive, 28 in. wheels, magneto ignition, 4.34 horsepower, $3^5/_{16}$ in. bore, 4 in. stroke, 35 cu. in., motor numbers followed by letters AB, BA or B.
Model X8A: single-cylinder, single-belt drive, 28 in. wheels, magneto ignition, free-wheel control (clutch), 4.34 horsepower, $3^5/_{16}$ in. bore, 4 in. stroke, 35 cu. in., motor numbers followed by letters AB, BA or B.
Model 8D: twin-cylinder, single-belt drive, 28 in. wheels, magneto ignition, $6^1/_2$ horsepower, 3 in. bore, $3^1/_2$ in. stroke, 49.48 cu. in., motor numbers followed by letter D.
Model X8D: twin-cylinder, single-belt drive, 28 in. wheels, magneto ignition, free-wheel control (clutch), $6^1/_2$ horsepower, 3 in. bore, $3^1/_2$ in. stroke, 49.48 cu. in., motor number followed by letter D.
Model X8E: twin-cylinder, single-belt drive, 7 to 8 horsepower, $3^5/_{16}$ in. bore, $3^1/_2$ in. stroke, 60.34 cu. in., motor number followed by letter E.

1913
Model 9A: single-cylinder, single-belt drive, 28 in. wheels, magneto ignition, $3^5/_{16}$ in. bore, 4 in. stroke, 35 cu. in., motor numbers followed by letter C.
Model 9B: single-cylinder, single-chain drive, 28 in. wheels, magneto ignition, 4.34 horsepower, $3^5/_{16}$ in. bore, 4 in. stroke, 35 cu. in., motor numbers followed by letter D.
Model 9E: twin-cylinder, single-belt drive, 28 in. wheels, magneto ignition, 8.68 horsepower, 3 in. bore, $3^1/_2$ in. stroke, 49.48 cu. in.
Model 9G: twin-cylinder, single-belt drive, 28 in. wheels, magneto ignition, free-wheel control (clutch), 8.68 horsepower, 3 in. bore, $3^1/_2$ in. stroke, 49.48 cu. in.

1914

Model 10A: single-cylinder, single-belt drive, 28 in. wheels, magneto ignition, 4.34 horsepower, $3^5/_{16}$ in. bore, 4 in. stroke, 35 cu. in., motor number followed by letters CF.

Model 10B: single-cylinder, single-chain drive, 28 in. wheels, 4.34 horsepower, $3^5/_{16}$ in. bore, 4 in. stroke, 35 cu. in., motor number followed by letters DG or D, single speed.

Model 10C: single-cylinder, single-chain drive, 28 in. wheels, magneto ignition, 4.34 horsepower, $3^5/_{16}$ in. bore, 4 in. stroke, 35 cu. in., motor number followed by letters DG or D, two speed.

Model 10E: twin-cylinder, twin-chain drive, 28 in. wheels, magneto ignition, 8.68 horsepower, 3 in. bore, $3^1/_2$ in. stroke, 49.48 cu. in.

Model 10F: twin-cylinder, twin-chain drive, 28 in. wheels, magneto ignition, 8.68 horsepower, 3 in. bore, $3^1/_2$ in. stroke, 49.48 cu. in.

Model 10G: twin-cylinder, twin-chain drive, 8.68 horsepower, magneto ignition, $3^5/_{16}$ in. bore, $3^1/_2$ in. stroke, 60.34 cu. in.

1915

Model 11B: single-cylinder, single-chain drive, 28 in. wheels, magneto ignition, 4.34 horsepower, $3^5/_{16}$ in. bore, 4 in. stroke, 35 cu. in., motor number followed by letter J, single-speed.

Model 11C: single-cylinder, single-chain drive, 28 in. wheels, magneto ignition, 4.34 horsepower, $3^5/_{16}$ in. bore, 4 in. stroke, 35 cu. in., motor number followed by letter L, two-speed.

Model 11E: twin-cylinder, twin-chain drive, 28 in. wheels, magneto ignition, 8.68 horsepower, 3 in. bore, $3^1/_2$ in. stroke, 49.48 cu. in.

Model 11F: twin-cylinder, twin-chain drive, 28 in. wheels, magneto ignition, 8.68 horsepower, 3 in. bore, $3^1/_2$ in. stroke, 49.48 cu. in.

Model 11G: twin-cylinder, twin-chain drive, 8.68 horsepower, magneto ignition, $3^5/_{16}$ in. bore, $3^1/_2$ in. stroke, 60.34 cu. in.

Model 11H: twin-cylinder, twin-chain drive, 8.68 horsepower, generator, $3^5/_{16}$ in. bore, $3^1/_2$ in. stroke, 60.34 cu. in.

Model 11J: twin-cylinder, twin-chain drive, 8.68 horsepower, generator, $3^5/_{16}$ in. bore, $3^1/_2$ in. stroke, 60.34 cu. in.

1916

Model 16B: single-cylinder, single-chain drive, 28 in. wheels, magneto ignition, 4.34 horsepower, $3^5/_{16}$ in. bore, 4 in. stroke, 35 cu. in., motor number followed by letter L, single-speed.

Model 16C: single-cylinder, single-chain drive, 28 in. wheels, magneto ignition, 4.34 horsepower, $3^5/_{16}$ in. bore, 4 in. stroke, 35 cu. in., motor number followed by letter L, three-speed.

Model 16E: twin-cylinder, twin-chain drive, 28 in. wheels, magneto ignition, $6^1/_2$ horsepower, 3 in. bore, $3^1/_2$ in. stroke, 49.48 cu. in.

Model 16F: twin-cylinder, twin-chain drive, 28 in. wheels, magneto ignition, $6^1/_2$ horsepower, 3 in. bore, $3^1/_2$ in. stroke, 49.48 cu. in.

Model 16J: twin-cylinder, twin-chain drive, 7 to 8 horsepower, generator, $3^5/_{16}$ in. bore, $3^1/_2$ in. stroke, 60.34 cu. in.

1917

Model 17B: single-cylinder, single-chain drive, 28 in. wheels, magneto ignition, 4.34 horsepower, $3^5/_{16}$ in. bore, 4 in. stroke, 35 cu. in., motor number preceded by 17S, single-speed.

Model 17C: single-cylinder, single-chain drive, 28 in. wheels, magneto ignition, 4.34 horsepower, $3^5/_{16}$ in. bore, 4 in. stroke, 35 cu. in., motor number preceded by 17S, three-speed.

Model 17E: twin-cylinder, twin-chain drive, 28 in. wheels, magneto ignition, $6^1/_2$ horsepower, 3 in. bore, $3^1/_2$ in. stroke, 49.48 cu. in.

Model 17F: twin-cylinder, twin-chain drive, 28 in. wheels, magneto ignition, $6^1/_2$ horsepower, 3 in. bore, $3^1/_2$ in. stroke, 49.48 cu. in.

Model 17J: twin-cylinder, twin-chain drive, 7 to 8 horsepower, generator, $3^5/_{16}$ in. bore, $3^1/_2$ in. stroke, 60.34 cu. in.

1918

Model 18B: single-cylinder, single-chain drive, 28 in. wheels, magneto ignition, 4.34 horsepower, $3^5/_{16}$ in. bore, 4 in. stroke, 35 cu. in., number preceded by 18S, single-speed.

Model 18C: single-cylinder, single-chain drive, 28 in. wheels, magneto ignition, 4.34 horsepower, $3^5/_{16}$ in. bore, 4 in. stroke, 35 cu. in., number preceded by 18S, three-speed.

Model 18E: twin-cylinder, twin-chain drive, magneto ignition, 8.68 horsepower, $3^5/_{16}$ in. bore, $3^1/_2$ in. stroke, 60.34 cu. in., number preceded by 18T, single-speed.

Model 18F: twin-cylinder, twin-chain drive, magneto ignition, 8.68 horsepower, $3^5/_{16}$ in. bore, $3^1/_2$ in. stroke, 60.34 cu. in., number preceded by 18T, three-speed.

Model 18J: twin-cylinder, twin-chain drive, magneto ignition, 8.68 horsepower, $3^5/_{16}$ in. bore, $3^1/_2$ in. stroke, 60.34 cu. in., number preceded by L18T, three-speed.

1919

Model 19F: twin-cylinder, twin-chain drive, magneto ignition, 8.68 horsepower, $3^5/_{16}$ in. bore, $3^1/_2$ in. stroke, 60.34 cu. in., number preceded by 19T or 19A, three-speed.

Model 19J: twin-cylinder, twin-chain drive, magneto ignition, 8.68 horsepower, $3^5/_{16}$ in. bore, $3^1/_2$ in. stroke, 60.34 cu. in., number preceded by L19T or L19A, three-speed.

Model: Sport, front-to-back opposed twin, $2^3/_4$ in. bore, 3 in. stroke, 35.64 cu. in., three-speed transmission.

1920

Model 20F: twin-cylinder, twin-chain drive, magneto ignition, 8.68 horsepower, $3^5/_{16}$ in. bore, $3^1/_2$ in. stroke, 60.34 cu. in., number preceded by 20T, three-speed.

Model 20J: twin-cylinder, twin-chain drive, magneto ignition, 8.68 horsepower, $3^5/_{16}$ in. bore, $3^1/_2$ in. stroke, 60.34 cu. in., number preceded by L20T, three-speed.

Model: Sport, front-to-back opposed twin, $2^3/_4$ in. bore, 3 in. stroke, 35.64 cu. in., three-speed transmission.

1921

Model 21F: twin-cylinder, twin-chain drive, magneto ignition, 8.68 horsepower, $3^5/_{16}$ in. bore, $3^1/_2$ in. stroke, 60.34 cu. in., number preceded by 21F, three-speed.

Model 21FD: twin-cylinder, twin-chain drive, magneto ignition, 9.5 horsepower, $3^{7}/_{16}$ in. bore, 4 in. stroke, 74 cu. in., number preceded by 21FD, three-speed.

Model 21J: twin-cylinder, twin-chain drive, generator, 8.68 horsepower, $3^{5}/_{16}$ in. bore, $3^{1}/_{2}$ in. stroke, 60.34 cu. in., number preceded by 21J, three-speed.

Model 21JD: twin-cylinder, twin-chain drive, generator, 9.5 horsepower, $3^{7}/_{16}$ in. bore, 4 in. stroke, 74 cu. in., number preceded by 21JD, three-speed.

Model: Sport, front-to-back opposed twin, $2^{3}/_{4}$ in. bore, 3 in. stroke, 35.64 cu. in., three-speed transmission.

1922

Model 22F: twin-cylinder, twin-chain drive, magneto ignition, 8.68 horsepower, $3^{5}/_{16}$ in. bore, $3^{1}/_{2}$ in. stroke, 60.34 cu. in., number preceded by 22F, three-speed.

Model 22FD: twin-cylinder, twin-chain drive, magneto ignition, 9.5 horsepower, $3^{7}/_{16}$ in. bore, 4 in. stroke, 74 cu. in., number preceded by 22FD, three-speed.

Model 22J: twin-cylinder, twin-chain drive, generator, 8.68 horsepower, $3^{5}/_{16}$ in. bore, $3^{1}/_{2}$ in. stroke, 60.34 cu. in., number preceded by 22J, three-speed.

Model 22JD: twin-cylinder, twin-chain drive, generator, 9.5 horsepower, $3^{7}/_{16}$ in. bore, 4 in. stroke, 74 cu. in., number preceded by 22JD, three-speed.

Model: Sport, front-to-back opposed twin, $2^{3}/_{4}$ in. bore, 3 in. stroke, 35.64 cu. in., three-speed transmission.

1923

Model 23F: twin-cylinder, twin-chain drive, magneto ignition, 8.68 horsepower, $3^{5}/_{16}$ in. bore, $3^{1}/_{2}$ in. stroke, 60.34 cu. in., number preceded by 23F, three-speed.

Model 23FD: twin-cylinder, twin-chain drive, magneto ignition, 9.5 horsepower, $3^{7}/_{16}$ in. bore, 4 in. stroke, 74 cu. in., number preceded by 23FD, three-speed.

Model 23J: twin-cylinder, twin-chain drive, generator, 8.68 horsepower, $3^{5}/_{16}$ in. bore, $3^{1}/_{2}$ in. stroke, 60.34 cu. in., number preceded by 23J, three-speed.

Model 23JD: twin-cylinder, twin-chain drive, generator, 9.5 horsepower, $3^{7}/_{16}$ in. bore, 4 in. stroke, 74 cu. in., number preceded by 23JD, three-speed.

1924

Model 24FE: twin-cylinder, twin-chain drive, magneto ignition, 8.68 horsepower, $3^{5}/_{16}$ in. bore, $3^{1}/_{2}$ in. stroke, 60.34 cu. in., number preceded by 24FE, three-speed, aluminum pistons.

Model 24FD: twin-cylinder, twin-chain drive, magneto ignition, 9.5 horsepower, $3^{7}/_{16}$ in. bore, 4 in. stroke, 74 cu. in., number preceded by 24FD, three-speed, cast iron pistons.

Model 24FDCA: twin-cylinder, twin-chain drive, magneto ignition, 9.5 horsepower, $3^{7}/_{16}$ in. bore, 4 in. stroke, 74 cu. in., number preceded by 24FDCA, three-speed, aluminum pistons.

Model 24FDCB: twin-cylinder, twin-chain drive, magneto ignition, 9.5 horsepower, $3^{7}/_{16}$ in. bore, 4 in. stroke, 74 cu. in., number preceded by 24FDCB, three-speed, iron alloy pistons.

Model 24JE: twin-cylinder, twin-chain drive, generator, 8.68 horsepower, $3^{5}/_{16}$ in. bore, $3^{1}/_{2}$ in. stroke, 60.34 cu. in., number preceded by 24JE, three-speed, aluminum pistons.

Model 24JD: twin-cylinder, twin-chain drive, generator, 9.5 horsepower, $3^{7}/_{16}$ in. bore, 4 in. stroke, 74 cu. in., number preceded by 24JD, three-speed, cast-iron pistons.

Model 24JDCA: twin-cylinder, twin-chain drive, generator, 9.5 horsepower, $3^{7}/_{16}$ in. bore, 4 in. stroke, 74 cu. in., number preceded by 24JDCA, three-speed, aluminum pistons.

Model 24JDCB: twin-cylinder, twin-chain drive, generator, 9.5 horsepower, $3^{7}/_{16}$ in. bore, 4 in. stroke, 74 cu. in., number preceded by 24JDCB, three-speed, iron alloy pistons.

1925

Model 25FE: twin-cylinder, twin-chain drive, magneto ignition, 8.68 horsepower, $3^{5}/_{16}$ in. bore, $3^{1}/_{2}$ in. stroke, 60.34 cu. in., number preceded by 25FE, three-speed, iron alloy pistons.

Model 25FDCB: twin-cylinder, twin-chain drive, magneto ignition, 9.5 horsepower, $3^{7}/_{16}$ in. bore, 4 in. stroke, 74 cu. in., number preceded by 25FDCB, three-speed, iron alloy pistons.

Model 25JE: twin-cylinder, twin-chain drive, generator, 8.68 horsepower, $3^{5}/_{16}$ in. bore, $3^{1}/_{2}$ in. stroke, 60.34 cu. in., number preceded by 25JE, three-speed, iron alloy pistons.

Model 25JDCB: twin-cylinder, twin-chain drive, generator, 9.5 horsepower, $3^{7}/_{16}$ in. bore, 4 in. stroke, 74 cu. in., number preceded by 25JDCB, three-speed, iron alloy pistons.

1926

Model 26F: twin-cylinder, twin-chain drive, magneto ignition, 8.68 horsepower, $3^{5}/_{16}$ in. bore, $3^{1}/_{2}$ in. stroke, 60.34 cu. in., number preceded by 26F, three-speed, iron alloy pistons.

Model 26FD: twin-cylinder, twin-chain drive, magneto ignition, 9.5 horsepower, $3^{7}/_{16}$ in. bore, 4 in. stroke, 74 cu. in., number preceded by 26FD, three-speed, iron alloy pistons.

Model 26J: twin-cylinder, twin-chain drive, generator, 8.68 horsepower, $3^{5}/_{16}$ in. bore, $3^{1}/_{2}$ in. stroke, 60.34 cu. in., number preceded by 26J, three-speed, iron alloy pistons.

Model 26JD: twin-cylinder, twin-chain drive, generator, 9.5 horsepower, $3^{7}/_{16}$ in. bore, 4 in. stroke, 74 cu. in., number preceded by 26JD, three-speed, iron alloy pistons.

1926–1927

Model A: single-cylinder, single-chain drive, magneto ignition, 3.31 horsepower, $2^{7}/_{8}$ in. bore, $3^{1}/_{4}$ in. stroke, 21.098 cu. in., number preceded by A, side by side valves, iron alloy pistons.

Model AA: single-cylinder, single-chain drive, magneto ignition, 3.31 horsepower, $2^{7}/_{8}$ in. bore, $3^{1}/_{4}$ in. stroke, 21.098 cu. in., number preceded by AA, overhead valves, aluminum pistons.

Model B: single-cylinder, single-chain drive, generator, 3.31 horsepower, $2^{7}/_{8}$ in. bore, $3^{1}/_{4}$ in. stroke, 21.098 cu. in., number preceded by B, side by side valves, iron alloy pistons.

Model BA: single-cylinder, single-chain drive, generator, 3.31 horsepower, $2^7/8$ in. bore, $3^1/4$ in. stroke, 21.098 cu. in., number preceded by BA, overhead valves, aluminum pistons.

1927

Model 27F: twin-cylinder, twin-chain drive, magneto ignition, 8.68 horsepower, $3^5/16$ in. bore, $3^1/2$ in. stroke, 60.34 cu. in., number preceded by 27F, three-speed, iron alloy pistons.

Model 27FD: twin-cylinder, twin-chain drive, magneto ignition, 9.5 horsepower, $3^7/16$ in. bore, 4 in. stroke, 74 cu. in., number preceded by 27FD, three-speed, iron alloy pistons.

Model 27J: twin-cylinder, twin-chain drive, generator, 8.68 horsepower, $3^5/16$ in. bore, $3^1/2$ in. stroke, 60.34 cu. in., number preceded by 27J, three-speed, iron alloy pistons.

Model 27JD: twin-cylinder, twin-chain drive, generator, 9.5 horsepower, $3^7/16$ in. bore, 4 in. stroke, 74 cu. in., number preceded by 27JD, three-speed, iron alloy pistons.

1928

Model 28A: single-cylinder, single-chain drive, magneto ignition, 3.31 horsepower, $2^7/8$ in. bore, $3^1/4$ in. stroke, 21.098 cu. in., number preceded by 28A, side by side valves, Dow metal pistons.

Model 28AA: single-cylinder, single-chain drive, magneto ignition, 3.31 horsepower, $2^7/8$ in. bore, $3^1/4$ in. stroke, 21.098 cu. in., number preceded by 28AA, overhead valves, Dow metal pistons.

Model 28B: single-cylinder, single-chain drive, generator, 3.31 horsepower, $2^7/8$ in. bore, $3^1/4$ in. stroke, 21.098 cu. in., number preceded by 28B, side by side valves, Dow metal pistons.

Model 28BA: single-cylinder, single-chain drive, generator, 3.31 horsepower, $2^7/8$ in. bore, $3^1/4$ in. stroke, 21.098 cu. in., number preceded by 28BA, overhead valves, Dow metal pistons.

Model 28F: twin-cylinder, twin-chain drive, magneto ignition, 8.68 horsepower, $3^5/16$ in. bore, $3^1/2$ in. stroke, 60.34 cu. in., number preceded by 28F, three-speed, iron alloy pistons.

Model 28FD: twin-cylinder, twin-chain drive, magneto ignition, 9.5 horsepower, $3^7/17$ in. bore, 4 in. stroke, 74 cu. in., number preceded by 28FD, three-speed, iron alloy pistons.

Model 28J: twin-cylinder, twin-chain drive, generator, 8.68 horsepower, $3^5/16$ in. bore, $3^1/2$ in. stroke, 60.34 cu. in., number preceded by 28J, three-speed, iron alloy pistons.

Model 28JD: twin-cylinder, twin-chain drive, generator, 9.5 horsepower, $3^7/17$ in. bore, 4 in. stroke, 74 cu. in., number preceded by 28JD, three-speed, iron alloy pistons.

Model 28JXL: twin-cylinder, twin-chain drive, generator, 8.68 horsepower, $3^5/16$ in. bore, $3^1/2$ in. stroke, 60.34 cu. in., number preceded by 28JXL, three-speed, Dow metal pistons.

Model 28JDXL: twin-cylinder, twin-chain drive, generator, 9.5 horsepower, $3^7/17$ in. bore, 4 in. stroke, 74 cu. in.,

number preceded by 28JDXL, three-speed, Dow metal pistons.

Model 28JH: twin-cylinder, twin-chain drive, two cams, generator, 8.68 horsepower, $3^5/16$ in. bore, $3^1/2$ in. stroke, 60.34 cu. in., number preceded by 28JH, three-speed, Dow metal pistons.

Model 28JDH: twin-cylinder, twin-chain drive, two cams, generator, 9.5 horsepower, $3^7/17$ in. bore, 4 in. stroke, 74 cu. in., number preceded by 28JDH, three-speeds, Dow metal pistons. (Note: all 61 and 64 cu. in. models were offered with 25×3.85 tire sizes; the JD models were offered with these sizes standard and with 27×3.85 tires optional. Tire size for the singles was 26×3.30.)

1929

Model 29A: single-cylinder, single-chain drive, magneto ignition, 3.31 horsepower, $2^7/8$ in. bore, $3^1/4$ in. stroke, 21.098 cu. in., number preceded by 29A, side by side valves, Dow metal pistons.

Model 29AA: single-cylinder, single-chain drive, magneto ignition, 3.31 horsepower, $2^7/8$ in. bore, $3^1/4$ in. stroke, 21.098 cu. in., number preceded by 29AA, overhead valves, Dow metal pistons.

Model 29B: single-cylinder, single-chain drive, generator, 3.31 horsepower, $2^7/8$ in. bore, $3^1/4$ in. stroke, 21.098 cu. in., number preceded by 29B, side by side valves, Dow metal pistons.

Model 29BA: single-cylinder, single-chain drive, generator, 3.31 horsepower, $2^7/8$ in. bore, $3^1/4$ in. stroke, 21.098 cu. in., number preceded by 29BA, overhead valves, Dow metal pistons.

Model 29D: twin-cylinder, twin-chain drive, generator, no horsepower given, $2^3/4$ in. bore, $3^{13}/16$ in. stroke, 45.32 cu. in., number preceded by 29D, three-speed, Dow metal pistons.

Model 29F: twin-cylinder, twin-chain drive, magneto ignition, 8.68 horsepower, $3^5/16$ in. bore, $3^1/2$ in. stroke, 60.34 cu. in., number preceded by 29F, three-speed, iron alloy pistons.

Model 29FD: twin-cylinder, twin-chain drive, magneto ignition, 9.5 horsepower, $3^7/17$ in. bore, 4 in. stroke, 74 cu. in., number preceded by 29FD, three-speed, iron alloy pistons.

Model 29J: twin-cylinder, twin-chain drive, generator, 8.68 horsepower, $3^5/16$ in. bore, $3^1/2$ in. stroke, 60.34 cu. in., number preceded by 29J, three-speed, iron alloy pistons.

Model 29JD: twin-cylinder, twin-chain drive, generator, 9.5 horsepower, $3^7/17$ in. bore, 4 in. stroke, 74 cu. in., number preceded by 29JD, three-speed, iron alloy pistons.

Model 29JXL: twin-cylinder, twin-chain drive, generator, 8.68 horsepower, $3^5/16$ in. bore, $3^1/2$ in. stroke, 60.34 cu. in., number preceded by 29JXL, three-speed, Dow metal pistons.

Model 29JDXL: twin-cylinder, twin-chain drive, generator, 9.5 horsepower, $3^7/17$ in. bore, 4 in. stroke, 74 cu. in., number preceded by 29JDXL, three-speed, Dow metal pistons.

Model 29JH: twin-cylinder, twin-chain drive, two cams, generator, 8.68 horsepower, $3^5/16$ in. bore, $3^1/2$ in. stroke, 60.34 cu. in., number preceded by 29JH, three-speed, Dow metal pistons.

Model 29JDH: twin-cylinder, twin-chain drive, two cams, generator, 9.5 horsepower, 3^7/$_{17}$ in. bore, 4 in. stroke, 74 cu. in., number preceded by 29JDH, three-speed, Dow metal pistons. (Note: 45 cu. in. model offered with 25 × 3.85 tires, standard; 61 and 74 cu. in. models offered with 27 × 3.85 tires, standard. No optional sizes listed.)

1930

Model 30-V: 74 cu. in. Big Twin.
Model 30-VL: 74 cu. in. Big Twin, high compression.
Model 30-D: 45 cu. in. side-valve V-twin.
Model 30-DL: 45 cu. in. side-valve V-twin, high compression.
Model 30-DLD: 45 cu. in. side-valve Special Sport solo.
Model 30-C: 30.50 cu. in. single.

1931

Model 31-V: 74 cu. in. Big Twin.
Model 31-VL: 74 cu. in. Big Twin, high compression.
Model 31-D: 45 cu. in. side-valve V-twin.
Model 31-DL: 45 cu. in. side-valve V-twin, high compression.
Model 31-DLD: 45 cu. in. side-valve Special Sport solo.
Model 31-C: 30.50 cu. in. single.
Model 31-VC: 74 cu. in. Big Twin Commercial.

1932

Model 32-V: 74 cu. in. Big Twin.
Model 32-VL: 74 cu. in. Big Twin, High Compression.
Model 32-R: 45 cu. in. side-valve V-twin.
Model 32-RL: 45 cu. in. side-valve V-twin, High Compression.
Model 32-RLR: 45 cu. in. side-valve V-twin, Special Sport solo.
Model 32-C: 30.50 cu. in. single.

1933

Model 33-V: 74 cu. in. Big Twin.
Model 33-VL: 74 cu. in. Big Twin, High Compression.
Model 33-VLD: 74 cu. in. Big Twin, Y manifold.
Model 33-R: 45 cu. in. side-valve V-twin.
Model 33-RL: 45 cu. in. side-valve V-twin, High Compression.
Model 33-RLR: 45 cu. in. side-valve V-twin, Special Sport solo.
Model 33-C: 30.50 cu. in. single.

1934

Model 34-B: 21 cu. in. side-valve single.
Model 34-C: 30.50 cu. in. side-valve single.
Model 34-CB: B model with the 30.50 cu. in. motor.
Model 34-RL: 45 cu. in. V-twin, high compression.
Model 34-R: 45 cu. in. V-twin, low compression.
Model 34-RLD: 45 cu. in. V-twin, Special Sport solo.
Model 34-VLD: 74 cu. in. side-valve twin, Special Sport solo, TNT motor.
Model 34-VD: 74 cu. in. side-valve twin, solo, low compression.
Model 34-VDS: 74 cu. in. side-valve twin, low compression, sidecar gears, TNT motor.
Model 34-VFDS: 74 cu. in. side-valve twin, heavy-duty commercial TNT motor.

1935

Model 35-RL: 45 cu. in. V-twin, high compression.
Model 35-R: 45 cu. in. V-twin, low compression.
Model 35-RS: 45 cu. in. V-twin, low compression, sidecar gears.
Model 35-RLD: 45 cu. in. V-twin, Special Sport solo.
Model 35-VLD: 74 cu. in. side-valve twin, Special Sport solo.
Model 35-VD: 74 cu. in. side-valve twin, solo, low compression.

1936

Model 36-RL: 45 cu. in. V-twin, sport solo, high compression, solo bars.
Model 36-RLD: 45 cu. in. V-twin, sport solo, extra high compression, solo bars.
Model 36-RLDR: 45 cu. in. V-twin, competition special.
Model 36-R: 45 cu. in. V-twin, low compression, solo bars.
Model 36-RS: 45 cu. in. V-twin, low compression, sidecar gears.
Model 36-VLD: 74 cu. in. side-valve twin, Special Sport solo.
Model 36-VD: 74 cu. in. side-valve twin, low compression.
Model 36-VDS: 74 cu. in. side-valve twin, low compression, sidecar gears.
Model 36-VLH: 80 cu. in. side-valve twin, Sport solo.
Model 36-VHS: 80 cu. in. side-valve twin, low compression, sidecar gears.
Model 36-EL: 61 cu. in. overhead valve twin, Special Sport solo.
Model 36-E: 61 cu. in. overhead valve twin, medium compression.
Model 36-ES: 61 cu. in. overhead valve twin, medium compression, sidecar gears.

1937

Model 37-WL: 45 cu. in. twin, Sport solo.
Model 37-WLD: 45 cu. in. Sport solo, extra high compression.
Model 37-WLDR: 45 cu. in. twin, competition model.
Model 37-W: 45 cu. in. twin, low compression.
Model 37-WS: 45 cu. in. twin, sidecar gearing.
Model 37-UL: 74 cu. in. twin, Special Sport solo.
Model 37-U: 74 cu. in. twin, solo, medium compression.
Model 37-UHS: 80 cu. in. twin, medium compression, sidecar gears.
Model 37-EL: 61 cu. in. twin, overhead valve twin, Special Sport solo.
Model 37-E: 61 cu. in. twin, overhead valve twin, medium compression.
Model 37-ES: 61 cu. in. twin, overhead valve twin, medium compression, sidecar gears.

1938

Model 38-WLD: 45 cu. in. twin, Sport Solo, extra high compression.
Model 38-WL: 45 cu. in. twin, Sport Solo, high compression.
Model 38-WLDR: 45 cu. in. twin, competition model.
Model 38-UL: 74 cu. in. twin, Special Sport solo.
Model 38-U: 74 cu. in. twin, solo, medium compression.
Model 38-US: 74 cu. in. twin, medium compression, sidecar gears.
Model 38-ULH: 80 cu. in. twin, Special Sport solo.

Model 38-UH: 80 cu. in. twin, solo, medium compression.
Model 38-UHS: 80 cu. in. twin, medium compression, sidecar gears.
Model 38-EL: 61 cu. in. overhead valve twin, Special Sport solo.
Model 38-ES: 61 cu. in. overhead valve twin, sidecar gears.

1939

Model 39-WLD: 45 cu. in. twin, Sport Solo, extra high compression.
Model 39-WL: 45 cu. in. twin, Sport Solo, high compression.
Model 39-WLDR: 45 cu. in. twin, competition model.
Model 39-UL: 74 cu. in. twin, Special Sport solo.
Model 39-U: 74 cu. in. twin, medium compression.
Model 39-US: 74 cu. in. twin, medium compression, sidecar gears.
Model 39-ULH: 80 cu. in. twin, Special Sport solo.
Model 39-UH: 80 cu. in. twin, solo, medium compression.
Model 39-UHS: 80 cu. in. twin, medium compression, sidecar gears.
Model 39-EL: 61 cu. in. overhead valve twin, Special Sport solo.
Model 39-ES: 61 cu. in. overhead valve twin, sidecar gears.

1940

Model 40-WLD: 45 cu. in. twin, Special Sport solo.
Model 40-WL: 45 cu. in. twin, high compression.
Model 40-WLDR: 45 cu. in. twin, competition model.
Model 40-UL: 74 cu. in. twin, Special Sport solo.
Model 40-U: 74 cu. in. twin, medium compression.
Model 40-US: 74 cu. in. twin, medium compression, sidecar gears.
(Aluminum head optional on all 74 cu. in. twins.)
Model 40-ULH: 80 cu. in. twin, Special Sport solo.
Model 40-UH: 80 cu. in. twin, solo, medium compression.
Model 40-UHS: 80 cu. in. twin, medium compression, sidecar gears.
(Aluminum heads standard on 80 cu. in. twins.)
Model 40-EL: 61 cu. in. overhead valve twin, Special Sport solo.
Model 40-ES: 61 cu. in. overhead valve twin, sidecar gears.
(Four-speed transmission standard on 61, 74, 80 cu. in. twins.)

1941

Model 41-WL: 45 cu. in. twin, high compression.
Model 41-WLD: 45 cu. in. twin, Sport solo.
Model 41-WLDR: 45 cu. in. twin, Special Sport solo.
Model 41-UL: 74 cu. in. twin, Special Sport solo.
Model 41-U: 74 cu. in. twin, medium compression.
Model 41-ULH: 80 cu. in. twin, Special Sport solo.
Model 41-UH: 80 cu. in. twin, medium compression.
Model 41-EL: 61 cu. in. overhead valve twin, Special Sport solo.
Model 41-E: 61 cu. in. overhead valve twin, medium compression.
Model 41-FL: 74 cu. in. overhead valve twin, Special Sport solo.
Model 41-F: 74 cu. in. overhead valve twin, medium compression.

1942

Model 42-WLD: 45 cu. in. twin, Special Sport solo.
Model 42-WL: 45 cu. in. twin, high compression.
Model 42-UL: 74 cu. in. twin, Special Sport solo.
Model 42-U: 74 cu. in. twin, medium compression.
Model 42-EL: 61 cu. in. overhead valve twin, Special Sport solo.
Model 42-E: 61 cu. in. overhead valve twin, medium compression.
Model 42-FL: 74 cu. in. overhead valve twin, Special Sport solo.

1943

Model 43-UL: 74 cu. in. twin, high compression solo.
Model 43-U: 74 cu. in. twin, medium compression.
Model 43-EL: 61 cu. in. overhead valve twin, Special Sport solo.
Model 43-E: 61 cu. in. overhead valve twin, medium compression.
Model 43-FL: 74 cu. in. overhead valve twin, Special Sport solo.
Model 43-F: 74 cu. in. overhead valve twin, medium compression.

1944

Model 44-UL: 74 cu. in. twin, high compression solo.
Model 44-U: 74 cu. in. twin, medium compression.
Model 44-EL: 61 cu. in. overhead valve twin, Special Sport solo.
Model 44-E: 61 cu. in. overhead valve twin, medium compression.
Model 44-FL: 74 cu. in. overhead valve twin, Special Sport solo.
Model 44-F: 74 cu. in. overhead valve twin, medium compression.

1945

Model 45-WL: 45 cu. in. twin.
Model 45-UL: 74 cu. in. twin, high compression solo.
Model 45-U: 74 cu. in. twin, medium compression.
Model 45-US: 74 cu. in. twin, medium compression, sidecar gears.
(Aluminum heads a $7 option on all above models.)
Model 45-EL: 61 cu. in. overhead valve twin, Special Sport solo.
Model 45-E: 61 cu. in. overhead valve twin, medium compression.
Model 45-ES: 61 cu. in. overhead valve twin, medium compression, sidecar gears.
Model 45-FL: 74 cu. in. overhead valve twin, Special Sport solo.
Model 45-F: 74 cu. in. overhead valve twin, medium compression.
Model 45-FS: 74 cu. in. overhead valve twin, medium compression, sidecar gears.

1946

Model 46-WL: 45 cu. in. twin.
Model 46-UL: 74 cu. in. twin, high compression solo.
Model 46-U: 74 cu. in. twin, medium compression.
Model 46-US: 74 cu. in. twin, medium compression, sidecar gears.
(Aluminum heads a $7 option on all above models.)
Model 46-EL: 61 cu. in. overhead valve twin, Special Sport solo.

Model 46-E: 61 cu. in. overhead valve twin, medium compression.
Model 46-ES: 61 cu. in. overhead valve twin, medium compression, sidecar gears.
Model 46-FL: 74 cu. in. overhead valve twin, Special Sport solo.
Model 46-F: 74 cu. in. overhead valve twin, medium compression.
Model 46-FS: 74 cu. in. overhead valve twin, medium compression, sidecar gears.

1947
Model 47-WL: 45 cu. in. twin.
Model 47-UL: 74 cu. in. twin, high compression solo.
Model 47-U: 74 cu. in. twin, medium compression.
Model 47-US: 74 cu. in. twin, medium compression, sidecar gears.
(Aluminum heads a $7 option on all above models.)
Model 47-EL: 61 cu. in. overhead valve twin, Special Sport solo.
Model 47-E: 61 cu. in. overhead valve twin, medium compression.
Model 47-ES: 61 cu. in. overhead valve twin, medium compression, sidecar gears.
Model 47-FL: 74 cu. in. overhead valve twin, Special Sport solo.
Model 47-F: 74 cu. in. overhead valve twin, medium compression.
Model 47-FS: 74 cu. in. overhead valve twin, medium compression, sidecar gears.

1948
Model 48-S: 125cc two-stroke single.
Model 48-WL: 45 cu. in. twin.
Model 48-UL: 74 cu. in. twin, high compression solo.
Model 48-U: 74 cu. in. twin, medium compression.
Model 48-US: 74 cu. in. twin, medium compression, sidecar gears.
(Aluminum heads an $8.35 option on all above models.)
Model 48-EL: 61 cu. in. overhead valve twin, Special Sport solo.
Model 48-E: 61 cu. in. overhead valve twin, medium compression.
Model 48-ES: 61 cu. in. overhead valve twin, medium compression, sidecar gears.
Model 48-FL: 74 cu. in. overhead valve twin, Special Sport solo.
Model 48-F: 74 cu. in. overhead valve twin, medium compression.
Model 48-FS: 74 cu. in. overhead valve twin, medium compression, sidecar gears.

1949
Model 49-S: 125cc two-stroke single (chrome rims $7.50 option).
Model 49-WL: 45 cu. in. twin (aluminum heads, $7.50 extra).
Model 49-EL: 61 cu. in. overhead valve twin, sport solo.
Model 49-ES: 61 cu. in. overhead valve twin, sidecar gears.
Model 49-FL: 74 cu. in. overhead valve twin, sport solo.
Model 49-F: 74 cu. in. overhead valve twin, medium compression.

Model 49-FS: 74 cu. in. overhead valve twin, medium compression, sidecar gears.
(All E- and F-series models equipped with Hydra-Glide forks beginning in 1949 model year.)

1950
Model 50-S: 125cc two-stroke single (chrome rims $7.50 option).
Model 50-WL: 45 cu. in. twin (aluminum heads, $7.50 extra).
Model 50-EL: 61 cu. in. overhead valve twin, sport solo.
Model 50-ES: 61 cu. in. overhead valve twin, sidecar gears.
Model 50-FL: 74 cu. in. overhead valve twin, sport solo.
Model 50-F: 74 cu. in. overhead valve twin, medium compression.
Model 50-FS: 74 cu. in. overhead valve twin, medium compression, sidecar gears.

1951
Model 51-S: 125cc two-stroke single (chrome rims $8.50 option, chrome handlebars $3.75 option).
Model 51-WL: 45 cu. in. twin (aluminum heads $10 option).
Model 51-EL: 61 cu. in. overhead valve twin, sport solo.
Model 51-ELS: 61 cu. in. overhead valve twin, sidecar gears.
Model 51-FL: 74 cu. in. overhead valve twin, sport solo.
Model 51-FLS: 74 cu. in. overhead valve twin, sidecar gears.

1952
Model 52-S: 125cc two-stroke single.
Model 52-ELF: 61 cu. in. overhead valve twin, sport solo, foot shift.
Model 52-EL: 61 cu. in. overhead valve twin, sport solo, hand shift.
Model 52-ELS: 61 cu. in. overhead valve twin, sidecar gears, hand shift.
Model 52-FLF: 74 cu. in. overhead valve twin, sport solo, foot shift.
Model 52-FL: 74 cu. in. overhead valve twin, sport solo, hand shift.
Model 52-FLS: 74 cu. in. overhead valve twin, sidecar gears, hand shift.
Model 52-K: 45 cu. in. twin, sports model.

1953
Model 53-ST: 165cc two-stroke single.
Model 53-K: 45 cu. in. twin, sports model.
Model 53-FLF: 74 cu. in. overhead valve twin, sport solo, foot shift.
Model 53-FL: 74 cu. in. overhead valve twin, sport solo, hand shift.
Model 53-FLEF: 74 cu. in. overhead valve twin, foot shift with traffic combination.
Model 53-FLE: 74 cu. in. overhead valve twin, hand shift with traffic combination.

1954
Model 54-ST: 165cc single-cylinder, two-stroke.
Model 54-STU: 165cc single-cylinder, two-stroke, modified carburetor.
Model 54-KH: 54 cu. in. twin, sport model.

Model 54-FLF: 74 cu. in. overhead valve twin, foot shift.
Model 54-FL: 74 cu. in. overhead valve twin, hand shift.
Model 54-FLEF: 74 cu. in. overhead valve twin, foot shift, traffic combination.
Model 54-FLE: 74 cu. in. overhead valve twin, hand shift, traffic combination.

1955
Model 55-Hummer: 125cc single-cylinder, two-stroke.
Model 55-ST: 165cc single-cylinder, two-stroke.
Model 55-STU: 165cc single-cylinder, two-stroke, modified carburetor.
Model 55-KH: 55 cu. in. twin, sport model.
Model 55-KHK: 55 cu. in. twin, sport model KH with special speed kit.
Model 55-FLF: 74 cu. in. overhead valve twin, sport solo, foot shift.
Model 55-FL: 74 cu. in. overhead valve twin, sport solo, hand shift.
Model 55-FLEF: 74 cu. in. overhead valve twin, foot shift, traffic combination.
Model 55-FLE: 74 cu. in. overhead valve twin, hand shift, traffic combination.
Model 55-FLHF: 74 cu. in. overhead valve twin, super sport solo, foot shift.
Model 55-FLH: 74 cu. in. overhead valve twin, super sport solo, hand shift.

1956
Model 56-Hummer: 125cc single-cylinder, two-stroke.
Model 56-ST: 165cc single-cylinder, two-stroke.
Model 56-STU: 165cc single-cylinder, two-stroke, modified carburetor.
Model 56-KR: 45 cu. in. side-valve twin, four-speed transmission, magneto ignition, flat-track racing motorcycle.
Model 56-KRTT: 45 cu. in. side-valve twin, four-speed transmission, magneto ignition.
Model 56-KHRTT: 45 cu. in. twin-cylinder TT racing motorcycle.
Model 56-KH: 55 cu. in. side-valve twin, sport model.
Model 56-KHK: 55 cu. in. side-valve twin, KH sport model with special speed kit.
Model 56-FLHF: 74 cu. in. overhead valve twin, super sport solo, foot shift.
Model 56-FLH: 74 cu. in. overhead valve twin, super sport solo, hand shift.
Model 56-FLF: 74 cu. in. overhead valve twin, sport solo, foot shift.
Model 56-FL: 74 cu. in. overhead valve twin, sport solo, hand shift.
Model 56-FLEF: 74 cu. in. overhead valve twin, foot shift, traffic combination.
Model 56-FLE: 74 cu. in. overhead valve twin, hand shift, traffic combination.

1957
Model 57-Hummer: 125cc single-cylinder, two-stroke.
Model 57-ST: 165cc single-cylinder, two-stroke.
Model 57-STU: 165cc single-cylinder, two-stroke, modified carburetor.
Model 57-KR: 45 cu. in. twin-cylinder, flat-track racing motorcycle.
Model 57-KRTT: 45 cu. in. twin-cylinder, TT racing motorcycle.

Model 57-KHRTT: 45 cu. in. twin-cylinder, TT racing motorcycle.
Model 57-XL: 55 cu. in. overhead valve twin, designated the Sportster.
Model 57-FLHF: 74 cu. in. overhead valve twin, super sport, foot shift.
Model 57-FLH: 74 cu. in. overhead valve twin, super sport, hand shift.
Model 57-FLF: 74 cu. in. overhead valve twin, sport solo, foot shift.
Model 57-FL: 74 cu. in. overhead valve twin, sport solo, hand shift.

1958
Model 58-XL: Sportster: 55 cu. in. overhead valve twin, medium compression.
Model 58-XLH: Sportster: 55 cu. in. overhead valve twin, 9:1 compression.
Model 58-XLC: Sportster: 55 cu. in. overhead valve twin, 9:1 compression.
Model 58-XLCH: Sportster: 55 cu. in. overhead valve twin, 9:1 compression, magneto ignition.
Model 58-FLHF: 74 cu. in. overhead valve twin, super sport, foot shift.
Model 58-FLH: 74 cu. in. overhead valve twin, super sport, hand shift.
Model 58-FLF: 74 cu. in. overhead valve twin, sport solo, foot shift.
Model 58-FL: 74 cu. in. overhead valve twin, sport solo, hand shift.
(F series motorcycles designated Duo-Glide, equipped with swinging arm and twin rear shocks.)
Model 58-Hummer: 125cc single-cylinder, two-stroke.
Model 58-ST: 165cc single-cylinder, two-stroke.
Model 58-STU: 165cc single-cylinder, two-stroke, modified carburetor.

1959
Model 59-XL, Sportster: 55 cu. in. overhead valve twin, medium compression.
Model 59-XLH, Sportster: 55 cu. in. overhead valve twin, high compression.
Model 59-XLCH, Sportster: 55 cu. in. overhead valve twin, high compression.
Model 59-FLHF: 74 cu. in. overhead valve twin, super sport, foot shift.
Model 59-FLH: 74 cu. in. overhead valve twin, super sport, hand shift.
Model 59-FLF: 74 cu. in. overhead valve twin, sport solo, foot shift.
Model 59-FL: 74 cu. in. overhead valve twin, sport solo, hand shift.
Model 59-Hummer: 125cc single-cylinder, two-stroke.
Model 59-ST: 165cc single-cylinder, two-stroke.
Model 59-STU: 165cc single-cylinder, two-stroke, modified carburetor.

1960
Model 60-XLH, Super H Sportster: 55 cu. in. overhead valve twin.
Model 60-XLCH, Super CH Sportster: 55 cu. in. overhead valve twin.
Model 60-FLHF: 74 cu. in. overhead valve twin, super sport, foot shift.

Model 60-FLH: 74 cu. in. overhead valve twin, super sport, hand shift.

Model 60-FLF: 74 cu. in. overhead valve twin, sport solo, foot shift.

Model 60-FL: 74 cu. in. overhead valve twin, sport solo, hand shift.

Model 60-BT, Super 10: 165cc single-cylinder, two-stroke, 9 horsepower.

Model 60-BTU, Super 10: 165cc single-cylinder, two-stroke, 5 horsepower, with carburetor restrictor.

Model 60-A, Topper scooter: 165cc single-cylinder, two-stroke, belt drive, automatic transmission, 9 horsepower.

Model 60-AU, Topper scooter: 165cc single-cylinder, two-stroke, belt drive, automatic transmission, 5 horsepower, with carburetor restrictor.

1961

Model 61-XLH, Super H Sportster: 55 cu. in. overhead valve twin.

Model 61-XLCH: Super CH Sportster: 55 cu. in. overhead valve twin.

Model 61-FLHF: 74 cu. in. overhead valve twin, super sport, foot shift.

Model 61-FLH: 74 cu. in. overhead valve twin, super sport, hand shift.

Model 61-FLF: 74 cu. in. overhead valve twin, sport solo, foot shift.

Model 61-FL: 74 cu. in. overhead valve twin, sport solo, hand shift.

Model 61-BT: Super 10: single-cylinder, two-stroke, 9 horsepower.

Model 61-BTU: Super 10: single-cylinder, two-stroke, 5 horsepower, with carburetor restrictor.

Model 61-AH, Topper scooter: 165cc single-cylinder, two-stroke, belt drive, automatic transmission, 9 horsepower.

Model 61-AU, Topper scooter: 165cc single-cylinder, two-stroke, belt drive, automatic transmission, 5 horsepower, with carburetor restrictor.

Model 61-C, Sprint: 250cc single-cylinder, four-stroke.

Model 61-KR-KRTT: 45 cu. in. side-valve racing motorcycle.

Model 61-XLRTT: 45 cu. in. side-valve TT racing motorcycle.

Model 61-CRTT: 250cc single-cylinder, overhead valve, four-stroke motor, 9.5:1 compression ratio, four-speed transmission, battery ignition, off-road racing motorcycle.

1962

Model 62-KR-KRTT: 45 cu. in. side-valve racing motorcycle.

Model 62-XLRTT: 45 cu. in. side-valve TT racing motorcycle.

Model 62-XLH, Super H, Sportster: 55 cu. in. overhead valve twin.

Model 62-XLCH, Super CH, Sportster: 55 cu. in. overhead valve twin.

Model 62-FLHF: 74 cu. in. overhead valve twin, super sport, foot shift.

Model 62-FLH: 74 cu. in. overhead valve twin, super sport, hand shift.

Model 62-FLF: 74 cu. in. overhead valve twin, sport solo, foot shift.

Model 62-FL: 74 cu. in. overhead valve twin, sport solo, hand shift.

Model 62-BT, Pacer: 175cc single-cylinder, two-stroke.

Model 62-BTH, Scat: 175cc single-cylinder, two-stroke.

Model 62-BTF, Ranger: 165cc single-cylinder, two-stroke.

Model 62, BTU, Pacer: 165cc single-cylinder, two-stroke, 5 horsepower, with carburetor restrictor.

Model 62-H Sprint H: 250cc single-cylinder, four-stroke.

Model 62-C: Sprint: 250cc single-cylinder, four-stroke.

Model 62-CRTT: 250cc single-cylinder, four-stroke road racer.

Model 62-AH, Topper scooter: 165cc single-cylinder, two-stroke, belt drive, automatic transmission, 9 horsepower.

Model 62-AU, Topper scooter: 165cc single-cylinder, two-stroke, belt drive, automatic transmission, 5 horsepower, with carburetor restrictor.

1963

Model 63 XLH, Super H Sportster: 55 cu. in. overhead valve twin.

Model 63-XLCH, Super CH Sportster: 55 cu. in. overhead valve twin.

Model 63-KR: 45 cu. in. side-valve twin, four-speed transmission, magneto ignition, designed for flat-track racing.

Model 63-KRTT: 45 cu. in. side-valve twin, four-speed transmission, magneto ignition, designed for TT racing.

Model 63-XLRTT: 55 cu. in. overhead valve twin, four-speed transmission, magneto ignition, 9:1 compression ratio.

Model 63-FLHF: 74 cu. in. overhead valve twin, super sport, foot shift.

Model 63-FLH: 74 cu. in. overhead valve twin, super sport, hand shift.

Model 63-FLF: 74 cu. in. overhead valve twin, sport solo, foot shift.

Model 63-FL: 74 cu. in. overhead valve twin, sport solo, hand shift.

Model 63-AH: Topper scooter: 165cc single-cylinder, two-stroke, belt drive, automatic transmission, 9 horsepower.

Model 63-AU: Topper scooter: 165cc single-cylinder, two-stroke, belt drive, automatic transmission, 5 horsepower, with carburetor restrictor.

Model 63-BT, Pacer: 175cc single-cylinder, two-stroke, three-speed transmission, street model.

Model 63-BTH, Scat: 175cc single-cylinder, two-stroke, three-speed transmission, trail model.

Model 63-BTU, Pacer: 175cc single-cylinder, two-stroke, three-speed transmission, 5 horsepower, with carburetor restrictor.

Model 63-C, Sprint: 250cc single-cylinder, four-cycle.

Model 63-H, Sprint: 250cc single-cylinder, four-cycle, trail model.

Model 63-CRTT: single-cylinder, four-stroke road racer.

1964

Model 64-KR: 45 cu. in. side-valve twin, four-speed transmission, magneto ignition.

Model 64-XLRTT: 55 cu. in. overhead valve twin, four-speed transmission, magneto ignition, 9:1 compression ratio.

Model 64-CRTT: single-cylinder, four-stroke road racer.

Model 64-XLH, Super H, Sportster: 55 cu. in. overhead valve twin.

Model 64-XLCH, Super CH, Sportster: 55 cu. in. overhead valve twin.

Model 64-FLHF: 74 cu. in. overhead valve twin, super sport, foot shift.

Model 64-FLH: 74 cu. in. overhead valve twin, super sport, hand shift.

Model 64-FLF: 74 cu. in. overhead valve twin, sport solo, foot shift.

Model 64-FL: 74 cu. in. overhead valve twin, sport solo, hand shift.

Model 64-BT, Pacer: 175cc single-cylinder, two-stroke, three-speed transmission, street model.

Model 64-BTH, Scat: 175cc single-cylinder, two-stroke, three-speed transmission, trail model.

Model 64-BTU, Pacer: single-cylinder, two-stroke, three-speed transmission, 5 horsepower, with carburetor restrictor.

Model 64-C, Sprint: 250cc single-cylinder, four-stroke.

Model 64-H, Sprint: 250cc single-cylinder, four-stroke, trail model.

Model 64-AH, Topper scooter: 165cc single-cylinder, two-stroke, belt drive, automatic transmission, 9 horsepower.

Model 64-AU, Topper scooter: 165cc single-cylinder, two-stroke, belt drive, automatic transmission, 5 horsepower, with carburetor restrictor.

1965

Model 65-XLH, Super H, Sportster: 55 cu. in. overhead valve twin.

Model 65-XLCH, Super CH, Sportster: 55 cu. in. overhead valve twin.

Model 65-FLHFB: 74 cu. in. overhead valve twin, super sport, foot shift.

Model 65-FLHB: 74 cu. in. overhead valve twin, super sport, hand shift.

Model 65-FLFB: 74 cu. in. overhead valve twin, super solo, foot shift.

Model 65-FLB: 74 cu. in. overhead valve twin, super solo, hand shift.

(All F models were equipped with electric starting and designated Electra Glides. Last year for the Panhead motor.)

Model 65-BT, Pacer: 175cc single-cylinder, two stroke, three-speed transmission, street model.

Model 65-BTH, Scat: 175cc single-cylinder, two-stroke, three-speed transmission, trail model.

Model 65-C, Sprint: 250cc single-cylinder, four-stroke.

Model 65-H, Sprint: 250cc single-cylinder, four-stroke, trail model.

Model 65 M-50, single-cylinder, two-cycle, three-speed transmission.

Model 65-AH, Topper scooter: 165cc single-cylinder, two-cycle, belt drive, automatic transmission, 9 horsepower. Designated high compression.

1966

Model 66-FLHFB: 74 cu. in. overhead valve twin, super sport, foot shift.

Model 66-FLHB: 74 cu. in. overhead valve twin, super sport, hand shift.

Model 66-FLFB: 74 cu. in. overhead valve twin, super solo, foot shift.

Model 66-FLB: 74 cu. in. overhead valve twin, super solo, hand shift.

Model 66-XLH, Super H, Sportster: 55 cu. in. overhead valve twin.

Model 66-XLCH, Super CH, Sportster: 55 cu. in. overhead valve twin.

Model 66-C, Sprint: 250cc single-cylinder, four-stroke.

Model 66-H, Sprint: 250cc single-cylinder, four-stroke trail model.

Model 66-BTH, Bobcat: 175cc single-cylinder, two-stroke, three-speed transmission, offered in standard (street) and trail models without separate model designation.

Model 66-M-50: 50cc single-cylinder, two-cycle, three-speed transmission, magneto ignition.

Model 66-M-50 Sport: 50cc single-cylinder, two-cycle, three-speed transmission, magneto ignition.

1967

Model 67-XLH, Sportster: 55 cu. in. overhead valve twin, electric start.

Model 67-XLCH, Sportster: 55 cu. in. overhead valve twin, electric start.

Model 67-FLHFB: 74 cu. in. overhead valve twin, super sport, foot shift.

Model 67-FLHB: 74 cu. in. overhead valve twin, super sport, hand shift.

Model 67-FLFB: 74 cu. in. overhead valve twin, super sport, foot shift.

Model 67-FLB: 74 cu. in. overhead valve twin, super sport, hand shift.

Model 67-H, Sprint: 250cc single-cylinder, four-stroke, trail model.

Model 67-SS, Sprint: 250cc single-cylinder, four stroke.

Model 67-M-65, 65cc single-cylinder, two-cycle, three-speed transmission.

Model 67-M-65, Sport: 65cc single-cylinder, two-cycle, three-speed transmission.

Model 67-M-50: 50cc single-cylinder, two-cycle, three-speed transmission.

1968

Model 68-XLH, Sportster: 55 cu. in. overhead valve twin.

Model 68-XLCH, Sportster: 55 cu. in. overhead valve twin.

Model 68-FLHFB: 74 cu. in. overhead valve twin, super sport, foot shift.

Model 68-FLHB: 74 cu. in. overhead valve twin, super sport, hand shift.

Model 68-FLFB: 74 cu. in. overhead valve twin, super sport, foot shift.

Model 68-FLB: 74 cu. in. overhead valve twin, super sport, hand shift.

Model 68-H, Sprint: 250cc single-cylinder, four-stroke, trail model.

Model 68-SS, Sprint: 250cc single-cylinder, four-stroke.

Model 68-M-125, Rapido: 125cc single-cylinder, two-stroke, four-speed transmission.

Model 68-M-65: 65cc single-cylinder, two-cycle, three-speed transmission.
Model 68-M-65, Sport: 65cc single-cylinder, two-cycle, three-speed transmission.
Model 68-M-50, Sport: 50cc single-cylinder, two-cycle, three-speed transmission.

1969

Model 69-XLH, Super H, Sportster: 55 cu. in. overhead valve twin.
Model 69-XLCH, Super CH, Sportster: 55 cu. in. overhead valve twin.
Model 69-FLHFB: 74 cu. in. overhead valve twin, super sport, foot shift.
Model 69-FLHB: 74 cu. in. overhead valve twin, super sport, hand shift.
Model 69-FLFB: 74 cu. in. overhead valve twin, super sport, foot shift.
Model 69-FLB: 74 cu. in. overhead valve twin, super sport, hand shift.
Model 69-SS, Sprint: 350cc four-cycle, overhead valve single.
Model 69-ERS, Sprint Scrambler: 350cc overhead valve, four-cycle, four-speed transmission, magneto ignition.
Model 69-ML-125, Rapido: 125cc single-cylinder, two-stroke. (1,000 street models built; Rapido then continued as a trail model.)
Model 69-M-65: 65cc single-cylinder, two-stroke.
Model 69-M-65 Sport: 65cc single-cylinder, two stroke.
Model 69-XLRTT: 55 cu. in. overhead valve twin, 9:1 compression ratio, four-speed transmission, magneto ignition.

1970

Model 70-FLHF: 74 cu. in. overhead valve twin, super sport, foot shift.
Model 70-FLH: 74 cu. in. overhead valve twin, super sport, hand shift.
Model 70-FLPF: 74 cu. in. overhead valve twin, super sport, foot shift.
Model 70-FLP: 74 cu. in. overhead valve twin, super sport, hand shift.
Model 70-XLH, Super H, Sportster: 55 cu. in. overhead valve twin.
Model 70-XLCH, Super CH, Sportster: 55 cu. in. overhead valve twin.
Model 70-SS, Sprint: 350cc single-cylinder, four-cycle.
Model 70-MLS, Rapido: 125cc single-cylinder, two-stroke.
Model 70-M-65 Sport, Leggero: single-cylinder, two-cycle.
Model 70-ERS, Sprint Scrambler: 350cc overhead valve, four-cycle.
Model 70-MSR, Baja: 100cc single-cylinder, two-cycle, four-speed transmission.

1971

Model 71-FLHF: 74 cu. in. overhead valve twin, super sport, foot shift.
Model 71-FLH: 74 cu. in. overhead valve twin, super sport, hand shift.
Model 71-FLPF: 74 cu. in. overhead valve twin, super sport, foot shift.
Model 71-FLP: 74 cu. in. overhead valve twin, super sport, hand shift.

Model 71-FX, Super Glide: 74 cu. in. overhead valve twin, foot shift.
Model 71-XLH, Super H, Sportster: 55 cu. in. overhead valve twin.
Model 71-XLCH, Super CH, Sportster: 55 cu. in. overhead valve twin.
Model 71-SX, Sprint: 350cc single-cylinder, four-cycle, off-road model.
Model 71-SS, Sprint: 350cc single-cylinder, four-cycle.
Model 71-MLS, Rapido: 125cc single-cylinder, off-road bike.
Model 71-M-65 Sport, Leggero: 65cc single-cylinder, two-cycle.
Model 71-ERS, Sprint Scrambler: 350cc overhead valve, four-cycle.
Model 71-MSR, Baja: 100cc single-cylinder, two-cycle.

1972

Model 72-FLHF: 74 cu. in. overhead valve twin, super sport, foot shift.
Model 72-FLH: 74 cu. in. overhead valve twin, super sport, hand shift.
Model 72-FLPF: 74 cu. in. overhead valve twin, super sport, foot shift.
Model 72-FLP: 74 cu. in. overhead valve twin, super sport, hand shift.
Model 72-FX, Super Glide: 74 cu. in. overhead valve twin, foot shift.
Model 72-XLH, Super H, Sportster: 1000cc V-twin.
Model 72-XLCH, Super CH, Sportster: 1000cc V-twin.
Model 72-MLS, Rapido: 125cc single-cylinder, two-cycle.
Model 72-M-65 Sport, Leggero: 65cc single-cylinder, two-cycle.
Model 72-ERS, Sprint Scrambler: 350cc overhead valve, four-cycle.
Model 72-MSR, Baja 100L (lights): single-cylinder, two-cycle.
Model 72-MSR, Baja 100 (no lights): single-cylinder, two-cycle.
Model 72-MC-65, Shortster minicycle: 65cc single-cylinder, two-stroke.

1973

Model 73-FL: 74 cu. in. overhead valve twin.
Model 73-FLH: 74 cu. in. overhead valve twin.
Model 73-XLH, Super H, Sportster: 1000cc V-twin.
Model 73-XLCH, Super CH, Sportster: 1000cc V-twin.
Model 73-FX, Super Glide: 74 cu. in. overhead valve twin.
Model 73-SS, Sprint: 350cc single-cylinder, four-stroke, electric start.
Model 73-SX, Sprint: 350cc single-cylinder, four-stroke, electric start.
Model 73-TX: 125cc.
Model 73-Z-90: 90cc single-cylinder, two-stroke, automatic gas-oil mix.
Model 73-X-90: 90cc single-cylinder, two-stroke, automatic gas-oil mix.
Model 73-SR-100: 100cc single-cylinder, two-stroke, automatic gas-oil mix.
Model 73-XRTT: 45 cu. in. aluminum engine, racing motorcycle.

1974

Model 74-FLH-1200: 74 cu. in. overhead valve twin.

Model 74-FLHF: 74 cu. in. overhead valve twin.
Model 74-FL, Police: 74 cu. in. overhead valve twin.
Model 74-FX, Super Glide: 74 cu. in. overhead valve twin.
Model 74-FXE, Super Glide: electric start, overhead valve twin.
Model 74-XLH, Super H, Sportster: 1000cc V-twin.
Model 74-XLCH, Super CH, Sportster: 1000cc V-twin.
Model 74-SS 350: 350cc single-cylinder, four-cycle.
Model 74-SX 350: 350cc single-cylinder, four-cycle.
Model 74-SX 175: 175cc single-cylinder, two-cycle.
Model 74-SX 125: 125cc single-cylinder, two-cycle.
Model 74-Z-90: 90cc single-cylinder, two-cycle.
Model 74-X-90: 90cc single-cylinder, two-cycle.
Model 74-SR-100: 100cc single-cylinder, two-cycle, off-road bike.
Model 74-XR: 45 cu. in. racing motorcycle.

1975

Model 75-FLH-1200: 74 cu. in. overhead valve twin.
Model 75-FLHF: 74 cu. in. overhead valve twin.
Model 75-FL Police: 74 cu. in. overhead valve twin.
Model 75-FX, Super Glide: 74 cu. in. overhead valve twin.
Model 75-FXE, Super Glide: electric start, 74 cu. in. overhead valve twin.
Model 75-XLH, Super H, Sportster: 1000cc V-twin.
Model 75-XLCH, Super CH, Sportster: 1000cc V-twin.
Model 75-SX-175: 175cc single-cylinder, two-cycle.
Model 75-SX-125: 125cc single-cylinder, two-cycle.
Model 75-Z-90: 90cc single-cylinder, two-cycle.
Model 75-X-90: 90cc single-cylinder, two-cycle.
Model 75-XR: 45 cu. in. racing motorcycle.
Model 75-SX-250: 250cc single-cylinder, two-cycle, five-speed transmission.
Model 75-RC-125: 125cc single-cylinder, two-cycle.
Model 75-SS-250: 250cc single-cylinder, two-cycle, five-speed transmission.

1976

Model 76-FLH-1200: 74 cu. in. overhead valve twin.
Model 76-FX, Super Glide: 74 cu. in. overhead valve twin.
Model 76-FXE, Super Glide: electric start, 74 cu. in. overhead valve twin.
Model 76-XLH, Super H, Sportster: 1000cc V-twin.
Model 76-XLCH, Super CH, Sportster: 1000cc V-twin.
Model 76-SS-250: 250cc single-cylinder, two-cycle.
Model 76-SX-250: 250cc single-cylinder, two-cycle, off-road.
Model 76-SXT-125: 125cc single-cylinder, two-cycle.
Model 76-SS-175: 175cc single-cylinder, two-cycle.
Model 76-SS-125: 125cc single-cylinder, two-cycle.
Model 76-MX-250: 250cc single-cylinder, off-road racing cycle.
Model 76-RR-250: 250cc two-cylinder, liquid-cooled racing cycle.

1977

Model 77-FLH-1200: 74 cu. in. overhead valve twin.
Model 77-FLHS: 74 cu. in. overhead valve twin.
Model 77-FX, Super Glide: 74 cu. in. overhead valve twin.
Model 77-FXE, Super Glide: electric start, 74 cu. in. overhead valve twin.
Model 77-FXS, Low Rider: 74 cu. in. overhead valve twin.
Model 77-XLT, Sportster: electric start, 1000cc V-twin.
Model 77-XLCR, Cafe Racer: 1000cc V-twin.

Model 77-XLH, Super H, Sportster: 1000cc V-twin.
Model 77-XLCH, Super CH, Sportster: 1000cc V-twin.
Model 77-SS-250: 250cc single-cylinder, two-cycle.
Model 77-SX 250: 250cc single-cylinder, two-cycle.
Model 77-SXT 125: 125cc single-cylinder, two-cycle.
Model 77-SS 175: 175cc single-cylinder, two-cycle.
Model 77-SS 125: 125cc single-cylinder, two-cycle.
Model 77-RR 250: 250cc two-cylinder, liquid-cooled racing cycle.

1978

Model 78-FLH-1200: 74 cu. in. overhead valve twin.
Model 78-FLH Anniversary: 74 cu. in. overhead valve twin.
Model 78-FLH 80, Electra Glide: 80 cu. in. overhead valve twin.
Model 78-FX, Super Glide: 74 cu. in. overhead valve twin.
Model 78-FXE, Super Glide: electric start, 74 cu. in. overhead valve twin.
Model 78-FXS, Low Rider: 74 cu. in. overhead valve twin.
Model 78-XLH, Super H, Sportster: 1000cc V-twin.
Model 78-XLH Anniversary, Sportster: 1000cc V-twin.
Model 78-XLCH, Super CH, Sportster: 1000cc V-twin.
Model 78-SX 250: 250cc single-cylinder, two-cycle.
Model 78-XLT, Sportster: electric start, 1000cc V-twin.
Model 78-XLCR, Cafe Racer: 1000cc V-twin.
Model 78-XLS, Roadster: 1000cc V-twin.
Model 78-XR 750: 45 cu. in. V-twin flat-track racer.

1979

Model 79-FLT, Tour Glide: 80 cu. in. V-twin, solid-state ignition.
Model 79-FLHC, Electra Glide Classic: 80 cu. in. V-twin, solid-state ignition, sixteen-spoke wheels, MT90 by 16 in. rear tire; TourPak standard.
Model 79-FLHC with sidecar, Electra Glide Classic, sidecar standard.
Model 79-FLH 80, Electra Glide: 80 cu. in. V-twin; fairing/windshield, saddle bags with safety guards, luggage rack, passing lights, safety bars, running boards, all standard.
Model 79-FLH 1200, Electra Glide 74: 1200cc V-twin; fairing/windshield, saddle bags with safety guards, luggage rack, passing lights, safety bars, running boards, all standard.
Model 79-FLH 80, Police: 80 cu. in. police motorcycle.
Model 79-FLH 1200, Police: 74 cu. in. police motorcycle.
Model 79-FXS 1200, Low Rider: 1200cc V-twin, solid-state ignition, two-into-one exhaust; stash pouch, sissy bar standard.
Model 79-FXS 80, Low Rider: 80 cu. in. V-twin, solid-state ignition, two-into-one exhaust; stash pouch, sissy bar standard.
Model 79-FXEF 1200, Fat Bob Super Glide: 1200cc V-twin, solid-state ignition, buckhorn handlebars.
Model 79-FXEF 80, Fat Bob Super Glide: 80 cu. in. V-twin, solid-state ignition, 3.5-gal. twin gas tanks with instrument pod in middle, two-into-one exhaust.
Model 79-FXE 1200, Super Glide: 1200cc V-twin, solid-state ignition, two-into-one exhaust.
Model 79-XLH, Sportster: 1000cc V-twin, XR750-derived frame, 16 in. rear tire, nine-spoke aluminum wheels, buckhorn bars.

Model 79-XLCH, Sportster: 1000cc V-twin, XR750-derived frame, 16 in. rear tire, nine-spoke aluminum wheels, buckhorn bars.

Model 79-XLCR, Cafe Racer: 1000cc V-twin.

Model 79-XLS, Roadster: 1000cc V-twin, solid-state ignition, siamese exhaust system, cast aluminum wheels, 16-in. drag-style rear tire, tooled leather stash pouch, highway pegs; termed by factory "a Sportster version of the FXS Low Rider."

1980

Model 80-FLT, Tour Glide: 80 cu. in. V-twin, solid-state ignition.

Model 80-FLHC, Electra Glide Classic: 80 cu. in. V-twin, solid-state ignition.

Model 80-FLHC with sidecar, Electra Glide Classic.

Model 80-FLH 80, Electra Glide: 80 cu. in. V-twin, solid-state ignition.

Model 80-FLH 1200, Electra Glide: 1200cc V-twin, solid-state ignition.

Model 80-FLHS, Electra Glide: 80 cu. in. V-twin, solid-state ignition.

Model 80-FLH 80, Police: 80 cu. in. police motorcycle.

Model 80-FLH 1200, Police: 74 cu. in. police motorcycle.

Model 80-FXB, Sturgis: 80 cu. in. V-twin, solid-state ignition, primary and secondary belt drive.

Model 80-FXWG, Wide Glide: 80 cu. in. V-twin, solid-state ignition.

Model 80-FXS 1200, Low Rider: 1200cc V-twin, solid-state ignition.

Model 80-FXS 80, Low Rider: 80 cu. in. V-twin, solid-state ignition.

Model 80-FXEF 80, Fat Bob Wide Glide: 80 cu. in. V-twin, solid-state ignition.

Model 80-FXE 1200, Super Glide: 1200cc V-twin, solid-state ignition.

Model 80-XLS, Roadster: 1000cc V-twin, solid-state ignition, spoke wheels standard, cast wheels extra.

Model 80-XLH, Sportster: 1000cc V-twin, solid-state ignition, spoke wheels standard, cast wheels extra.

1981

Model 81-FLTC, Tour Glide Classic: 80 cu. in. V-twin, solid-state ignition, crossover exhaust system.

Model 81-FLT, Tour Glide: 80 cu. in. V-twin, solid-state ignition, crossover exhaust system.

Model 81-FLHC, Electra Glide Classic: 80 cu. in. V-twin, belt drive, four-speed transmission, 7 in. quartz halogen headlight; TourPak and back rest standard.

Model 81-FLHC with sidecar, Electra Glide Classic: 80 cu. in. overhead valve V-twin, belt drive, four-speed transmission, 7 in. quartz halogen headlight; TourPak and back rest standard.

Model 81-FLH 80, Electra Glide: 80 cu. in. V-twin, solid-state ignition.

Model 81-FLHS, Electra Glide: 80 cu. in. V-twin, solid-state ignition.

Model 81-Heritage, Electra Glide: 80 cu. in. V-twin, solid-state ignition.

Model 81-FLH 80, Police: 80 cu. in. police motorcycle.

Model 81-FXB, Sturgis: 80 cu. in. engine, primary and secondary belt drive.

Model 81-FXWG, Wide Glide: 80 cu. in. V-twin.

Model 81-FXS 80, Low Rider: 80 cu. in. V-twin.

Model 81-FXEF 80, Fat Bob: 80 cu. in. V-twin.

Model 81-FXE 80, Super Glide: electric start, 80 cu. in. V-twin.

Model 81-XLS, Roadster: 1000cc V-twin.

Model 81-XLH, Sportster: 1000cc V-twin.

1982

Model 82-FLT, Tour Glide: 80 cu. in. V-twin.

Model 82-FLT Classic, Tour Glide: 80 cu. in. V-twin.

Model 82-FLH, Electra Glide: 80 cu. in. V-twin.

Model 82-XLS, Roadster: 61 cu. in. V-twin.

Model 82-FXS, Low Rider: 80 cu. in. V-twin.

Model 82-FXWG, Wide Glide: 80 cu. in. V-twin.

Model 82-XLH, Sportster: 61 cu. in. V-twin.

Model 82-FXE, Super Glide: 80 cu. in. V-twin.

Model 82-FXB, Sturgis: 80 cu. in. V-twin, primary and secondary belt drive.

Model 82-FXR, Super Glide II: 80 cu. in. V-twin, five-speed transmission.

Model 82-FXRS, Super Glide II: 80 cu. in. V-twin, five-speed transmission, computer-designed frame.

Model 82-FLH 80: 80 cu. in. police motorcycle

1983

Model 83-FLHT, Electra Glide: 80 cu. in. motor, fork-mounted fairing, halogen headlamp and dual spot lamps, tubeless tires, five-speed transmission.

Model 83-FLHT Classic, Electra Glide: 80 cu. in. motor, fork-mounted fairing, halogen headlamp and dual spot lamps, tubeless tires, five-speed transmission, TourPak standard.

Model 83-FLT, Tour Glide: 80 cu. in. motor, adjustable footboards, tubeless tires, rear fender engine vents, 22-amp alternator, spin-on oil filter.

Model 83-FLT Classic, Tour Glide: 80 cu. in. motor, adjustable footboards, tubeless tires, rear fender engine vents, 22-amp alternator, spin-on oil filter.

Model 83-FLH, Electra Glide: 80 cu. in. motor, secondary belt drive, automotive type spin-on oil filter.

Model 83-XLH, Sportster: 61 cu. in. motor, two-stage ignition, 8.8-1 compression ratio, oval air box, FXE-style 3.3-gallon gas tank, ribbed primary chain cover.

Model 83-XLS, Roadster: 61 cu. in. motor, two-stage ignition, 8.8-1 compression ratio, oval air box, 3.8-gallon Fat Bob-style gas tank, nine-spoke cast wheels.

Model 83-XLX-61: 61 cu. in. motor, two-stage ignition, 8.8-1 compression ratio, oval air box, peanut gas tank, nine-spoke cast wheels.

Model 83-FXSB, Low Rider: 80 cu. in. motor, four-speed transmission.

Model 83-FXWG, Wide Glide: 80 cu. in. motor, four-speed transmission.

Model 83-FXE, Super Glide: 80 cu. in. motor, four-speed transmission.

Model 83-FXR, Super Glide: 80 cu. in. motor, five-speed gearbox, low-maintenance calcium alloy grid battery, spin-on oil filter.

Model 83-FXRS, Super Glide II: 80 cu. in. motor, five-speed gearbox, low-maintenance calcium alloy grid battery, spin-on oil filter.

Model 83-FLH 80: 80 cu. in. police motorcycle.

Harley-Davidson Production 1903-1991

The following was gleaned from several sources, all within the Harley-Davidson, Inc. More complete figures are not available.

1903 1	**1922** 12,759
1904 2	**1923** 18,430
1905 8	**1924** 13,996
1906 50	**1925** 16,929
1907 150	**1926** 23,354
1908 450	**1927** 19,911
1909 1,149	**1928** 22,350
1910 3,168	**1929** 21,142
1911 5,625	**1930** 17,422
1912 9,571	**1931** 10,500
1913 12,904	**1932** 6,841
1914 16,284	**1933** 3,703
1915 16,645	**1934** 10,231
1916 17,439	**1935** 10,368
1917 19,763	**1936** 9,812
1918 19,359	**1937** 11,674
1919 24,292	**1938** 9,934
1920 28,189	**1939** 8,355
1921 10,202	**1940** 10,855

1941
18,428

1942
29,603

1943
29,243

1944
17,006

1945
11,978

1946
15,554

1947
20,392

1948
31,163

1949
23,740

1950
18,355

1951
14,580

1952
17,250

1953
14,050

1954
12,250

1955
9,750

1956
FL: 836
FLE: 671
FLH: 224
FLF: 1,578
FLEF: 162
FLHF: 2,315
(Total F series, 5,786)
G: 467
GA: 736
KHK: 714
KH: 539
KR: 29
KRTT: 18
XL: 1
KHRTT: 13

ST: 2,219
B: 1,384
TOTAL: 11,906

1957
FL: 1,579
FLH: 164
FLF: 1,259
FLHF: 2,614
(Total F series, 5,616)
G: 518
GA: 674
KH: 90
XL: 1,983
XLA: 418
(Total XL series, 2,401)
KR: 16
KRTT: 9
KHRTT: 4
ST: 2,401
B: 1,350
TOTAL: 13,079

1958
FL: 1,591
FLH: 195
FLF: 1,299
FLHF: 2,953
(Total F series, 6,038)
G: 283
GA: 643
XL: 579
XLH: 711
XLCH: 239
(Total XL series, 1,529)
KRTT: 26
KR: 9
XLRTT: 26
ST: 2,445
B: 1,677
TOTAL: 12,676

1959
FL: 1,201
FLH: 121
FLF: 1,222
FLHF: 3,223
(Total F series, 5,767)
G: 288
GA: 524
XL: 42
XLH: 942
XLCH: 1,059
XLR: 5
XLRTT: 13
(Total XL series, 2,061)
KR: 10
KRTT: 23

ST: 2,311
B: 1,285
A: 73
TOTAL: 12,342

1960
A: 3,801
74: 5,967
Servi-Car: 707
XLH: 2,765
B, BT: 2,488
TOTAL: 15,728

1961
A: 1,341
74: 4,927
Servi-Car: 628
XLH: 2,014
BT: 1,587
TOTAL: 10,497

1962
74: 5,184
45: 1,276
XLSS: 1,998
G, GE: 703
B: 1,983
TOTAL: 11,144

1963
BT: 824
BTU: 39
BTH: 877
AH: 972
AU: 6
XLH: 432
XLCH: 1,001
(Total XL series, 1,433)
KR: 80
FL: 1,096
FLF: 950
FLH: 100
FLHF: 2,100
Sprint C: 150
Sprint H: 1,416
TOTAL: 10,043
(Factory reported 10,407 bikes produced; no reason given for discrepancy.)

1964
FL: 2,775
FLH: 2,725
(Total FL series, 5,500)
BT: 600
BTH: 800
BTU: 50
AH: 800
AU: 25
XLCH: 1,950
XLH: 810
XLA: 100
(Total XL series, 2,860)
GE: 725
XLRTT: 30

KRTT: 30
KR: 20
CR: 50
Sprint C: 230
Sprint H: 1,550
TOTAL: 13,270

1965
FL: 2,130
FLH: 4,800
(Total F series, 6,930)
BT: 500
BTH: 750
AH: 500
XLCH: 2,815
XLH: 955
(Total XL series, 3,770)
GE: 625
XLRTT: 25
KRTT: 10
KR: 8
CR: 35
CRS: 175
Sprint H: 2,500
Sprint C: 500
M50: 9,000
TOTAL: 25,328

1966
FL: 2,175
FLH: 5,625
(Total F series, 7,800)
BTH: 1,150
XLCH: 3,900
XLH: 900
(Total XL series, 4,800)
GE: 625
KR: 10
KRTT: 10
XLRTT: 25
CR: 50
CRS: 350
Sprint H: 4,700
Sprint C: 600
M50: 5,700
M50S: 10,500
TOTAL: 36,310

1967
FL: 2,150
FLH: 5,600
(Total F series, 7,750)
XLCH: 2,500
XLH: 2,000
(Total XL series, 4,500)
GE: 600
Sprint H: 2,000
Sprint SS: 7,000
CRTT: 35
CRS: 50
M65: 2,000
M65 Spt: 3,267
TOTAL: 27,202

1968
FL: 1,718
FLH: 5,354
XLH: 1,995
XLCH: 4,889
GE: 617
M-65: 1,200
M-65 Sport: 1,700
SS-350: 4,150
ML: 5,000
ERS: 125
TOTAL: 26,748

1969
FL: 1,800
FLH: 5,500
XLH: 2,700
XLCH: 5,100
GE: 475
M-65: 950
M-65 Sport: 1,750
SS-350: 4,575
ML: 1,000
MLS: 3,275
ERS: 250
TOTAL: 27,375

1970
FL: 1,706
FLH: 5,909
XLH: 3,033
XLCH: 5,527
GE: 494
M-65 Sport: 2,080
SS-350: 4,513
MLS: 4,059
ERS: 102
MSR-100: 1,427
TOTAL: 28,850

1971
FL: 1,200
FLH: 5,475
XLH: 3,950
XLCH: 6,825
GE: 500
M-65 Sport: 3,100
SS-350: 1,500
MLS: 5,200
ERS: 50
MSR-100: 1,200
FX: 4,700
SX-350: 3,920
TOTAL: 37,620

1972
FL: 1,600
FLH: 8,100
XLH: 7,500
XLCH: 10,650
GE: 400
M-65 Sport: 3,708
SS-350: 3,775
MLS: 6,000
ERS: 50

MSR-100: 900
FX: 6,500
SX-350: 2,525
XR: 200
MC: 8,000
TOTAL: 59,908

1973
FL: 1,025
FLH: 7,750
XLH: 9,875
XLCH: 10,825
GE: 425
SS-350: 4,137
FX: 7,625
SX-350: 2,431
MC: 95
TX-125: 9,225
Z-90: 8,244
X-90: 8,250
SR-100: 986
XRTT: 10
TOTAL: 70,903

1974
FLH-1200: 5,166
FX: 3,034
FXE: 6,199
XLH: 13,295
XLCH: 10,535
SS-350: 2,500
SX-350: 2,085
SX-175: 3,612
SX-125: 4,000
Z-90: 7,168
X-90: 7,019
SR-100: 1,396
XR: 100
FLHF: 1,310
FL-Police: 791
TOTAL: 68,210

1975
FLH-1200: 7,400
FX: 3,060
FXE: 9,350
XLH: 13,515
XLCH: 5,895
SX-175: 8,500
SX-125: 2,500
Z-90: 2,562
X-90: 1,586
XR: 100
FLHF: 1,535
FL-Police: 900
SX-250: 11,000
RC-125: 4,500
SS-250: 3,000
TOTAL: 75,403

1976
FLH-1200: 11,891
FX: 3,857
FXE: 13,838
XLH: 12,844

XLCH: 5,238
SX-250: 3,125
SS-250: 1,416
SXT-125: 6,056
SS-175: 1,461
SS-125: 1,560
MX-250: 87
RR-250: 2
TOTAL: 61,375

1977
FLH-1200: 8,691
FX: 2,049
FXE: 9,400
XLH: 12,742
XLCH: 4,074
SX-250: 558
SS-250: 144
SXT-125: 48
SS-175: 110
SS-125: 488
RR-250: 5
FLHS: 535
FXS: 3,742
XLT: 1,099
XLCR: 1,923
TOTAL: 45,608

1978
FLH-1200: 4,761
FX: 1,774
FXE: 8,314
XLH: 11,271
XLCH: 2,758
XLH Anniversary: 2,323
SX-250: 479
FXS: 9,787
XLT: 6
XLCR: 1,201
FLH-80: 2,525
XLS: 2
XR750: 80
FLH-1200 Anniversary: 2,120
TOTAL: 47,401*

1979
FLT: 19
FLHC: 4,368
FLHC and sidecar: 353
FLH-80: 3,429
FLH-1200: 2,612
FLH-80 Police: 84
FLH-1200 Police: 596
FXS-1200: 3,827
FXS-80: 9,433
FXEF-1200: 4,678
FXEF-80: 5,264
FXE-1200: 3,117
XLCH: 141
XLCR: 9
XLS: 5,123
XLH: 6,525
TOTAL: 49,578*

1980
FLT: 4,480

FLHC: 2,480
FLHC and sidecar: 463
FLH-80: 1,625
FLH-1200: 1,111
FLHS: 914
FLH-80 Police: 391
FLH-1200 Police: 528
FXB: 1,470
FXWG: 6,085
FXS-1200: 3
FXS-80: 5,922
FXEF-80: 4,773
FXE-1200: 3,169
XLS: 2,926
XLH: 11,841
TOTAL: 48,181*

1981
FLTC: 1,157
FLT: 1,636
FLHC: 1,472
FLHC and sidecar: 152
FLH-80: 2,131
FLHS: 1,062
Heritage: 784
FLH-80 Police: 402
FXB: 3,543
FXWG: 5,166
FXS-80: 7,223
FXEF-80: 3,691
FXE-80: 3,085
XLS: 1,660
XLH: 8,442
TOTAL: 41,606*
(Factory total, 41,586; no reason given for discrepancy.)

1982
FLT Tour Glide: 1,196
FLTC Tour Glide Classic: 833
FLH 80: 1,491
FLC FLH Classic: 1,284
FLC (+sidecar): 95
FLHF Heritage: 313
FLHS Electra Glide Sport: 948
8SDX1C sidecar: 81
8SEX1c: 17
FXE Super Glide (electric start): 1,617
FXS Low Rider (first factory chopper): 1,816
FXB Sturgis (belt drive): 1,833
FXWG Wide Glide (wide front fork): 2,348
FXR Super Glide: 3,065
FXRS Super Glide (with extras): 3,190
XLH Sportster (electric start): 5,015
XLHA Anniversary: 932
XLS Roadster Custom Sport: 1,261
XLSA Anniversary: 778
FLHP (police 80: 161
FLHP Police) 80: 156

FLHP 80: 1,261
FLHP (deluxe): 270
FLHP Shrine: 19
FLHP: 282
TOTAL: 30,262

1983
FLT Tour Glide: 565
FLT: 1
FLTC: Tour Glide Classic: 475
FLTC (+sidecar): 37
FLH 80: 1,272
FLHT Electra Glide: 1,426
FLHTC Electra Glide Classic: 1,302
FLHTC: 2
FLHTC (+sidecar): 75
FLHS Electra Glide Sport: 985
8SAX1D1 sidecar: 4
8SBX1D1: 1
8SEX1D1: 19
8SFX1D1: 90
8SGX1D1: 12
FXE Super Glide (electric start): 1,215
FXWG Wide Glide: 2,873
FXSB Low Rider (rear belt): 3,277
FXDG: 810
FXR Super Glide: 1,069
FXR: 60
FXRS Super Glide II (extras): 1,413
FXRT Tour Glide (fairing, bags): 1,458
XLH Sportster (electric start): 2,230
XLS Roadster Custom Sport: 1,616
XLX: 4,892
XR 1000: 1,018
FLHP Police Standard: 334
FLHP Deluxe (birch white): 414
FLHTP (chain): 341
FLHP Shrine: 11
FLHP (belt): 112
FLHTC (chain): 211
TOTAL: 29,620

1984
FLTC Classic Tour Glide: 446
FLTC: 855
FLTC (+sidecar): 11
FLTC (+sidecar): 24
FLHTC Classic Electra Glide: 974
FLHTC: 1,517
FLHTC (+sidecar): 14
FLHTC (+sidecar): 22
CLE sidecar: 19
TLE (with motorcycle): 57
FLH 80: 155
FLH 80: 1,828
FLHX: 791
FLHX: 467
FLHS Electra Glide Sport: 499
FXE (single tank): 1
FXE (single tank): 666
FXE (twin tank): 1,076
FXE (twin tank): 364
FXST: 3,303
FXST: 2,110

FXB: 942
FXB: 1,935
FXWG: 2
FXWG: 2,225
FXRS: 1,079
FXRS: 1,731
FXRT: 834
FXRT: 1,196
FXRDG: 853
FXRSDG: 3
FXRSDG: 7
XLH (alternators): 2,278
XLH (331 with alternators): 2,164
XLS (alternators): 678
XLS (191 with alternators): 457
XLX (alternators): 2,165
XLX (alternators): 2,119
XR1000 (generators): 759
FLHTP Police: 100
FLHTP: 53
FLH (belt): 216
FLH (belt): 173
FLH: 565
FLH: 123
FXRP: 43
FXRP: 588
FXRP CHIPS: 189
FLHT Shrine: 36
FLHT: 19
FLH: 5
FLH: 10
TOTAL: 38,741

1985
FLTC Classic Tour Glide: 1,602
FLTC (chrome): 205
FLTC (+ sidecar): 40
FLHTC Classic Electra Glide: 3,409
FLHTC (chrome): 598
FLHTC (+ sidecar): 51
FLH 80: 41
FLHX: 80
FXEF: 2,324
FXST: 4,529
FXSB: 2,359
FXWG Wide Glide: 4,171
FXRS Low Rider: 3,476
FXRT: 1,252
FXRS (high performance): 1,008
FXRS (chrome): 299
FXRC (candy and orange chrome): 1,084
XLH: 4,074
XLS: 616
XLX: 1,824
FLHTP Police: 216
FLH (belt): 296
FXRP: 341
FXRP CHIPS: 161
FXRP (fairing): 474
FLHTC Shrine: 102
TOTAL: 34,632

1986
FLTC Classic Tour Glide: 1,039

FLTC Special Anniversary: 202
FLTC Liberty: 160
FLTC (+ sidecar): 41
FLHTC Classic Electra Glide: 1,879
FLHTC Special Anniversary: 536
FLHTC Liberty: 810
FLHTC (+ sidecar): 62
FLHT: 711
FLST: 2,510
FXST Softail: 2,402
FXSTC: 3,782
FXWG Wide Glide: 573
FXWG Wide Glide (California): 626
FXR Super Glide: 2,038
FXRS Low Rider: 1,846
FXRS Special Anniversary: 962
FXRS Liberty: 744
FXRT Sport Glide: 591
FXRS Low Rider Sport Edition: 1,247
FXRD: 1,000
XLH-1100 Sportster: 3,077
XLH-1100 Liberty: 954
XLH-883 Sportster: 8,026
XLH-883 (upgrade): 2,322
XLH-1200 Sportster: 14
FLHTP (fairing): 239
FLHTP (windshield): 71
FXRP (windshield): 252
FXRP (fairing): 252
FLTC Shrine: 14
FLHTC: 134
TOTAL: 39,116

1987
FLTC Classic Tour Glide: 699
FLTC Special/Anniversary: 125
FLTC (+ sidecar): 32
FLHTC Classic Electra Glide: 2,858
FLHTC Special/Anniversary: 800
FLHTC (+ sidecar): 146
8SFX1H (with motorcycle): 1
8SHX1H: 1
FLHT Electra Glide Sport: 87
FLHS: 1,054
FLST: 2,794
FLST Special: 1,545
FXST Softail: 2,024
FXST Special: 398
FXSTC Softail Custom: 5,264
FXR Super Glide: 1,265
FXRS Low Rider: 784
FXRT Sport Glide: 287
FXRS Low Rider Sport Edition: 1,142
FXRC Special: 736
FXLR Low Rider Custom: 3,221
XLH-1100 Sportster: 4,018
XLH-1100 Anniversary: 600
XLH-883 Sportster: 4,990
XLH-883 (upgrade): 2,260
XLH-883 (low): 2,106
FLHTP (fairing): 194
FLHTP (windshield): 203
FXRP CHIPS: 171
FXRP (windshield): 149

FXRP (fairing): 245
FLTC Shrine: 68
FLHTC: 411
TOTAL: 41,678

1988
FLTC Classic Tour Glide: 745
FLTC Special/Anniversary: 50
FLTC (+ sidecar): 44
FLHTC Classic Electra Glide: 3,958
FLHTC Special/Anniversary: 715
FLHTC (+ sidecar): 207
8SFX1J sidecar: 103
FLHS Electra Glide Sport: 1,677
FXST Softail: 1,467
FXSTC Softail Custom: 6,621
FLST Heritage Softail: 2,209
FLSTC Heritage Softail Classic: 3,755
FXSTS Springer Softail: 1,356
FXR Super Glide: 1,205
FXRS Low Rider: 2,637
FXRS Special/Anniversary: 519
FXRS-SP Low Rider Sport Edition: 818
FXLR Low Rider Custom: 902
FXRT Sport Glide: 243
XLH-883 Sportster: 5,387
XLH-883 DeLuxe: 1,893
XLH-883 Low (Hugger): 4,501
XLH-1200 Sportster: 4,752
FLHTP Police (fairing): 278
FLHTP (windshield): 343
FXRP (fairing): 348
FXRP (windshield): 230
FXRP CHIPS: 217
FLTC Classic Tour Glide (Shrine): 9
FLHTC Classic Electra Glide: 136
TOTAL: 47,325

1989
FLTC-Ultra Classic Tour Glide: 530
FLTC-Ultra (+ sidecar): 38
FLTC Classic Tour Glide: 588
FLTC (+ sidecar): 15
FLHTC-Ultra Classic Electra Glide: 2,653
FLHTC-Ultra (+ sidecar): 237
FLHTC Classic Electra Glide: 3,969
FLHTC (+ sidecar): 128
8SFX1 sidecar: 161
8SFX1 sidecar: 275
FLHS Electra Glide Sport: 2,330
FLSTC Heritage Softail Classic: 5,210
FLST Heritage Softail: 1,506
FXSTS Springer Softail: 5,387
FXSTC Softail custom: 6,523
FXST Softail: 1,130
FXRT Sport Glide: 255
FXLR Low Rider Custom: 1,016
FXRS-Convertible: 292
FXRS-SP Low Rider Sport Glide: 755
FXRS Low Rider: 2,096
FXR Super Glide: 1,821
XLH-1200 Sportster: 4,546
XLH-883 DeLuxe: 1,812
XLH-883 Hugger: 4,467

XLH-883 Sportster: 6,142
FLHTP (fairing): 342
FLHTP (windshield): 318
FXRP (clear windshield): 214
FXRP (fairing): 379
FXRP CHIPS: 187
FLTC Classic Tour Glide (Shrine): 3
FLTC-Ultra: 11
FLHTC Classic Electra Glide: 80
FLHTC-Ultra: 91
TOTAL: 55,507

1990
FLTC-Ultra Classic Tour Glide: 575
FLTC-Ultra (+ sidecar): 37
FLTC Classic Tour Glide: 476
FLTC (+ sidecar): 9
FLHTC-Ultra Classic Electra Glide: 3,082
FLHTC-Ultra (sidecar): 323
FLHTC Classic Electra Glide: 3,497
FLHTC (+ sidecar): 100
8SJX1 sidecar: 139
8SJX1 sidecar: 360
FLHS Electra Glide Sport: 2,410
FLSTF Fat Boy: 4,440
FLSTC Heritage Softail Classic: 5,483
FLST Heritage Softail: 1,567
FXSTS Springer Softail: 4,252
FXSTC Softail Custom: 6,795
FXST Softail: 1,601
FXRT Sport Glide: 304
FXLR Low Rider Custom: 1,143
FXRS-Convertible: 989
FXRS-Low Rider Sport Edition: 762
FXRS Low Rider: 2,615
FXR Super Glide: 1,819
FXDS: 28
FXDB: 10
FXDS: 4
FXDB: 2
FXDS-Convertible: 1
XLH-1200 Sportster: 4,598
XLH-883 DeLuxe: 1,298
XLH-883 Hugger: 4,040
XLH-883: Sportster: 5,227
FLHTP (fairing): 467
FLHTP (windshield): 218
FXRP (clear windshield): 221
FXRP (fairing): 572
FXRP CHIPS: 15
FLTC Classic Tour Glide (Shrine): 3
FLTC-Ultra: 8
FLHTC Classic Electra Glide: 94
FLHTC-Ultra: 122
TOTAL: 59,706

1991
FLTC-Ultra Classic Tour Glide: 458
FLTC-Ultra (+ sidecar): 41
FLTC Classic Tour Glide: 250
FLTC (+ sidecar): 9
FLHTC-Ultra Classic Tour Glide: 3,204
FLHTC-Ultra (+ sidecar): 311
FLHTC Classic Electra Glide: 3,117

FLHTC (+ sidecar): 108
8SJX1 sidecar: 170
8SJX1 sidecar: 372
FLHS Electra Glide Sport: 2,383
FLSTF Fat Boy: 5,581
FLSTC Heritage Softail Classic: 8,950
FXSTC Softail Custom: 1
FXSTS Springer Softail: 4,265
FXSTC Softail Custom: 7,525
FXRT Sport Glide: 272
FXLR Low Rider Custom: 1,197
FXRS-CONV Convertible: 1,721
FXRS-SP Low Rider Sport Edition: 683
FXRS Low Rider: 2,183
FXR Super Glide: 1,742
FXDS Dyna: 1
FXDB Dyna: 1,546

XLH-1200 Sportster: 6,282
XLH-883 DeLuxe: 3,034
XLH-883 Hugger: 3,487
XLH-883 Sportster: 4,922
FLHTP (fairing): 509
FLHTP (windshield): 263
FXRP (clear windshield): 248
FXRP (fairing): 483
FXRP CHIPS: 1
FLTC Classic Tour Glide (Shrine): 3
FLTC-Ultra: 26
FLHTC Classic Electra Glide: 90
FLHTC-Ultra: 113
TOTAL: 65,548

*Does not include production for Harley-Davidson International.

Grand National Champions

Past AMA National Champions
1946: Chet Dykgraff, Grand Rapids, MI, Norton.
1947: Jimmy Chann, Bridgeton, NJ, H-D.
1948: Jimmy Chann, Bridgeton, NJ, H-D.
1949: Jimmy Chann, Bridgeton, NJ, H-D.
1950: Larry Headrick, San Jose, CA, H-D.
1951: Bobby Hill, Grove City, OH, Indian.
1952: Bobby Hill, Grove City, OH, Indian, Norton.
1953: Bill Tuman, Rockford, IL, Indian, Norton.
1954: Joe Leonard, San Jose, CA, H-D.
1955: Brad Andres, San Diego, CA, H-D.
1956: Joe Leonard, San Jose, CA, H-D.
1957: Joe Leonard, San Jose, CA, H-D.
1958: Carroll Resweber, Cedarburg, WI, H-D.
1959: Carroll Resweber, Cedarburg, WI, H-D.
1960: Carroll Resweber, Cedarburg, WI, H-D.
1961: Carroll Resweber, Cedarburg, WI, H-D.
1962: Bart Markel, Flint, MI, H-D.
1963: Dick Mann, Richmond, CA, BSA, Matchless.
1964: Roger Reiman, Kewanee, IL, H-D.
1965: Bart Markel, Flint, MI, H-D.
1966: Bart Markel, Flint, MI, H-D.
1967: Gary Nixon, Cockeysville, MD, Triumph.
1968: Gary Nixon, Cockeysville, MD, Triumph.
1969: Mert Lawwill, San Francisco, CA, H-D.
1970: Gene Romero, San Luis Obispo, CA, Triumph.
1971: Dick Mann, Richmond, CA, BSA.
1972: Mark Brelsford, Woodside, CA, H-D.
1973: Kenny Roberts, Modesto, CA, Yamaha.
1974: Kenny Roberts, Modesto, CA, Yamaha.
1975: Gary Scott, Springfield, OH, H-D.
1976: Jay Springsteen, Lapeer, MI, H-D.
1977: Jay Springsteen, Lapeer, MI, H-D.
1978: Jay Springsteen, Lapeer, MI, H-D.
1979: Steve Eklund, San Jose, CA, H-D, Yamaha.
1980: Randy Goss, Hartland, MI, H-D.
1981: Mike Kidd, Euless, TX, H-D, Yamaha.

1982: Ricky Graham, Seaside, CA, H-D.
1983: Randy Goss, Hartland, MI, H-D.
1984: Ricky Graham, Seaside, CA, Honda.
1985: Bubba Shobert, Carmel Valley, CA, Honda.
1986: Bubba Shobert, Carmel Valley, CA, Honda.
1987: Bubba Shobert, Carmel Valley, CA, Honda.
1988: Scott Parker, Swartz Creek, MI, H-D.
1989: Scott Parker, Swartz Creek, MI, H-D.
1990: Scott Parker, Swartz Creek, MI, H-D.
1991: Scott Parker, Swartz Creek, MI, H-D.

AMA Dirt Track National win leaders
(Make most often ridden is listed first.)
1. Scott Parker, Swartz Creek, MI, H-D, 48 wins.
2. Jay Springsteen, Lapeer, MI, H-D, 40.
3. Bubba Shobert, Lubbock, TX, Honda, H-D, 33.
4. Bart Markel, Flint, MI, H-D, 28.
5. Ricky Graham, Salinas, CA, H-D, Honda, 25.
6. Joe Leonard, San Jose, CA, H-D, 19.
6. Gary Scott, Springfield, OH, H-D, Triumph, 19.
8. Hank Scott, Findlay, OH, H-D, Yamaha, Honda, 17.
8. Steve Eklund, San Jose, CA, Yamaha, H-D, Can-Am, Rotax, 17.*
8. Steve Morehead, Findlay, OH, H-D, Honda, 17.
8. Chris Carr, Valley Springs, CA, H-D, Wood-Rotax, 17.
12. Carroll Resweber, Cedarburg, WI, H-D, 16.
12. Randy Goss, Hartland, MI, H-D, Honda, 16.
14. Mert Lawwill, San Francisco, CA, H-D, 15.
14. Kenny Roberts, Modesto, CA, Yamaha, 15.
16. Everett Brashear, Beaumont, TX, H-D, BSA, 14.
17. Dick Mann, Richmond, CA, BSA, Matchless, Yamaha, Ossa, Honda, 12.
17. Mike Kidd, Decatur, TX, H-D, Triumph, Honda, Yamaha, 12.
17. Jim Rice, Palo Alto, CA, BSA, H-D, 12.
20. Gene Romero, San Luis Obispo, CA, Triumph, Yamaha, 10.

AMA Grand National wins, by make

Harley-Davidson, 406.
Honda, 122.
Yamaha, 97.
Triumph, 67.
BSA, 58.
Suzuki, 22.
Kawasaki, 20.
Matchless, 10.
Can-Am, 6.
Bultaco, 5.
Ossa, 3.
Norton, 2.
Rotax, 2.
Wood-Rotax, 2.
(By the end of the 1992 season, Harley-Davidson probably will have won more AMA Grand National races than all other makes combined.)

Index